ST. KILDA PORTRAITS

i

ST. KILDA PORTRAITS

by DAVID A. QUINE, FLS

Drawings and Photographs by the author except where acknowledged.

To my Wife, Mary.

1988 by D. A. Quine

ISBN 0 9508135 3 2

CONTENTS

Natives of St. Kilda by Sands

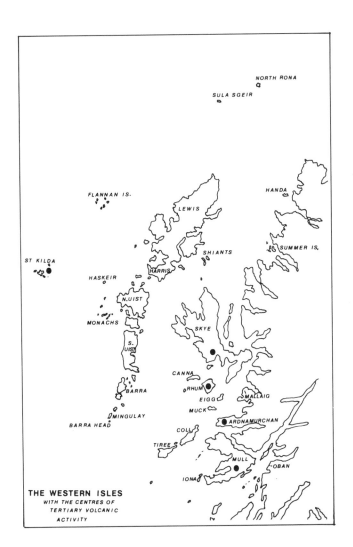

ILLUSTRATIONS

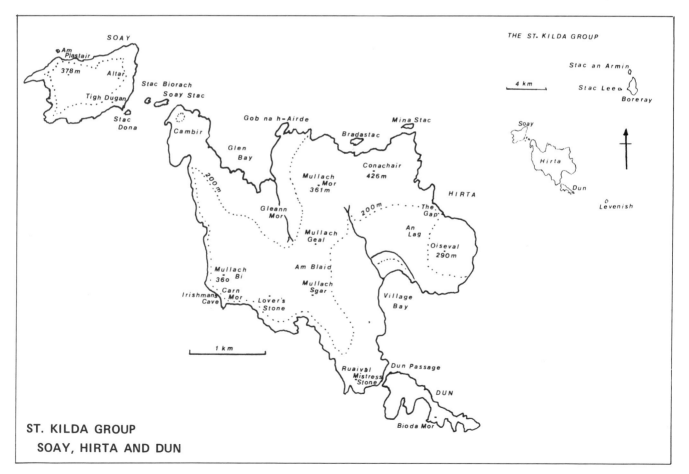

ST. KILDA GROUP
SOAY, HIRTA AND DUN

x

Foreword

Many books have been written about St. Kilda in the past and world attention was focussed on this beautiful archipelago when it was designated. "A World Heritage Site" in a ceremony in the Kirk on Hirta on August 10th 1987. I was delighted to be present. However, for some time now, I personally wanted to know more about the people who lived and worked on the island – people who were just names to me. Before it was too late I thought it would be good to collect information about each of the families who were present at the Evacuation, where possible letting those still alive tell their own story. It has been a great pleasure to talk with many of the St. Kildans.

I have also had access to diaries and memoirs of others who have worked on the islands – teachers, missionaries and scientists. Especially, I have had the privilege of seeing and reproducing the charming watercolours of Sir Thomas Dyke Acland – the first known paintings of St. Kilda dating back to his visit in 1812.

Acknowledgements

Collecting material over the last five years for "St. Kilda Portraits" has been an extremely stimulating and evocative experience and I am greatly in debt to many people for their co-operation and generosity in lending material and allowing me to quote at length. Firstly, I must thank Sir Richard Acland and Lady Anne for their encouragement and generous permission to include reproductions of the twelve beautiful watercolour paintings executed in 1812 by their relative, Sir Thomas Dyke Acland. These paintings add an extra dimension to the book.

Professor Bill Lawson has been most helpful in putting his St. Kilda file at my disposal which has been invaluable in tracing the families and in many other ways.

In each chapter I have acknowledged my debt to people like Kelman MacQueen in Australia, Susan MacLachlan in Zimbabwe, Marie MacDonald in London, Mrs. S. Barker and Robert Gladstone in Scotland who have supplied me with precious photographs, memoirs and diaries. I am also most grateful to Lachlan MacDonald for all his time and patience in answering my many questions and allowing me access to his own collection of photographs. In addition my thanks go to the Rev. Donald John Gillies for all his assistance, to Alick MacLeod for his thoughtful contribution and the loan of a photograph which enabled me to draw his father's home in Berneray, to Morton Boyd whose photograph enabled me to draw the bothy on Stac Lee and to David Royle whose panoramic view included Stac an Armin and Stac Lee from the east. Robert Atkinson kindly allowed me to include the lovely character study of Finlay MacQueen, Elizabeth Ogilvie three photographs from her Collection and Ralph Wright four from his.

I am most grateful to the National Trust for Scotland for their permission to reproduce some of A. M. Cockburn's photographs and to use copies of R. Jobling's sketches owned by the Marchioness of Bute and photographed by Susan Forbes and to the School of Scottish Studies for permission to publish photographs from their collections, two taken by R. C. MacLeod of MacLeod.

Dowland Press have taken great care in publishing the book and setting it out so attractively.

Last, but, by no means least, to my wife Mary, who knows St. Kilda well and has shown unlimited patience over many years and has advised and supported me in this fascinating project.

Sir Thomas Dyke Acland, A Painter's Portrait

Family Background
1812 Visit to St. Kilda
1834 Visit to St. Kilda
Lady of St. Kilda – further escapades

Sir Thomas Dyke Acland (1787-1871) made two extremely important visits to St. Kilda. The first one in 1812 was remarkable for the fascinating record he has left us through his beautiful watercolour paintings, some of which are reproduced in this book. His second visit in 1834 was momentous for St. Kilda as his gift of £20, left with the minister, was the stimulus for the demolition of the old village and the rebuilding of the new planned settlement.

"St. Kilda 2½ miles from the North". Showing Oiseval, Conachair and the Cambir. Acland.

1

FAMILY BACKGROUND

Sir Thomas was one of those rare beings who was larger than life, in fact, he became known as "the Great Sir Thomas". His father, Sir Thomas Dyke Acland, the 9th Baronet, died when "Tom" was only 7 years of age – he had hoped that his son would have taken after him to become a famous stag hunter. His mother, Henrietta, was the daughter of Sir Richard Hoare, the eminent banker, she took very seriously the upbringing of "Tom". One year after the death of her husband she married Captain Matthew Fortescue, RN; the family increased to seven children, and "Tom" went off to Harrow School and then to Oxford. Matters other than stag hunting occupied his attention. "By the time Tom was twenty-one a new century had started, and a more serious climate of opinion was beginning to influence both private and public life. There was no more hunting at Holnicote: instead politics and philanthropy absorbed the energy and enthusiasm which he had inherited from his forebears". (Acland, 1981).

Francis Nicholson, the artist, visited their home from time to time and both Matthew and Henrietta developed skills as landscape painters. "Tom" must have inherited some of these gifts, which he was to develop by the daily practice of illustrating his travels. As soon as his time at Oxford University was completed he went on a sketching tour in Norway, leaving on July 17th 1807. Here he was caught up in the Napoleonic Wars and cast into prison in Kongsberg. After two months he was released; he left £500 to relieve those suffering as a result of the war, and returned home safely. He had made some new friends and brought back a collection of sketches. "So ended an adventure which revealed at the very outset of his career all his main characteristics. No doubt the most apparent to casual observers were his impatient energy, reckless love of adventure, and disregard of the feelings and advice of others, but it was more significant that he showed so early the concern of the underdog, the courage to speak freely, even when it put him in danger, and the warm generosity to those in need, which were to be his best qualities throughout life." (Acland, 1981).

After two weeks he was off to Edinburgh – "the Athens of the North" where he attended the university lectures on moral philosophy and political economy. Did he meet there Henry Lord Brougham, who frequented Edinburgh and who had visited St. Kilda only a few years before in 1799? A member of his party wrote a full and interesting unpublished account of the visit (see "St. Kilda Revisited", Quine, 1982). "Tom" returned from Edinburgh, had his 21st birthday party and was married to Lydia Hoare on April 7th. 1808. Lydia's father was Henry Hoare, a friend of William Wilberforce.

During the next few years most of Sir Thomas's time and energy were taken up with matters relating to education and to his estates in Devon, working from his family home at Killerton, near Exeter.

In September 1808 he was heading North again to spend the winter in Edinburgh, attending the lectures at the university and debating with his friends from Christ College, Oxford. He was seeking "to form a Course in life which a wise Man would not repent and which a Christian would not fear". He was to spend a second winter in Edinburgh but then returned to Devon for the birth of their first child on May 25th 1809. He was to be Christened after his father – Thomas Dyke Acland.

1812 VISIT TO ST. KILDA

On the 3rd June, Sir Thomas, his wife Lydia and the young Thomas, aged three years, set off for their summer holidays, first visiting County Wicklow where they enjoyed sketching and the opportunity to rest in the stimulating company of the Latouche family and their friends at Belle View. They then travelled to Scotland visiting the Falls of Clyde, Loch Lomond, Inverary, Loch Awe, Loch Etive, Staffa, Skye and Strontian. Each place is recorded beautifully in Sir Thomas's sketch-books. At the height of their holiday they made the adventurous voyage to St. Kilda, reaching the islands on July 17th. Sir Thomas was clearly thrilled by the majestic scenery surrounding him and immediately set to work on his first painting at 3.30 in the morning. His title for the finished work was "The Island of Borera and the Rock of the Solan Goose – Stack Levenish.". (He had been wrongly informed about the name of the Stack which was in, fact, Stack Lee).

On the whole of the Scottish holiday he completed three sketch-books, one of which was given over to St. Kilda. This contains twelve delightful water colour paintings, 12 x 9 inches, on rough textured, oatmeal coloured paper. He used a limited palette to great effect. His blues, greys and browns were particularly suitable to express the St. Kilda scenes in which he caught the grandeur of the cliffs and stacs with all the evocative play of light and shade. Since many of the paintings were executed from sea level, the towering cliffs of Boreray, Soay and Conachair are seen in their full stature, scale being given by tiny figures climbing the rocks and the sight of distant boats under sail. After sketching on site he would work up the paintings in the evenings. Because of the accuracy of the paintings, they are not only of artistic merit but also are of great historic value. Here are to be seen the earliest known pictures of St. Kilda. As his boat entered Village Bay

Sir Thomas painted the great amphitheatre formed by the surrounding mountains, with the river – Amhuinn Mhor to the west of the little cluster of bee-hive like houses, all grouped together showing the compact community.

The next painting was a detailed study of the village which he titled, "The Principal Square in the Capital City of St. Kilda". Here we are surprised by the proximity of the houses to each other, huddled together, some butting onto their neighbours, sheltering each other from the savage elements. The pattern shown is so different from the open plan which was to develop as a result of Sir Thomas's second visit. The visitors can be seen, the lady with a bonnet, and the islanders sitting around in the square. Lady Anne Acland in her book, a Devon Family comments. "Acland was shocked by the islander's poverty and spoke earnestly with them before sketching their wretched huddle of thatched huts (the main square), and returning to his boat with a firm promise to come again. Lydia, his wife, was reputedly the first Lady ever to land on St. Kilda, and it must have been a great adventure for her; as for Tom aged three, it remained his earliest memory." (Acland, 1981). Bearing in mind the unfortunate Lady Grange who was exiled to St. Kilda for seven years, we ought to say that Lydia was the first Lady to voluntarily visit St. Kilda!

On their return they stopped at Fort William and climbed Ben Nevis. Then they received a message from home requesting them to return immediately as there was likely to be an opportunity for Sir Thomas to stand for Parliament. It was the seat for North Devon which he was to win on October 15th. 1812.

1834 VISIT TO ST. KILDA

Sir Thomas was now under financial pressure caused by elections, the maintenance of his estates, the demands of his ten children and massive contributions to worthwhile projects in his constituency and to charity. With his love of painting and travel he concluded that the purchase of a yacht would be an economically viable proposition. During the years 1832-34 he had caught yachting fever through his close friendship and association with Captain Fairfax Moresby RN, who had moved into a house only half a mile from Holnicote on the North Devon coast. Captain Moresby had commanded one of the ships engaged in suppressing the slave trade at Mauritius during 1821-23. He was later to become Admiral of the Fleet, in 1870. On August 9th, 1832 they hired a yacht. "The Arrow" from Porlock Weir and during the next two weeks made four voyages in the Bristol Channel – some in extremely rough weather. "Everything about the adventure – freedom from convention, new opportunities for sketching – appealed enormously to Sir Thomas." (Acland 1981). Next summer they hired another yacht, "Vansittart", and with Captain Moresby they went to Ireland for three weeks and then to Northern Spain (1833). The sketches of the mountains, including Mount Bergan, which he climbed, were some of the best he ever did.

Anne Acland takes up the story. "During the winter, which was spent mostly at Holnicote (Exeter again being visited by cholera), Acland resolved to acquire a boat of his own. With the encouragement of Captain Moresby and his own midshipman son, Baldwin, on the 6th. May 1834 he bought at Dartmouth, a two-masted schooner of 186 tons, built for the fruit trade, and converted her into a yacht capable of accomodating the whole family as well as a paid crew. The equipment on board included enough cutlery and glass to supply a large household, as well as Lady

Route Round Britain of The Lady of St. Kilda in 1834.

Acland's piano. On the 2 August 1834 "The Lady of St. Kilda", as she was named in honour of Lady Acland's earlier exploit, sailed on her maiden voyage, which was to be a circumnavigation of England and Scotland. Except for Tom who was travelling in Europe, the entire Acland family was on board, and Captain Moresby was in command." The schooner had been engaged in carrying fruit from the Levant for sale in the London markets, a passage which had to be improvement otherwise: he left behind a prize of £20 for the islander who first built himself a proper house." (Acland 1981). The minister at this time was the Rev. Neil MacKenzie, the first to be resident for over 100 years. During the 1820's Dr. John MacDonald made several visits to St. Kilda and spent much energy collecting money to relieve the poverty of the inhabitants. He also collected £600 to build a Church, and also a manse. These were ready for the arrival and introduction of the Rev. MacKenzie on July 4th 1830.

One of Sir Thomas's sketches portrays the simple outline of the Church and manse. Another visitor in 1838 made the comment, "The first thing that strikes the eye is the manse, which is a neat one storey slated house, of four apartments, I think, about 100 yards from the beach, on the North East side of the bay. Endways to it, and forming a letter T, is the Chapel in tasteful keeping." (MacLean, 1838). Perhaps Sir Thomas was struck by the attractive new buildings of the Church and manse which had been built since his previous visit, and the stark poverty and unchanged state of the dwellings of the poor islanders.

The Rev. Neil MacKenzie described the developments that followed. "In 1834 Sir Thomas Acland visited the island, and, in order to encourage

Tray with sketching materials on the Lady of St. Kilda. Acland.

executed quickly, laden as she was with perishable fruit. She was designed for speed, clipper built, with sharp nose and high cut water.

"From the cabin roof swung a tray holding the sketching materials with which Acland made a pictorial log of the journey as the yacht sailed up the east coast and around Cape Wrath, making a special detour to visit the island of St. Kilda. Acland found a resident minister with a church and a manse, but little

New Church and Manse, drawing in 1834 by Acland.

the people to build better houses, left with me, as their minister, the sum of twenty pounds. I was to use it in any way which I might find best for that purpose. When I mentioned this generous donation to the people and explained his wish, they all at once resolved to build for themselves better houses, but, before beginning to do so, they wished to have the land (which they had hitherto held in common) divided among them, so that each may build upon his own portion. To this division the proprietor readily consented. As soon after as possible, the father of Mr. MacDonald, lately tenant of Kingsburgh, but now of Seaport in Skye, came to the island and divided the land among them. They were not, however, satisfied with his division, and a good deal of ill-feeling began to manifest itself, each thinking that the other's share was better than his own. With some difficulty I got them at last to agree to divide the land themselves, and when they had made the different portions as equal as possible, then to apportion them by lot. This they did and were satisfied."

"The following winter they began to build their new houses, but as they had only the wood of the old ones for roofing they could not make them much larger. At a later period we got a saw and built a saw-pit, so that any drift wood might be cut up for this as well as other

uses. It was not very often that a log fit for use was secured, as owing to the rocky nature of the shore and the constant surf, it was generally ground to matchwood. One great improvement in these new houses was that the beds were to be no longer recesses in the thickness of the walls, and that an opening was to be left for a small window which was one of the things which they resolved to buy with Sir Thomas's gift. At the same time they agreed to discontinue the custom of spreading over the floor the ashes and all kinds of filthy rubbish which they used to accumulate for manure, and which before they removed it in spring had risen as high as the wall, so that no one could stand upright even in the centre of the floor. This they all faithfully observed. At the same time they agreed to abolish the rubbish pit in front of the door, but in regard to this there were several relapses till it was finally abolished by order of the proprieter."

"When the houses were nearly finished it was necessary that I should go south in order to purchase with the money left by Sir Thomas the windows and other things needed for their completion. I soon found that the money which I had was not nearly sufficient to purchase the things of which they stood in immediate need. I therefore went to Mr. MacLeod of St. Columba's, and some other kind friends, and they entered so heartily into the matter that in a short time I had a good supply of windows, tables, bedsteads, kitchen dressers, chairs, stools, and crockery ready for shipment. At this stage the proprietor of the island, who had just returned from India, heard of what we were doing and sent twenty pounds to pay the expense of carriage." Dr. MacLeod accompanied MacKenzie on his return from Glasgow bringing with them 47 bedsteads, making two for every house paying rent, and one for each of the poor widows; also 24 chairs, 21 stools, 21 tables, 21 dressers, 21 glass windows, together with pieces of delft-ware.

MacKenzie continued, "After the houses were finished we next set to work on clearing the ground, draining it, and deepening and straightening the natural water courses. When this was completed we built a ring fence round the whole of the arable land, and, although it was not required as a fence, continued it on between the land and the sea. This latter portion was built still higher than the other, and proved of great use, not only in protecting the growing crops, but in preventing the gales from blowing away the seed and blowing the cut grain into the sea. Lastly, we built a massive stone wall around the burial ground. It was built oval in form and was rather troublesome to keep exactly in shape owing to the great inequalities in the levels of the foundation. It was the portion of our work in which I took the greatest personal interest, as there I buried three of my children who died in infancy." (MacKenzie, 1911).

When Wilson visited St. Kilda in 1841 the new village had been completed, he described it in detail (see St. Kilda Revisited) and his artist completed a drawing showing the new houses with Dun in the background. (Wilson, 1842).

So ended a most important stage in the history of St. Kilda, and Sir Thomas's £20 were put to extremely good use.

Sir Thomas spent less time sketching on his second visit – the paintings were smaller, less detailed and on a blue background, but many portray delightfully the outlines of the rocky skylines, stacks and islands. On leaving St. Kilda his party, aboard the "Lady of St. Kilda" sailed south via Liverpool and on to Devon where the boat was laid up for the winter at Porlock Weir.

Figurehead of the Lady of St. Kilda.

THE LADY OF ST. KILDA — FURTHER ESCAPADES

Sir Thomas later sailed in "The Lady of St. Kilda" to Lisbon and on a ten month Mediterranean tour staying in Rome for the winter of 1835-36; he could not remember a more enjoyable family occasion. After about five years he sold "The Lady of St. Kilda", but kept the figurehead, which can still be seen at the Acland's ancestoral home at Killerton, near Exeter. The schooner was sold in 1840 to Jonathan Curdy Pope of Plymouth, who soon transferred her to Sydney, Australia. She arrived in Port Phillip on July 6th 1841 under the command of Lieutenant J. R. Lawrence.

In the Port Phillip Herald for July 9th 1841 a news-paragraph read, "Lady of St. Kilda. This vessel arrived on Tuesday last from Plymouth which she left on 27th February. When south of the Cape of Good Hope she encountered very severe weather, her foreyard being carried away, and the gale continuing unabated she was compelled to strike her top masts. In point of sailing we understand she is a regular clipper. She brings no passengers." (Cooper, 1931). She had brought no less than 34 barrels of blacking. By August 20th her cargo had been discharged and by the 24th she was advertised for sale. During 1841 she was engaged in trade around Sydney and Launceston. One record reports a trip from Sydney to Port Phillip – on her return journey she brought a cargo of 72 tons of cedar obtained in the vicinity of the Tweed river in New South Wales. This was required in building operations in Melbourne. (Port Phillip Herald, 29/10/1841). She was soon off again to Launceston and in 1842 headed off to Canton.

St. Kilda – Australia

An intriguing question arises. How did this St. Kilda obtain its name? It was not, as many suppose, in honour of the St. Kildans who arrived on board the "Priscilla" on that fateful voyage of 1852 when 36 St. Kildans left Liverpool to seek a happier life. No less than 20 died on the journey through diseases from which they had no immunity, and several others died soon after their arrival. The evidence is that St. Kilda,

Melbourne, was so named ten years before, in 1842.

The early settlers in Australia were surveying the harbours and new land suitable for living quarters and for development. Cooper takes up the story "Governor Gidley King, R.N. of New South Wales, in the year 1802 sent a surveying party from Sydney to survey Port Phillip. The leader was Charles Grimes, Acting Surveyor of New South Wales. For purposes of transport Governor King lent to the party His Majesty's colonial schooner, "Cumberland". James Flemming was appointed to be the journal keeper of the expedition. Very probably the members of Grimes' surveying party were the first white men to see the lands whereon now is the city of St. Kilda. The schooner "Cumberland", anchored in Port Phillip Bay on Thursday, January 20th, 1803, upon which day it is recorded by Flemming that they had "hot winds most of the day". Grimes commenced his survey along the eastern shores of the Bay. On February 1st. the schooner was abreast of the lands of St. Kilda. On Grimes' survey plan at Elwood is marked "salt". It was at the swamp the surveyors "saw two large emus". Flemming states in his journal that, "the land appears to be covered with water in wet seasons. Came to a salt lagoon about a mile long, and a quarter of a mile wide, had no entrance to the sea." That swamp we know as Albert Park Lake. In some old maps the swamp, and marshy ground, are plotted close to Fitzroy Street, at the point where the St. Kilda Railway Station stands." (Cooper, 1931).

The next stage in the story takes place on August 20th, 1835 when the "Enterprise", a craft of 55 tons burden, stood off Red Bluff and landed a good five-oared whale boat with a shore party. They had noted the gum trees on the edge of the creek and were sent to see if there was water and if the land was suitable for a settlement. The owner, John Pascoe Fawkner, was not present at the time but wrote later how his men saw, "lovely knolls around lagoons on the flats or swamps,

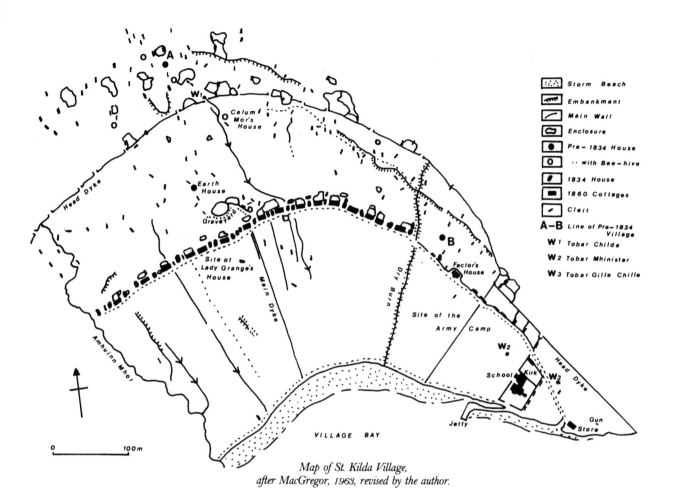

Map of St. Kilda Village,
after MacGregor, 1963, revised by the author.

and how the flocks, almost innumerable of teal, ducks, geese and swans and minor fowls filled them with joy". Fawkner's men in the "Enterprise" were the first settlers who landed at or about what was soon to become known as St. Kilda. By the residents of Melborne this locality was known as the "Green Knoll". A small village community grew up there and it was known as Fareham. However, by July 15th. 1842 the area had been carefully surveyed, a new plan for the locality drawn up and presented to the Executive Concil - and approved. On August 29th. 1842 the name St. Kilda was also approved.

What was the reason for the change of the place name? It should be explained that "The Lady of St. Kilda" was often moored off the shore in this locality and occasionally some of the crew got into trouble with too much to drink. However, it wasn't the crew but the schooner running into trouble which prompted the change in the name! Edward M. S. Stafford of Carlisle Street, St. Kilda explained what happened to the editor of the Argus newspaper.

"Sir,

For Mr. Cooper's information I beg to state that it was my father, Mr. John Stafford, Customs House Officer, appointed in England in 1835, who named St. Kilda, after a yacht called St. Kilda, owned by Mr. Acland. The yacht came ashore on a sandbank, and my father went out to her in one of his boats and had an interview with the captain, and then said, "I call this the St. Kilda foreshore." Later he told Governor Latrobe, who said it was a very appropriate name.

Yours

Edward M. S. Stafford."

"At the St. Kilda sale of the allotments a block of land containing 2 acres, 2 roads, and 16 perches was bought by Lieutenant J. R. Lawrence, the late Captain of the schooner – "The Lady of St. Kilda". The block was situated at the corner of the Esplanade and Fitzroy Street, and it was Lieut. Lawrence who named Acland Street in honour of Sir Thomas Dyke Acland." (Cooper, 1931).

"The Lady of St. Kilda" was to appear in a number of shipping news bulletin reports, some are included here:-

7/2/1843 Left Canton, cleared Manilla on March 4th

7/5/1843 Arrived in Port Phillip Bay

23/5/1843 Sailed for Sidney with 14 passengers

20/6/1843 Moored at her old anchorage in St. Kilda waters. Daily advertised for sale.

31/10/43 New owners registered in Sydney.

16/1/1844 "The Lady of St. Kilda" left Aukland for Tahiti and the Sandwich Islands on 16 Ultimo. (Sydney Morning Post, 24/1/1844).

12/6/1844 The Sydney Morning Herald reported that she was sold to the French authorities at Tahiti and later references state that she was used as a police boat between the islands to prevent the smuggling of arms by the natives of Tahiti. The last reference to the schooner was in the Sydney Morning Herald of 6/8/1844 where she is referred to in an account of the conflicts between the French and the natives of Tahiti. A final note appeared later in the Shipping Register that "the schooner sailed from Sydney and was wrecked at Tahiti – date unknown."

Another St. Kilda Saga closes in which "The Lady of St. Kilda" provided a link between the development of the new planned settlement in St. Kilda, Outer Hebrides, Scotland and the newly named and established settlement of St. Kilda, Melbourne, Australia.

Malcolm MacQueen,
(1828-1913)
An Emigrant's Portrait

"Principal Square in the Capital, St. Kilda". Acland.

Finlay MacQueen on St. Kilda. R. Atkinson.

SETTING THE SCENE

The MacQueens

The MacQueens have been a distinguished family linked with St. Kilda over many generations, probably arriving from the Uists at the time of the resettlement soon after 1730. "A family of MacQueens now in Tigharry, North Uist, claim a relationship with the St. Kilda family, which corroborates the suggestion of a Uist origin". (Lawson, 1981). Some members had outstanding gifts of strength and cliff climbing skills. Finlay, who left at the time of the Evacuation, was an imposing looking elder statesman with a long black beard. He was an amateur taxidermist and was proud of the puffins and gannets which he had specialised in stuffing. He became a legend in his own life-time for his skills on the rocks, considered by many to be Britain's greatest cragsman. He accompanied Heathcote and his sister during their visit to the islands and stacs in 1898 and 1899. With Finlay's help they both climbed Stac Lee. Heathcote described the landing, "With the assistance of a rope and a sufficient amount of confidence, any active man could walk up the side of a house; but it needs a St. Kildan to get a foot-hold on an overhanging rock covered with slippery sea-weed and draw himself to the top. The first time I landed there the tide was fairly high, and it was possible to get some foot-hold on the upper part of the rock where it is not quite perpendicular, but the next time ten or twelve feet of slimy sea-weed clinging to the absolutely overhanging cliff were exposed. How Finlay MacQueen got up is still a marvel to me".

(Heathcote, 1900). When the evacuation finally came Finlay was, understandably, very reluctant to leave the island which had been his lifetime home.

The Emigration to Australia in 1852

It was an earlier member of the MacQueen family, Malcolm, whose story we follow. He was to take his place with other members of his family and another family of MacQueens on the ill-fated voyage in the "Priscilla" to Australia in 1852. Ill-fated in that half of the 36 St. Kildans died on the voyage or during quarantine within weeks of landing. Their departure was a loss that the St. Kildan community was never able to overcome. The population in 1830 was 110, and in 1856 it had dropped to 73, having lost many of its young active members as a result of this emigration and further losses due to "eight day sickness".

Ann Holohan has recently made a careful study of the voyage and the problems faced by the St. Kildans on their journey. "In 1852 the Highland and Island Emigration Society listed 17 ships and 2,605 passengers who were to leave Liverpool for Australia, many assisted by the Highlands and Islands Emigration Society. Included among these 17 ships was the barque "Priscilla", which departed from Liverpool on 13 October 1852 with 298 passengers on board including 36 St. Kildans . . . The "Priscilla" passenger list, on arrival in Melbourne on 24 February 1853, after a voyage of over four months, had increased from 298 to 302 with the births of at least four infants, and there were 41 deaths; female children were at greatest risk. This percentage was greater than on any of the other 1852 emigrant ships; for example in the "Marco Polo", which also contained emigrants from the Highlands and Islands, 52 passengers were to die, from a total list of 887. Who were these thirty six St. Kildans who decided to make this epic journey to the

Malcolm MacQueen's Family Portrait taken 1885-90 in Melbourne. Left to Right:- Standing – Neil, John, Christina, Donald, Ewan. Seated – Finlay, Mary (nee MacSwain) and Malcolm.

Australian gold fields, so peculiarly alien to their island beliefs and life-style? Were they at special risk to disease and death on the voyage? Scrutiny of both the emigration and immigration lists provides the following information:-

MacQueen	Finlay (senior)	58	–	survived
	Chirsty	50	–	survived
	Malcolm	24	–	survived (subject of this chapter)
	Rachel	19	–	died, measles 6 November 1852
	John	13	–	survived
MacQueen	Finlay	44	–	died, dysentery, 26 November 1852

13

Surname	Name	Age		Notes
	Catharine	44	–	died, mesenteric fever, 30 Nov. 1852
	Donald	18	–	survived
	Marion	16	–	survived
	Catharine	12	–	survived
	Ann	9	–	survived
	Neil	7	–	survived
	Finlay	4	–	died, marasmus, 21 February, 1853
	Mary	1	–	died, dysentery after measles, 2 Dec 52
Ferguson	Malcolm	31	–	survived
	Catharine	23	–	died, scarletina 9 February 1853
	Mary	3	–	died, dysentery after measles, 6 Dec 52
Morrison	Mary	57	–	died, gastric fever 9 Nov 1852
Ferguson	Hector	35	–	survived
	Mary	22	–	survived
Gillies	Ewan	27	–	survived
	Margaret	28	–	survived
	Mary	1	–	died, dysentery after measles, 3 Dec 52
McCrimmen	Donald	32	–	died, diarrhoea 14 Nov 1852
	Ann	32	–	died, debility 25 Jan 1853
	Marion	9	–	died, dysentery after measles, 23 Nov 52
	Mary	6	–	died, dysentery after measles, 22 Nov 52
	Donald	5	–	died, dysentery after measles, 22 Nov 52
	Chirsty	1	–	died, dysentery 27 Nov 1852
MacDonald	Roderick	47	–	died, diarrhoea after measles, 11 Nov 52
	Marion	48	–	died, diarrhoea after measles 14 Nov 52
	Chirsty	18	–	survived
	Neil	15	–	survived
MacDonald	Neil	22	–	survived
	Catharine	51	–	died, dysentery after measles, 17 Nov 52
	Ann	15	–	survived

"In this carnage, eighteen of the thirty-six St. Kildans were to die on the voyage, the majority from an epidemic of measles, which raged on board the "Priscilla" in November 1852, and these 18 deaths contributed disproportionately to the total of 41 deaths aboard the "Priscilla". Both St. Kildan adults and children fell victims to disease contrary to the deaths on other ships where adults were less susceptible than children; of the total of 12 adults who were to die on the "Priscilla" 10 were from St. Kilda and of the 29 children to die, 8 were from the island. The islanders' much ridiculed beliefs as to their susceptibility to the 'strangers' cold was to prove deadly in the fetid, miasma aboard the "Priscilla". (Holohan, 1986).

When the Factor, Osgood MacKenzie, visited St. Kilda in early June 1853 he had this to say of his arrival. "Nearly all the male inhabitants were assembled to meet us when we landed, as well they might welcome us, for they had not seen a creature but themselves for nine long months and they were very anxious for news from Australia about their friends who had emigrated the previous autumn. Eight families containing thirty-six souls had then gone". We can hardly imagine the over-whelming sadness with which the inhabitants would receive the news of the deaths of so many of their relatives and friends.

Australian Newspaper Report, 1853

The Australian Newspaper, "The Argos", published daily in Melbourne, dated Friday, February 25th 1853 carried the following under the title of Shipping Intelligence. "The Priscilla, which left Liverpool October 15th, arrived at the Port Phillip Heads January 19th, since which time she had been in quarantine on account of a number of deaths that had taken place, which were as follows:- 12 adults, 24 children, 5 babies, principally from general causes. The classification of the emigrants now on board is as follows:- 32 married females; 44 single men, 58 single women, and 66 children: 3 married men, 3 married women, 1 single man, 7 single women and 16 children, still remain on board the Lysander at the Sanitory Station, but are all convalescent. The Priscilla carries no cargo for this port, but coals for Bombay".

Other articles in the same paper give some inklings about the environment into which the St. Kildans were to attempt to settle and make their own homes. One hard hitting article by a member of the Colonial Reform Association challenged the Government of the day to release more land at reasonable prices for incoming families. "The throwing open of the lands of the Colony is a matter that holds a very high place on the list of important duties of the Association. Upon that being done, and done NOW, our future as a people very materially depends. The members of this Association can see, although a wilfully blind Government cannot see, that thousands of people are being driven from our shores who would willingly settle here, and would become the best and most useful colonists we have. They can see, although the Executive cannot see, that millions of our wealth are being taken away from amongst us to enrich neighbouring, and, to some extent, rival colonies, simply because the owners of these millions cannot find a foothold in Victoria. They can see that life in this Colony is little better than one wild, eager scramble for gold; that we are fast becoming a nation hungry for adventurers, rushing to a gold mine, seizing a few nuggets and away again to some worse country, happily supplied with better government. They can see, although to this, our mockery of a government is blinder than to aught else, that a rancorous spirit of disaffection is being rapidly developed, and encouraged amongst us, by bad management of public affairs, and profound general contempt for the authorities . . . The case is urgent. It is perfectly monstrous that so overpowering a want should be so trifled with, or its gratification denied us altogether. The lands must be unlocked. If they cannot in one way, they must be in another. We are not to be starved, driven about, and rendered homeless vagabonds, to please any government or governor. The present peddling system must be discarded, by fair means if possible – but is must be discarded for ever. Very large quantities of land must be thrown into the market; large quantities of land of suitable sizes, in suitable localities. The plough and the spade must have fair play; and men with wealth to spend must have a chance of spending a portion of it in the most natural way, in securing a home for themselves, and for their wives and families".

In the same newspaper their Sydney correspondent reported, "The arrival of the Overland Mail this morning, brings a letter from a highly respectable commercial firm in your city of a gentleman stating that at the Canadian Gully three more monster nuggets (of gold) had been found, one weighing 77 lbs, one 69 lbs and one 175 lbs weight. Although some doubt exists as to the authenticity of this statement, it had excited a great deal of sensation here, and will probably have some effect on mercantile affairs, as it will certainly turn the table of emigration in your direction." The price of gold at the time was £3.13s. 9d per ounce.

Other prices are interesting, "Flour remains steady at £23, but I do not think it is so steady as it was. Bottled Beer is still on the rise, and for the most inferior brands excessive rates are asked. None can be bought under 14s 6d. Beer in wood is almost unobtainable. Some lots of wool at yesterday's sale realised 1s 11d per pound – these prices must be looked on as extremely speculative. Tallow is also very high, being sold at £27 and £28, while hides fetched as much as 8s 6d to 9s 1d. Sugar – although during the week has been increased by 40,000 bags the price continues firm, Pampangas may be quoted at 22s. Teas – a thousand chests have been taken in from sea-board during the week, without affecting former rates. Hysonskin 80s. Cigars – although nearly 300,000 have arrived during the week, rates will remain nearly unaltered. They may be quoted 2's and 3's, together at 75s to 80s. Our large export of gold is beginning to be met by a corresponding importation of European goods."

In the crime report a number of offences were recorded – murder, stealing clothes and a horse, many instances of drunkenness and some of sly-grog selling.

"James Booth and Chilton Newburne, seamen of the "Allison", were sentenced to twelve weeks with hard labour, for desertion. Donald McInnes was fined 5s for drunkenness. Robert Doyle, for the same offence, and whilst in that state refusing to pay a waterman his fare of 5s from this place to the Beach, was fined 15s; 10s of which was to go to the waterman . . ."

Such was the atmosphere into which the surviving St. Kildans were to step out after their frightful voyage in search of their new life in the developing Country in February 1853. However, we must let Malcolm MacQueen tell his story, beginning with his life on St. Kilda.

LIFE ON ST. KILDA BEFORE 1852

Family Background

Malcolm MacQueen survived all the traumas of the voyage, carved out a new way of life in Australia, facing many problems, and, at the turn of this century, dictated his "Life Story" to the Rev. Finlay MacQueen, a task which must have taken many hours. The original document resides with Malcolm's great grandson, Kelman McQueen in Australia, who makes the point that they should be considered as "the thoughts of an old Gaelic man." A remarkable man indeed from a remarkable family. Kelman has kindly donated a copy to the Bute Box at the National Trust for Scotland headquarters in Edinburgh. The following extracts have been taken from that copy. Kelman pointed out that, "his grandfather, the Rev. Finlay McQueen changed the spelling of the surname to McQueen, although some descendents have reverted to the MacQueen spelling."

"I was born in St. Kilda on December 25th 1828. My father's name was Finlay MacQueen and my mother was Christina Ferguson. Four children died in infancy.

One brother John and two sisters, Ann and Rachel, all younger than I, made up the family.

My father was the son of John MacQueen and he had a brother Donald and sisters, Mary who married John Ferguson (five sons and one daughter) and Rachel who died about 25. Catharine married Sandy Gillies – four sons and two daughers, one son went to America (Canada). Ann married Donald McCrimmon and was a widow with one child when I came here.

My grandfather was three years in College. His father Finlay MacQueen was not a native of the island. I think he came from Uist, but I am not sure. He was well-to-do when he came. He fell in love with my great-grandmother, I think she was a MacDonald. My grandmother, the wife of John MacQueen, was Catharine MacDonald. My grandmother was 52 years when my father was born.

My father was about 28 years of age when he married Christina, daughter of John Ferguson by his first wife. The marriage was performed by the Rev. John MacDonald of Ferintosh on his first visit (1822), on his last visit he baptised me (1830). I was able to walk down to the Church by myself. My father went several times to the mainland when a young man in the company of Malcolm MacDonald, first cousin of his and father of Mrs. MacLeod of Colac (Victoria).

My mother's father was John Ferguson. He had a family by his first wife Annie McDonald, my mother (Christina), and by his second wife Mary MacQueen, my aunt, Donald, Finlay, Neil, Hector, Bessie and Malcolm. Malcolm and Finlay came to Victoria and died here. John Ferguson's father was mate or captain of a ship trading to the island. His name was Finlay Ferguson. He fell in love with my grandmother (a McDonald) and settled in the island.

At the time of my father's marriage (1822) the houses were grouped together, but when I was about 8 or 10, surveyors cut the place up in lots, and lots were cast and each man had to go onto his own lot and new houses were put up. My father had more sheep than anyone else on the island, some of them (about 200) were on Borero, an island about eight miles off. He had six or seven horses, he used to breed and sell, also several head of cattle. The wool woven into cloth was the main source of income. We had two spinning wheels and one weaving machine, and we used to work at this all the winter and most of the summer. The spinning was mostly done by the women and the weaving by the men.

The island of St. Kilda was precipitous, there were cliffs 1,000 ft high round the cultivation, and this meant in summer it was very hot. In summer the islanders seldom wore boots except on Sundays and when visitors came. It snowed much in winter. I have seen drifts 40 ft deep. Each man cultivated 8 to 10 acres. There was 10 acres in the glebe. Oats and barley were grown, also potatoes, vegetables were also grown. Cows and sheep were milked, butter and cheese were made and cheese was sometimes sold. The cheese fetched a very good price as it was extra good. Before the disease came in the potatoes (about 1847) we had more potatoes than we could use and we used to feed them to the cows. After that they were scarce. It was never so bad as the first year and ultimately disappeared. The people raised all the corn they needed for their own use in those days when the population was so great, and rent and taxes were paid for in corn.

Island of Soay

In the shearing season ten or twelve men would go for a week at a time to the island. The island of Soay was capable of carrying 1300 or 1400 sheep belonging to the proprieter and the men used to shear for him, getting only food as a rule, but some consideration would be made in other ways. There were no white sheep on this island. They were miserable creatures. The islanders would get them at 2/6d a head. The best sheep at this time fetched only 6/- each. The wool was reddish and fetched 2/6d per pound but there was not a great weight of it. They were allowed to breed as they pleased and deteriorated. We always killed a sheep for New Year's Day.

Island of Dun

Another island, the island of Dun, belonged to the proprietor, on this also were sheep. It was evident from furrows that at one time this has been cultivated. On some parts of St. Kilda also were traces of ground having been ploughed. In my time there was no ploughing. In those older days all payment had to be by corn. There was a terrific outbreak of small-pox when near 200 people died of it. In all my time no one was drowned, one man fell over the cliffs and was killed.

Fulmar and other Birds

A deal was made out of feathers of sea-birds, especially the fulmar. From the fulmar we got oil also, from young ones especially. Most of this oil was used for lamps but much was sold at 1/- a gallon to the factor. The oil from the old fulmar was not so plentiful, but was more valuable, being used for lotion, it brought 1/- a bottle. They did not care to kill the old birds. They laid only one egg in nests in the cliffs. We never gathered eggs of this bird, a fine was inflicted for this. When after the young fulmar, ropes were used sometimes to let the men down, sometimes the rope was tied to a peg and the man let himself down; sometimes a mate on top let the man down, and sometimes two men tied together with a rope between would help one another down. We got from the young

fulmar feathers and oil. They used to hunt them in parties of four or five, each party having its own hunting ground. The oil was clear like kerosene, but darker if the young fulmar saw you coming, he would spit oil at you, some would spill a pint of oil this way. When caught and killed the bird was held head down

Fulmar Cliffs at the Gap, Boreray and the Stacs.

and the oil was run into receptacles. This was not the oil sold at 1/– a gallon but was mostly burnt. The birds were cleaned and salted and when boiled the better oil was got. The flesh was then often used for food.

The penguin (he must mean the guillemot, D.A.Q.) and many other birds were killed for their feathers. The Solan Geese were sometimes eaten. The eggs of birds were also a source of food supply – the eggs of the penguin (guillemot) were about the size of hens' eggs, and almost as good. These eggs were gathered by going in boats to the foot of the cliffs and climbing.

Paying the Rent

The island was owned by Sir John McPherson McLeod. I remember seeing him on the island with his wife and servants. He was the son of Colonel McLeod and was Chief Justice of Calcutta for 22 years. We paid rent to him through the factor. For every sheep we had running on the island, except for 10 for each crofter, we had to pay 1/– per annum and each yearling 6d. Also for every head of cattle, except one cow for each crofter, 7/– per annum, and the people between them paid £35 for the privilege of killing the birds. It was very hard to tell exactly how many sheep etc. we had as all were mixed together, each had his own ear-mark and the factor had to take the word of each man. It was easy for the crofters to cheat, but I never knew of this being done. We could tell only by the number shorn. It (the wool) usually lifted off like a blanket. The people paid £5 per annum for the grass on Borera. Previous to my time vessels used to come and steal the sheep. The people at that time were very suspicious of all strange vessels and used to retire and hide in inaccessible spots. The crofters paid about 30/– each or more for the land they cultivated. This meant some £25 or more for the land. We paid nothing for the privilege of fishing. The factor bought all the fish we could catch at 4d per head. Of herrings we caught usually only what we wanted. The men fished with nets and lines but in winter it was usually too rough. We used to set the long net in the evening and take it up in the mornings. The lines we fished off the rocks also and caught schnapper and salted any surplus. In twelve months they were just as good as ever. We caught also "lieu" (probably "liugh" – lythe). Fishing smacks were always about there. They would fill their ship in two to three days.

Church and School

The visits of the Rev. John McDonald of Ferintosh resulted in a revival, but about 1841 there was a great revival. The people did very little work for two years. There were meetings almost every night in the Church with the minister. The regular services all along on Sundays were at 7am. Gaelic, 11am. Gaelic and before separating – the English service, and in the evening. At one time there was a Bible class at 2pm for 1½ hours for married men and women. (At the Day School there was a class of 16 married women taught by the minister).

During the week the men were usually away in boats at one or the other of the islands around, looking after sheep or birds, or occasionally fishing.

One Wednesday night the minister was preaching, at a meeting in the Church. The minister was the Rev. Neil McKenzie, a good man and a faithful preacher, it was McDonald of Ferintosh who inducted him on his last visit, when I was baptised. In the meeting I remember hearing Mrs. Gillies crying. There were nine or ten men in the meeting. I afterwards heard one of the men tell some who were arriving with the boats from their day's work, "I believe the Spirit of God was formed upon our congregation tonight." This was the beginning of the revival.

There was a meeting every Tuesday in one cottage or another to explain the Shorter Catechism. On Wednesday evenings there was a service in the Church, Thursday evening a meeting for all communicants by themselves, Friday evening, a preparatory class.

Whenever the minister was absent the elders kept the services going. John Ferguson was the preacher since before I remember and remained so till he was over eighty, in both Gaelic and English.

The father of Mrs. Ewen Gillies (second) was my first teacher – Donald MacQueen, a cousin of mine. We had no introductory books and we didn't make much progress.

One Donald McKinnon, a native of the island, whom Dr. McDonald of Ferintosh had taken away and sent to College was next. He was at the same time the factor. He married a school-mistress who was in Harris. She was a very fine woman. Some benefactor in past times had left £25 per annum to pay for a school-master and we thought it was a great sum. He and the minister did not get on very well, but the people placed their faith in the minister. Complaint was made of his factorship and he was moved away. Rory, who was here when Finlay Ferguson came, was a son of his.

The minister next took it. He had also to farm his glebe and was a good farmer. He was very vigorous in looking up absentees. On one occasion he missed one woman and on calling and enquiring as the reason he was told that she stayed at home to keep the crows away from the house – the crows used to make great holes in the thatch after the corn. About this time a school house was built about a quarter of a mile from the Church and we went there for four or five years. Sir John McPherson McLeod and some others came on a visit and they thought it was better to hold school in the Church as the minister had charge and it would be more convenient and it was so held until after I left.

Gaelic and English were both taught.

After McKenzie left no minister was settled till I came away, but other school-masters came. One Carmichael started singing lessons to which I went and one McEwan was two years there. The islanders at the Disruption came out and joined the Free Church. These masters belonged to the Established Church and the £25 was in the hands of the Established Church. When McEwen came he found the elders carrying on services regularly and he wanted to take the service on an equal footing with the elders but the people resented this. One family kept away from this meeting and then Finlay Gillies (grandfather of the present Finlay), then MacDonald (married to Betty Scott from Sutherlandshire) – these three families gathered in our house, then we got double the congregation. At least my Uncle Neil came and we went to a larger place to Roderick Gillies' house, a larger room. We were there for nearly six months and all the people except 15 or 16 came there. Among those going to the Church were 9 who got benefit from the minister's glebe and thought McEwen might have some control over the glebe.

The factor, Norman McRail then came out and was vexed at the state of matters. He threatened to evict any who refused to go to Church. In this he overstepped his powers and the owner was opposed to this conduct. A fortnight or three weeks after McEwen left and all went back to Church.

I remember the father of Ewen Gillies, Malcolm McDonald (Mrs. McLeod – Colac's father) and I were staying there. Gillies was excited over the land question and said he reckoned the people had made a mistake in coming out. If it were not for that (leaving the Established Church) we would have been on our own land from eternity to eternity. After he had gone out, Malcolm McDonald turned to me and said, "Is not that an ignorant man?" On another occasion he was speaking in this style and his son reminded him that he was the second to sign for the Free Church. "Yes," he said, "but I did not know what I was doing. I saw John Ferguson, my brother-in-law signing and I never knew him to make a mistake or do anything bad in his life and I thought I was quite safe following his example." Some folk had told him we were all to be put off the land and sent away. But McLeod had instructed the factor that on no account, for debt or anything else, were any of the people to be sent away. A deputation from the Free Church came every year and the Communion was then held. Ewen Gillies was one of the chief movers to come away.

When I was about 22 or 23 a deputation came, Mr. Alls Sinclair of Clunies and Breadalbane was one (Marquis of Breadalbane was one of his elders), Mr. McGilvray, from Glasgow was another. Mr. McGilvray bought all our tweed and gave us 2d per yard more than the factor. There were three to interview, Malcolm Ferguson, Finlay MacQueen (father of Mrs. Sommerville) and myself. The year before this, Ferguson about six years previously had been appointed by the people to teach for nine months while there was no teacher. Ferguson and MacQueen were both married. They asked the elders whom they would prefer and I was nominated. They took me out to the yacht and I was examined. They told me I had to teach English and brought me the English Bible to read, but especially to teach Gaelic. I was appointed and acted as school-master till three days before leaving. While master I did not get any of that £25 as it was in the hand of the Established Church. On my way to Australia I called to see Rev. Roderick McLeod of Skye (Master Rory) and he was not pleased at my leaving. I told him that I had appointed my Uncle Neil Ferguson and he was pleased at that. Master Rory and McDougall of Raasay inspected the school while I was there. I was laid in fever when they arrived."

A NEW START IN AUSTRALIA

During the decade prior to 1852 life on St. Kilda had become increasingly difficult. The potato blight having reached the island, fortunately died out fairly quickly. The period of progress and development under the Rev. Neil MacKenzie between 1830 and 1844, when the new village was carefully planned and completed, was followed by a time of considerable unrest after his departure. In 1846 the St. Kildans became members of the Free Church in the presence of a Deputy who visited the island. At the same time the Established Church sent out teachers and were responsible for the Church building and the glebe. This tension was felt very deeply and divided the community. Rumours abounded that they were going to be forced off their land and would have to leave the island. The rent also continued to be a heavy burden on each family, although the owner made it quite clear that no one was to be evicted from the island, even if they were in debt. At the same time plans drawn up by the Highland and Island Emigration Society reached St. Kilda. The sense of dissatisfaction continued to wrankle until eventually 36 of the inhabitants decided to leave and to seek a better way of life in Australia.

Malcolm MacQueen takes up the story:-

The Voyage – St. Kilda to Australia

"We left St. Kilda in a sailing ship belonging to Mrs. Sarah McDonald and came to Skye. We called at Harris on the way and stayed about a fortnight in Skye and the neighbourhood. From there we went by steamer to Glasgow. We were there some twenty-four hours and shipped aboard a steamer for Liverpool. The owner of St. Kilda, Sir John McPherson McLeod, met us in Glasgow and was speaking to all the St. Kildans till we came to Liverpool. In Liverpool he offered to send them all back in a steamer to St. Kilda and give them all they needed for two years. We told him probably the rest of the inhabitants would come

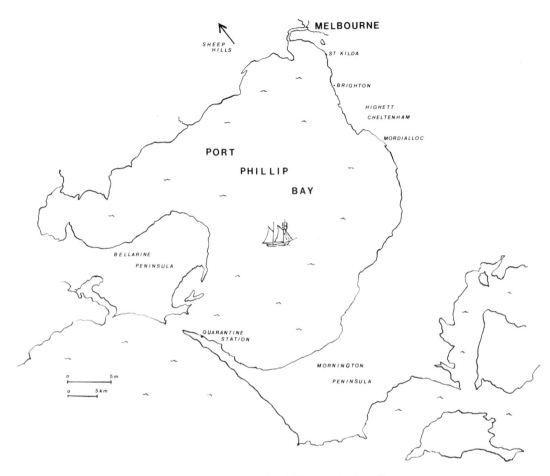

Map Port Phillip Bay and Neighbourhood, Australia.

away shortly. He asked what he had better do to retain them. The people were not pleased because the Established Church sent catechists and schoolmasters, while the people themselves belonged to the Free Church. We suggested that the Manse and Church should be given to the people. He replied that he had no power to do that as, although built on his land, they belonged to the Established Church, but he would see what he could do. We afterwards learnt that

he purchased them from the Established Church and presented them to the Free Church and the people are now in the Free Church.

We were in Liverpool some three or four weeks and shipped on board the "Priscilla" bound for Port Phillip. We saw no land or vessel till we came near the Heads after 13 weeks. Three weeks after leaving measles broke out and many died, about 80 old and young, largely owing to the ignorance of the doctor.

He used to drive them on deck and they would be dead in the next morning. At last the passengers rebelled and refused to allow the doctor to have his own way, no one died after that. I was the last man to take ill with it. My mother was laid up at the same time as I was. A young widow and another woman were very kind. Frank McKenzie and Alex McDonald were very kind to me. They did not live long after getting here. Passengers were landed at the quarantine station but those who were ill were kept aboard and the vessel was made a quarantine hulk. Scarlet fever was aboard when we arrived. Many who were healthy when landing got ill at the quarantine and most of them died. The old quarantine station was at Elwood about Point Ormond. That accounts for my father meeting Wymmes and McMillan both of whom lived on North Road.

Settling In

The year we landed here, 20,000 landed in Victoria from the Highlands.

All our family came on here. We built Mia-Mia's of Ti-trees, I saw no buildings. Dr. McDonald of Baerald Hill was there when we landed. He had got there some weeks previously on the "Allison". He left with the other passengers about a fortnight afterwards. A marquee was sent from Melbourne and services were being conducted there before we landed. I attended a service held by Dr. McDonald there, and I conducted a Gaelic service after he had gone. There were about 1,000 people there, mostly Highlanders.

We came after about five weeks in the same vessel up to Melbourne, about the month of February. I was in Melbourne a week. In our ship were a number of passengers who had paid their fares. We thought we should have better treatment on that account as the rest were emigrants whose fares were paid. When we landed we all went together, I was complaining to the man in charge of something and he asked my name, on telling him he said, "Oh we have nothing to do with you for you are not an emigrant. We could turn you out tomorrow if we like to, but we won't." Thus the tables were turned. My father paid £120 or £130 passenger money. McLeod paid for all who were unable to pay their way.

Finding Work

Uncle Malcolm, Gillies and I were engaged by Walstab of Brighton, my father and mother and uncle John came with me. Gillies' wife was with him but Ferguson's wife died in the quarantine ship. We were splitting wood for brick-burning. We were there about six months.

Wymmes was living at Brighton. Mrs. McMillan and Mrs. Wymmes were both very kind to my mother. Wymmes was at the digging while we were at Walstab and Mr. McMillan was at home. The women folk were very kind. Walstab sacked Gillies because he thought he was lazy; he caught him sitting on his hayrack one day. When sacked Gillies got no money given him but he went to Lachlan McKinnon of the Argus Office who had been appointed as agent of the Society which was sending out the Highlanders. McKinnon told him to demand the money and if he didn't get it to come back. When Gillies went next day Walstab was waiting for him with the money – I don't think Walstab meant to keep him out of his money. My father died while we were with Walstab and was buried in the English Church ground (the main Church in Brighton, in New Street).

When I finished with Walstab we went to McDonald of Mordiallic (Uncle Malcolm, Ewen Gillies and a Neil McDonald joined us) to make bricks for the Hotel now standing there. But we had never made bricks. So he got a Mr. Straker to instruct us and then afterwards to come and burn them with us. We made 40,000. He was a splendid employer. They were dairying there. We were in a large tent about the present cricket ground. A McLeod, afterwards of Cheltenham, was living in Mordiallic. There were some McKenzies there, one of whom was a boat builder. We were there about three months and then came here to see the land Wilkinson was selling, afterwards called "Gaelic Town". I bought one acre at that time for £50. Uncle Malcolm and Gillies also bought. Gillies getting the acre next to us. The day I bought the land I agreed with Malcolm McLean to bring our luggage up with his bullock dray and we lived there in tents.

We agreed to work for Wilkinson draining a swamp – "The Double Lagoon". (Kelman McQueen commented, "As the name "Double Lagoon" is shown on Malcolm's marriage certificate, and as he bought his land before he married, I would say that it is pretty certain it was in the area of Spring Road, Highett, where his land was and where he set up house and family. Spring Road was named from the number of water springs in the area, which would tie in with "Double Lagoon"). We were taking the stuff out and putting it on the land. He was a good farmer and a good master. We spread the stuff and he planted potatoes. The first crop was no good – all top. The next year he put them in again without manure and got a great crop. Wilkinson had houses in Richmond, prices were very high for land at that time but then came a great slump. Gillies left and went into Melbourne for a while and then went off to the diggings and we heard nothing of him for several years. We got 10/– a day at Wilkinsons.

McMillan of Brighton sent for me and asked me to go and make bricks for him. While Malcolm and I went down and found he was not quite ready to commence. He was to pay £5 a 1,000 for making them. As he was not ready, a Mr. Masawell, who had the contract for making the Brighton Road about Elsternwick, got us to help him giving us 14/– a day for several weeks. We then started at the bricks.

Marriage and Visit to St. Kilda, Melbourne

At that time I was courting (Mary MacSwain from the Island of Raasay in Scotland, who had also emigrated). We got Uncle Donald and Uncle Malcolm to help us at the bricks. Mr. Chisholm got us to make some giving us 48/–. Uncle Malcolm married about that time. He used to knock off when we had made 1,000. He reckoned we were doing well enough.

I came back to South Brighton a little before Christmas and put a fence around this block and built four rooms with weatherboard with a view to getting married. The house was lined with laths and filled in between with clay, the roof was shingles. We were married at McMillan's house at Brighton by Dr. MacKay of St. Andrew's Gaelic Church. He had been preaching there the previous evening. August 22nd. 1855 was the date of the marriage. We went to Church on the Sunday after the marriage, but coming home we took a cab as far as St. Kilda. We were here only about five weeks after getting married and then went to Sheep Hills, together with my mother and John with Uncle Malcolm and his wife (Auntie Sarah). We had a cart for the women and were driving a good few cows up with us. It took nine days going up. We halted a day and a half at Glen Wyllen, 50 or 60 miles this side of Sheep Hills. We passed another station of theirs called "Cattle Station" about 12 miles from Glen Wyllen; it was the other side of the river and they used to send most of the sheep down there in the summer as water was scarce at Sheep Hills. For the first six months we lived at the "Home Station" and then went out to a hut close to a big water hole, about 3½ miles towards the present Warraacknabeal, then called "Scots Station".

We were there for a time by ourselves and then my mother came to live with us. When the water dried up we went to the "Homestead". I worked with Neil one of the brothers, putting up huts and when idle used to go out sometimes with the sheep. My mother was not satisfied up there and so we came back. We had taken our own horse and cart but the horse was killed up there. We bought another from a man name Stewart for £36.

When I was returning with the horse and cart (from Sheep Hills Homestead), about 10 miles before I came to the Warmera I saw a dog come out and start to bark and saw a small tent by the side of the road and a man came out who was so ill he could not speak. He was dying for want of water. I took him to the water. When he saw the water he ran off to it and I never saw him again. I camped a few days at the "Cattle Station" and set off again via Glen Wyllen. There Uncle Malcolm and his wife joined us. It was summer and the road was good so we did not take long coming down. We got here on an afternoon and we found Mrs. Gillies, whom we had left in charge of the cottages, had gone into town. McDonald got Malcolm and me to put up a mile of fencing. He got the Hotel built while we were up country. We were camped up at Long's Water Hole on the Carrum, where we were getting the posts and we both came in once a week.

Things were very bad before we went up country. They were opening soup kitchens about town and there was very little work. After my return I worked for three months with a man named Burrows who was where Elizabeth Arnott afterwards lived. We then heard of a contract that a Mr. Campbell and Russell had, and then went up past Kilmore, road making. We were there three months, Norman McLean (afterwards of Framlingham) was with us there. Before going to Kilmore, Backhouse who lived below Uncle's house came to me and offered me the 6 acres in the paddock for £70. I said I would take it if the deeds were given the clear. After my return I did some work on the road making on Main Road over here. While there they had a strike. They were getting 5/- per day and struck for 1/- extra. The contractor gave it, but on Saturday night he paid off 30 of them. Most of these men went to Queensland where the gold-fields just broke out, scarcely any of them every returned.

We cleared the face of the hill and sowed oats. Padwick offered me £9 for the hay and I wished to sell. I had potatoes also. John and I were partners in the land and John went to market. When Malcolm Ferguson went to Mordiallic we bought his land and when Murdoch McLean went to Purman we bought that acre; we bought the two acres (the little paddock) from a Mrs. McLean and afterwards we got Backhouse's land.

Church Life

The day after I landed in Victoria (about Feb. 20 1853) I went to the Protestant Hall in Stephen St. (now Exhibition St.) Brighton to a Gaelic service. After 12 months the preacher gave out that a committee was about to wait on the authorities to get a site for a Gaelic Church. We met in that hall for two years, I did not get in regularly. One Sabbath the announcement was made that Dr. MacKay was on his way out. There were about 13 Gaelic families here at that time and they called the place "Gaelic Town". I remember the first time I heard Dr. MacKay. His text was "Let your conversation be as becometh the gospel of Christ." He made a sensation that day. Dr. MacKay came out to go to Sydney, he travelled throughout the country.

They earlier took steps to build a Church but it was not easy as stone masons were getting 35/- a day. Alex McLean was engaged as Clerk of Works to look after these buildings. Dr. MacKay came out to Mr. McMillan's once a month on a week day. He was a

very thoughtful preacher and I remember several of his texts. He preached ten sermons on the Parable of the Sower.

Uncle Malcolm and I used to conduct a service at McSwain's and we used to go into town at least every Sunday. The Church, St. Andrew's, Brighton cost I believe £12,000. I was at the opening day in 1855 and Dr. MacKay preached one sermon. His text was "I rejoiced when they said unto me, I will go up to the House of God". Another sermon was preached by Mr. William McIntyre of N.S.W. in English in the morning and in Gaelic in the evening. The collections were £456 for the day at the opening. Less than three weeks after the Church was opened I was married by Mr. MacKay on August 22nd 1855. Uncle Malcolm was married more than 15 months before me.

We heard before we returned from the country that Dr. MacKay left and went to Sydney. Times were very hard now and many of the Highlanders had scattered in search of work and he was disappointed by the smallness of the congregations. For 7 years after that I went in to the Gaelic service at 2 o'clock. After Dr. MacKay left they were a good while without a minister. Uncle Malcolm and I used to carry on the service between us. We also carried on the prayer-meeting on the Thursday night. The Rev. Fraser came out to take charge of the Church. He was a better preacher in English than in Gaelic. He was followed by a Mr. Beggs from Warrnambool and Mr. McGregor, then Mr. Wade and a Mr. McEachran from Cromarty.

By this time, 1886 or 87, the service was going regularly at Cheltenham and as the rest of the family were going there I did not go regularly to St. Andrews. There was no service here when we came. About this time I was elected with Hugh Brewer, Mr. McCallum and Mr. Milburn as the first session at Cheltenham. Mr. Kay prepared the plans for the new Church. It was Hugh Brown and my brother John who started the Sunday School. Some years after I went there we had about 73 scholars and I took the Bible Class. After Mr. Brown left I acted as Superintendant and was there for 17 years (Superintendant of the School and Secretary), also Secretary of the Board of Management and Senior Clerk. I was going to Westerport once a month for about 10 years and once a fortnight for sometime afterwards. I left when a minister was settled in Dandenong.

Mr. Gordon from Invercargill was called to Brighton. When I left Cheltenham I went there. Mr. Gordon was in the old church for 2 years but the congregation grew rapidly and it was decided to build a new Church. Mr. Gordon was a man in a hundred and drew a great congregation. When we went down the congregation were worshipping in the Town Hall. I was representative elder at Brighton for 20 years. Professor Dr. McDonald of Ormond College opened the New Church – your mother and I were at the opening, His text was, "He shall come down as rain upon the mown grass." He preached a splendid sermon. Gordon drew great congregations there, the Church was filled until the crash came after the land boom. We were going to Brighton for 11 years and then came back to Cheltenham about the time Gordon resigned."

Malcolm MacQueen's account ends rather abruptly but not before he has given us a fascinating glimpse into life on St. Kilda before 1852, the horrors of the voyage in the "Priscilla", and the many and varied problems which had to be faced by the St. Kildans and other Scottish emigrants as they attempted to forge their new way of life and to make their homes in Australia.

Both Malcolm and his wife died in Melbourne, Mary on the 14th of July 1905 and Malcolm, aged 85, on the the 16th. November 1913. Kelman McQueen kindly sent me the two family photographs.

The Gillies
A Family Portrait

"Town and Harbour, St. Kilda." Acland.

The Gillies have been an important, influential and much travelled group of families on St. Kilda, probably arriving to repopulate the island after the terrible small-pox outbreak in 1727 which had decimated the island. Prof. Lawson comments that they "almost certainly came from Skye, as that surname is not found in Uist or Harris at that date and the later families in these islands have a Skye origin. MacDonald (1822) has five sets of Gillieses: Alexander (3), Angus (13), John (6), John (10) and Roderick (9). Mitchell's notes (1865) require at least two different sets of Gillieses. Since Alexander, Roderick and John (10) all called their eldest sons Finlay, it is tempting to assume that they could be brothers, sons of the original Finlay,

Three Generations of Gillies – Finlay, Ewen, Neil. A. M. Cockburn.

leaving Angus and John (6) as the sons of the other Gillies, probably Donald. John (6)'s family went to Claddach Illeray in North Uist and Angus had no sons and so it would appear that all the later Gillieses in the island were of the same family." (Lawson, W. M. St. Kilda Mail, 1981). At the time of the Evacuation in 1930 nearly half the population bore the name Gillies – the sixteen members came from five households. Many have been colourful characters and five pen-portraits are included here to represent the families.

EWEN GILLIES – Born 1825, Emigrated to Australia, New Zealand and Canada
FLORA GILLIES – Born 1919, Left St. Kilda at the Evacuation. Father died on Boreray
NORMAN JOHN GILLIES – Born 1925, Left St. Kilda at the Evacuation
NEIL GILLIES – Born 1896, Left St. Kilda in 1919, Worked in Glasgow
REV. DONALD JOHN GILLIES – Born 1901, Left in 1924, Canada, Army and Prison Chaplain

EWEN GILLIES

Ewen's father, John Gillies was born in 1778, he was first married to Betsy Ferguson, and later to Mary Gillies, Ewen being the fifth of the six children born to Mary. On the 10th. July 1849 he married Margaret MacDonald and on the ill-fated emigration to Australia their baby Mary died on the voyage. Ewen also features in the MacQueen story.

While John Ross was the Schoolmaster on St. Kilda in the summer of 1889 he met up with Ewen Gillies who had returned from his travels to visit his native haunts and his friends. Ross in his memoirs, written in beautiful copperplate style, about his time on St. Kilda

tells his story having received it at first hand. Here is his account:-

"One man, "Ewen Giliies" or as he was latterly termed "California" although he had as good a right to "Victoria", "Melbourne", "Rocky Mountain" or "New Zealand" had some wonderful migrations and it may not be out of place to give a few here as I drew them from himself.

Born in November 1825 he remembers at eight years of age about the first tea introduced to the island. He was offered a cup by the Factor but doubting his benefactor's motives took it with the exclamation, "If I am killed you will be blamed for it." Have it he would, it seems, even should it kill him.

Emigration to Australia in 1852

He married an elder's daughter when twenty three years of age and three years after, he determined to leave the island. He sold all his effects for £17 and with his wife and thirty six other St. Kildans set sail for Melbourne by Skye, Glasgow, and Birkenhead. His thoughts on never seeming to come to the end of the journey can better be imagined than described.

This was a fatal voyage to many St. Kildans as no less than twenty six died from the effects of some fever contracted on board ship. It is noticeable that St. Kildans are very liable to smit disease at any time for if one takes ill the cause passes through their community like an electric shock passing through all the parts of the human body. What is this owing to? Is it consanguity?

But to follow my man who was one of those with his wife who escaped the dread enemy. After landing, he with five others, was employed by an Englishman in Melbourne at brickmaking. They were very glad to leave this at the expiry of their term of engagement –

six months – and for the next two years wandered over a great part of Victoria digging for gold with very little success. But wishing to have his "better half" with him, who was all this time at Melbourne, he started shepherding with a Skye gentleman, Colin MacKinnon Esq. "nephew to the minister who used to preach to Lord McDonald of the Isles."

After staying here fifteen months he thought he had sufficient to start for himself, so he took a small farm. But probably owing to a limited capital and a St. Kilda training, this did not turn out a good speculation and he had to give up in two years.

New Zealand and Canada

Not pleased with Australia he packed off to the New Zealand gold diggings in 1861 leaving his wife and three children at Melbourne. He was not so successful in New Zealand as he expected although he could not do much in the time for he returned to Australia in less than two years. Short as his stay was, it was too long for his wife who, probably never expecting his return, married a Melbourne man and, as Ewen had no money, he left them undisturbed and crossed to North America.

Here he took the step, so often resorted to by the unsuccessful – "Listed". Yes, our St. Kildan has listed in the Union Army but as in every place and work made a short stay. For after carrying the colours for two years he made for the "Californian" gold mines. "Fortune favours the brave" the old proverb says and it came true in our brave soldier's case as he spent six years here attended with great success.

Then possessing some money he went back to Australia to claim at least his children. After some trouble he was successful and not wishing to stay longer at that time sailed to London, thence to St. Kilda. Possibly the children were not satisfied with such small limits for in five weeks he and they returned to California. There he got them all settled and after spending other eleven successful years thought he would betake himself to his native rock and take his ease for the remainder of his life. He returned, but only like Sinbad, to stay for a few months. The charm of another St. Kildan proved too much for he married her and sailed again for Melbourne. This climate did not agree with his second bride as well as with the first which caused them to return in eight months for another breath of St. Kilda air. This was in 1886. From then 'till June 1889 he tried in various ways to work reformation among his less travelled brethren but with even less success than attended him at his first gold digging, for they actually made him leave the place, having no faith in such a prodigal. He is now with his wife again in Canada. Where he will go or what he will do next is a mystery."

FLORA GILLIES

I have very much enjoyed talking with Flora on a number of occasions. She is very reticent to talk about life on St. Kilda as she was only 11 years old at the Evacuation and feels that she cannot add to the St. Kilda Portraits. However, a number of things she said seem well worth telling.

Family

Flora is the youngest of four daughters living in No. 14. Her father Donald Gillies had married Annie MacQueen, the daughter of Finlay who had married Mary Otter Gillies. The family had to overcome one tragedy after another on St. Kilda. The first was the death of Donald on the 26th. June 1922 at the age of 36. He was on Boreray with a group of men minding the sheep when he took seriously ill with appendicitis.

Neil Gillies and nieces, Rachel Johnson and Flora Craig, both Gillies'.

Flora commented, "As far as I know he was the only St. Kildan to die on Boreray. My sister Chrissie was over there with him at the time. She would only be nine." Chrissie was to contract mumps, "Her neck was all swollen, and she caught a cold after it and died, she was only 13 when she died in 1926."

Mary

The third member of the family to die on St. Kilda, and that within the space of 8 years, was Mary, she was the oldest of the daughters. She caught T.B. and was very ill during the winter of 1929-30. Her condition deteriorated. An article in the Times for 23rd May 1930 told the story of the attempt to save her life.

TRAWLER'S ERRAND OF MERCY
From our Correspondent – Fleetwood
May 22nd, 1930

It was related, when the steam trawler "Chorley" arrived in port today, that the vessel had abandoned its fishing voyage during rough weather on the high seas in order to bring help to a 23 year old girl of St. Kilda who was dying. The trawler was steaming passed the island on Saturday morning when signals of waving sheets were observed and the vessel drew in. Islanders rowed to it and asked that a message from the island's Nurse, Miss Barclay, should be put on the trawler's wireless at once. The message was addressed to the Scottish Board of Health at Edinburgh, and stated that Mary Gillies was seriously ill, and asked for Medical advice. An immediate reply came from the board who asked if the "Chorley" could put into Leverburgh, South Uist, and await the arrival of a doctor. When the consent of the owners, the Palatine Steam Trawling Company Limited of Fleetwood, had been sought and obtained, the vessel picked up Dr. Alexander Shearer, of Edinburgh, and a health inspector who had been sent by the authorities the same evening. Then began the dash of 50 miles back to St. Kilda, where the trawler arrived late the same night, but the gale had increased so much that it was impossible to approach until 10 on Sunday morning. After that the vessel was stormbound until Monday morning, when the Doctor and inspector were taken to Leverburgh. Unfortunately, it was found that the condition of Mary Gillies was hopeless; and she was so dangerously ill that she could not be moved to hospital on the mainland."

Mary died on the 21st, July 1930. This sad event added confirmation to the islanders that they were doing the right thing in asking to be taken off the island and to be rehoused on the mainland.

Rachel Annie

Rachel Annie was the second daughter to be born to the family. During 1927 she was helping Mrs. MacLeod, the wife of the Missionary, at the Manse.

When Mrs. MacLeod left on a trawler bound for Fleetwood, to begin her holiday in the following year, Mary went with her, seeking a job. The newspapers of the day were fascinated. The Daily Mail for 30th. May 1928 carried an article:-

RACHEL IN WONDERLAND
ST. KILDAN SEES HER FIRST TREE
LAUGH AT TRAFFIC POLICEMAN

A 17 year old girl who has never before seen a tree, a horse, a motor-car, a railway train, a cinema picture, a telegraph pole, or, indeed the majority of the civilised amenities which are now commonplace, was taken for a motor-car ride through Blackpool by a Daily Mail reporter on Saturday.

She is Miss Rachel Gillies, a native of St. Kilda, the lonely island in the North Atlantic, and she is paying a brief visit to Fleetwood with Mrs. MacLeod, the wife of the island Missioner, and Mr. John McDonald. It is the first time Rachel has left her island home. During the greater part of the journey she sat in silence, spellbound, too delighted to speak. Her bright eyes missed nothing. Occasionally she would ask a rapid question in Gaelic or broken English. "What makes the car move? . . . Is that a tree? . . . I have only seen them in pictures . . . And what are those funny wires hanging on the poles for?" She shook her head in dismay when she was told they were telegraph poles. "I don't understand." she said.

"But your 'sheep!" she exclaimed. "They are very dirty, and the cows in your fields are nothing like the St. Kildan cows." A windmill at Thornton, near Blackpool, with its huge sails, mystified her. "What is it?" she asked.

She laughed when she saw a policeman in uniform with white sleeves directing the traffic. "Isn't he funny?" she exclaimed, "I have never seen anything like him before." Motor-cyclists with side-cars and pillion riders amused her but she had no words with which to describe her astonishment when she saw Blackpool Tower and the Big Wheel. Rachel's brow knitted in bewilderment at the electric tramways-car which moved without any visible methods of traction. "How do they go like that?" she asked. At the South Shore Fair-ground Rachel was filled with alarm that people should go for amusement on contrivances which seemed to her so dangerous and mysterious. "I would NOT like to go on that," she exclaimed with finality when she saw the Big Dipper.

Rachel is trying to grasp the conditions which prevail in England. She has still to speak on a telephone and see a cinema picture. At present she feels like Alice in Wonderland, but she finds the pursuit of knowledge in modern England the most entrancing experience she has ever had."

Another report commented, "She stopped a moment to gaze enraptured at a florist's shop full of madonna lilies, daffodils and tulips, "They are lovely – lovely," she said. "I have never seen flowers before." Rachel's life at present is just one big thrill after another. Mrs. Parker, of St. Peter's Place, with whom she is living, said to me, "I am afraid she will become ill with all the excitement of seeing tramway-cars, shops, motor-cars, and fresh people. "How I envy Rachel!"

Rachel's stay in Fleetwood didn't last long. She took up domestic work for a short period, but she soon became restless and homesick and returned to her native St. Kilda. She stayed on until the Evacuation, living with her mother and sister, Flora, before marrying Robert Milne in 1942. They have no children but still live happily in Culross in Fife.

Flora

"My earliest memories were of just going to school, we went to Church and to Sunday School. My best friend lived next door at No. 13, Cathy Gillies, we were the same age and we were always playing together, which meant that her sister, Rachel (now Rachel Johnson) was always left out. At school we learnt English and Gaelic. I remember carrying peats for my grandfather – bringing them down from Mulloch Mor – we had several cleits up there. In the Village we had two cleits down by the sea wall on the croft directly below No. 14, this one is still standing, the other below No. 15 has fallen down. I remember the evenings of waulking the tweed . . . pulling it across the table.

"I don't remember my father, I was only three years old when he died. My mother's name was Annie, she was a MacQueen." (Gladstone commented, "She only lived to make people happy.") With so many sad events happening so close at hand I asked if they had been depressed on St. Kilda? Flora replied, "We were only very young – we did not realise at the time." Asked if she had photographs of her parents, she ruefully said, "I had just one of my father. I lent it to a man, together with one of my mother and he was going to put the two together into one photograph. I have never seen them since. I have never seen another photograph of my father. People said he was very like his brother."

About the Evacuation, Flora said, "I remember very clearly seeing the sheep being loaded up. It was a gorgeous day when we left, lovely and sunny and calm. I remember looking back and seeing all the chimneys smoking – it was very sad. We went to Lochaline, my mother, Rachel and myself, and we stayed with Mrs. MacQueen from No. 11 for nine months. Later we moved to Culross in Fife where a number of St. Kildans had made their homes and had found work – the MacQueens and the Fergusons. We moved into a big house where we could be nearer together. In Morvern we were far from each other."

Flora married Richard Craig in 1943 and they have lived in Kincardine for the last 30 years. They are both very happy and active – they climbed Ben Nevis together in 1986. They have a daughter Christine and a son Harry. Flora has been back to St. Kilda several times, "In a way it is just the same – there are some new buildings – in some ways nothing has changed. It brings back all the memories – it is such a lovely place."

NORMAN JOHN GILLIES

Norman John was born on 22nd. of May 1925 in No. 15. His home was to be in No. 10, but later he moved back to No. 15 after his mother died. His father was John, the third son of John Gillies and Annie Ferguson, the Queen of St. Kilda. His mother was Mary MacQueen, (the daughter of Donald MacQueen and Marion MacDonald), sadly she died on the 26th. of May 1930 just before the Evacuation. Norman John was so named after his mother's two brothers, who were both drowned in the boating accident off the Dun, together with Donald MacDonald Lachlan's father, in 1909. Norman John told me that, "When I was born seemingly I was not breathing. The nurse, mother and grandmother kept putting me in baths of cold water, then in warm water, but still there was not a sign of life. My mother kept holding me, but they said, 'you might as well lay him down – he's dead'. Fortunately, someone thought of turning me upside down and gave me a good smack, so consequently here I am in September 1987 still alive!"

"My childhood memories of St. Kilda are of my mother standing on the large dyke in front of No. 10, and calling me home to dinner (in Gaelic). It didn't matter which end of the village I was, she could still see me. I also remember being locked in No. 10, I'd

Mary Gillies, nee MacQueen and son Norman John and father John outside their home on St. Kilda. L. MacDonald Collection.

crying, sitting on my mother's knee and the whole village coming to see me that night at No. 15. While recovering Nurse Barclay taught me a verse or two of "Gentle Jesus".

I remember being on the boat at evacuation time, seeing the people at Lochaline and my grandmother taking me across the fields to school at Lochaline. In 1931 we moved to Larachbeg, to No. 4, in No. 3 lived my Uncle Donald and Aunty Chrissie and cousins Cathie and Rachel. The MacKinnon Family lived in No. 5 until 1939 when they moved to the Black Isle. Three of their family are still alive, Chrissie, Mary and Neil. During this time I was educated at Claggan School by the one teacher, Miss Robertson. She must have had great patience because I could only speak Gaelic – when she asked me something in English I recall I answered her back in Gaelic. During the summer holidays from 1931-38 I spent at Kincardine with mother's sister Annie and Uncle Neil Ferguson. Also in this large house lived Neil Ferguson junior and his wife and her father, Finlay MacQueen. After leaving school in 1939 I worked in a sawmill, at a sand mine and then with the Forestry Commision.

In November 1943 I joined the Royal Navy. I began training at the Butlins Holiday Camp at Skegness before being moved to Doonfoot in Ayrshire, H.M.S. Hornet, Portsmouth and Fort William. I joined the Motor Torpedo Boat 489 as signalman in Lowestoft about August 1944 and served there and at Felixstowe and Ostend. We were one of a flottila of boats that went to accept the surrender of the E-boats just before V.E. Day.

In June 1945 I came to Shotley, H.M.S., Ganges, to learn American signals and was there for V.J. Day. Here I met Ivy for the first time and was invited home shortly afterwards. I joined H.M.S. Cossack on 14/10/45 and went to serve in Malta, Alexandria and Port Said. While I was in Alexandria I had chicken-pox but all the Naval doctors thought it was small-pox so I was

probably been asleep and Mum and Dad had probably been away cutting the peats or something. I was crying and I remember Mrs. N. MacQueen of No. 11 coming and talking to me at the window. I remember too being in Church and one occasion when my grandmother – the Queen of St. Kilda – carried me home on her back, probably from the Glen. I remember when I was burned on my back when someone threw red hot coals over me. I remember

Norman John Gillies in the Royal Navy, Second War. N. J. Gillies Collection.

escorted by Naval dispatch riders in a field ambulance to an isolation hospital. After a few days, thankfully, it turned out to be chicken-pox! In 1946 I was serving on a minesweeper at Trieste – it was a very dangerous mission sweeping and shooting mines. While there I had an eight day holiday in Venice. I also served for a short while on H.M.S. Magpie before coming home overland via Austria, Germany, and France by train. I was demobbed from Chatham barracks in September 1946.

I came to lodge in Ipswich where I married Ivy Knights on 27th, November 1948. I had various jobs after demob, including work at Brown's Saw Mill, Trolley Bus Conductor, Ironmongers and Builders, Paint and Decorators Merchants. I am still working in 1987 and have never been on the dole. Ivy and I have three children, Bridget Mary, John Donald and Shirley Joy.

I revisited St. Kilda in 1980."

NEIL GILLIES

Family Background

Neil's home was at No. 15 Main Street, St. Kilda. His parents, John Gillies (son of Donald Gillies and Margaret MacCrimmon) and Annie Ferguson (the daughter of Donald Ferguson and Rachel Gillies) had been married on St. Kilda by the visiting minister, the Rev. Angus Stewart of Whiting Bay, Arran on 24th June 1890. Visiting St. Kilda in May of the same year was the artist R. Jobling who drew a quick pen and ink sketch of the bride and the groom, the latter he called

Sketch of the Bride and Groom, Annie Ferguson and John Gillies by R. Jobling in 1890.

Red Gillies, on account of his red beard. They had five sons. Donald was the first to be born in 1891, he later married Christine MacKinnon on July 10th 1916 and they lived in No. 13. They had two girls, both still alive, Rachel married to Mr. Johnson and Catharine who is unmarried and lives in Oban. Donald died aged 83. John was the second son, born in 1893 and married Mary MacQueen in 1924. They had one son Norman John and lived in No. 14. Mary died in Feb. 1930. Norman John married Ivy Knights in 1948 and they have three children, Bridget, Shirley and John. John died aged 55.

The third son born to John and Annie is Neil, the fourth is now the Rev. Donald John whose story is told later in this chapter. The youngest son was Donald Hugh (Ewen), born in 1902 and who died on St. Kilda on 26/1/28 having contracted T.B. whilst working in Glasgow; he returned to St. Kilda and died a year later.

Neil's father died on St. Kilda after a severe bout of Influenza on the 23rd May 1926, one of four deaths in the same week. His mother Annie lived on in Morvern after the Evacuation and died at the age of 86.

Annie Gillies outside her home. D. J. Gillies Collection.

Neil's Story

Neil was born on St. Kilda on 26th April 96. Anyone meeting him today would hardly believe that as a boy he was rushed off to Oban hospital and the report came back that he was too weak to operate on. He is now 91. When I visited him in his home in Glasgow I found him a little deaf and still limited by his damaged leg, but remarkably alert with a good memory for detail – places, names and events in the past.

His leg trouble started on his way to school. "Yes, it was an accident, playing on the way to school, one of the boys had me, I fell and he fell on top of me. At first it seemed nothing – I went to school but the pain was awful and I couldn't walk. I got home and they poulticed it – the leg came up and the knee – the poison went into the blood – I lay there. There was a doctor on the island, on holiday and he lanced it – the pain was terrific and I was crying. I was only 10 years old at the time. My uncle in Glasgow took me to the Western Royal Infirmary in Glasgow but the Chief was on holiday. I saw Dr. Kennedy and he wanted to amputate my leg but my father wouldn't allow it. He gave me a dose of chloroform, opened my leg and put weights on it. I lay in the centre of the ward and a nurse attending me.

The Chief, Sir William MacEwen (who had been sent for and operated on the King when he had appendicitis and who kept on operating until he was 76) came back from his holiday – on St. Kilda! He looked at the leg and said, "You're for the operating table tomorrow – the poison is still there!" He operated and later said I would be better in the side ward and told a nurse to be with me all the time. He also said, "I am very very sorry not to be here when you came in or I could have saved that leg." It was a very big operation and my leg was all over in Plaster of Paris. He told me that I would not be able to climb the rocks but he would straighten my leg. I lay in the Western Hospital for seven months and then he sent me to the Lanark Home for six weeks. I was able to climb the hills but I had to keep off the cliffs."

When he returned to the island Alice MacLachlan cared for him, dressing his leg regularly – see her diaries.

About life on St. Kilda he commented, "Stac an Armin was easy to climb compared with Stac Lee. But if the weather was good they would climb Stac Lee at night for the gannets. If you caught the watchman gannet you would have a good night. It was in the Spring we used to go at night when the Shearwater came to Carn Mor. You would get them when they hit the rock. You might get six in the night. The Puffin was very sweet meat when they came at first. Once they had laid eggs, they were no good after that. Whales were moored to a buoy in the Bay. When they burst the smell was terrible. Mind you it was handy having the whalers coming in – you could get away nearly every day to Harris – and there was no charge. I had heard that there was a whaling station planned. It was to be near the Store – just beyond there – but it didn't materialise – the numbers of whales became less. The saw-pit was in the Head Dyke above the Glebe (Neil demonstrated as if he were sawing from below and the other fellow above).

The day the German submarine came in 1918 I was one of four Watchmen that night up in a hut on Mullach Mor – the others were John and Donald MacQueen and John MacDonald. We were up there – we made hot tea, we would sleep and take it in turns to watch. We spotted the submarine coming in very slowly – we watched – and he stopped over by the Dun. He came in closer and fired 75 shots and knocked down the aerials. He wasn't aiming for the people and only one lamb had to be done away – its legs were badly damaged. The people were away at the top of the hill. Two Naval trawlers came in at one o'clock the next morning from Stornoway. The Navy men kept watch on Oiseval. Three weeks later an Admirality trawler came, and he was fishing, laying his lines when a submarine came and fired at him. They were both firing at each other. The trawler killed three of the submarine crew and the trawler got £200 or £300 for putting it out of action. He wouldn't have got anything if the authorities knew he had been out fishing!

A long time ago there were two thieves who burnt down the church with all the people in it except one old woman who hid in the rocks opposite the Dun. She watched for their lights and when they moved away she crept in to get their food. One day they went to the Dun and one said he smelt fire, "No," said the other, "you're just smelling the fire you left." The Factor's boat arrived – she didn't move until the small boat came in – then she appeared and told the whole story. They were all amazed! One thief was taken to Soay and the other to Stac an Armin, but he wouldn't stay there – he plunged into the sea and drowned.

After St. Kilda

I left the Island in 1919 because there was no work there. I started work in the yard at Old Kilpatrick to serve my apprentice as a ship's wheelwright at Napier and Millers, Glasgow. I stayed a few years and then I was paid off. During the Second World War I got a job with Donald MacKinnon at Renfrew as a ship's wheelright making naval ships – Motor-torpedo boats, launching one nearly every month. I was working on "blocking up", putting the blocks under the hulls – you had to keep altering them to keep them level. All the yards are now closed.

I became Bird Watcher to Lord Dumfries from 1931-39 when the War broke out. He had put nine watchmen on the island to stop some of the foreign trawlers taking all the stuff out of the houses. I would go out in May and stay until August. I stayed in No. 11. I had no trouble. There would be quite a lot of visitors. Lord Dumfries used to come for 2-3 days or a week at a time with Lady Dumfries and his mother. They would go up the hill ringing the birds with the brother of Lord Dumfries.

In December 1942 I married Ellen Nichol, we didn't have any children and she died in 1975."

THE REV. DONALD JOHN GILLIES

I first met the Rev. Donald John at one of the St. Kilda Club meetings in Edinburgh. Having corresponded with him several times in Canada I was delighted to receive a telephone call from him to say that he was staying with relatives in Barrow-in-Furness, could he come over for a chat. He came for lunch and we had four fascinating hours together discussing life on St. Kilda and his own intriguing life story. He is a sprightly 86 years old, very alert with a wonderful memory and extremely knowledgeable about all things to do with St. Kilda – somewhat surprising since he left St. Kilda at the age of 24 and has lived most of his life in Canada. Wherever Donald John went remarkable things seemed to happen – but let him tell his own story.

Rev. Donald John Gillies.

Life on St. Kilda

"I was born on the 29th. May 1901 at 3am in No. 15 Main Street St. Kilda. In the summer after my birth the Rev. Ross came over to the island for the Communion, I guess he baptized me too. I was told that he looked down at me in my cradle and said, "This man will be preaching the gospel of the unsearchable riches of Christ in America." People probably looked at each other, perhaps they had never heard the name of

America mentioned before, perhaps it was the first time it was introduced!

My father, John Gillies, was an elder of the Kirk for many years. In appearance he was medium height, well built and of a ruddy countenance, he had a red beard. In fact, he had the appearance of a man who could endure hardness. He had a powerful voice and that saved his life and the life of others in the accident at the Dun. My father was very spiritual, all along the line. I don't think I am living as well as my father was. I was often wondering, when I was a very young kid, when we were carding the wool and all that – when the clock struck seven, I don't suppose he missed one night that he didn't go outside and I was wondering what it was. Then I discovered that it was a time of prayer – he was going into the barn. When the Church came out at twelve o'clock on Sunday you didn't see anyone standing and talking – you'd see them scattering here and there down on the beach – prayer first. On the Lord's Day you only heard the barking of dogs – that was about all the noise. My father was not the owner of many books, but those he read. The works of Boston and Pilgrim's Progress and Robert McCheyne were on the same shelf as the Bible. He made great use of those books – he read them over and over again. His own soul was fed on strong spiritual meat. He died of the virus of the flu. When the virus got there, there was nobody there and nothing could be done. I saw the whole village down with the flu at one time and nobody looking after the cows for a day or so.

During my twenty four years on the island there were sixteen homes and one thatched roof cottage, next to No. 1, where Rachel MacCrimmon lived. She was a relative of ours (my father's mother was Margaret MacCrimmon) and my father was very interested in her. She was offered a house at the time of the others but she said, no. I remember going with my father and mother there. As you entered this cottage facing you were the stall for the cow and nearby the

Rachel MacCrimmon outside her 1834 House. By R. C. MacLeod of MacLeod.

stall for the sheep. The hens were sheltered in the same area. The living area consisted of one big room with an open fireplace in the centre – the house was something desperate. She had a bed in the wall with a mattress of the chaff of the oats – the old fashioned way – she wouldn't have anything else. One day as everyone was going out of Church Rachel stood at the door and she was preaching to all those going out, "Let not your heart be troubled – you believe in God, believe also in me, Jesus said." She died at the age of 81 (on 8/4/1914; Euphemia died aged 88 on 31/5/1869). A holy hush seemed to descend on the island when it became known that Rachel MacCrimmon had departed to be for ever with her Lord. As far as the Lord's cause on the Island was concerned indeed she was a remarkable Christian.

I started school with the MacLachlans, my brother Neil was there too – they were very fine people. On his way to school my brother Neil fell on the stones. He came to Glasgow and they operated but they didn't make a very good job of it. I am sure nowadays it would have been straightened out, without a doubt. In those days things were entirely different.

Tragedies on the Island

I remember, I was very young at the time at school, there was this brother, a Gillies, Norman and he was going to fish and he asked permission from the teacher to leave school a little early. They were passing Oiseval, going in that direction and he was anxious to join them fishing. She would always close the school with a hymn. I did not see the tremendous meaning of it until later on in life, but she closed the school a little earlier on account of him leaving before she dispersed the class and it was "Till we meet again". He was drowned. None of them could swim – the sea was calm enough and if anyone could have swum or given him a rope – he would have been saved.

One of the greatest sea tragedies that took place in Village Bay was in March 1909. Five men, Donald MacDonald (Lachie's father), John Gillies (my father), the two brothers MacQueen and Neil MacKinnon. These men went to the Island of Dun to attend sheep – they were in a skiff – they went a distance of approximately two miles. It was a beautiful sunny day, the sea extremely calm. As they were preparing to land the boat struck a rock and capsized with the result that the two MacQueen brothers and Donald MacDonald were drowned. Donald MacDonald's body was recovered. My father clung to the boat, Neil MacKinnon to the two oars. My father's powerful voice saved his life and that of McKinnon that day – he was heard two miles distance. The boat – the skiff – was different from what they were used to, and that was the cause and they were overloaded – there were too many of them. It was a thin boat and easily turned over. These years, Scotland used to produce clogs, Donald MacDonald had these on, they were made of wood and they brought his feet up and his head down. That was the reason. And I remember as a young man seeing all this and a friend of his taking Lachie's father on his back – the body to the house. I can still see the road – I can still see all this.

Regarding the other MacDonald tragedy (17th. August 1916), John was newly married – (only 5 weeks), when the Fulmar Harvest started. He and Ewen Gillies took to going into the cliff on the first day. To send the big man down, instead of keeping the big man up – it would have made the biggest difference in the world if Ewen was up – you couldn't move him – but it was the opposite way round. Tragedies of that nature – they could have been prevented.

I remember an incident, my father taking me as a young fellow to the rocks to get Fulmars, after the season was closed. He let me down because I was young – by gosh – I was climbing and the rope broke! I had to stop where I was – carelessness. Now if I had been in a slippery place I would have had no chance – no chance in the world!

The medicines on St. Kilda. There were five boys of us and there used to be in a little press a whisky bottle, a brandy bottle and a rum bottle – and none of us touched it! I suppose if father or mother had locked it, you would be curious, but there it was. They just said what the dangers were and they were not drinkers. They were the medicines and they did the trick!

I think at the time we were neglected, there is no doubt about it. Berneray in Uist is quite a number of miles from the mainland and they have representatives on the Council and I fully believe that if St. Kilda had been involved as it ought to have been, with a representative and had a voice, the whole thing would have been changed. But we were just like a boat without a rudder. Nobody to direct you. That would have directed you and you would have got what was owing to you. When you come to think of it they didn't even provide mail communication – just for the summer months. MacBraynes did it from Glasgow but it was just for their own profit because they were running tourists. This was stopping in August and then you depended on the kindness of fishermen.

Then I remember the starvation time. His Majesty's Ship "Achilles" coming and sending prepared food ashore first and asking us to eat at the pier – I remember that. And then there was another company that came afterwards from London with loads of goods from one of the millionaires that had his yacht. It was before the war – I would be only 13 or 14.

I always thought that if we were living in this generation with new modern techniques and equipment, I think you could have made something of St. Kilda – with the helicopter to land there and that you were sure that you were connected if anything happened to the home – accident or otherwise.

The First World War

When the War came we were never so well on St. Kilda. You were even working sometimes and being paid for it, and you were getting mail every week or twice a week. You would start building for the gun and get 2/6 a day. We were never so well. There were four civilians engaged during the war itself – my brother Neil, Finlay MacDonald, John and Donald MacQueen. They were on a watch and they built a place on Mullach Mor and were round the clock on there watching the North Bay. They had just rifles and some secret books they had to guard and guide.

The most exciting day on the island was May 15th. 1918. It started at about 9 am in the morning. At 10 o'clock word was received from the outlook on Mount Oiseval that a submarine was 1½ miles from Village Bay – nationality unknown. At 11 am the submarine entered Village Bay. The civilians were not aware that it was an enemy with the result that no-one made a move for shelter. I was there myself. One of the fellows was short of tobacco – he with the black beard – Finlay MacQueen – he was going down to the quay to see if he could get some off the crew. We never thought that it might be a German. The German Captain was decent enough – he called out with his megaphone for everyone to keep away – then he started firing. The first shot was a warning – the inhabitants scattered here and there. As a matter of fact some islanders were at a loss as to know what to do – they had no previous practice in any way as to what to do in case of an attack. One of the first shells hit the Church – I don't blame him for that – he was aiming at the wireless aerial which was in direct line. The fellow manning the radio just had time to put out an S.O.S. message to Stornoway before the mast was struck and the communications were put out of action. Stornoway was not able to answer and assumed something had happened. He fired 70 shells. People hid in the cleits, no-one was killed or hurt, one or two houses were damaged but not too seriously. The only casualty was a wee lamb. All this time, Mrs. MacKinnon, the Missionary's wife was stuck in the Manse. A few days before she had given birth to a baby son and she couldn't get out – and all these shells were flying over the Manse. According to the information that I received this lad later graduated as a Medical Missionary and was sent out to Africa as a Missionary of the United Free Church of Scotland. After a short period of service he was crossing a bridge and was accidentally killed. The day the submarine came – was a day to remember!

There was only one St. Kildian as far as I could ascertain in the First World War and it was a fellow by the name of John MacDonald, one of William MacDonald's sons – the oldest son. He was in the Mainland, and I remember as a 13 year old lad, he came from Stornoway in a little drifter and the people of the island had gone to Soay to get sheep, my father wasn't there, but two of our family were. John was only going to be there for a couple of hours – he came to see his people – and his father was away. My father went all the way to the Cambir. There's the Cambir here, and Soay there on the other side, and he called from this point and the man in the boat on the other side heard him and got the people into the boat in order to say "Farewell" to this soldier. Well, he survived – he was going to the Dardanelles at that time.

Some Reasons for Leaving

On St. Kilda you were taught to handle the loom, to handle the cliffs, to recognise your sheep – you had to do that and to train your dogs – all this and that. Before the War there was very little material and very little reading done to advertise what was going on in the outside world. But during the War there were sixteen people from various parts of Scotland and England and they would sit down and talk to you and picture life elsewhere than in St. Kilda – green pastures here and there that looked very attractive. I fully believe that had a big say – a big reason for leaving St. Kilda. Here you had a picture. And you were carrying everything on your back – you were going into the cliffs – you were carrying your peat home – you were fed on salt diet (fulmars) all the winter, unless by a mere chance at times you would find a trawler that you might get a cod or something like that – that would help your diet.

Then again, on account of the open nature of Village Bay to the south and south-east wind it was hazardous to land. At times it would be disappointing – there is no question about that.

So under those circumstances you were separated from the rest of the world. But today the story is different – you have a helicopter that can land on any part of the island – telephone and radio. This is the ridiculous thing – the moment the Army moved in. St. Kilda and the St. Kildians were surely neglected – there's no question – they were forgotten people. The moment the Army came in – look at the difference – they got lights up, they got roads, they got cars running – I saw all this. I never thought I would ever see this in my life on St. Kilda. They did this in no time – why in the whole wide world wouldn't they do it for their own subjects? This is what we come to think of the injustice of it.

Important Influences

The islanders owed a great deal to the Rev. Dr. John MacDonald – they admired and worshipped him. He went and gathered money and built the Church and Manse – that is his monument – the most important building on the island. MacDonald changed the whole life of the St. Kildians – not only in Church but in loving one another and sharing with one another. For instance, if there were widows, if you were coming in with a boat-load of fulmars, you would put the widows' share there, just the same as your own so that no-one would be missed. When you started shearing or planting you saw that your neighbour, who wasn't in a position to do so – was looked after. I give MacDonald the credit – it comes in the Gospel, of course.

I was converted under the ministry of Mr. Cameron in 1923. He had a text on one of the Wednesdays from the New Testament, "What are you come out to see – is it a tree shaken by the wind?" This was my first thought – seriously – of a decision for Christ. I remember that. Cameron was a great guy – a dedicated preacher – so was his wife and two daughters.

To me the greatest event of the year was the Communion Service, which was celebrated in the month of July. The head quarters of the Church of Scotland in Edinburgh arranged for a Gaelic speaking clergyman to come who not only conducted the Communion, but also Weddings and Baptisms. The Service commenced on the Thursday, called the day of Fasting (in Gaelic – La Traisg) and as such was literally observed by the faithful, who abstained entirely from food, until the afternoon, and then indulged only in light refreshments. Friday was known as the Question Day (Gaelic – La Ceist), after the preliminary singing and the invocation of the Divine blessing, the minister called for the Question. Immediately some elderly Christian stood up and read or quoted a Bible verse and asked for its interpretation which virtually meant a different diagnosis, between saint and sinners. The minister invariably led off the discussion that followed. Then he would call on the various members to speak on this topic. I can recall him calling on the first man, my grandfather Donald Ferguson, then my father John Gillies, Finlay Gillies, Finlay MacQueen, Ewen Gillies, William MacDonald, Finlay Gillies, Norman MacKinnon, Neil MacKinnon, Neil Ferguson, John MacDonald, Donald MacDonald and Angus Gillies. These were the men that spoke on the Question at the July Communion in 1924.

On Saturday afternoon, at the conclusion of the preaching for the day, the members for Sacramental Admission presented themselves for examination, as to their knowledge of the doctrines of the Gospel, their experience of its saving power and their performance of religious duties. If the presiding minister and elders were satisfied with the answer, the member was given a token that permitted the member to partake of the Lord's Supper on Sunday.

Matters reached their culmination on Sunday, when the Sacrament was dispensed. The Service would start as usual with the singing of the 103rd Psalm, with the sermon and so on. The minister stands there and calls for two verses of a Psalm, and he will say it in Gaelic, in the language they understood there. "While those verses are being sung, come forward and take your place at the Lord's Table." The table would be filled. The common cup was the only thing used. Nobody, however flippant, could gaze upon the slowly advancing men and women, most passed middle age, who rose from their seat and proceeded, while a psalm was being sung, to the two white covered tables – I can truly say that nobody could gaze upon these people without being impressed with the sincerity and seriousness, with their conviction, that their experience was a blessed reality and not a vanishing dream. It was one of the most sublime sights – as far as I am concerned – the world ever beheld. It compelled one to think of Him who preached to the multitude on the shores of Gennesaret, with the ripple of the waves on the strand as the undertone of the words of life that fell from His lips.

On Monday you had the Thanksgiving Service and the congregation, when the minister came along, presented the missionary where the minister was staying, with a wether – a sheep, in order to have the meat for the man to have during his stay on the island.

That was a habit that was adhered to right on to the very end. That was a sacred service that was looked forward to with great expectation and prayer. Yes, indeed.

Leaving St. Kilda – 1924

It was Mr. Barr who was over for the Communion Service in July 1924 who introduced me to the thought that I should go to the Bible Training Institute in Glasgow – that was his recommendation. On a Saturday afternoon the Reverend gentleman spent an hour with me, outlining the opportunities that were available on the mainland. He finished the discussion by saying, "If you moved to the City of Glasgow there was the possibility of entering the Bible Training College on Bothwell Street and becoming a missionary. I feel sure that the Church of Scotland would help in this direction." He also mentioned the possibility of getting work and attending evening classes at the Bible Training College. This interview got me thinking seriously as to what I really should do. I prayed about it.

The same month the whole MacDonald family from No. 3 had left the island – that left a very very big blank. The population was on the decline. To see a home that had the largest family closed was indeed a sad sight. This MacDonald family moved to Stornoway, Lewis. Another home closed on account of a fowling accident. Also my neighbours, Lachie's brothers – Angus and Donald had gone. As I looked around I discovered that all my school chums and playmates had left for various places on the mainland and St. Kilda looked to me as a desolate place without any future. I was just left practically alone and all of a sudden I made up my mind that the time was right to go. When the "Hebrides" arrived in Village Bay on that Thursday morning in the first week in August on her last trip for the season – I had not planned to go. As she dropped anchor, I made up my mind that I would leave that day for the City of Glasgow. It was just an hour and a half before she left that I said to my mother and father that I might as well take the step forward. I had never been off the island before. We had a friendly discussion and my parents answered, "If this is your wish, we will not hinder you leaving." They handed me all the cash they had in the house – four pounds. My fare from St. Kilda Bay to Broomelaw in Glasgow was one pound. I saw my first car and wondered what the dickens it was – four wheels in Lochmaddy coming towards me. I used the remainder of the money for food, arriving in Glasgow on Monday noon. A cousin of mine met me and took me to my uncle's home in Old Kilpatrick. I have no regrets that I left on the spur of the moment.

Life in Glasgow – 1924-27

I was 24 when I left St. Kilda – it was for the first time. On arriving in the big City of Glasgow, I was met by my first cousin, Donald Ferguson, who accompanied me to my uncle's home, Alexander Ferguson the Tweed Merchant, who had a very attractive home in Old Kilpatrick, in the area of Dalmuir. I stayed with my uncle and aunt approximately one week. I was hired by the Clyde Trust Company and assigned as deck-hand on a dredger on the river Clyde. I enjoyed my first week – nevertheless, I was not satisfied. I was still looking forward to a college education and training for the ministry of the United Free Church of Scotland. After working a year for the Clyde Trust Company, I resigned my job and entered the Bible Training College on Bothwell Street. Glasgow aiming to become a missionary. When I left St. Kilda finances were the problem and I still felt that I had the opportunity, if I could used it, for a better education, bit by bit.

During my training in the college, I was in charge of

the Mission in Govan, belonging to the Free Church, at a salary of one pound a week. I remember my father being with me when I had the Mission – he took the Service on a Sunday at South Govan. He was quite capable of doing that in the Gaelic language. He was at all times very close to his Lord – speaking to Him at all times – that's my impression. I remained in this Mission approximately one year. The training at the college was a great help to me and I used to attend Skelly's College in the evenings trying to get the English – we didn't hear any English. When I came to Canada it proved its worth to me because I was able and capable of presenting a sermon in Gaelic and then in English in the afternoon without any difficulty.

The first Sunday in March 1926, an opportunity presented itself that I could hardly miss. On this Sunday I decided I would go and hear a Canadian Minister by the name of the Rev. John McKay, DD, who was a guest speaker in the Govan Free Church of Scotland. Before he pronounced the benediction, he made an appeal for Theological students who would be prepared to emigrate to Canada and serve in the Continuing Presybterian Church in Canada. Dr. McKay was a Gaelic speaker, and I can recall addressing him at the door of the Church in Gaelic. I had a very short conversation, but made an appointment to meet him at his lodgings on the Govan Road on Monday night. The appointment was kept. After a profitable hour of discussion I filled in an application to become a student of the Presbyterian Church of Canada. After the application was completed, the Rev. Dr. McKay led in prayer. Dr. McKay was minister of the Presbyterian Church in London, Ontario, Canada – the new St. James Street Church.

At the beginning of March 1927, I received a communication from the office of the Presbyterian Church in Toronto, Canada notifying me that my application was accepted and that I was appointed to the Presbytery of Cape Breton, Nova Scotia and to report to the Rev. Dr. Thomson, minister of the Bethel Presbyterian Church, Sydney, Cape Breton. I was appointed to a bilingual congregation.

Canada

I sailed from Glasgow on the "Metagama" on the last day of April 1927. When we were about 3-4 days out in early May – out on deck I met some other Lewis people, on the way, emigrating, too. I met this fellow, Alick MacLeod, my own age, and we started talking and he said, "Where are you going?" I told him, then he showed me a letter. I said, "By Jove – I have a letter by the same name!" We were reporting to the same man in Sydney, Nova Scotia! I lost track of Alick later.

I arrived in the city of Quebec on Sunday May 7th, 1927 with only one sixpence in my possession. After satisfying the emigration authorities I met an Anglican clergyman at the dock. I told him my story and also my frustration that I had no money or ticket to take me to my destination that was stated in the letter I received from headquarters of the Church in Toronto. He looked at my letter and assured me right there that I had no worry in the world. He went over to a phone and contacted the Rev. Gordon, minister of St. Andrew's Presbyterian Church, Quebec. He handed the address of the manse and a diagram as to how to arrive there. I remember my first impression – on the way I met this guy – I never thought I was in the French area – and he couldn't answer me! I said to myself, 'I think the Church has made a mistake – I would far rather die in the Old Country where the people could understand me. If the whole of Canada is like this – What am I doing here?' I continued and finally I went into a store where I found a man who could understand me. He came out and showed me how to go and when I came round the corner sure enough I could see the round collar of the Minister in the narrow Quebec street. I had a very good lunch with him and I showed him the letter. He came and got my bags and gave me a ticket to Sydney, Nova Scotia and gave me 20 dollars. I arrived in Sydney on May 10th 1927 and contacted Dr. Thomson who arranged transport to North River, which I reached on Saturday May 13th.

On Sunday May 14th I preached a Gaelic sermon at 11 am in St. Andrew's Presbyterian Church, North River Bridge and at 3 pm an English service in the same Church. The parish was like being in the Highlands of Scotland – the Highlands of Nova Scotia. I remember the first Sunday at North River, it was the Gaelic Service and I was trying to figure out which part of the Old Country the people belonged to. When I came down to North Shore – once I gave out the Psalm from the pulpit, and you had your precentor – I knew then the difference between the one end of the parish and the other. I said – these folk are from Lewis – the Lewis singers – and they were!

On Sunday May 14th, I was notified by one of the elders from Knox Presbyterian Church, Indian Brook, that I was to conduct a funeral service at 1 pm on May 15th. this was something I had never done before. However, finding myself with the representative elder of the congregation, I asked him to outline for me the manner they conducted funerals in Cape Breton. This he did and I discovered that it was very similar to the custom we had on St. Kilda. However, on entering the room the body was in the casket. I immediately discovered that the body was not dressed in a shroud, the custom I was used to in St. Kilda and Glasgow. Apparently the Canadians dressed the body with the man's best Sunday suit with collar and tie. This shocked me. Let me share with you the first thought that came to my mind, "The elderly gentleman all dressed up and nowhere to go!" So I learnt my first lesson of a change as to the Canadian Custom.

When I got to Nova Scotia – when you're in a new country and amongst new people and everything is new to you – there was a fisherman there one day, and he said to me, "Why not come out fishing?" There was an island there not too far away – so we went. And the first thing that I saw, that I rejoiced in it, and my heart went to it – was a Puffin! It was unbelievable, but it was true. That was the first I had seen since leaving my native island – a Puffin!

I spent a very happy two summers in this congregation in 1927-28. One could travel a great distance before coming into contact with people as hospitable as the congregation of North River and North Shore, Victoria County, Cape Breton, Nova Scotia. During the summer I met the Principal of the Montreal Theological College and that helped me. At that time you were only paying a very small portion for your winter board in the College, for fees and tutoring.

Off Duty Puffins on Carn Mor.

Not only was I satisfied with the college but I had a great friend from one of the islands, he was a school teacher and he was going in for a doctor and he took a great interest in me. We used to discuss and use his ability also in the higher education - Dr. Crozier - I thought the world of him. He became a doctor and practised in the States, but he died young. The opportunity also came at the week-ends, you had work to do - you could go out preaching and you got so much remuneration and I took advantage of that. So bit by bit, and the generosity of the congregation of North River and North Shore paid practically for the training in Montreal. We would struggle along that way. Having the Gaelic was an advantage at that time because not far from the College there were two or three Gaelic speaking congregations where you could fill in. I took it step by step like that.

In September 1927 I commenced to study for the ministry of the Presbyterian Church in Canada at the College in Montreal and graduated from there in April 1933. I was ordained in 1934 in Knox Presbyterian Church, Carberry, Manitoba by the Presbytery of Brandon. On May 29th 1935 I married Lillian Gilmore of Carberry - she is an Aberdonian and a good one at that! The whole family were in the congregation and very interested in the Church. Her father was a cabinet-maker and he learned his trade in the Old Country. We have a daughter, Margaret, who married Donald Askew, a native of Barrow-in-Furness, England. They have a family of three - Jamie, Robert and Lauren, they live in Colquitlam, British Columbia.

In September 1935 I received an invitation from the congregation of North River and North Shore in Victoria County, Cape Breton to become the resettled pastor. I accepted this invitation and was inducted into the pastoral charge on May 27th. 1936 in St. Andrew's Church, North River. It was the same Church where the board of World Mission of the Presbyterian Church of Canada had appointed me in May 1927, and now inducted me 9 years later. I remained in this parish for four years.

In September 1939 I received a call from the congregation of Mira Ferry and Catalone. The parish was situated in Cape Breton County on the main highway leading towards the Great Fort of Louisburg, Cape Breton. My induction took place in the Church on Oct. 1939 but my pastorate was of a short duration.

Army Chaplain – 1942-46

I enlisted as a Chaplain in the Army in April 1942 in Sydney, Nova Scotia. I was appointed Chaplain to the Pictou Highlanders, they were stationed at Dartmouth, Nova Scotia. One afternoon I was out for a walk when this motor-cycle passed me, he stopped and he came right by me. Who was this but Alick! I could hardly believe it. What a reunion we had and I took him over to the mess and we had supper together. He had started in the oil business, married a Baptist and they were very happy. In May 1942 this Regiment was dispatched to St. John's, Newfoundland. I was assigned with them and after two months they were transferred to Gander where I spent two months with them. They sent me with the Paratroopers that were returning from the Old Country and were recuperating. I was their Chaplain and I started taking their training programme. I was a little too fat before that, but, by gosh, I soon lost weight. I remember the officer looking into my room in the evening and saying, "Padre, would you like to go on a 5 mile route march – it would be 10 miles, 5 on the road, 2½ on another and back?" "Yes." I said. Well! What a hot day on the prairie! With a uniform on - but the other poor fellows, they had their packs and everything on - I only had my uniform on. I was panting - but - by golly I lost 2lbs that day itself! I went up for a check up and I went up from Grade "B" to Grade "A" so the officer said, "Your time is up to go on holiday." My wife was only

50 miles away in Calgary so he says to go tomorrow morning – make arrangements. So I started out and went on holiday. I was talking to my wife, I wasn't in the house 2 hours when he phoned from the barracks to return to base and cancelling the holiday. So, this I did, and that night I was away to Winnepeg and on to Halifax. Nova Scotia and then to Sydney Harbour where we boarded a troopship. We joined a convoy of sixty ships. We were away with nurses, doctors and a re-inforcements of medicals and chaplains and all kinds. We landed in Liverpool, England in November 1943 and I was six months as Chaplain to the hospital at Aldershot. Then I was turned back to HQ, and I found myself in London one morning with a great number of others to go across the Channel. They landed us from Kent into Belgium. I was not very long there, a week or so, when they took an Anglican out and put a Presbyterian in – they put me in at HQ, I got a car, batman and driver. I was talking with the Senior Chaplain and he said, "Oh yes, you'll be happy, you're going with the 27th. Canadian Armoured Regiment – stationed at Whinshouten, Holland. You go down this side of Holland – this side of the river and you are supposed to find the Regiment in a spot somewhere. But – don't go on the other side!" Well, anyway, I tried to follow as best I could. I was wishing again that I should have taken more attention to the Map Reading than I ever did! Anyway, we were on the go and finally, I was sitting in the front with the batman and I saw a water-truck with the Regimental markings on it. I said, "Follow him!" We followed him and stopped him and found the information we wanted and he said, "Are you the Padre coming in?" "Yes." I said. That's how we found the Regiment. I was with them from May 1944 until the end of hostilities, until the armistice was signed.

We couldn't get into Hitler's Germany because of the crossing to Leer – they blew up the bridges and we had to wait patiently until we found pontoon bridges to cross to Leer. Before we went over to Leer – what destruction. I didn't need to take my binoculars to look and see where the bombs were falling. I could see them – our own planes over the river. We were on this side and Germany was over on the other side. You could see the bombs falling. The devastation when I went over – the sight! After all I was wondering, as a young man I went in with the Canadian Forces for experience – this was not the type of experience I was looking for. In Leer – one big grave – pretty near half a mile long, just with a bull-dozer, bringing the corpses in bags and laying them there – who knows who we were burying there. I remember a man meeting me in Leer, and he says, "Is the War over?" "Yes," I says, "a couple of days ago." He says, "I don't know, I've been in the basement for ages – what a War! I've lost everything – car, family – I don't know where they are." He was a German in Leer.

They sent us over to Leer with the Advance Party and they would put the German civilians out and they had given me a house with the Padre's sign on it. I went there and a few of the boys were celebrating there and I went back to my truck. You had sleeping quarters in the truck, seeing you were in the city – if you were in the field you slept outside – if you got any sleep. Then we went out and we took prisoners in at Willemshaven – they were coming in with their hands on their heads. At the hour of the Armistice we found ourselves in Willemshaven.

I was six months in Germany after that. I remember organising a Church Service on a Sunday and I went to see the Minister in a part of Germany that the English had – he was very nice but he couldn't speak very much English. I had been in Church in the morning and it was German that they had and a really good congregation there. Anyway, he said, 'wait a minute,' and he came with a woman and she was from the United States and she could talk English just as well as I could. She said we would be very welcome to have a service after they had theirs, but something was wrong with the organ – a bit of shell went into it. And said if we had anyone in our outfit to look at the organ they would appreciate it. Well, I said I would see what we could do. Sure enough, we got a man and he fixed it and we had our Church Service there. I was talking to this woman, I was curious to find out what was the reason for the turmoil of Germany in this way. Well, this was her interpretation, she said, "When Hitler came into. power, his aim and object was to get everybody to work – and he got everybody to work. And they all worshipped him for that. But then he started against the Church. He organised Hitler's Youth and they met at the same time as the Church Services – and they did not know that there was such a thing as a Church." And I believe it.

We returned to Aldershot, England and in the beginning of February 1946 I returned to Canada and on the last day of February I was discharged at Little Mountain, Vancouver, B.C.

After the War – Canada – Parishes and Prisons

One of the ministers was talking to me and asked if I was interested in staying at the coast. "There is a vacancy at a Church there. I will arrange for you to go and preach for a couple of Sundays and have a look at." My wife was with me and we had this one daughter and we left her with her grandmother. I took the service for two Sundays on this East side of Vancouver. I went back to Winnipeg and they wired me – would I take the Church? I accepted and in April 1946 I was inducted into the pastoral charge of Vancouver Heights Presbyterian Church, remaining in this parish until 1952. The years after the war were hard years – especially in the cities – anyway I was happy in that congregation.

Then I got a wire, "Would you accept the chaplaincy of the Westminster B.C. Penitentiary?" I took it and resigned the Church, and was appointed Prison Chaplain in October 1952. How it came about – the Warden of the Prison and one or two fellows came over on a Sunday, I didn't know, to hear this fellow at Vancouver Heights – he was a returned Army Chaplain. They said after that it could be all right. So that's where I landed for 15 years. In the Penitentiary you had a good congregation – it's unbelievable. I used to organise choirs from outside for them to see civilians taking part and I had a chapel that would seat 400 and I would have 200. Statistics were taken – the attendance of the Protestant Chaplain was better than the Church at South Side! I could understand it – you were shut up in that cell – to get out was a welcome release!

I was in the Federal Penitentiary – when you got over 2 years you were coming to us; the Provincial responsibility was for those up to 1 year 11 months. When the death penalty was abolished, it meant that those in death row were coming to us. You saw one or two who were rewarding. You were trying your very best to change the life of the individual from perhaps burglary, robbery, murder. How we worked it was – there was a social part and they interviewed the individual first. You went down and read his records and you had one or two fellows each day, you knew him according to his history and you were studying whether he was telling the truth or otherwise. He wasn't aware of the fact that you were in the know! I said it was rewarding – I remember a couple of instances. They used to send us those individuals who were down hearted. One day the fellows downstairs in the office phoned me and said there was a fellow there who was about to be discharged and he had a Bible – there was no name in it. They mentioned the name of the man and I looked him up and I couldn't recall him. The man said, 'It's not a very good one – it's a delapidated book.' I said, "Send the man up with his

Bible, I'm in my office and I'll see what can be done." He came up – his Bible was delapidated all right! He sat down and I said, "Apparently, you've made it, you're going to be discharged and I am glad you are. I'll take this Bible and give you a new one. I'm sure the Gideons will not mind you having a Bible." Well, now, he didn't want to part with his old Bible. "Well," I said, "give me the reason why you want to keep this Bible." "Well," he said, "I have a mother and she is 80 years of age, up in the north and she has been praying for my conversion for many years and when I came into this place I found this Bible in my cell and I started reading it." I saw to it that there was a Bible in each cell. He had a verse all marked out and he said, "It is my mother's favourite verse and I am sure she was praying and a light came into the cell and struck me onto this verse and I would like very much to take this and show it to my mother." The verse was 'I have fought a good fight, I have finished my course, I have kept my faith.' "Yes," I said, "you can have it." So we had a word of prayer and I put my name in the book. I had a great respect for the Gideons – they came every 5th Sunday and they took the service.

In July 1967 I was inducted into the pastoral charge of Knox Church, Sooke, B.C. on Vancouver Island. In 1969 I retired from the ministry of the Presbyterian Church. I still thought of the Correctional and I went back with the Mounties and to the Correctional. In 1969 I was appointed Chaplain of the the Royal Canadian Legion, Chapter 148.

In 1986, on September 28th I travelled to where I started my ministry in Canada on May 14th 1927, 59 years before and celebrated the 50th year of my induction by preaching in the first Church, St. Andrew's Presbyterian Church, North River Bridge. The text I shared with the congregation, the church was filled to capacity, was from the prophecy of Isaiah Chapter 40 verse 31. "But they that wait upon the Lord shall renew their strength, they shall mount up with wings as eagles. They shall run and not be weary and they shall walk and not faint." A surprise reception was held in the Church hall after the service and they presented me with a plaque, "Presented to the Rev. Donald John Gillies on September 28th. 1986 to commemorate 50 years since he was inducted into the North River and North Shore Pastoral Charge of the Presbyterian Church of Canada on May 27th. 1936. In recognition of his ongoing interest, and continued concern for this charge over the last 50 years." In addition to this a purse was also presented with $300. I can truly say the years that I served in Cape Breton congregations was served with great delight."

EXTRACTS FROM THE REV. DONALD JOHN'S ST. KILDA SERMON IN 1980

"I am pleased to be here today on this important occasion celebrating the 50th. Anniversay of the Evacuation of the Island and the Rededication of the Church – the most important building on Hirta – the House of God. This particular spot where we find ourselves gathered today is sacred to the memory of many. It was here that they received their early education and religious training and since have gone forth to other parts of the Empire, for that matter, to other parts of the world, and have made a mark for themselves in their new homes.

We live in a time when much of what is old and cherished is being questioned and doubted, but it seems to me that there are a few matters which should be beyond dispute – the value of the great Scottish virtues of honesty, and pride, of self-reliance and of independence of spirit, of deep religious sense, of love and of education – surely these are beyond all doubt. I am proud of the National Trust for Scotland, of the marvellous efforts they are putting forward in the restoration of abandoned places of great religious and historic life. All men of Scottish blood have a just pride in the land of their fathers and forefathers. No matter where they are found, no matter what country in which they live – speak of Caledonian, land of mountains, lochs and glens – the eye brightens, the pulse quickens and the heart thrills with a deep love of country. . .

The Islanders owed a great deal to the late outstanding theologian, called the Apostle of the North, the Rev. Dr. John MacDonald, Minister of Ferintosh in the Black Isle. According to what I remember, discussed on many occasions by my father and grandfather, he was the first missionary in the early 19th. Century to bring the true message of salvation to the island. He was also responsible for the building of this Church and School-house 150 years ago. He made four trips to the island, and in his first trip he found he was unable to land in Village Bay and was welcomed ashore by the islanders at the North Glen. Several feet from his landing spot he noticed a small well, removed his hat and drank. I tell you, it is no different and stands to this day and is named – the Eternal Well – in the Gaelic language – Tobar nam Buadh. . .

St. Kilda, since the Evacuation, has attracted many visitors from all walks of life, even our gracious Queen and the Royal Family in 1971.

In closing I must offer a sincere "Thank you" to Allan Aitken, for his interest, effort, energy and guidance, for the tireless work parties that have come to St. Kilda year after year. All the buildings by now would be in ruins but instead we see trim cottages, rebuilt walls and cleits, the Church and School stand in humble pride as silent tribute both to the character of the people of the past, but also to the skill and enthusiasm of the the new St. Kildians who have given of themselves to the island's long story.

Now the text, Philippians 3 verse 13, "Brethren, I count not myself to have apprehended, but this one thing I do, forgetting those things that are behind and reaching forth to those things that are before." Thank you."

Alice MacLachlan –
A Teacher's Portrait
On St. Kilda 1906–09

*The Gap with
Oiseval. Acland.*

CALL TO ST. KILDA

Alice MacLachlan spent three years on St. Kilda with her husband Peter who was the Missionary. During that time she kept a daily diary from the time of rising in the morning until bedtime. The originals are in the possession of her daughter Susan who was born on St. Kilda. A typescript of the diaries was in the possession of the National Trust for Scotland but was mislaid for about 30 years. However, during a search for information on the Store, an envelope fell out of the archives onto the floor – it contained the typescript of the diaries of Alice MacLachlan. Her daughter very kindly let me see the originals and these contain material leading up to their time on St. Kilda as well as the treatments she administered to patients while on the island.

These diaries are very special as they record, over a long period, the happenings of each day – visiting trawlers and yachts, kindnesses and frustrations, tragedies and joys – they are full of vitality, courage, humour and honesty. They also

Alice with her spinning wheel outside the Manse, 1908. S. MacLachlan Collection.

record certain poignant events – Neil Gillies in hospital in Glasgow (Sept. 06) and his return (May. 07), the death of young Norman Gillies (Oct. 06), the terrible drowning tragedy (Mar. 09), as well as lovely days – the birth of her daughter (Apr. 09), – beautiful sunny days and moonlit nights, the plan for the whaling station (Aug. 07) and the imprisonment of the trawler skipper (Apr. 07), the man with a hair-pin in his beard, and the girl who was not 'Willin'!

Alice Scroggie was born in Haddington near Edinburgh and went to school in Lincoln. She later qualified as a teacher and began her career in York where she taught art, sewing and the piano; she also had a very good singing voice. Her husband Peter, she nick-named 'Duine' (Gaelic-Man), was born on the Isle of Mull. He studied law at Glasgow University and then, with other Highland students, followed Professor Blackie to Edinburgh University when he took the Chair of Greek Philosophy. Peter considered emigrating to Canada but then, through differing circumstances, felt the call of God to become a missionary. He became a missionary to the Highlands and Islands. After their marriage they worked in Garve and lived in the Manse. They received a shock on 9th January 1906 when they were told that they must be "prepared to leave the Manse at any time as the 'Wee Frees' have got the Church and the Manse." It was a great disappointment to them and Alice felt much depressed. They continued in their work of preaching and sick visiting until they received another letter on April 26th, Alice recorded "Got a letter from Mr. Lee telling us to be prepared to move out of Garve on May 28th and to Peter to meet him in Dingwall tomorrow between 1-2 o'clock. We were very sorry indeed about it but it couldn't be helped. Mr. Lee wishes a talk so he may have some places to discuss." For April 27th Alice reported "Going on the first train to Dingwall. Saw Mr. Lee at the station (with Mr. Johnston, Strathpeffer). Mr. Lee offered us Jura or ST.

Copy of part of Alice's diary.

KILDA (What a cheek!!!)"

The next few weeks were fully occupied:-

May 21 – 26th. "Busy all the time preparing for our flitting."

June 6. "Time so much taken up with schools in Inverness that there is no time for my diary – so will leave it until we get to St. Kilda.

EXTRACTS FROM ALICE'S DIARIES ON ST. KILDA. August 1906-July 1907
AUGUST 1906

St. Kilda Aug. 16, 1906 (Arrival). We left for St. Kilda on Tuesday (Aug.14) from Tobermoray by the S.S. "Hebrides", and arrived here at 1 o'clock midnight, Wednesday night, but did not land until Thursday morning. The Inspector, Mr. Beaton, came with us and inspected the school at 7 o'clock in the morning, and by 9 o'clock the "Hebrides" was off and we were left on our island home. The men and quite a lot of the girls were on the pier and all escorted us up to the gate of the Manse, where Kate (sister of the wife of Donald McQuien) was waiting. We went in and had some breakfast, at least, tea, and went in to see the Inspection of the School. The children are very far back but answered fairly intelligently the questions about the poetry they had been learning during the year, viz. "Waterloo" and "Lochiel's Warning". Kate, our servant, is very nice and kind. I do not know what we should do without her. One or two days we have been seeing the people; but did not see them all, as the men were so busy away at the fulmar hunting, while many of the women had also gone to carry home the birds. We went first to see Rachel McCrimmon, who is the only one who still lives in the same old house and would not have a new house. The hens just live in the same room. Peter found her most intelligent, and spoke very good Gaelic. There are several other old folks, one Bess, who is older than Rachel and is pretty helpless having burned herself very badly. One other is very bad with nerves. The others are all in good health. All are recovering from vaccination, having been vaccinated by two Doctors who have been on the island for a fortnight, but who left by the boat with which we came.

Tues. Aug 21st. (Climb Conacher). The men being still at fulmar catching, we went to the top of the highest hill, Conacher, Kate with us. The women and girls were there on the top and overtook us as we came home, with their loads of birds. I rolled a bag of fulmars a long way down Conacher with the help of my walking stick. Then on Wednesday we went and saw the rest of the folks, those who were not away at the fulmars.

Thurs. Aug 23rd. (Unpacking). It was wet and windy so we stayed in and I sewed my curtains and Friday did the same. We have been very busy unpacking all our boxes and getting things in order. We have people coming to see us every day and all who come bring us a pair of fulmars, plucked and ready for the pot.

Sat. Aug 25th. (Whaler in Bay). This is a lovely fresh day. The Big Whaler came into the bay last night as we were going to bed and today they are unloading coal which they have brought for the people here. Duine has been busy all day being Saturday, while I have been doing odd jobs. The St. Kildans have been busy taking in coals all morning. The Captain of the Big Whaler has kindly given them five tons in a present, and they gave him a suit of clothes. In the afternoon the men took home the coals and after tea they went fishing and we got several presents of fish (caravanach). This has been a glorious day. The Dune and the surrounding hills looked lovely in the sunset tonight. Got curtains up in the dining room (the white ones).

Sun. Aug 26th. (Sunday). Went to both services and Sunday School. Children fearfully shy. Good congregations and singing slightly better than on previous Sunday.

Mon. 27th. (Whale brought in). Busy all morning. In the afternoon Duine and I went to visit and see nearly all the folks. Precentor's wife very poorly. Also the Queen's son, but neither serious, I think. In the evening we had intended going to fish but it was too wet so we stayed in and wrote letters. One boat brought in an enormous blue whale worth hundreds of pounds. It was longer than the whaler. The big steamer came in from Harris and took the whale away and in the morning another whale was tied to the buoy.

Tue. 28th. (On board the whaler). Wet all day. Mrs. William MacDonald better a little but the boy Gillies is not any better. We were in all day until evening when we went out to the pier to meet a little boat which came from the whalers. We sent out milk to both boats and the Captain of the Brymwolf took us out in his little boat to see the whales, one was 65ft long, then we were taken out on the whaler and saw all through, and were down in the cabin. The Captain showed us his wife's and children's photo and gave us a loaf of their newly baked bread. We were seeing the supper which was being cooked and which looked very tempting. We saw how the harpoon works and I shot one to see how it went. Then the Captain took us home. He gave me prunes and was very kind. It was jolly seeing the strangers. When we came in Annie Gillies and Mrs. Norman McQuien were having a ceilidh. Duine's stomach bothering him a little.

Thurs. 30th. (Hebrides – last call). We were aroused at midnight by the welcome whistle of the "Hebrides". I was so excited I could hardly sleep for the remainder of the night. The first sirens sounded at 5.15am and we jumped out of bed. The mails had been brought ashore at mid-night, and our letters, papers and parcels were on the parlour table. What an array! Upwards of 40 letters. Papers and Magazines and Picture Post Cards galore. Every one of our friends wrote. We went out just as the first boat-load of passengers came ashore. There were some nice people among them and I took them into the church and they sang, "Oh for a closer walk with God" to the tune St. Kilda. It sounded so pretty. I am so glad the church was cleaned out on Tuesday by the girls. Duine went out to the boat with the men and bought a big quantity of bread (4/- worth). Flora sent us potatoes (as ordered). The "Hebrides" left about 10 o'clock and we waved gaily to her as she went out of sight. We didn't feel a bit lonely. We will feel worse when the whalers stop. Later on in the day several of the younger St. Kildans left with the "Johanna" for Scalpay, the "Happy Hunting Ground". They won't return till next week.

Fri. 31st. (Lads to Glasgow). Another wet day. Great excitement prevails. Three young fellows are going off by the whalers to Glasgow. They will go as far as Tarbert by the whaler and then to Glasgow next week by the "Johanna". The whole crowd of youths were in the afternoon and wanted a loan of a bag from Duine which they got with great pleasure for the Glasgow trip. We gave them an order to bring back from Cooper's with them for us. We all went down to the pier at 8 o'clock to see them off. They went off in great glee – Norman McQuien, Neil Gillies and Ewen

Gillies. There was lamenting at the pier, and embracing and kissing any amount.

SEPTEMBER 1906

Sat. Sept 1st. (St. Kilda by Moonlight). A change in the weather. Simply a glorious day. Did a little cooking in the morning, but spent the whole afternoon out of door in the sun which was blazing hot. It was delightful on the pier . . . What an exquisite night! Duine called me to the door and we went out as far as the pier. I have never in my life seen such a picture as the bay presented tonight. There was a full (or nearly so) moon. At the left hand Oshavale stood guarding the bay – on the other side rose the towering heights of Dune. Between in a clear, cloudless sky shone the moon. It made a broad clear path on the rippling water, and the night was so bright altogether we could have stayed out for hours. The other hills rising so high behind the houses were so clearly outlined in the bright moonlight. It was altogether most beautiful. I never wished so much to be able to paint from nature as tonight. Bed 10.30.

Sun. 2nd. (Loveliest Day). Loveliest day this summer – so warm and bright. No boats in this morning, but when we came out of church tonight the old man's boat was in with two whales. We had rather fewer in church today as we missed those who are away at Scalpay and Glasgow. Donald Ferguson prayed after some pressing. Neil MacKinnon came in after church on ceilidh. Read quite a lot today. Duine keeping better.

Mon. 3rd. (Visit of Luxury Yacht). Another glorious day. We were to have started school today, but it is the monthly morning service so we do not have school that day. We went in to the service at 12 o'clock and were in about an hour and a half when Donald Ferguson rose up in the meeting and said, "We'll be finishing now!!!" He came up after and told Duine that there was a yacht in the bay, and so there was. What excitement! A little boy had come to the door during the prayer and brought news. It was a lovely large steam yacht, the "Vendura", owned by Mr. Mann Thompson. His sister, Mrs. Heneage of Underwood, Kilmarnock was there, also Mrs. Robinson of Dunvegan Castle, another lady and two other gentlemen. They were so nice, we took them up to the village cemetery and to see the Fairy's House. They were so kind to the people and bought up nearly every available bit of cloth in the place, also socks and stockings. We were taken aboard to tea on the "Vendura" and had an awfully good time. We got papers and flowers etc, and Mr. Mann Thompson took us all through the yacht. It was quite luxurious. The bedrooms lovely and fitted up with every convenience – lovely bathroom, bedrooms with double beds etc. The dining room was lovely with oil paintings all round, and the drawing room opening off

St. Kildans, taken just before the Maclachlan's arrived. Left to Right:- Standing – Unknown, Finlay MacQueen, Alec Ferguson (light jacket), Unknown, Unknown, Norman MacKinnon, Ewen MacDonald (killed on rocks), Unknown, William MacDonald, Unknown, Donald MacDonald (Lachlan's father), John Gillies, Malcolm MacDonald, Unknown, Malcolm MacDonald (from No.13). Seated – Unknown, Unknown, Unknown, Donald Ferguson and the Rev. Angus Fiddes. Photo about 1903, Lawson Collection.

it. There was a pianola, and everything in the way of luxury. Two of the crew rowed us home. It was quite a red letter-day. The yacht stayed all night and left at four Tuesday morning. Had a good evening with our papers and magazines.

Tues. 4th. (School Opened). Opened school at 10 o'clock this morning with twenty, two pupils being absent. I went in during the morning but was only in for a little while when we heard the siren of a yacht so there was confusion. We made them sit still for a little and then dismissed them, as is usual in such events. We all rushed down to the pier and there was a lovely steam yacht in the bay. The men put out the boat, when to our disgust, the yacht turned and went steaming at full speed out of the bay. It was an awful shame, and the poor people here were so disappointed. After dinner we took Kate and went off to the Female Warrior's Glen and the Lover's Stone. Got home feeling very tired, but refreshed by tea. Duine and Kate went to try out the new scythe. Duine agreeably surprised. Kate is a grand hand with the scythe. I went, but to applaud. Spent evening getting seams ready for children sewing tomorrow. I am giving them specimens to see what they really can do for practice. Bed 10.30.

Thurs. 6th. (Hay-making). Was in school all of the afternoon helping with the little ones. After school went into the field where Kate has been very busy cutting the hay. Duine and she cut alternately and I raked. It looked like rain so Kate carried what was driest into the "Clet". This is a most ingenious method of drying the grass. These "Clets" are loosely built stone houses with earthen roofs. The grass is kept in there and pushed in between the stones in huge quantities. The rain can't get near it and the winds whistle through the stones and quite dry it, although it might be quite damp when put in. The boys went fishing for red mullet and brought us some.

Fri. 7th. (Exhaustion). Kate so tired with yesterday's work that she is useless today. Very tired today myself.

The "Botoch" has just arrived. No school in the afternoon. Three boats came in and all the men came home. None went to Glasgow as Mr. Herlofson (Tarbert) dissuaded them on account of the weather. Our order which was to have come by them from Glasgow was given by Norman McQuien to Capt. Ritchie of the "Evening Star" which they saw at Harris yesterday. The three Captains and the engineer all came ashore and had tea with us. We had great fun. The old Captain (at least, the father, for he is not old) teases Kate that he is to take her back to Norway with him for his wife is dead. This is a fib as his wife is alive and he has nine of a family. He speaks in broken English and Kate in Gaelic, and it is too comic. She is telling him to tell his wife to hurry up and die and she'll go with him. Mr. Herlofson has very kindly sent us 4 tons of coal which we ordered. It is awfully kind of him. The St. Kildans are very busy bringing them ashore tonight. With the last load the boat collapsed slightly and it was with great difficulty they could get ashore. The boat was half full of water and was so heavy. Poor men, they did work well. Bed 10.30.

Sun. Sept 9th. ("Evening Star" returns). When we woke up there was a new red boat in the bay, and sure enough this was the "Evening Star". Soon after breakfast we saw a boat-load coming in and we went out. Capts. Morris and Ritchie were there. Then the crew of the "Star" came in and all came to church. We had an English service in the morning, and at night it was partly English and partly Gaelic. The Norwegians were there also. It was an awfully nice day. "Evening Star" left very early Monday morning.

Mon. 10th. (A Day at the Hay). A splendid day for the hay. I had breakfast in bed as I had not slept well. I did all the housework as Kate was out all day at the hay. Two boats came in with whales. Kate and Duine still at hay after school and Norman MacKinnon and Finlay Gillies came and helped. They came in and had supper in the kitchen.

Thurs. 13th. (Stormy night). One of the stormiest possible nights. I really thought the house was to be blown down. The boats evidently expected this as they shifted from here to the other bay. Kate said this morning that we could not have a worse storm in winter than we had last night; so it's a consolation that it can't get worse! Put in Hyacinth bulbs from Mrs. Heneage. Kate busy hay making (as on Tues and Wed). Donald og (og = young) and Norman McQuien went over Oshaval for one of Kate's sheep. They brought it during the morning. It was quite exciting, the killing and skinning which was done at the back door. It is a nice sheep and it is nice to have a plentiful supply of mutton. The whalers have come to this bay again. Gave scholars first singing lesson today.

Fri. 14th. (Whalers Away). All whalers away today. The people are afraid that they are away for the season. We are so sorry that we won't see them till next May. Lovely day. Had nice dinner of mutton, broth and our own potatoes. Was in school taking Duine's place all afternoon. The men came and helped with the hay tonight. Kate spinning. I did some carding.

Some of the MacLachlans pupils. Photo Lawson Collection.

Sat. 15th. (Indoor Work). A very wet day, for which I was devoutly thankful, as it kept Kate in (from the hay) and at her housework, and Duine got rest from the hay too, which was good, as he was busy with his Sunday work. Donald og came and cut up and salted the sheep. Later on in the day the "Diadem", Fleetwood came in. "Diadem" left.

Sun. Sept 16th. (Good Services). A very good day. The hay will dry. Good services. Finlay McQuien had to go out of church with a pain in his side. Lovely night. No boats.

Mon. 17th. (Battle in School). Miserably wet day. Was in school in the afternoon. Had a scene with John Gillies as to who was to be master, or mistress, rather. Kept him in and talked plainly to him. He stayed in for an hour and finally said he was sorry. Went to see all the folks after that. Got quite a lot of red mullet tonight. Had it salted.

Tues. 18th. (Better Day). Duine and Kate did a little at the hay. Had Sheep's Head Broth (for the first time in my life for dinner). A. Gillies came to ask me to help her with her blouse. Was in school this afternoon. Gave Singing lesson. Children behaving better. Got more fish.

Wed. 19th. (Men to Boreray). The men went to Boreray and Stack an Armine today. They were not home in time for the Prayer Meeting. We went out between 8 and 9 to see them on their arrival. They had caught three sheep and a lot of gannets, young ones. These birds are huge, even the younger ones.

Thurs. 20th. (Fishing). Two men came home from fishing and it seems they had lost a rod, so had to take a boat and go to get it. We went too and took the rod. I caught a cuddie right away, and when we got to the fishing ground I caught a fine big red mullet myself, and coming home two tiny cuddies! Two boats went out today, one to Boreray and one to Soay. We went out to see the sheep but it was so dark we could not see properly.

Fri. 21st. (Goods and Letters). A very good day. Duine and Kate on for the hay with all their might. "Evening Star" had come in, in the night, and brought all our goods and some letters. They are coming in again tomorrow. Men busy all day killing and salting sheep. After tea went down to see the sheep the men had brought from Boreray today. Got a piece of mutton from Callum and a piece from Finlay McQuien. Went to see John Gillies and his wife who have had bad news from Glasgow about their little boy Neil who is in hospital there. The Doctors are afraid they cannot operate on his leg as he can't stand it. He is in decline. It is very sad. I am so sorry for them.

Sat. 22nd. (About the House). Doing little things about the house. Got six pieces of Soay mutton sent in. Busy in the evening making puddings, as the "Evening Star" is expected in tonight. Came in 10.30.

Sun. Sept 23rd. (Sunday and Shoes). One of the loveliest days of the year. Capt. Ritchie only came ashore in the morning and had dinner. He sent us two nice ling (fresh). The other two came in the evening to service, and all came in after and sang a little. Capt. R. took my shoes to be soled, also a good big order. Don't know when they will be back.

Mon. 24th. (Thieving Cat). A splendid day for the hay. Duine and Kate at it before breakfast. Duine went to school in the morning. I did housework and took school in the afternoon. The people all at their corn and finished the cutting. We got a lot more cut. Duine busy salting fish and the remainder of the meat. Left some fresh fish for breakfast, which cat ate in the night.

Thurs. 27th. (More Haymaking). Another lovely day (as were Tues and Wed). Kate and Duine very busy all day with the hay. I am sick and tired of hay and wish it was at the bottom of the sea and Cruvack (the cow) too. Kicked up a row about house duties as everything is being neglected by D. and K. for the accursed hay. But got better later on. Got present of coileach from Angus Gillies.

Fri. 28th. (Splendid Day). Of course nothing but hay again. I fished a little at the pier tonight but wasn't successful. Kate busy plucking coileach and baking for Sunday. No school now until Tuesday!!!

Sat. 29th. (Fine Weather). Kate busy as usual with "feur". Duine busy with his sermons. I made a very fine pan-cake in the afternoon. Had to go to bed after tea as I was so tired. Finlay Gillies came to get something for Catharine who has a very swollen face; I got up and went to see her. Stayed up and finished my white gloves.

Sun. Sept 30th. (Time Flies). Last day of the month. How time is flying, Church twice and Sunday School. Big attendance. Felt very hungry at supper time.

OCTOBER 1906

Tues. Oct 2nd. (Death of Norman Gillies). School as usual today. Went in in the afternoon. As we were finishing our tea, we heard a great shouting and other confused noises. In a few moments the men were down, and in less time than it takes me to write they launched the boat. The women were screaming and wringing their hands. It seemed that poor Norman Gillies (who had gone away from school a little earlier than usual to go to the Point of Coll to fish mullet) had fallen from the rocks into the sea. There is a fearful current there and although the only man there (Hugh Gillies) had flung him a rope, the current carried him out beyond it. Some of the bigger boys had run off home to give the news. Norman MacKinnon went to the place on foot but only in time to see poor Norman sink. He was clinging to the fishing rod. He never made a sound. The boat was too late even to see him. We went up to the house with the men and women and stayed till nine o'clock and the sight was pathetic in the extreme. It was terribly sad. The poor mother was very quiet and sensible though in an awful state. The father was in a frenzy. I was so sorry for them all especially as the poor girl Catharine was in bed. Came home with a splitting headache and was very sick.

Wed. 3rd. (No School). No School today (or this week I suppose) owing to poor Norman's death. Good day although not much wind. Went up after dinner to see the Gillies family and Bess. The Gillies very sad and no wonder. Took Bess gloves.

Thurs. 4th. (Knitting). Knitted stockings. Visited people after dinner. They are slightly better and Finlay Gillies himself seems more resigned. Had boys, John MacDonald and Donald og, in all the evening. Boiled piece of ham and knitted a lot. Reading a "Modern Mercenary". Not bad. Very calm today.

Fri. 5th. (Bits and Pieces). Very calm night. People wishing more wind to dry the hay in the cleits. Boat in sight fishing. Hope it will come in during the day. Had a nice lentil soup for dinner. D. and K. busy with hay for a little. Went up the village to see people.

Sat. 6th. (Feeling Ill). Very wet and blowy day. Not feeling at all well. Duine went to see the people in the afternoon himself. I had to go to bed early, didn't sleep.

Sun. Oct 7th. (Bed All Day). Bed all day and side sore. Had a reception in bed. People so kind. A little better in the evening.

Thurs. 11th. (Feeling Better). Felt very weak on Mon and Tues, much better on Wed. There hasn't been such a lovely day this year. Perfect. Men went to the Dune. Kate and Mary Mhor span a lot of white wool for gloves for Minnie. Feeling much better today.

Fri. 12th. (Feeling Myself). Changeable day. Knitted a good deal of glove. Feeling quite myself again. Wish one of the boats would come as our potatoes are finished today. Very cold night. Everyone wishing boat would come.

Sun. Oct 14th. (Dinner Burnt). Wet day but wind changed which they say is favourable to trawlers. Was at church in the morning. Duine took Sunday School himself. Had hymns for the first time. Dinner burnt whilst we were at church, but had nice plum pudding

last night. All the Finlay Gillies family out, poor souls.

Mon. 15th. (Spinning and Carding). A fine fresh day. Glass pretty low and continues to fall. Fearful night of wind, did not sleep literally one wink. Went to School (first time for a fortnight) this afternoon. After tea we both went up the village and saw most of the natives. All fairly well. Seeing about sheep. All busy spinning and carding. Cross with Duine as he slept all night in the chair. He seems to have no inclination to improve his mind, and reads so little, which keeps him "small" in mind. Men and boys were away bringing home the sheep today.

Tues. 16th. (Sheep for Salting). Duine was very successful in his search after sheep tonight. He got the promise of four. He arrived home, with Norman MacKinnon and sheep No. 1 which was promptly despatched in the back lobby; after which Norman was entertained to supper. Splendid sheep.

Wed. 17th. (Puddings and Tripe). Lovely day though cold. Kate and I busy getting rid of the inside of the sheep. We made white and black puddings and sheep tripe. A great success . . . busy cutting up and salting sheep. Made mince for rissoles and also made resolve to rise early.

Thurs. 18th. (Duine's Hair-Cut). Lovely day. Finished "Campion Court". Very good old fashioned story of the time of Charles 11. Precentor came before supper to cut Duine's hair. Took my hyacinths out of the dark today. Forgot to say I kept last night's resolve.

Fri. 19th. (Potting Bulbs). This has been a lovely clear cold day. Kate washing today (flannels). School in the afternoon. Men after sheep. Potted nearly all the hyacinths, tulips, and snowdrops, scyllas etc. and put them in dark cupboard. Settled down to a nice quiet evening by the fire when Neil MacKinnon came for us to go to Finlay McQuien's who it seems very ill. We both went up and did what we could. He was in great pain. Stayed about 1½ hours and came home. Duine and Kate went up again about 9 o'clock pm. and didn't get back until nearly 12 o'clock.

Sat. 20th. (Finlay McQuien Ill). Finlay McQ. just the same, very poorly. Sent Kate up with pudding (arrowroot) for his breakfast. Then Duine went up. Callum MacDonald arrived soon after with a sheep for us (the second, we are to get two more). He killed and skinned it.

Sun. Oct 21st. (Donald Ferguson Preaching). A very good day. Was twice in church and Sunday School. Finlay McQuien is a little better but very poorly. Donald Ferguson preached at night for Duine and did very well. He was very vigorous. We like him very much indeed. Duine went after church again to see Finlay.

Thurs. 25th. (Hay on Conacher). Finlay McQuien much better. Liner from N. Shields sent us a lovely little fish by Donald og yesterday. Liner left this morning. Men cutting "feur" on Conacher. I don't like that as it is so dangerous. Lot of children kept in today.

Fri. 26th. (Cheese Making). Terrible storm of wind and rain last night. No sleep for hardly any of us. Bad headache. Got breakfast in bed. Made butter in morning. School in the afternoon. Children very good. Settling down in the evening when Lachlan MacKinnon came to say his mother was going to make cheese and I was to go up and see her. Duine and I went up and got a lesson; then called on Finlay (who is better) and Rachel. Home and sewed a blouse. Bed 10.30.

Sun. Oct 28th. (Food for Fishermen). Men from little liner came ashore, wanting food. Gave four of them a good dinner after church (lentil soup, mutton and plum pudding). Their food is done, they having brought 14 days' food and they having been out 17 days. They are the "Coquette" from North Shields. The people gave them some flour, meal, sugar, and we gave them meat, tea, coffee, milk, butter, white puddings etc., and they went away to their boat quite pleased. They sent us a lovely halibut and large ling. Church at night. A good night.

Mon. 29th. (Sheep No.3). Good day. The "Coquette" left for home, I am glad to say. Thanksgiving Day. No school. Service at 12 o'clock. Went and visited faraway houses. Finlay McQuien in bed again with relapse. Sent milk and cotton wool. Finlay Gillies came down, poor man, to register Norman's death. We gave him some tea and who arrived then but Neil Ferguson (with Neil Junior) and Neil Gillies with another sheep which they killed in the back passage. They are very nice fellows, especially Neil Ferguson. Piece of whale washed up today on beach. Lovely moonlight night and so calm. Surely the "Evening Star" is on her way.

Wed. 31st. (Catching the Sheep). Last day of another month. Beautiful calm day. After dinner, before School, went to watch them (the Natives) catching the sheep (they call it ruaging) on Oshaval, which is at the back of the Manse. When catching them Donald Gillies got a terrible bad fall over a stone, which pierced and cut his leg badly. Had him brought into the Manse. Duine and I washed and dressed his leg and sent him home. Then school. Heard Finlay McQuien was worse. Prayer Meeting, then up and stayed with Finlay McQuien and Finlay Gillies' Donald till after 9 o'clock. Supper, and washed hair. Bed 11.30. No signs of the "Evening Star".

NOVEMBER 1906

Thurs. Nov 1st. (Odd Jobs). Sewing and doing odd jobs in morning, but Duine and I went up to see Finlay before school and went to dress Donald Gillies' leg. School in the afternoon. Then after tea to visit two patients again and Donald Ferguson. Home and bed 11.30.

Fri. 2nd. (Sheep on Dune). Men putting sheep on Dune. The old men went themselves today with a boat – two miles and rescued a sheep which had fallen into the sea. Went visiting our two patients. Finlay McQuien much better . . . worse at night.

Sat. 3rd. (Lifting Potatoes). Kate and I were busy all morning with the inside of the fourth sheep (which I forgot to say in yesterday's entry came yesterday. Neil Ferguson and Neil Gillies brought it). Both patients much better. People all busy lifting their potatoes. Very windy all day, indeed quite a gale. No boat could come into the bay today.

Sun. Nov 4th. (Stormy Days). Nothing "on". Church three times. Cross.

Mon. 5th. (Question Day). Fine day. Church Service being first Monday in month, also "ceisd" day. It was rather interesting. One man introduced a difficult passage from the Bible. First Duine spoke and then called on every member to say something on it, which they all did except two. Some spoke very well. Then the one who wanted light on the question finished up by praying. Then a collection was taken up for the church cleaning. After dinner A. Gillies came for her blouse. Kate and I then made cheese, our first on St. Kilda (and I am sure the last as the milk is getting so scarce). Took one pot of flowers from the cupboard. Donald og and Iain McDonald came to ceilidh. Made them help with the butter as we were going to churn. Took them to the sitting room after supper and showed them my bulbs, which surprised them.

Tues – Fri. (Nothing special recorded. The usual visits, no boats, reading "Bleak House", finished making bedroom slippers.)

Sat. 10th. (Men to Dune). Lovely day. Wind has now changed to the south. Wish the "Diadem" or "Evening Star" would come. If the latter doesn't come tonight we needn't expect her any more this season. Men went to Dune with lambs and to bring back the gentlemen sheep. Refooting socks. Two hens laying this last month.

Sun. Nov 11th. (Trawlers Sighted). Fine day, very calm, west wind, church in the morning. After dinner we were settling down for a nap, great excitement was caused by Kate's rushing in to tell us that the Fleetwood Trawlers were at the mouth of the bay. We went out and saw two. They passed and went to trawl but of course will call tomorrow. Hope to get mails. Duine better, has been a bit off with stomach for a week.

Mon. 12th. (Letter Writing). Writing letters all morning on chance of the boat calling today. Duine doing up registers with last teacher's work in it all wrong – gives Duine an awful lot of work. Making a Tam-o-shanter for myself of Uist wool. We hear that the two wretched boats seen yesterday went away again. One boat is still fishing at Boreray. It is maddening. When I came in from school got glorious surprise. Duine and Kate had put in Garve stove.

Tues. 13th. (Toothache). Duine bad with toothache all night. Men went to Dune with a sick sheep. Rather windy and stormy day.

Wed. Nov 14th. Duine had awful night with neuralgia. I went into school for him . . .

Thurs. 15th. (Trawler Calls). Just dressed when Kate came to say she saw a steamer in the distance. I also saw it coming nearer and nearer. To our great joy we saw it making for the Bay. It turned out to be the long looked for Fleetwood boat and had our mails at last. What rejoicing and no wonder, the first letters since the beginning of September. Duine and I got nearly two dozen letters besides papers innumerable. Bride cake and letters from Mrs. McWalter (Newport) and parcel from Inverness. It wasn't the usual boat but the "Kathleen", however, Capt. Wright was there and he is to bring our goods. The boat waited for letters. All are well at home. "Evening Star" we hear is sold and we shan't see her any more this year at any rate. We wrote and sent off several letters. No more school that day. Duine a little better. Went to see John McQuien's finger.

Fri. 16th. Duine a better night. School all day. Reading papers every opportunity.

Sat. 17th (Bits and Pieces). Duine improving. Very wet day. Finished socks (refooting). Baked oven scones and cakes (rock). Great success. Hens doing fairly well, three eggs and one huge one today. Salt herrings for dinner, very good. Killed red coileach tonight (the young one). Butter making yesterday.

Sun. Nov 18th. (Burst Gum-boil). Terrible storm of wind and rain. Duine's face very bad still but he went out twice; but had no Sabbath School. Did not go out at night. Duine's gum-boil burst after supper and toothache went at once.

Mon. 19th. Duine went to School today and is better.

Tues. 20th. Bathed Neil Gillies' hurt foot, dressed Mary MacDonald's burn.

Wed. 21st. Children specially wicked today. Getting on well with counterpane.

Thurs. 22nd. Kate started spinning herself today. I was vomitting from 2 till midnight. Awfully bad. No sleep.

Fri. 23rd. Feeling a little better. In bed all day. Finished "Bleak House".

Sat. 24th. (Duine so Kind). Simply awful day. Bed until after dinner, but still feeling very seedy and glad to get to bed. Duine so kind all these days, kinder than I am to him when he is sick I'm afraid, but I'm always so nervous when he is ill and can't help it. Scalpay!!!!!

Sabbath Nov. 25th. (Visitors). Got up just before dinner. Lovely day. After tea while the S.S. was in I "received" simply the whole of the village who came to enquire. It was awfully kind of them. Then all the Sunday School scholars came in. I am heaps better tonight.

Mon. 29th. (Kate's Courtiers). Got up to dinner and took some. Time taken up all day with visitors. Donald Ferguson and Finlay McQuien have been here today courting Kate. Ewan Gillies was here too, and we tease her, he is also after her, but we all suspect it is cupboard love with him, but the two botoch are in earnest right enough and it is awful fun.

Thurs. 29th. (Spinning). Dry wind, wind pretty high. Rose for breakfast. Busy all morning. Try spinning. Tongue for dinner. Writing letters. Put Barley in store-room today to make it last longer.

Fri. 30th. (Wintry Weather). Last day of Nov. and a very wintry day. Showers of hail (first of the year). Writing letters and cooking mutton in the morning. In the afternoon made bread. In the evening spun and crocheted. Got on better with spinning tonight.

DECEMBER 1906

Sat. Dec 1st. (Good Day). So good that Duine thought I might go for a walk. We climbed Oshaval, at least a bit of it and it was lovely.

Sun. Dec 2nd. (Stormy). Very stormy again. Terrible rain and wind, yet I got to church in the morning. Duine wouldn't let me out a second time.

Mon. 3rd. Still as stormy. Was spinning after dinner, then rested till tea.

Tue. 4th. In evening saw A. McQuien who has a bad burn of her face.

Wed. 5th. (Window Smashed). Most awful gale. Garden gate blown down and bedroom window smashed. Writing letter during morning to be sent off by real St. Kilda Mail.

Thurs. 6th. (Spinning Wheel on Loan). Donald MacDonald's baby *(Lachlan)* has been very ill but he is now better. When we came home Callum was in, he had brought down a spinning wheel for me to practice on.

Fri. 7th. (Letter Writing). Rachel Ferguson sent me down piece of mutton by Neil Junior. School in afternoon then letter writing and spinning. Boiled a huge pot of barley for the hens. It is splendid for them.

Sat. 8th. (St. Kilda Boat). Boys sent away St. Kilda Mail as the wind was from the right direction. William MacDonald came to mend the slates and to dip Kate's sheep. To our great joy Kate had him kill one of her sheep for us. It was awfully kind of her. Reading "Vicar of Wakefield". Don't care much for Goldsmith.

Sun. Dec 9th. (Snow). Very stormy. Showers of snow.

Hills white. Church twice but no Sunday School. Roenig ill all week with bad headache. Annie Gillies (Finlay) ill also.

Mon. 10th. (Raw Meat). Stove "grot" and mutton half raw, this and Duine made me cross all day.

Tues. 11th. (Variety). Just a glorious day. Spinning, cooking, school, visiting, knitting, reading "Chamber's" Annual, cutting up sheep and salting, finished first glove.

Wed. 12th. (Dog Bite). Hear Angus Gillies got badly bitten by his little dog last night. Reading "Gabriel Garth, Chartist" by E. Everett-Green. Kate busy spinning. Girls doing well with sewing. No visitors.

Thurs. 13th. (Duine not Well). Very cold day. Showers of snow. Up the Village with Duine to visit sick . . . D. Gillies was down weighing my wool for coat. Duine has a nasty turn of his stomach.

Fri. 14th. (More Snow). Hills covered with snow. Fine

The atmosphere of the Village Street by Heathcote, 1898.

starry night. Duine better.

Sat. 15th. Fearfully cold day. Showers of snow occasionally. Very rough night.

Sun. Dec 16th. Twice to Church. Very wet.

Mon. 17th. Breakfast in bed as no sleep. Up village ceildhing.

Tues. 18th. Very wet. Stayed at home all day. Started blouse.

Wed. 19th. Another wet day. School in afternoon. P. Meeting, first time for 6 weeks.

Thurs. 20th. (Wool Promised). Much better day. Got promise of wool from Angus Gillies.

Fri. 21st. (Rams on Dun). Men catching rams these days to put them back on the Dune. Spinning today and making new blouse. Trawler working behind the island.

Sat. 22n. (Making Butter). No sign of rotten boat. Men went to Dune this morning with gentlemen sheep. Cruvag got things cut out of her mouth by the Precentor. Kate killed second last coileach (for Xmas) this morning. Lovely day. Finished blouse for New Year. Duine and I very well. Only two eggs in dairy. Made butter today, fearful business, took two hours.

Sun. Dec 23rd. (No Boat Calling). No boat and men think she has gone. It is such a disappointment having all letters written. Church twice. Very stormy. Good attendance.

Mon. 24th. (Christmas Eve). Very stormy still. Cut blouse for New Year present for Kate. Got 2 eggs today. Kate went to Angus for wool for my jacket, got 4lbs and 1lb for white gloves. Spinning tonight and combing wool. Made plum pudding tonight. North wind. No hope of trawler coming now.

Tues. Dec 25th. (Christmas Day). Xmas Day on Hirta!!! Heavy snow all day. Busy in kitchen all morning cooking Xmas pudding and roasting fowl. Had capital dinner. School in the afternoon. Busy with Kate's blouse. Quite happy in Hirta this Christmas with my dear Duine. I don't mean all the things I say in this book in other places, because I love him. So funny to see snow here. I wonder what they are all doing at home and in Tobermoray and in Garve. In the evening went up to see Angus Gillies' wife who is ill just now again, or at least worse than usual. Got her to rise, or rather lifted her out of bed and took her to the fireside. She took some tea and was better then, a little. Angus was so pleased. Called at D. Ferguson's. Snow very deep in drifts.

Wed. 26th. (Sheep Dying). Snow worse than ever, and still falling and drifting. Duine clearing paths etc. Fearful weather but I like it if the sitting-room chimney wouldn't smoke so much. No visitors at all during the day. Men came down and put up the big black boat. Some of the men went over the hills after sheep. We hear they are dying.

Thurs. 27th. (Drifting Snow). Day worse than yesterday. Drifts fearful and wind so high. I am sorry for the poor sheep. The children have got holidays until after the New Year.

Fri. 28th. (Worse Than Ever). Storm still continues. It cleared up a little in the afternoon and Duine waded through the drifts and got to the village. The people, save Finlay Gillies, are all well. The people, even the oldest, all say they never saw the like of this.

Sat. 29th. (Arctic Appearance). More snow fallen in the night but the wind has gone down, still it looks like continuous snow. It is very serious. I don't know if there can be any services tomorrow. On the cliffs, opposite the sitting-room window, the long icicles are hanging from the rocks; it looks like the pictures one sees of Arctic regions.

Sun. Dec 30th. (Thaw Begins). Last Sunday of this year! Better day and gentle thaw enabling the folks to come out to church. Very good congregation. All the old folks nearly out.

Mon. 31st. (Close of 1906). Last day of 1906. My diary has been now kept for one year. It is so strange to find ourselves at this time out in this lonely island in the

Atlantic. Busy making scones (currant) for Children's Tea in School tomorrow. After dinner we went (Duine and I) to ask the children to come tomorrow, all so pleased, took ⅛lb tea to Bess who is ill, also jar Liebig to Beau Angus. I will also give ½lb tea to Rachel MacKinnon. Finished Kate's blouse tonight. Kate spinning. Lovely moonlight night but with showers of rain.

ST. KILDA 1907 – Alice MacLachlan, The Manse, St. Kilda

JANUARY 1907

Tues. Jan 1st. (Children's Tea). Got up and wished Kate, "Bleadus mhath whr" and presented her with her new blouse. She was greatly pleased with it and SO surprised. Had breakfast and went to church at 12 o'clock. Great hurry to get ready for the Children's Tea which was at 3 o'clock. They all came and got on very well. They left as it was growing dark. Kate went up to village to spend the New Year, and we (Duine and I) had a nice quiet evening to ourselves. I made another plum pudding for tomorrow's dinner, as I have asked Roenig to come and get dinner with us. So our first New Year in St. Kilda has passed. Duine better and I am alright. Kept NEW YEAR!

Wed. 2nd. (Queen's Kindness). Nice quiet day but stormy out of doors. Duine's stomach very bad. The Queen came down and brought me some flour, which was very kind of her. She was afraid the school treat had left us short.

Thurs. 3rd. (Duine Ill). Duine rather ill and still on sick man's diet. I was spinning quite a lot tonight. I finished "The Fair God" by Wallace and enjoyed it immensely. Now I am reading the bound volumes of "Chambers' Journal" and find these splendid. Kate up at Meirut's tonight at a carding party, which are all on the go just now. My hens are not laying a single egg just now.

Fri. 4th. (Change of Plans). Fine day. Wind changed from NE to S. If the N wind had continued the boys were going to Soay for sheep today but Alas! the wind has changed. However, the trawlers may come with the present wind. Duine much better today.

Sat. 5th. (Longing for a Boat). A very wet day, but with the trawler's wind. Kate informed us as she came home from carding at Callum's last night that she "smelt" a steamer! She thinks it will be about Barra Head!!! I am so much wearying for a boat to come through. I am looking for letters, potatoes, bacon etc., not to speak of newspapers, parcels. Duine keeping better, but still on arrowroot diet. He pled for "feoil" (flesh) tonight but I was obdurate. No eggs yet. I firmly believe they are laying and eating the eggs.

Sun. Jan 6th. Fairly good day, but very cold. Church twice. Duine well.

Mon. 7th. Days getting suitable for boat; will come be hoping for her any time now.

Tus. 8th. Nothing special. School in afternoon. Duine bad last night with stomach.

Wed. 9th. Not very well myself, took cascara. Went to prayer meeting.

Thurs. 10th. (Trawler at Last). Not well in night. Breakfast in bed. When dressing and looking out of the East, what to my delight should I see coming round the Point Coll but the long looked for Trawler from Fleetwood with mails. What joy! He brought us mails but no provisions. He says his brother may be here any day with them. How glad we should be if this were so. We are too glad to get our mails to think of anything else just now. I went to school and let Duine go out with the men as I wish him to see the Captain himself. Duine got a lovely pair of lemon soles and a small cod, which were priceless to us as we have seen nothing but salt beef for nearly two months. We are hoping Capt. Wright will bring the side of bacon which has been lying somewhere for us since SEPTEMBER. Plenty of home letters. Went up the village. Home and had a good read of the newspapers. Just exactly two months as today since the mails came before. Sorry our letters bring news of Doctor Rainy's death in Australia.

Sat. 12th. (New Recipes). Lovely day with a good deal of sunshine. Went for an hour's walk on the shore and enjoyed it very much. Came home to dinner and went to see Annie McQuien, she is much better today, but is still in bed. Busy all the evening trying to get through my newspapers and cutting recipes out of the "Weekly Scotsman".

Sun. Jan 13th. Duine speaking in church this morning about Doctor Rainy.

Mon. 14th. Took calendar to Angus – he was very pleased. Went to Donald Ferguson's to see about oil. Got promise of some, and flour when we need it. Went to Mary Gillies to ask her to come and card with Kate for my coat tomorrow.

Tues. 15th. (Extra Paraffin). Another lovely day. Got five gallons of paraffin from the store today and very glad to get it. Mary Gillies carding today. I see to the food for them and do little things.

Thurs. 17th. (Boat brings Supplies). To our great joy a boat came today. I was the first to see it coming at about 12.30. It was the "Kathleen" from Fleetwood (Capt. Wright) and brought our long looked for flour, Indian Meal, coffee, potatoes, but no bacon yet. The tide was pretty far out but it was an awful job getting the big boat out. There was great fun between old Donald McQuien and John Gillies, and McQuien had the rope and was on the rocks and wanted into the boat, while John Gillies was as determined he wouldn't go with them. J.G. pulled the rope and Donald fell half into the water. Such bawling at one another. Duine went with them. It was a terrible business, but they got out alright and returned with everybody's things, but it was difficult to get out and worse to get in. In fact, we who were on the shore were afraid that they were not going to get in at all. Got a lot of letters. All are well at home, also Tobermoray. Got jolly parcel of books

from Miss. Cram, also from Mrs. Stirling. Big parcel from a Mr. Johnston in Fleetwood on "Sunday Magazine's Circle" for "Hirsleach". Grand night's reading of newspapers.

Tues. 18th. Very stormy day. We hear the trawler is in the Glen.

Sat. 19th. Fearful day. Trawler in the Glen so they have evidently got fish.

Sabbath. Jan 20th. Lovely day. Trawler came in while we were in church. The men went out in the afternoon with the mail-bag.

Mon. 21st. Didn't sleep yesterday through shutting my thumb nail in the window.

Tues. 22nd. (High Pressure). Out all the morning about the hens. Got three eggs. Glass at its highest point. It couldn't go any higher.

Wed. 23rd. Neil Ferguson and Lachlan MacKinnon ill with trouble like diarrhoea. My hens now laying splendidly.

Thurs. 24th. (Mysterious Illness). Only 10 children in School this aft. Nearly all laid up with this mysterious illness.

Fri. 25th. Kate went up to see her sister (Donald McQuien's wife) who is now getting better.

Sat. 26th. Snow again. Ground white. Neil Ferguson's baby is very poorly, also the Precentor's.

Sun. Jan 27th. (Too Cold to Lay). Very blowy all day and so cold. Hens stopping laying again with the cold. Snow away. Several more have had to go to bed with the Gripe.

Mon. 28th. (Storm and Keating's Powder). Fearful day. Disturbed night with awful wind. Thought the roof would be lifted off and windows blown in. Duine says it is the beginning of the "Favilleach". Too stormy to have School. Hurricanes terrific. The glass is very low. One of the worst this winter. Had great fun at old Bess's. She had asked Duine to bring her some Keating's Powder. Almost the first thing she asked was, "Did you bring the powder?" Duine said "Yes" and produced it. "Oh" she said, "Put it on me!" She is old and in bed. She heaved herself up and waited for Duine to put it under her. We fairly shrieked. She herself couldn't see the joke. Fortunately, Catrione was in and took the job in hand. Duine and I were fairly convulsed with laughter. Catrione and I couldn't behave while Duine prayed! Got three eggs today. Started gloves for self, dark brown.

Tues. 29th. Had a jolly evening by the fireside. Very rough night indeed. Reading "The Double Marriage" by Charles Reade.

Thurs. 31st. Lovely day. Spent greater part of morning outside. Donald og got the "Lady of Hirta" and "Naighven Fireanneach" away.

FEBRUARY 1907

Fri. Feb 1st. (Men to Soay). Simply glorious day. To our great joy the men went today to Soay. Nearly every house turned out, and a large boat load set off. We had an early tea and then Salana accompanied the Duine and I went to the top of Ruadval. It was a lovely walk. We sat on the tops of the cliffs and watched the fulmars on the rocks below. They have such a funny scream which sounds so weird. We thought we should see the boat coming back from Soay but we didn't. On our way home we went down to look at the Dun passage. It was all magnificent, unutterably so. On our way home we went to ask for Donald Gillies and Norman McQuien. Both are very poorly yet especially the latter. Straight home. Just in time to meet the boat. Got a nice sheep for killing, also a lovely little pet lamb, which we have put in the byre along with Salana.

Sat. 2nd. Another lovely day. Spent most of the morning in the byre watching my new sheep. Got three eggs. Went to see all the sick folks in the afternoon. Very tired tonight. Went to bed early.

Sun. Feb 3rd. Blowy, fresh day, cold. Church twice. Finished "Red Morn" by Pemberton, and have enjoyed it very much.

Mon. 4th. (More Illness). Wakened early by Kate coming into the bed-room to say Donald og was in the kitchen (8 o'clock) saying Toromich was very very ill and had been all night. Duine went up before church and found Norman very poorly. I went up after dinner to see Norman and took eggs. My pet Soay sheep in the byre is thriving nicely.

Sun. Feb 10th. (Strange Noises in the Night). Better day, church twice. Sent Kate up with eggs to Toromich who I think is a little improving. Kate telling us of a curious sound (we put it down to an owl) heard by many people on Oshaval. They say that poor Norman's blood is still about the place and is calling out. The superstition is appalling. Got eight eggs today. Did without light at S.S. for the first time.

Mon. 11th. (More Snow). Ground heavily coated with snow today, and still failing. Kate put her second sheep in the byre today; it came home itself from Oshaval. Sending eggs daily to Norman. We hear there is a steamer fishing at Boreray. Blood was drawn from John MacDonald today for his leg. Toromich a bit better. Donald Gillies came down before tea to have his foot dressed. Wrote letters.

Tues. 12th. (Trawler Called). Frosty and more snow. To our great delight, just as we were finishing dinner a boat came in, the one which has been fishing off Boreray for a day or two. It was the "Knowsie" of Aberdeen. Duine went out with the men and found the Captain so kind. He gave Duine a huge basket of haddocks and a fine big cod. Gave the men large pipes of tobacco and X Ale. He took all our letters to post in Aberdeen (where he hopes to be on Saturday or Sunday). He will be coming here till the end of May. He returns here in a week (tomorrow). The men all nearly, gave him orders and Duine ordered a bag of potatoes.

Thurs. 14th. (First Loom). Very stormy day. "Kathleen" due today but no sign of her. Finlay Gillies put up looms today. He is the first.

Sat. 16th. (Nasty Fall). Forgot to say I had nasty fall yesterday morning and wrenched my shoulder. It is awfully sore (fell off the table in the store room). Hugh Gillies put up his loom yesterday and Callum preparing. My hyacinths are lovely.

Sun. Feb 17th. Fine day. Church twice. Hear that Toromich is just as bad as ever. His father Donald McQuien is also ill. Sent daily supply of eggs by Kate.

Mon. 18th. (Trawler Calls – Cheese Mountain!) Breezy day but fine all the same. Going about morning's work as usual and was in the bedroom about 12.15 when to my great delight the "Knowsie", Aberdeen, came round the Point of Coll. He only left here at mid-day on Wednesday last and returned in two days less than a week and brought back all the things ordered. The men bungled their order and instead of bringing some small pieces of cheese he brought two huge cheeses – one of 84lbs and another of 96lbs at 10d. per lb. The people wanted us to take them, or rather one, but what could we do with so much. Besides we ordered some from Fleetwood and so did most of the people and some got some pieces with their order yesterday. Saw Callum and Neil Gillies weaving. Very stormy. The "Knowsie" had to stay in the bay all night. We got 8 stones of lovely potatoes. Splendid.

Tues. 19th. (Dinner on Board). Fearful night. "Knowsie" still in the bay. As it quietened down a little in the morning some of the men went out to the boat (to see about the mistake in the cheese). They got dinner on board and the Captain was very kind to them.

Wed. 20th. Again a fearful night. So dreadful with snow and wind and rain that we could not think of having School. William came down to mend church door and window. Donald Ferguson came in to ceilidh. Had great fun with him and Kate. It seems he proposed to her 13 years ago.

Thurs. 21st. Better day, a little. The "Knowsie" went out as far as Boreray and trawled but returned as it was rough. Duine and I went up the village and saw

MacDonalds (both Neil and Donald's families), Ian Phau, Bess, Toromich, Christina MacKinnon, and Christina McQuien, and home, took a big cheese supper. Donald MacDonald has also got his loom now.

Fri. 22nd. Fine frosty night last night and day. Started the "Mother Tongue" in School today with big boys. "Knowsie" left at 7 o'clock this morning.

Sat. 23rd. Fine fresh day. Knowsie I hear is still fishing at Boreray. Reading "His Brother's Keeper" by Sheldon, and enjoy it very much.

Sun. Feb 24th. Church twice. Reading "In His Steps". Toromich a bit better.

Mon. 25th. Fine day. Made last butter of the season today, which has been very good indeed.

Wed. 27th. (Gift of Fulmar). Another lovely day. My crocuses are very nice just now and hyacinths also. Went to Prayer Meeting, first time for 6 or 7 weeks. Got a fulmar sent down from William today. (It was delightful. Thurs.).

Thurs. 28th. Hear the "Knowsie" went off on Tuesday.

MARCH 1907

Fri. March 1st. March has come in so nice and mild, whichever way it will go out. We hear that there are some liners in the neighbourhood. Donald Gillies (MacFinlay) came down for my wool and is to put it into the loom at once.

Sat. 2nd. (Kindness of Hull Trawler Crew). Glad of a holiday. Shortly after breakfast a fine trawler came into bay and whistled for a pilot. After a long delay our men went out and didn't return till well on in the afternoon, and brought with them the Captain and most of the crew of the Hull trawler. The Capt. came to tea. He and the crew were awfully kind to our men and gave them coals, paraffin, medicine for the sick men, jam, butter, string, lamp glasses, and everything they needed – biscuits, bread etc. they are going to try for fish and if successful will come for a month. The men had got a splendid dinner on the boat "City of Hull". The Capt. sent us 9lbs of lovely BEEF, large loaf, and 4 beautiful plaice. So we are in luck. Hope they will get fish. Hear the invalids are better, a little.

Sun. March 3rd. (D. Ferguson Preached). Fine day though very blowy. Hull boat and another Hull boat and two other strangers in bay. Hulls went off but others stayed all day. (Forgot to say yesterday that Duine mended the window in bedroom and it is a great improvement although patchy). Twice to church. William came to ceilidh after church and told us·such a lot about Finlay and Callum and their love affairs. Donald Ferguson preached tonight with great vehemence (he does very well).

Mon. 4th. Hear that the four trawlers are all working at Boreray. Busy writing examination papers for 11 Class boys.

Tues. 5th. (Profitable Haul). The Aberdeen men say the "Knowsie" made £460 on her last trip here. Also that she put an advert into the paper saying she was going to St. Kilda and would bring letters and papers. Toromich up for the first time for nearly six weeks. Donald McQuien is a little better today. Donald Gillies came down with my cloth. I am very pleased with it. Made cakes (rock). Gave D. Gillies my scissors.

Wed. 6th. Fine breezy day. Two trawlers in the bay. There are five altogether, one from Hull, three or four from Aberdeen (one came yesterday). None came in. Reading "Westward Ho" (Kingsley).

Thurs. 7th. (Taking Toll). Wet, rather blowy. Rose first today, expecting the Fleetwood boat as it is now time she was here. It is two months, all but a week and next week the moon will not be so favourable. We are so much wanting letters and papers (and things ordered). The "Knowsie" came in just before dinner, while the men were out "Taking Toll" from the other boats. They went straight to her, but some of them

soon came in for their money. Duine came in from school and went out with the men to get our things and pay ours. Duine came in and brought a lot of people. This was the Capt. and Engineer of the "Knowsie" and another (Capt. Coull) of the companion boat to the "Knowsie". We got cheese, flour, jam, syrup, cream of tartar and sweets £1-7. I gave the three a grand tea and they went off so pleased. Duine took them up the baile. I am going to get lemon soles from them.

Fri. 8th. (Friendly Competition between the Trawlers). Very blowy. Six trawlers in the bay. Great fun among the trawlers. The "Knowsie" means to wait until the others are starved out as they are only provisioned for a week and "Knowsie" for three weeks, also the Hull boats. All the Aberdeen boats went to follow the "Knowsie" to see where she gets the fish. She made £460 last trip here. The Capt. (Wagner) was awfully kind and would give away anything. We got a bag of coals for Roenig and Capt. Coull promised one for Bess. But yesterday the men could not go out to the "Loch Lawyers" (Capt. Coull) as the tide was so far out. Got 10 eggs today – the best yet.

Sat. 9th. (Sermon Notes Lost). The "Knowsie" and "Ben Lawyers" both made a run round the island before dinner and after that they left immediately for a fishing ground. Duine and I went for a walk before tea to Beren-na-hahe (phonetic spelling) to get a view of Boreray. There were four boats fishing but which was which we could not tell. Duine put about as he must have lost all his papers up the hill during the afternoon so had, at the eleventh hour, to study new subjects. I was so sorry for him as he wasn't very well.

Sun. March 10th. (Infant Sunday School). Church twice. Started Infant Sunday School with three boys – Neil Ferguson, Donald Ian Ferguson and Donald Ian Gillies, but hope to have the girls next Sunday.

Mon. 11th. (False Alarm). Early this morning boat came round the bay and whistled. It only came in and steamed out again so our hopes sank to Zero! Made

Kate bake again to give the Aberdeen flour a fair trial. The scones are simply horrible and we can hardly eat them. Duine better. We heard yesterday that Ewen MacDonald is ill, and Norman McQuien is not so well. Everybody is giving up hope of Fleetwood this year.

Wed. 13th. Far too rough for fishing. We hear old Annie (at Finlay Gillies) was putting up blood last night and today.

Thurs. 14th. "Amy Dods" still here. Too rough to fish. Went up to see the sick folks.

Fri. 15th. "Amy Dods" went off this morning before we rose. Ewen MacDonald up but poorly yet. Norman better, Annie just the same, Meirut has been ill. Am getting on well with my spinning and did a whole pirn myself.

Sat. 16th. Fine day. "A. D. Dods" (Observe correct name of Capt. Richie's boat) in all day. Went to see the invalids after tea. Saw William's brother as he was going back to the boat – with his companion; brought them in and gave them 2 tins coffee and milk, 1 tin Swiss milk, and 1 tin corned beef, as I hear they are short of provisions. Tha mi bochd.

Sun. March 17th. (Sabbath Breakers). Fine day. Five of the "A. D. Dods" came in to church. A big trawler in the bay when the men (Hirst) were out with the "A. D. Dods" men, they went to it and got some things. In church Donald Ferguson was praying for the Sabbath Breakers!!! Not feeling very well.

Mon. 18th. (Trawlers off Rockall). Seedy all night and in bed all day up to 5.30. Forgot to say that the "Poloch Ruadh" who was in the bay on Saturday told the men that there were lots of fish at Rockall and that all the boats (trawlers) were off there. Men out at boat (A. D. Dods) tonight which has been out fishing all day.

Tues. 19th. Breakfast in bed. Feeling better. Spinning all day. Not out at all.

Wed. 20th. (Good Turbot Catches). Lovely day, glass going up. Two boats in, "Rambler" (North Shields), the other is the "Ben Lomond" (Aberdeen). They are getting lots of Turbot. Boiled the burner of lamp and improved it very much.

Thurs. 21st. Fairly good day but heavy showers. Spinning a good deal. School in the afternoon.

Fri. 22nd. (First Shearwaters). Fine day. No boats in today. Got a pair of shearwaters ("scrabillays") from John McQuien and one from Neil Ferguson. William got very sore foot cut – dressed it.

Sat. 23rd. (Sermon Notes Found). Duine and I went for a walk up Beren-na-hake. We were looking for the missing sermons lost a fortnight before, but we found them in a book when we came home. Went up (with very bad headache) to see William's wife who has got a very sore ear and Annie McQuien who is ill.

Sun. March 24th. Out twice to church myself and Sunday School. Had Rachel, Annabella and 3 boys. No boat. Toromich MacKinnon precented tonight as William was at home with his wife. My box of flowers is lovely.

Mon. 25th. (Boat Cold). All the baile have the steamer cold the last day or two very badly. They say it came by the last boat. It seems so funny! They believe implicitly in this. Everybody has it and all the School is in a constant cough and sneeze. Reading "A Naturalist's Voyage Round the World" by Darwin and enjoying it very much. Have an awful pain in my back today. Kate finished Angus Gillies' spinning today.

Tues. 26th. (Treacle Cake and Toffee). Very misty still. Fine rain, sun trying to peep through. I made some treacle cake and toffee. Both most successful. Everyone bad with cold.

Wed. 27th. ("Knowsie" Returns). Great excitment this morning during breakfast when our friend the "Knowsie" came in. She brought us our potatoes, toffee, sugared almonds, blacking. The Capt. brought me a bag of oranges and apples, 2 bts ginger beer and last but not least a big box of kippers from Stornoway. I shall never forget Capt. Wagner's kindness – never. He will call before he goes for letters. Set a hen with 12 eggs today. Two clucking hens but neither very satisfactory, I fear.

Thurs. 28th. (My Birthday). I got my present yesterday by Capt. Wagner. During the morning John McQuien came down to tell Kate to go up for the letters and parcels. We got about 10 between the two. Letters from everybody. William's wife very ill with ear and head.

Fri. 29th. Fine day. Not much news. No boats at all. Went to see the sick.

Sat. 30th. (Captain's Kindness). Rather blowy and fine rain. Went (Duine and I) to see Beau William and Donald MacDonald's wife and looked in a minute on Norman. About 7.30 the "Knowsie" came in. What fish the men brought in. A sack of the loveliest soles and flounders and plaice, and simply heaps of roes. I have enough to last me a month. Also ling. We packed them in ice in a tub. The Capt. (Waulkner) is simply kindness itself and sent word he wants to take back the flour and he is to take the invalids to Aberdeen.

Sun. March 31st. (Easter Day). The crew, five of the "Knowsie", came in to church and stayed to dinner. This is Easter Sunday. We kept them to dinner and gave them salt beef, boiled fish and potatoes besides tinned pine-apple. The Capt., Engineer, Cook and young boy came in at night to evening church and then to supper. The Capt. simply studies what he can do to be kind.

APRIL 1907

Mon. April 1st. "Knowsie" left about 8 o'clock. We went up the village and saw those who were ill. Set the second hen down with 13 eggs. The young pigeon is growing so quickly and there is another egg.

Tues. 2nd. We hear there are two liners in Glen Bay. I baked some ginger-bread. Very big sea and high wind.

Wed. 3rd. (Soap in the Eye). Hear Ewen Gillies has a bad eye, John (William's small son) threw some soft soap at him! Went to prayer meeting and entertained Don. Gillies and Don. Ferguson after.

Thurs. 4th. Boat came in at darkening which turned out to be the "Katy", Capt. Morris. The men went out and brought in a letter bag from Aberdeen. Nothing for anyone but me.

Fri. 5th. (A Perfect Hurricane and First Calf). Terrible gale today in the middle of which came in the "Knowsie". They blew their sirens, but of course it was impossible for our boats to venture. Stayed all day till evening when she sailed out in a perfect hurricane, the wind washing her from end to end and almost turning her over. Whether she went to the Glen or not for shelter we don't know or whether she went off straight to the Butt of Lewis. Went up to see the invalids. Finlay's (McQuien's) cow calved today.

Sat. 6th. Better day. "Knowsie" must have gone. "A. D. Dods" came in this evening. Capt. Ritchie sent us a nice little halibut. The "Katy" (Capt. Morris) also came in and two liners. William and Ewan very angry at "Knowsie".

Sun. April 7th. (No boats in today). Fine day though a little blowy. Bad headache. Church twice.

Mon. 8th. (First Lamb Born). Lovely weather. Capt. Ritchie left early but the men are expecting him on Wed. to take William and wife to Aberdeen. Brown hen sitting a week today. First lamb today (Finlay McQuien's).

Tues. 9th. (Men after Gannets at Boreray). Another lovely day. Out most of the day. Most of the people are finished with their weaving, at least nearly. Kate doing a little for Angus. A good few of the scholars absent from school, away bringing home the sheep which are to lamb soon. I went up to see William's wife. Very gearranach. While up the men came down and went off to Boreray after the Solan goose. Duine busy digging the back garden. The Rhubarb growing nicely.

Wed. 10th. (Fall from the Rocks). The beautiful weather continues. Went down on the pier after breakfast to see the gannets killed last night. There were a good few over 100. Each who went had about 30 apiece. We got a pair. I am collecting the large quills. They are lovely for hats. Donald Gillies (son of Finlay) and John MacDonald (son of Neil) had a nasty fall over the rocks today, got badly bruised. Went and dressed their wounds. Also small Donald Ian Ferguson who cut his foot badly with an old scythe blade. Everyone expecting the "A. D. Dods" to come in to take out cargo

Gannet Portrait – on Boreray. T. A. Quine.

of "H'iortach" to Aberdeen. If they don't get away now, they are not going at all.

Thurs. 11th. Went up the village in the morning and dressed the wounds and saw the sick folk. Roenig down to tea, got hay from Duine.

Fri. 12th. (Men Painting Boats). The men are all down at the Quay busy painting their boats. After School Duine and I went up the Glebe beyond the store and saying how nice it would be if the "Knowsie" would come in – didn't she just come in while he was saying it. There was a big rush out and I went too. Got bread, coffee, steak, biscuits, X Ale, a lovely turbot, a crab, and two large cod. Gave one away to men. Was very sick. Got letters and papers.

Sat. 13th. Still sea-sick and in bed till after tea. Cooked beef-steak pie.

Sun. April 14th. ("Knowsie" Arrested). Had breakfast. in bed. Did not go to church. When Duine and I were resting after dinner, the men came down. I went to the bedroom and to my great surprise saw a gun-boat. In a moment or two to our grief came the "Knowsie" and we knew that she had been arrested by the Government boat. A boat came in from the latter and on her were the Capt. (Murdoch) and the Fiscal from Lochmaddy. The latter came to make enquiry about Norman Gillies' death. Duine spoke up to them bravely. The men were all so pleased. We hear the "Knowsie" is to be taken to Lochmaddy tomorrow. Duine, Neil Ferguson, Donald Og, William all going to speak up for Capt. Walkner. We told them what he had done for us, what no-one would do. Capt. Walkner and the Engineer came in to hear. The "Minna" (Government Boat) brought us papers. The Fiscal brought sweets for the children.

Mon. 15th. (Sick Get Away by Boat). Up very early as the Fiscal and Capt. came in at 6.30 am. We gave the children a holiday. The scholars and us had our photos taken by the Fiscal, after which he gave them sweets. Capt. Walkner and the mate came in to dinner, after which the preparations were made for going off. William and his wife (the latter going to Aberdeen Infirmary), Ewan going to Aberdeen, Norman McQuien going to Greenock, with the "Minna", en route for the Infirmary in Glasgow. We had great scenes on the pier. It was very affecting the parting between Beau William and her baby. At last they got off, Duine and Neil Ferguson too. The poor old "Knowsie" went off first, the "Minna" following behind. When shall we see them back, and with what result? The "Knowsie" is going to Aberdeen before she comes back. Went up the village to see the sick folks. Took sweets to Roenig and Donald MacDonald who could not come for their share.

Tues. 16th. (Caught Guillemot Myself). Went to School for Duine, so I must do till he comes back. Went up after School to see Finlay MacDonald who is still ill in bed and also Annie McQuien. Had eight girls down for their blouse pieces. Black hen clucking. Today, caught a guillemot on the rocks myself.

Wed. 17th. *(Sewing Session).* Very cold day. Threatening snow. Very busy in school all day. After Prayer Meeting Annie and Catherine Gillies (Finlay) also their two cousins and Catharine MacDonald came and sewed till 10 o'clock. Having Aberdeen steak for dinner. Kate had guillemot which I caught yesterday.

Thurs. 18th. (First Chicken Hatch). Windy day. A Shields liner fishing straight out from Levenish all day. Busy in School all day. Got first brood of chickens out today. Set 12, 3 eggs bad. I am fearfully bilious for a week and suffer from awful headaches. The people started cleaning the cloth today at Neil MacDonald's. Very tired, bed 1 o'clock. What would Duine say if he were here. I wonder where he is. Set black hen with 13 eggs. She sits well so far.

Fri. 19th. Children all very bad with colds today and a lot of them away. "M. A. Dodds" came in at 12 o'clock. Letters.

Sat. 20th. (Boat Cold). Donald Gillies brought down the letters which came at midnight by "M. A. Dodds". Two pigeons out today. "Rambler" North Shields in all day. Nearly everyone ill with colds and headaches and many in bed. The "Rambler" sent a whole lot of Solan Geese ashore and the people were down on the beach gathering them at darkening. Chickens getting on nicely, also blouses. Very wet and windy.

Sun. April 21st. Fine day but very cold. Chickens take up a lot of time this weather. I wonder if the "Knowsie" will come today. D. Ferguson took both services. Was out twice. Read book called "Thompson's Progress" by Cutcliffe Hyne.

Mon. 22nd. Very blowy still. So many absent with bad colds. Chickens in second brood beginning to come.

Tues. 23rd. Wind a little down. Girls sewing at night. No news except old Annie at Finlay Gillies very ill. Dying, we all think.

Wed. 24th. ("Knowsie" Returns – Capt. in Prison). Much better day. Looking eagerly all day for "Knowsie". When we were in the Prayer Meeting at night and Donald McQuien praying, we heard first the dogs then the whistle (very welcome) of the "Knowsie". Everybody was down at the pier. At last they came. They had a fearful passage, and had been tossing about from Sat. last to today! They were all "green". Poor Duine looking fearfully ill and no wonder. Poor Capt. Walkner is in prison in Inverness for 30 days (or £90 fine). They were only one night in Aberdeen where the excitement was intense. All news in papers which I have. Capt. (Rowbottom temporary) and Engineer came in to tea. Lots of parcels. One of material from Edinburgh, one from Miss Rainy.

Thurs. 25th. Very cold day. School in morning. Duine went in afternoon. Neil MacDonald here helping Duine to put up garden gate. Kate dug half of plot today.

Fri. 26th. (Death of Old Annie Gillies). Very wet and cold. Duine very bad still with stomach and back. My own very bad too. School in afternoon. Old Annie at Finlay Gillies died this evening, just when we were up the village. Great lamentations.

Sat. 27th. (William MacDonald Returns). Fine day Duine very tired. He stayed at home all day. "M. A. Dodds" came in late – and William also came with her.

Sun. April 28th. Men from "M. A. Dodds" came in to dinner and church. My back so bad I did not go out. Capt. Ritchie sent us in a ling. Duine and I both broke Sabbath by writing letters, about seed to Mr. Laing, to County Council etc.

Mon. 29th. No school as it is old Annie's funeral day today.

Tues. 30th. Fine day but very cold. Duine in School himself all day, I stayed in and sewed. He and Kate got back plot all ready for oats. On Friday last we set eggs under "feathery-feet". "M. A. Dodds" in Capt. Ritchie sent fish. Posted Roenig's letters.

MAY 1907

Wed. May 1st. (Soay Lamb Born). Lovely day. Got a little lamb from my caora Soay this morning. Going to school today.

Thurs. 2nd. Fearful day. Kate washing as we could not put it off any longer.

Fri. 3rd. (News of the Whalers). Cleared up a lovely day. Boys (John MacDonald and Donald og) came and helped with the manure. Caora Soay out but is as wild as the heather. Hear the first whaling boat passed today, going away out after whales. Very late this year. Lot of my chickens dying. The first whaler came in this evening and the men went out to see who it was and to get news. It was the Eleazen (as near as I can spell). He said Scorndorp was at the Flannan Isles but would be there soon. Scorndorp's son will not be here as he has gone to China (Yappu), but the mate has got his boat.

Sat. 4th. Lovely day. Something like summer. No boats

in all day. Went up baile to see sick folks. Duine getting better.

Sun. May 5th. ("Knowsie" Returns Again). A real summer day. Out to church twice and to Sunday School. When Duine and I were sitting after supper at the fireside I heard a whistle and ran out. What did this turn out to be but the good old "Knowsie". Duine and the men went out at once and were anxious for news of the Capt. They saw Rowbottom, the mate who told Duine to go down to the cabin himself. Who was there but the good old Capt. Walckner himself. The petition had been to the Home Secretary.

Great rejoicing.

Piece torn out of diary

THE PETITION – (Susan MacLachlan has kindly lent me a copy of the petition mentioned above, D.A.Q.)

To – The Right Honourable,
    H. M. Secretary for Scotland,
    Scottish Office,
    Whitehall.

The Petition of the Reverend Peter MacLachlan, Minister of the United Free Church of Scotland, Neil Ferguson, Postmaster, William MacDonald, Ewen Gillies, and Donald McQueen, all of St. Kilda.

Humbly Sheweth,
    That upon Tuesday, the 16th. day of April current, in the Sheriff Court at Lochmaddy, Albert Walkner, Master of the Steam Trawler, "Knowsie" of Fraserburgh was, by the Honorary Sheriff-Substitute then officiating, fined the sum of £90, with the alternative of 30 days imprisonment, for having, on the Sunday preceeding, fished within three miles of the barren and uninhabited rock called Boreray, but well outside the limit of 3 miles from low water mark on the Island of St. Kilda.

The interest in the case of the whole of the inhabitants of the Island of St. Kilda, in whose name we speak, arises under the following circumstances:-

For nine months or thereby in the year, the inhabitants are without any recognised means of communication with the mainland, or even with the Hebridean Islands; and as a consequence we are often reduced to considerable straits for want of provisions, while luxuries are unknown. No one but ourselves can appreciate the seriousness of that position. Last year the potato crop was an utter failure, and we were, in consequence, so short of provisions that but for the succour we obtained from the "Knowsie", we should, without doubt, have suffered from the calamity of famine. We have endeavoured to obtain the Government's assistance, but despite the kind efforts of Mr. Weir, M.P., and Mr. Dewar, M.P., in the matter, no aid has been vouchsafed to us. In that state of affairs, with starvation threatening us, and the Government declining to afford us relief, Captain Walkner and his crew in the "Knowsie" relieved our distress, bringing from time to time provisions and other commodities to the Island, and carrying letters for us, all free of charge for freight or trouble. Further, at the time of his capture, Captain Walkner had arranged to convey on his vessel to Aberdeen, also free of charge, the wife of one of us, who was in need of immediate surgical aid, which, of course, she could not receive on St. Kilda.

Yet, although Captain Walkner was so often in a position to contravene the Statutes prohibiting trawling within 3 miles of the shore, we can aver that he never attempted to do so; and neither he nor we conceived that he was committing an offence by fishing on the far side of Boreray, from 6 to 7 miles off our coast.

The rock, Boreray, stands solitary and uninhabited, at a distance of 4 miles or thereby from St. Kilda, and no one from our Island has fished there within the memory of living man. Trawling in the vicinity of the rock cannot, we humbly submit, harm any person or community; and in our view, therefore, the charge against Captain Walkner was unfounded by law. But even assuming that it be held differently, we beg to represent that Captain Walkner's offence was so purely technical that an admission would, especially looking to his record and character, have properly and sufficiently met the requirements of justice. In place of this, however, the offence, such as it was, has been visited with a punishment not perceptibly less that the full money penalty, with an alternative of imprisonment which cannot but remain as a blot on the record of one who has displayed such high characteristics in his dealings with us, and has, to our knowledge, refrained from any breach of what he and we sincerely believed to be the reasonable meaning of the law.

We, therefore, humbly pray that you will take the circumstances we have mentioned above into consideration, and exercise your prerogative by ordering a total remission of, or a material reduction in, the punishment imposed upon Captain Walkner, by the Honorary Sheriff-Substitute, who, it seems to us, did not appreciate the peculiar circumstances under which Captain Walkner was arraigned before him.

And we, your humble Petitioners, will ever pray
(Signed) Peter Maclachlan
Neil Ferguson
William MacDonald
Ewen Gillies
Donald McQueen

Dated at Aberdeen, the Twentieth day of April, Nineteen hundred and seven years.

(The Petition must have been well received as Captain Walkner was released from prison and re-appeared on St. Kilda on May 5th to great rejoicing . . ! D.A.Q.)

Mon. 6th. (Men to Boreray and Stac An Armin).
Question meeting postponed till tonight as the folks are so busy washing the cloth at Donald MacDonald's and the men are off the Stac an Armin and Boreray after lambs. The "Knowsie" will bring them home. The men came home with some lambs and some bougies (puffins) and some gannet eggs, but they saw no sign of the "Knowsie".

Tues. 7th. No news.

Wed. 8th. Meeting night. Went up baile yesterday to see Finlay Gillies . . . making cloth, manure.

Piece torn out.

Fri. 10th. (St. Kilda Mail Boat Success). Very wet day. Busy with sewing and chickens. Who came into the bay tonight but Botoch-nam Borrom. He and mate came ashore to see us and stayed till all hours. Botoch brought me my sweets. All the boys came down to see them. William gave him a wire to send off to his wife and I gave him letters to post. Forgot to say the other day that Neil Gillies got word that the "Post" posted by sea on Dec. 8th had reached its destination, but no particulars yet.

Sat. 11th. (Men to Boreray and Stac Lee). The men went off to Boreray and Stac Lee – got gannet eggs. One boat went to the back of Conacher for lambs. They came home very tired. Lovely day.

Sun. May 12th. Not so fine day today. Everyone with fearful cold in church, Duine included. Donald og very poorly, also his father.

Mon. 13th. (Village Hospital). Rough Day. Busy with sewing. Went up baile after tea and never saw such a hospital, simply every house with someone in bed. Duine very bad but much better of Eucalyptus. Wind very high.

Tues. 14th. (Soay Lamb Killed – Working Crofts). Everyone busy with their crofts. Kate has been up every day helping Callum's people with their out-door work. Very sorry to say Finlay McQuien's dog killed and ate my little Soay lamb which is just a fortnight old. I am so cut up over it. The children got a holiday this afternoon as so many are absent at out-door work. Duine very bad with cold (Influenza).

Wed. 15th. (Herring Drifters in Bay). No School as so few came. When we looked out this morning we saw three drifters. The men came in later in the afternoon and we got lovely fresh herrings. The men came in a second time and brought some more herrings. We are so enjoying them. The "Scaligram" came in for the first time this year. Also a trawler from Hull.

Thurs. 16th. Drifters still in the bay. Duine a little better. No boat with potato seed yet.

Fri. 17th. (Chickens Hatch). Duine in school all day with good attendance. Kate cleaned out Post Office and best bedroom. Got 9 chickens out of 11 eggs from "feathery feet" today. Got bad cold myself.

Sat. 18th. (Cran Put Up). Lovely day. Men putting up cran, and building walls etc. getting ready for the "Dunara".

Sun. May 19th. (Hens Attacked by Dog). Blowy day but fine. No "Dunara" came after all, so the date had not been correct. When we were in S.S. a dog came and killed two of my hens, both of them with chickens. Duine was in a fearful state. However, none of them were any the worse. D. nearly killed the brute. We were much disappointed that the "Dunara" didn't come but we know that all's well, the "Hebrides" will be here on Wednesday.

Mon. 20th. ("Dunara" Arrives and Neil Gillies).
Awakened early by the siren of the "Dunara Castle". The factor, Mr. MacKenzie, and Alistair Ferguson and Neil Gillies all arrived. Only two visitors. Great excitement. The people got their first supply of meal and flour, while A.F. brought all sorts of luxuries in the way of eating and clothing. Went up the baile and dressed Neil Gillies' leg. Very bad, with wound pretty open yet. Called for Mr. MacKenzie, who came down late and spent some time with us.

Tues. 21st. Forgot to say lots of letters yesterday. In house myself now with bad cold and sore throat. Norman McQuien arrived home yesterday. Mr. McKenzie came to supper.

Wed. 22nd. (Treacle Toffee). Very blowy. Everyone says no hope of the "Hebrides". But it may clear up. Cold very bad. The Queen called with milk and had ceilidh. Also Annie (Aig Finlay) and Mary Mohr (also with milk). Made treacle toffee (great success) and entertained Mr. MacKenzie.

Thurs. 23rd. ("Hebrides" in a Hurricane). The night was blowing a perfect hurricane yet the "Hebrides" came in and blew her whistle hurriedly. We got up and with great difficulty the men got the boat out. They came back with the word that the boat would wait for nobody. They took out the Baile but the men here persuaded them not to venture. The little boat was nearly swamped each time. Dressed Neil Gillies' foot.

Fri. 24th. (Potato Planting). In bed all day with bad headache. Kate and Duine bad. People planting potatoes.

Sat. 25th. (Men to Soay and Boreray). Lovely day. Two boat loads went to Soay, one to Boreray, Alistair Ferguson etc. in the latter. It was a perfect day. Went down to the Pier at night to see the boats return. Got a lot of guillemot's eggs. The men had some fulmar too. Feeling rather seedy yet after the Influenza.

Sun. May 26th. Another day like yesterday. Not out in the morning, went to S.S. and evening Church. Good attendance.

Mon. 27th. (Peat Cutting). Cold day with biting east wind. People started cutting their peat today. Went to School in the afternoon, feeling almost alright. Dressed Neil Gillies' bad leg later on in the day. Had Alistair Ferguson's friend, Mr. Kirkland in. He stayed supper and had a long evening. We enjoyed his company very much.

Tues. 28th. (Food Getting Low). Cold east windy day. People busy with their peats. We hear there are a good few steam drifters in the neighbourhood, but of course, they never will come in with this wind. Our food supply is getting very low.

Wed. 29th. Very breezy. "Johanna" came in the morning from N.L. Tarbert. There is a whale in the bay and in the evening the Botoch and Scaligram came in, the latter with a whale. The "Johanna" left at once with them. A boat went out with letters. Very rough night.

Thurs. 30th. Wet a little and very blowy. Strong east wind. No peat cutting today. No boats in with this wind.

Fri. 31st. Blowy day, dull. Kate went off in morning to work at peats with Meirut. It came on to rain but they stayed all day. Finlay McQuien came in, made tea for him. Donald Gillies came in the evening.

JUNE 1907

Sat. June 1st. (Rough Weather). Another day like yesterday. No boats in yet. Did not go out all day. Cold bad. Fearful weather.

Sun. 2nd. Rather better day, but glass very low. Raining. "Johanna" and three whalers came into the bay to shelter. One whale. Finished salt mutton today.

Mon. 3rd. (Work at the Whaling Station). Much better day. Long lie in bed after bad night with coughing. Hear that Ewan Gillies is going away to work at the whaling station with Mr. Herlofson and leaves tonight, also Mr. Kirkland. Weather most unsettled. Doing little packing. "Johanna" left at 8 o'clock taking Ewan and Mr. Kirkland with them.

Tues. 4th. (Puffin and Fulmar Eggs). Fearful day. East wind and very high seas. However, the rain is pouring down in buckets, so that should settle the wind. Got three fulmars. Kate away at the peats all day. Donald Gillies brought me some puffin and fulmar eggs. Doing some packing, jars, eggs etc. Cold very bad, not out since Sunday.

Wed. 5th. (Hoping for the "Hebrides"). Very wet but sea

very calm with little or no wind. Very bad night again coughing. Last night. Good look out for "Hebrides" due tonight.

Thurs. June 6th. (Rough Departure on Holiday). Fearful morning. The "Hebrides" came in a perfect gale but yet the men went out for letters. They returned with mails and to say that the Inspector and Doctor were on board. We had left the fire in all night, so poked it up and had tea. The Inspector came in about 6 o'clock, a bit before, and we went out at about 7 o'clock. Think the children did fairly well. No tourists could come ashore, the weather so awful, and I don't know how in the world we got on board the "Hebrides". The weather unspeakably bad between St. Kilda and Lochmaddy. Never was so ill in my life. Had good night and next morning got to Castlebay and had a walk ashore. Saw Mr. Grant, Deputy to Fleet of Herring boats. Got news and invitation to Inverness. Got to Tobermoray at 7 o'clock at night. Forgot to say we got heaps of letters and post cards and also photos, three from the McRaws, of Jeannie in her M.A. Cap and Gown. Mr. Levack and Campbell called.

August 1907 – June 1908
EXTRACTS FROM THE DIARY
AUGUST 1907

Thurs. Aug 1st. (Return from Holiday). Arrived here this morning after a delightful holiday. Had rather a stormy passage. The "Hebrides" acting up to her reputation for pitching and rolling. We were not particularly taken up with the crowd aboard. Saw Mr. McKenzie Sen. and Jun. at Dunvegan, also Dr. MacKenzie's brother. Order wool (Cheviot) and wheel from factor. Found on arrival that Rachel MacKinnon (Roenig) had fallen down a great side of Conacher and was very badly hurt. Her thumb broken shockingly – with bones protruding. Head terribly cut

and body badly bruised. There was a Doctor (McKintosh) from Edinburgh who came and saw her but was unable to do anything as it had to be amputated at once if anything was done. Had a busy day and what with sea-sickness etc. it was fearful. (Mr. McKenzie (Factor) introduced me to two young gentlemen (Messrs. Milne and Clarence from Oxford) who were coming to St. Kilda and who have taken up their abode with us.

Fri. 2nd. A bright day to begin but showery. Mr. McAllister took the gentlemen for a long walk as yesterday, while Duine and I were busy unpacking. I found my little Soay sheep nicely. She is a great pet and so pretty, nor is she shy. Killed calf today. Paid two visits to Roenig.

Mon. 5th. Capt. Ritchie kindly sent me in a fine halibut and the "Hope" sent in two fine ling.

Thurs. 8th. Had the three of the "Ornulf" (the Botoch, Mate and Engineer) to tea.

Sat. Aug 10-24th. (Sat). (Too Busy to keep Diary). For the last fortnight I have been so awfully busy I have no time to keep up my diary. There were five new women members "joined" the church – Kate, Mor (her sister), Bhen Donald MacDonald, Bhen Ian Gillies, and Bhen Toromich. It was a very busy time altogether having the gents. They left on Thursday morning by the "Hebrides", I was very sorry parting with the two Sassenachs. Kate also left for Tobermoray. The people started killing the fulmar on Friday (Aug. 16th.) and have had very good weather so far. The "Alekto" is the new boat in place of the "Johanna" which is at the bottom of the sea. There is a new Capt. and crew. Yesterday Aug. 23rd. we had a lovely day – the "Alekto" came in bringing Mr. Herlofson and Mr. McKenzie with them to measure out ground for the new fishing station (whales). They came to us for lunch and tea. We went altogether by boat to the Dun in the afternoon and had some awfully good fun – scaling the rocks. The Capt. of the "Alekto" is a big and stout man and in his efforts to come down gracefully into the boat he split his trousers! Mr. Herlofson was awfully kind with coals etc. I forgot to say last week we had a little sailing yacht in called the "Silver Bell" with a Doctor Wolfenden and party; he is a scientific man and is partly on errands of science and partly on pleasure. He is an M.D. and very kindly came to see Roenig's finger with me. Made cheese today, and butter last Wed. I ought to have said that we got 6 tons of coals from Mr. Herlofson on the day Kate left.

Sun. Aug 25th. People are nearly all very bad with a cold. Potatoes in the garden are growing splendidly.

Mon. 26th. "Alekto" goes off tonight with three whales.

Thurs. 29th. High wind. "Hebrides" called for last trip. Kate came. Got bacon and plenty of parcels. Botoch here to tea.

Sat. 31st. "Alekto" in and men got their coals and we got two more tons from Mr. Herlofson. The men brought them all up.

SEPTEMBER 1907

Sun. Sept 1st. "Knowsie" in, got halibut and haddocks.

Tues. 3rd. People busy dipping sheep these days.

Wed. 4th. Four or five whales in the bay. Men busy dipping sheep.

Fri. 5th. William swept sitting room chimney this morning, "Alekto" went off this morning and Botoch with 8 whales, huge ones, between them. Very stormy day. An illness very like the measles is going the round. Kate and Duine at the hay in the Glebe above the store.

Sat. 7th. (Ruaging and Dipping). Lovely day. "Scaligram" and other boat in but the "Alekto" and Botoch have not come in. Men busy ruaging and dipping all day. Three sheep went over Ruadval in the ruaging, two belonging to Roenig and one to Callum. One of Roenig's dead but the others will get better.

Mon. 9th. (Men on Dun). Simply a charming day. The "Alekto" was in and had four whales. Finlay McQuien's Donald and Donald (Ian Bhan) and John

MacDonald McQuien went over to the Dun in the black boat with some small sheep. Did Neil Gillies' leg. Do it every two days.

Tues. 10th. (Alekto to Glasgow). Very misty morning. The "Alekto" goes to Glasgow on Saturday with 1,600 barrels of oil, whalebone etc.

Wed. 11th. No Prayer Meeting as the men were away at the Glen dipping sheep. Misty tonight again.

Thurs. 12th. Three whalers came into the bay this afternoon. Men went out to fish, others went to the Dun with lambs.

Fri. 13th. ("Knowsie" Lost Anchor). Bright lights from the "Knowsie" which had come in after dark last night. She had lost her anchor and 16 fathoms of chain when they were here before, so the boats were out looking for it. Both Captains Eleasen and Skortorp came ashore after tea and cut grass, and stayed to supper. The "Skaligram" left for the Station to get her boilers cleaned. "te-steele" Norwegian – Keep quiet.

Sat. 14th. Two boats in the bay, the Botoch and Eleason.

Sun. Sept 15th. (Norwegian Kindness). There were two jolly letters from Mr. Herlofson wanting us to go for a trip to Harris to see him. I wish we could. He also returned the last coal money. He really is awfully kind. The Botoch and Eleason's boats came in loch.

Mon. 16th. (Men on Dun). Find breezy day, grand for the hay. The Botoch and "Scalligram" in, also "Katie" and a trawler from North Shields. Men at Dun today.

Tues. 17th. (Lessons To Learn). Capt. Skortorp went to the Station last night or this morning. Men put new lamps in church today. They are very nice. Had row with Finlay Mor today over Ian who is not learning his lessons at all well and who is such a clever boy when he likes.

Fri. 20th. The three Bata Na Nunc left the bay just as we were rising early, so we have no boats in at all now.

Sat. 21st. (Learning Norwegian). The whalers all came in after tea into the bay. Botoch and Paulsen came in to the Manse at darkening. Botoch brought a book to teach me Norwegian. It seems quite easy. Lovely day.

Sun. Sept 22nd. (First Liner). Beautiful all day. No boats in all day until evening when a liner (the first of the season) came in. It came to Levenish this evening, also another boat in the Bay. Did some Norwegian.

Mon. 23rd. (Measles Raging). Eleason (Kuendulf) came into the bay. So we surmise Skortorp and Paulsen must have got whales and gone to the Station. Roenig keeping better. Measles raging. Stretched shawl.

Tues. 24th. Eleasen went to fish but returned minus whales. Botoch and Paulsen returned from the Station, the former bringing letters. Botoch came ashore and certified that all the patients are suffering from measles! Liner from Grimsby in and sent us herrings and a nice small ling. Botoch stayed with us for supper and read English with Duine. He also presented me with the Norwegian grammar which he is very anxious to learn.

Wed. 25th. The Botoch's son from Tonsberg has now joined him and is on board. Skortorp and Paulsen came ashore this evening.

Thurs. 26th. (Plans Changed). Amid great excitement and barking of dogs, the men came down and made preparations to go to Boreray. Only one boat set out with loud talk but they were not away more than an hour when they returned. It seems they had some hot words about the number who were to go and they found out they could not bring any sheep with the number of men – not to speak of dogs. So they came back.

Fri. 27th. (Men on Boreray for Sheep). Fine day. Two boats left by 9.30 for Boreray. No other boat in the bay but the Grimsby liner left the bay about a quarter to eight for Levenish.

Sun. Sept 29th. (Botoch with Letters). Was going to rest at home this evening and was in bed when the siren of a boat began to sound. I flew into church for fear it was

the Botoch and indeed it turned out to be as he arrived with letters as we came out of church, and also with Peter's boots from Flora.

Mon. Sept 30th. (Grey Crows Shot). Made cheese and butter and went to Roenig's. Cooked roast of mutton when Botoch and Paulsen arrived. Paulsen and Eleasen came into bay today. Botoch and P to dinner and tea. They brought gun and shot 3 grey cows. Did a lot of carding.

OCTOBER 1907

Wed. Oct 2nd. (Whalers away for the Winter). Still a very stormy day with high east wind. The whalers left the Bay early but came in about 12 o'clock with flags flying and sirens sounding. I am sorry to say this is their good-bye (Tha mi bochd). There is still the chance we may see Captain Skortorp, if he makes one more trip before the "Ornulf" leaves for South Africa. Liner passed mouth of the bay this morning. We shan't see many more boats now. Neil MacDonald's wife in bed with swollen leg and Neil Ferguson's wife (measles).

Boreray and the Stacs, Flannan Isles in the background.

Thurs. 3rd. (Men to Boreray). The men came down just before school and went in Boreray. Two boat loads of them. Men came home before darkening with lots of wedders.

Fri. 4th. (Men to Soay). Men down cleaning the boats. Two liners have just come to fish at Levenish this morning. The men all went to Soay today. Poor luck, only 8 sheep. Making "Marracken geal" and using up all the pieces of inside of sheep. It is a splendid one with 10 or 12lbs of "gair" ("geir" to be correct.)

Sat. 5th. (Busy Spinning). Grimsby (or N.S.) liners in

bay all day. Fine Boreray chops today for dinner. Kate busy spinning my white gown. At second pirn today.

Sun. Oct 6th. (Boats to Rockall). Another boat in bay from Grimsby going to Rockall. 2 eggs.

Mon. 7th. Three boats in the Bay, two from N. Shields, including the "Rambler" and one from Grimsby.

Wed. 9th. (The Hay!) Duine and Kate at hay. I don't know whether it is anxiety to get the hay in or a wish on the part of the one to get off school and the other to escape housework. Corn from back put in barn today in good condition without any rain. Two liners at the back of Dun.

Sat. 12th. (Ruaging). Two liners into shelter last night. One, the "Rambler" from N. Shields has been here for the last 3 weeks or so. The people were cutting Bess' lot today and finishing Angus' corn. Ours finished now, the cutting, some hay to cut. Much interested to see the men ruaging. Saw one of William's, on Osheval at Coll Point, a very cross sheep, slip down into the sea. It was drowned. The men soon had a boat out and got its carcase.

Tues. 15th. (Kate with Measles). Kate has got the measles!!! Very stormy night. One Grimsby boat in Bay – a new one.

Fri. 18th. (Neil Gillies – More Leg Trouble). Kate rose from her bed this morning. Little Neil Gillies' leg turned very sore today coming to school and he simply could not walk home. His father had to carry him from the Glebe right home. We are afraid there is a disease in the bone.

Tues. 22nd. A little liner fishing out Levinish. "Rambler" came in and we got fish.

Thurs. 24th. In the middle of the day a trawler came in from Grimsby, the "General", Captain Bantock. He sent us some fish.

Fri. 25th. (Hay Harvested). Lovely morning. All of us in good form. The "General" fishing off Boreray, we hear. Three liners fishing (S.Shields). HAY FINISHED TODAY, I AM THANKFUL TO RECORD. Men

went out to liners and sold them some skins. They also ordered goods. I ordered a stone of apples. They have only been fishing four days and are full up. Duine taking up potatoes – very good.

Sat. 26th. (Finest Day of the Year). Simply perfect day. In the afternoon which was baking hot and the sun so strong, Duine and I went up Beren-a-hake and sat for a long time watching the sea below us which was as calm as glass. The fulmars were fluttering round us and we had a delicious time. We came home and I went up the village to see the sick people. Saw two liners off Levinish today and two further out . . . left for home. Men cutting grass on Conacher. Finest day this year.

Tues. 29th. (Cutting Grass). Fine breezy day with boistrous east wind. Splendid for drying hay in the cleits. People all busy cutting grass on Conacher, Glen and elsewhere.

Thurs. 31st. Very bad night. Grimsby boat fishing in the vicinity.

NOVEMBER 1907

Sat. 2nd. (Sore Throat). Throat very sore. This morning a boat was seen in the neighbourhood of Levinish but mysteriously disappeared.

Sun. Nov 3rd. Feeling better. Had nearly all "Hirta" calling for me! Duine specially kind.

Tues. 5th. Chance trawler passed mouth of bay and whistled but went straight away to Barra Head. A liner at Levinish, but has not yet come in. 5 eggs.

Wed. 6th. (Stock in Garden, Men to Soay). Simply glorious day, so sunny and warm. All our stock are in the front garden. Most of the "Hirsteach" went off in great spirits to Soay today. Men came home with lots of Soay sheep. We got a splendid molt. Just as they arrived the little liner came from S. Shields bringing all the things the men ordered, also my apples (3/- for a stone and rotten at that!) Donald Gillies came down and skinned Soay sheep. Gave him shoes to mend.

Thurs. 7th. (Rescue Operation). Lovely day. Three liners working at Levinish. the "Botoch Ruadh" came from Barra Head today on her way to Rockall. Finlay Mor stranded on Dun and had to be rescued by Donald og and Norman (brothers). Forgot to say Captain of the "Rambler" yesterday sent us a lovely big ling. Feeling better. 6 eggs.

Fri. 8th. Trawler, the men think from Fleetwood, came from Barra Head. There are several liners and trawlers about.

Sat. 9th. (Soay Sheep Over Rocks). Soay chops for breakfast. Just starting new bag of flour. The last has done since the middle of August. Men went to Dun for second or third time with lambs. Made butter today. Feeling very well. The "Rambler" in the Bay every night. My oldest Soay sheep has gone over the rocks of Oshaval! Bad luck indeed.

Mon. 11th. (Harvest Thanksgiving). The "Rambler" left about 9 o'clock. I'm afraid she is gone for good, as it is an awful storm of wind and rain today. Harvest Thanksgiving Day.

Wed. 13th. (Keeping Fit). Started skipping exercises today to keep down the "fat" and feel very stiff indeed. Duine busy working at the School Registers.

Fri. 15th. (Boats Secured). Men busy these days putting boats secure against the wind. Turning them upside down. Washed my hair tonight.

Sat. 16th. (No Luck). A real November day. So misty and wet. A Liner, the "Viceroy" from Grimsby came in this afternoon. It came from Aberdeen where it had been disposing of its fish. The men went out but got nothing for their pains. We hear there is a trawler from Fleetwood trawling at the back of Oshaval.

Sun. Nov 17th. Fine winter day. A liner working out and a trawler at Boreray.

Mon. 18th. ("Knowsie" Calls). Great excitement. Awakened by Kate shouting, "The Knowsie" and by hearing the ever welcome hoot. I got three letters. I

didn't expect any more but got a whole heap more, also parcels. One from Robertson (Inspector) with work for the girls, Medicines from Dr. Wolfenden, Medical from Mr. Coats, Paisley. Papers galore. Capt. Walkner sent me a case of "Scotch".

Wed. 20th. Another stormy day. "Knowsie" and N.S. Liner in bay all day.

Thurs. 21st. (Good Fishing). Still blowing a gale. "Knowsie" crew in great glee as they have got heaps of fish, £200 in a day or so.

Fri. 22nd. (Fishing at Night). The "Rambler" arrived again from North Shields and the other liner which was fishing has come in with brilliant lights, showing she has fish. "Knowsie" still working at night.

Sat. Nov 23rd. (First Snow). Snow on Conacher and other hills. First of the season. Both well. Hear "Knowsie" left and "Cornelian", Hull (Capt. Amazon) is working at Boreray.

Sun. Nov 24th. Bitterly cold day. Three liners "Rambler", "Roamer" also "Craigside" – Trawler "Cornelian" all in bay all day.

Mon. 25th. (Trawlermen Food Shortage). Had deputation of men from "Craigside" (N. Shields) in, who required food, having been out in the stormy weather for a fortnight. The Captain asked Duine and I how many children we had. Duine thought he meant in School and answered "Twenty one at present!" The man's face fell as he said he wanted to give them 1/- apiece! I saw the two sides and explained. It was awfully funny. One man came in with a bruised finger and I washed it with carbolic water and gave him bandages. Duine and I combed until 1 o'clock and did almost a whole fleece.

Fri. 29th. (Men to Soay). Splendid day. The men went to Soay today for sheep. We got a nice wedder. My pet lamb is getting so nice and tame and will run anywhere after me, and eat anything out of our hands. We hear there are five trawlers working at Boreray.

Sat. 30th. (Men to Boreray). As soon as we awoke Kate

came to the door to say "Knowsie" was in the Bay. Got my goods from Aberdeen. Capt. Walkner gave me a case of "Scotch". The Cook also brought me papers, also the Engineer brought me a huge parcel of People's Friend. I got some letters and parcels of papers. We also got a splendid turbot. We got post-cards galore from Africa, from Mr. Herlofson, also from Capt. Skortorp (two) and Paulsen. They are now going to Cape Verde Islands. Some of the men went to Boreray for sheep and the "Knowsie" towed them home at night. Capt., Engineer and brother of Mrs. Walckner came in and had dinner. The people gave the Capt. a Soay sheep. The "Lucy" from Fleetwood (Capt. Wright) was at Boreray.

DECEMBER 1907

Sun. Dec 1st. (Lovely Day). Church all day. Good congregations. "Knowsie" and other trawler in the Bay at night.

Mon. 2nd. "Knowsie" passed mouth of Bay on way to Soay Bank to fish. She gave us a salute as she passed. Lovely day.

Tues. 3rd. "Knowsie" and three other boats in bay tonight.

Wed. 4th. "Knowsie" and other boat in Glen bay.

Thurs. 5th. "Knowsie" and other boat in our Bay. Killed coilleach for Capt. Walckner and sent out cocoanut for his kiddies. The other boat is the trawler, the "Loch Ness" from Aberdeen. The Capt. of her and the engineer with Capt. Walckner and brother in law all came in to dinner. Turbot, potatoes, ham and eggs, also tea.

Sat. 7th. Having a lazy day. "Knowsie" and "Loch Ness" trawling round the point. The "Cygnet" (Jack Wright) returned today.

Sun. Dec 8th. Everyone bad with the "cratan".

Mon. 9th. The sea is a sight today and is breaking over the pier.

Tues. 10th. (Huge Hauls of Fish). "Knowsie" and Rowbottom (late mate of the "Knowsie") came in at breakfast time with their boats. It seems the boats got splendid hauls of fish at the point last night of huge cods. The nets were breaking and they had to throw some fish away. The sea was very rough and the old men were down in a wax at the young ones. Got a cod and some delicious flat fish soles, plaice etc.

Wed. 11th. ("Knowsie" to Aberdeen). Lovely day. "Knowsie" left for Aberdeen this morning with a splendid cargo. Rowbottom's boat working all night but in Bay today. The men out line fishing all day and only got two lings and a lot of eels which count for nothing. Two liners have come from S. Shields.

Thurs. 12th. Rowbottom's boat in bay all day. Tonight another boat came in.

Fri. 13th. Still glorious weather. We hear there are eight boats working out between Boreray and Levinish.

Sat. 14th. (Like Summer). Such a glorious day. Duine and I went up Beren-na-hake to see the trawlers working. It was beautiful up there – just like summer and we had such fine views of the outer islands. Beautiful moonlight night.

Tues. 17th. Men went over to Dun with lambs (or for lambs).

Thurs. 19th. (Presents for Children). When Duine came into School he was accompanied by the Capt. of the "Mercury". I recognised the Capt. as I had doctored his leg once (last Aug). The engineer was with him. They had brought a box of oranges and apples for the kiddies. The two came in and had tea and told us that the "Cornelia" had had a large haul last week and was coming back with another box for the children and one for the old folks.

Sat. 21st. ("Knowsie" with Burst Boiler). "Knowsie", much to our delight, came in. The excitement was intense. While the men were out the "Cornelia" came in! Duine came in with plenty of stuff – my case of

"Scotch", a leg of pork, presents from Capt. Walckner. The delay was due to the bursting of the "Knowsie's" boiler three hours after arriving in Aberdeen. Lots of letters and parcels in bag.

Mon. 23rd. (Hairpin In Beard!). Finlay Gillies came down and cut a pair of pants (present) for Duine – very amusing, the measuring and marking. Forgot to say D.F. found a hairpin in his beard!!!

Tues. 24th. (Tame Soay Lamb). Xmas Eve. No boats. Very blowy! Kate very busy washing. My little lamb so tame and following me about into the house and all round. Duine up the village again. I busy sewing.

Wed. Dec 25th. (Christmas Day). Xmas Day. Nothing on save a bad attack of neuralgia. Gave the children a treat of oranges, apples, nuts and sweets this afternoon and let them home early. Had cold port, hot salt fheoil and plum pudding for dinner. There are six trawlers in the Glen. The people were over that way and the boats were all whistling.

Fri. 27th. ("Knowsie" in Trouble Again). Neil Ferguson sent down for the letters as the "Knowsie" and six other trawlers, among them the "Princess Melton" with Johnnie (William's brother) are in the Bay. John came across to see the relations in the afternoon and Neil took our bag over to the "Knowsie". The boiler of the latter is leaking badly and the Capt. and crew say they are all going to leave her.

Sat. 28th. No boats in. Very stormy. In all day with neuralgia. Busy sewing. New bag of flour

Mon. 30th. (Latest Engagement). Lovely day. We have had no rain for a long time and a good deal of frost. "Cornelia" went home today. "Knowsie" went out yesterday. The "Avon" with the nice Capt. Bantock of the "General" is out there. Forgot to say on Saturday that Callum came down to give us the news that he had just got engaged to Annie Gillies (Ewan's sister). All busy just now cutting grass on the back of Conacher. Duine started smoking a month ago and finished the Craven Mixture that Mr. Clarence left.

Tues. 31st. (Men to Soay). Simply a perfect day. The men went to Soay today for sheep. We got a sheep for killing and a lamb which we put with my other pet. Busy making puddings for the children's treat tomorrow. Duine and I busy getting the children's presents ready.

ST. KILDA 1908

JANUARY 1908

Wed. Jan 1st. (Children's Treat). Glorious day – bright sun and so calm. Gave Kate her presents. After the Children's treat, which passed off with great success, we had in Capt. Craig of the "Melton Princess" and John (William's brother). My neuralgia bothering me very much.

Thurs. 2nd. Men of "Princess M." again in but only the Capt. in the Manse for tea. Will and Neil Gillies out trawling.

Fri. 3rd. Another lovely day. In the afternoon I went up the baile and distributed all the peppermints. I was in every house and got treated to tea, wine, biscuits and cheese.

Sun. Jan 5th. (Village Pays Visit). Had very bad night with tooth-ache so had breakfast in bed and received all the village. Did not go out today, but had the wee ones in to Sabbath School and they were such darlings. They said their Psalm and finished up by singing. I did love them so.

Mon. 6th. Very stormy day. The "Cygnet" dodging about the bay but does not come in.

Tues. 7th. (Matrimonial Affairs). Rough day. Did not go further than the byre to see the cirries. Both are now eating oil cake. Great gossip as to matrimonial affairs, as to who Finlay Mor is to get, whether Bellac or Kate will win!

Sat. 11th. ("Knowsie" – A Week To Reach Aberdeen). Quite a lot of boats in when we waked. The "Princess Melton" among the rest so we got news of the

"Knowsie" which had broken down and took a week to get back to Aberdeen. Capt. Walckner trying to get another boat. Got soles from "Cornelia" thanks to Donald Gillies.

Mon. 13th. Stormy day. Boats, eight or nine, sheltering in the bay.

Tues. 14th. "Princess Melton" in and two ashore. Capt. Craig in for little.

Wed. 15th. (Walckner's New Boat). First thing a new boat came in with great whistling. The men all thought it was Capt. Wackner and so it was and we were so glad. I got such a parcel of sketches of all sorts. Got a cake from Dundee, Dunie got "Omar Kyam" and Kate a Picture Post-card Album.

Fri. 17th. (Children's Entertainment). Better day. Two or three boats in. Capt. of "Princess Melton" came in and gave the children a gramophone entertainment, which delighted and charmed them. Children got oranges. "Cornelia" in bay. Had the skipper and William MacDonald to tea.

Sat. Jan 18th. – Feb 2nd. (Influenza Through Village – No Diary Kept). Between these dates owing to being ill myself with neuralgia and everything else under the sun. The whole village has been ill with a kind of influenza. It got its grip on poor old Bess and carried her off in less than two days. It comes on with shivering and one has a very sore head. This is one of the chief symptoms together with very sore back and bones. The majority of the people had violent vomiting. School of course closed from Jan 22nd – Feb 4th. Bess (MacDonald, aged 78, widow, D.A.Q.) died on Tues. night Jan 28th. and was buried on Jan 31st. Bessie has been very bad as well. Far the worst case at present is Beau Finlay Gillies, who has a most fearful incessant cough. This cough with (sac) as they call it is one of the symptoms of the sickness. My latest caora from the Soay died in the interval from water in the head. We have had such heaps of boats in the bay, sometimes fourteen. Capt. Walckner is now away from Fraserborough Tr. Co. and is on the "St. Machar", same line as the "Princess Melton".

FEBRUARY 1908

Mon. Feb 3rd. (Services Hit). Yesterday there was only one service as everyone was so sick. The previous Sunday there was none. The "Cornelia" and two other boats in bay today. My hyacinths, in water, are doing splendidly.

Wed. 5th. (School Re-opens). School re-opened yesterday after being closed for a fortnight for influenza. Rowbottom came into bay today on one of Bookless boats. They had an accident it seems on board and one man was hurt by the anchor. Gave him bandages and embrocation. He sent a huge cod and halibut.

Sat. 8th. "Craig Miller" came into bay, also the "Dreadnought" (Capt. Morris). Heard that the "Princess Melton" had been sold and the wee Capt. was waiting for another boat. Also that Ewan was in Aberdeen staying with Capt. Craig. Capt. Craig and Walckner are waiting for Bookless boats.

Sun. Feb 9th. "Craig Millar" in all day.

Thurs. 13th. It is the first time I have been up the village with Dunie, or out at night, for six or seven weeks. All are making progress.

Fri. 14th. (St. Valentine's Day). Still no boats. Gave VI Boys an object lesson today on the hyacinth, one of my own which I took to School. I made toffee for the coughs up the village, and oven scones. Shower of snow and Conacher is covered.

Sat. 15th. Neil Gillies (Finlay's) came for medicine. Also William MacDonald's son John to have his hand dressed. It had been slightly bitten by a dog.

Sun. Feb 16th. (Tension Mounts). Two steamers came into bay last night and had such bright lights showing that they had fish. We were awakened about 8 o'clock by the loud whistling of one of the Bookless boats, the

"Bannerdale" on which was Capt. Walckner. He hadn't brought the letter bag as he was not pleased with the St. Kildans for giving the last one to Donald Craig. He had Ewan Gillies with him as deck-hand. Ewan's sister came down and gave him a fearful wigging and took him home in triumph. He was rigged out at Capt. Walckner's expense. His mother could not let him go away again and the men had to go out and tell Capt. Walckner. So Capt. Walckner was awfully cross with the Hirteach and no wonder. Capt. Walckner now refuses to bring anything to anyone except ourselves and Neil Ferguson and William! Great storm in a tea-cup. "M. A. Dodds" in, also "Cornelia" and another. Church three times today!

Mon. 17th. Angus and Donald G down drowning "Bussy", poor Bess's dog. Capt. Ritchie in the bay.

Wed. 19th. Men went out to the "Cornelia" and "Bannerdale" and brought ashore Capt. Amazon and Walckner. They had dinner and tea with us.

Thurs. 20th. (First Loom Up Today). Donald MacDonald put up his loom today. He is the first. Dunie got his hair cut (William). Donald Ferguson's cow calved today and William's on Monday last. Kate up doing her "big carding" at Meirut's.

Fri. 21st. (New Outbreak Of Boat-cold). Rough day. Hens doing better. "Dreadnought" (Morris) in, also "Bannerdale", "Cornelia" and a lot of others. Dunie tells me there is hardly anyone in school today with a fresh "cratan" which Ewan is getting the blame of having imported!!! The men heard that Morris had been taken ill en route with pleurisy and had to be sent home from Stornoway.

Sat. 22nd. (Boiling Sea). Worst day we have ever seen in St. Kilda. Wind simply fearful, and roof of house rising up and down. Sea just like a boiling pot. Five boats in the bay trying to get shelter and finding none. Seedy myself. So stormy that the men came down and hauled up the boat.

Sun. Feb 23rd. Weather worse than ever. Five boats in.

"Creda" (?) Hull left, but "Tubal Cain" Grimsby arrived.

Mon. 24th. Bad morning but calmed down sufficiently to let trawlers out to fish "feasgai". Finlay Gillies' loom up today.

Tues. 25th. (Reading Nansen). Deeply interested in Nansen's "Farthest North", reading it aloud in evenings. "Clydesdale", "Dreadnought", "Bannerdale" and "Minerva" in bay. Too rough for trawling but they were out last night and had good catches, we think, from the amount of birds around.

Wed. 26th. Very stormy day. Boats doing nothing, but the men went out to the "Clydesdale" and got some fish.

Thurs. 27th. (Snow Storm). Our first storm of snow today and high wind. On rising this morning we looked on to a white world. Only three or four turned up to School so they were allowed to go home. Dunie and I had a splendid day at home and I read Nansen till I was hoarse. We have yet to follow the movements of the "Fram" with Svendrup as Commander. It is most exciting.

Fri. 28th. (Cloth From Donald). More snow. No School. Morris' boat "Dreadnought" left, so did the three others. We saw a lovely huge steamer today, evidently on its way to America. How we wished it would come in. Donald Gillies, our faithful friend, came down bringing with him my cloth which they had very kindly woven first. We looked at my white piece first. The texture is very satisfactory, but I can hardly say what it will be like until it is washed, as it is so dirty with the loom and the oil, but I think it will be splendid. Then there are 33 yds in the big piece, which is really beautiful. The small piece has about 15½ or 16 yds. There was so much "dluth" (warp of the web) over that if we buy a couple of pounds from Angus, what with ours left, Finlay G. says we shall have another little piece of eight yards! Mrs. Gillies ill now with "cratan". Made toffee today.

Sat. 29th. (Cold and Stormy). Last day of Feb and a fearful day to! Wind has gone round to E or N.E. and it is fearfully cold and stormy. No boat could stay in our bay with such a sea. Where is the "Bannerdale" I wonder today?

MARCH 1908

Sun. March 1st. Out at church twice. Everyone is speaking about the severe weather.

Tues. 3rd. (Clothes Out At Last). Great change in weather for the better. Quite warm today and occasional blinks of warm sunshine. Kate and I put out clothes which have been in the tub a fortnight. Men over at Dun for "waavi" – guillemots. We have had no letters for two months, since Jan. 11th.

Wed. 4th. A huge boat, as if on its way to America, whistled as she passed quite close to Hirst today. A liner and the "Clydesdale" are fishing at Boreray.

Thurs. 5th. The "M. A. Dodds" came in and the men went out. Capt. Ritchie sent us a nice ling. Days getting nice and long.

Fri. 6th. (Captain's Kindness). When I had Cruvack, Rosie and my cirrie at the well, to my great delight the "Bannerdale" came in and brought us such a lot of letters, papers and everything. Capt. Walckner as kind as ever. He brought me a leg of pork, ½ box of finnan haddies, and a box of Scotch. I got my heavy shoes which are splendid.

Sat. 7th. Who came in but "Fear Big" (Donald Craig) with his new boat. Lovely weather.

Sun. March 8th. Fine day. Only Capt. Ritchie in the bay.

Wed. 11th. (Cows to Oshaval). Glorious sunny day. I put cows up Oshaval myself.

Sat. 14th. (A Glorious Day). We were awakened early by the "Bannerdale's" whistle (7 o'clock). Got letters and seed order sent off. In the afternoon Kate, Dunie and I went up Berenahake. From there we climbed

Oshaval and I shall never forget it all my life. The day was perfect. – not a breath of wind, and we could see the outer islands so plainly. There were two trawlers working at Boreray. We sat on the top of Oshaval a long time and saw the bad places where in one of them "Mor Big's" brother was killed. He and his sister, it seems, were down cutting peats (or getting them) and he saw a guillemot or puffin a little way down. He slipped and fell hundreds of feet.

Thurs. 19th. (Men to Boreray). Simply a glorious day. Men all went to Boreray today for dead sheep and raven's eggs. The men got a nest with seven. It is the only nest in Boreray. The men showed them to me. They are very small for such a large bird – blue speckled with black.

Guillemots on a ledge on Ruaival.

Fri. 20th. (Men after the Guillemots). It has been a good night for the St. Kildans who were away last night for the guillemots. They got a lot. Mary McQuien brought one, also Mary MacDonald, also Donald (F) Gillies, Bellac and Finlay Mor, so we shall have "waavi"

tomorrow for dinner. Poor Meirut Ferguson is having her big carding today. She has not been well for a bit. We hear there is a small trawler in the Glen. Made toffee today.

Sat. 21st. Very stormy day. There are four boats in the Glen today. South wind.

Wed. 25th. (Seed But No Mail). Awakened early by the whistle of the "Bannerdale" (Capt. of "Knowsie"). It was only 6.15 am. We all rose at once. He brought seed but we were very much disappointed that he did not bring the letter bag. I went for a splendid walk up Ruadval and from that up Mullach Sgail and home the Glen road.

Sat. March 28th. "Thananois orm ceart galore, au dhu." I don't feel old though. Very stormy night and showery day. Busy spinning for Angus dluth. Hens doing very well at present. Three liners still in.

Mon. 30th. (Fearful Day). Stormy and wet. Three liners in bay, but had to change round to Glen as the wind came round to the south. At night the wind changed again and they came back. Poor fellows. Katharine MacDonald brought me down some milk.

Tues. 31st. Capt. Walckner came in but I was away up the other end of the village and did not see him. Got lovely soles. They are getting plenty of fish and will soon be back.

APRIL 1908

Wed. April 1st. (Ceilidhing – Stories about the Islands). Lovely day. Had Finlay Mor, Ian Bahn and old Donald McQuien in ceilidhing and got great fun. Donald was in great form and was telling us heaps of stories about the island – pirates etc. I wished I had had more Gaelic to understand better. He told us about men falling over the rocks at Soay – boys being stolen away from Boreray, and robbers coming to the island. His gestures were so funny and if any of the others dared to dispute anything he said he almost devoured them.

Entertained them to supper and gave Ian Bahn his "McCheyne", also presented others with "Grace Abounding" in Gaelic. They were delighted. No boats in.

Thurs. 2nd. North Shields liner came in and another from Inverness.

Fri. 3rd. (Daffodils). My daffodils are simply lovely just now.

Sat. 4th. Capt. Craig, "Fear Big", in and ashore most of the day. Here to dinner and tea. Sent ashore soles.

Mon. 6th. (Picnic In Great Glen). Three times to church yesterday. Today meeting in church. Then K., Dunie and I went for picnic to Tobar nan buadh and made tea. Glorious.

Tues. 7th. "Bannerdale" arrived with letters. Capt. Walckner brought our letters and parcels.

Wed. 8th. (Men After Gannets). Lovely day. The men all went away for gannets in the afternoon to Boreray.

Thurs. 9th. (Men Return From Boreray). The men returned about 2.30 this morning. Got dozen gannets each. Beau Donald MacDonald sent me half one. John MacDonald and Donald og came after dinner and put out the manure into the back buall for potatoes. In the evening the "Rambler", N. Shields in the bay for the first time this year.

Fri. 10th. Cold and blowy. Kate got first lamb today. No boats.

Sat. 11th. Glorious day! Lots of lambs.

Sun. April 12th. (Sickness Strikes). Donald Craig came in first thing this morning and sent me 1lb of chocolate walnuts. I had ordered them but he would not take any money for them. He says Capt. Walckner left last night – without our letters – if it is true. People, some few of them, ill with diarrhoea and vomiting. William tells us it is common at this time of the year.

Mon. 13th. (Spring Medicine). Made a mixture of sulphur, cream of tartar and syrup last night and am taking a dose of it every night. I think it will make a good Spring medicine as I am a bit out of sorts, so languid etc. Wet day. Beasts at home eating their heads off, and hay is getting short. It cleared up and Kate dug all the front.

Tues. 14th. (Oats and Potatoes). Beautiful day. Dunie sowed the front with oats today and Kate harrowed. Dunie put in two drills of early potatoes, the first two were put in yesterday.

Wed. 15th. (Men to Stac an Armine). Another lovely day. The men, about 8 or 10 went today to Stac an Armine to look after some lambs they have there. Hens are doing well just now but the ducks are a nuisance laying away somewhere.

Thurs. 16th. (Waulking and Mending Boats). Start of waulking the cloth today at Meirut's house. Dunie and Kate planting potatoes in the afternoon. The men are working at their boats mending, scraping, tarring and painting. Lovely day.

Fri. 17th. Waulking at Donald MacDonald's today. Boys putting out manure.

Sat. 18th. Waulking at Finlay Gillies.

Mon. 20th. (Red Herring Present). I forgot to say that on Thursday night at midnight Capt. Ritchie came in and brought 20 boxes of red herrings, one for each house, from a Mr. Thompson of Aberdeen. Fine day. Waulking at the "Bandraghs". Finlay Mor came in to ceilidh for a little and Donald Gillies came for my cloths which are to be waulked tomorrow.

Tues. 21st. Fine day. Got cloths nearly dried. Have one piece 33 yards fully, my white piece 16½ yds and Dunie's suit length 9 yds. which the Gillies are dyeing.

Wed. 22nd. (Potatoes Planted). Showers of snow. Large buall planted with potatoes today and looks splendid.

Thurs. 23rd. (Snow Storm). Fearful snow storm! Lots of boats in sheltering. Men went out to see strangers and sold lots of skins to the Hull boat. Got our letters away at last. Got nice soles and ling. I set my first hen, old Blackie, with 13 eggs today.

Fri. 24th. (Seed Spoilt). Days simply flying. Fearful night of snow and wind and today as bad as ever.

Dunie is afraid he will have to sow the corn over again as it is spoilt he is thinking, with the snow and frost. They were waulking at Donald Ferguson's.

Sat. April 25th. (Arctic Conditions). Another day like yesterday. Simply winter and Arctic cold. Waulking at Tigh Ian Bhan's. Wind came round in evening to West and no fewer than 10 boats came in to shelter. Too rough for the men to get out. Dressed and bandaged Annie McQuien's foot – she cut it away at the peats.

Mon. 27th. (Waulking). Waulking at Tigh William today and they were lucky in their day. They got all their cloth beautiflly dried. Took the dye for them for Dunie's suit. No boats.

Tues. 28th. Very wet and blowy. Waulking at Tigh Toromich McQuien but they will get none dried today. Heavy sea. South wind. Kate has now got four lambs in the Glebe and one in the Dun.

Wed. 29th. (Face Burnt). Waulking today at Finlay Mor's. He was in at the other end wanting Carron Oil for Norman big's face which was burnt with tar.

Thurs. 30th. (More Accidents). Very wet day and blowy. Waulking at Donald McQuien's. Went to see little Ian Ferguson who fell in the fire this morning and burnt his leg badly. I did not see him, however, as he was asleep and we thought it better to leave him as he had been crying so.

MAY 1908

Sat. May 2nd. (Waulking Finished). Lovely day but rather misty and blowy, Waulking finished today in Neil MacDonald's.

Tues. 5th. (First Whaler In). Simply an awful day. Rain pouring down in buckets. Beasts in again. In the evening the first whaler came in. It was the "Ornulf" – the Botoch's boat. Dunie and I waved but there was no response. So we knew there was something amiss. A trawler came in at the same time and whistled and the men hurried out. When they came in, alas, it was to tell us the poor Botoch was dead. He died in January about 3 weeks or a month after coming back from Africa. It is terribly sad and we shall miss him more than anybody as he was most of his time here. The mate of one of the boats is the new Captain. Paulsen is fishing on the "Scaligram" and Eleasen is in Norway yet waiting for the new boat the poor Botoch was to have had. Dunie and I are very sad. The boat whistled to give fish to the men.

Wed. 6th. The mate and one of the crew of the "Ornulf" came ashore wishing to get eggs for tobacco. They were telling us a lot about poor Škondorp. Set "Feathery Feet" with 13 eggs.

Fri. 8th. (Engine Trouble). "Ornulf" went off today, "Katy" in. The men went out and were told that Capt. Ritchie was as far as Loch Roag and had mails also, but had to go back to Aberdeen with broken engine and for bait. He may be back again tomorrow.

Sun. May 10th. At night after church the "Fear Big" (Capt. Craig), "Craigroy" came in and the men went out to see John.

Tues. 12th. (Croft Work Finished). The people all finished their crofts last night. Today they are

Crofts and the Village Street, Postcard, Photographer unknown. National Trust for Scotland.

93

spreading manure from the cleits where they have had sheep all the winter and putting it on their grass. Men went to Dun and brought home all last year's lambs.

Wed. 13th. (Men to Stac an Armine). Beautiful day. Men went to Stac an Armine for gannet and fulmar eggs. They got a lot. Small P.M. to which I went. Dunie and Donald MacDonald officiated. Got a lot of eggs.

Thurs. 14th. (Men to Soay). Cruvack got a lovely grey calf at breakfast time this morning. Men all away to Soay for eggs and fulmars. While they were away three boats came in. The "Botich" went out to the two, then the other, "Mercury" came in and whistled. Out went the "Botich", and the Capt. who we knew before. Men came home laden with eggs and birds. My first lot of chickens are coming out now.

Fri. 15th. (First Drifters of the Season). Glorious weather all this week. Men dividing eggs, putting up cran and building dykes. Kate and Dunie preparing turnip ground. Got a lot of fulmar and sular eggs. All the sheep out today I am thankful to say. Hear that the first drifter is in the neighbourhood. First day and evening without fire.

Sat. 16th. (Spring Cleaning). Men built our walls – of the Glebe today. I have only 10 of Blackie's chickens. Forgot to say set a black and white hen with 12 eggs on Thursday last. Everybody is doing a small spring clean.

Sun. May 17th. (Dunara's First Visit). The "Dunara" wakened us all at midnight last night. Men went out. Alistair Ferguson arrived with wife and family. Alistair came to the bedroom window at three in the morning with some of the Hirsteach.

Mon. 18th. Fine day. Went up village after "Dunara" left at 8.30 am. There is a new cargo boat coming. Factor very busy and having the usual hot time.

Thurs. 21st. ("Hebrides" Arrives). "Hebrides" arrived at 4.30 this morning. Fine day. Mrs. Ferguson (Alistair's Beau) and I went to Tobar nam buadh in the afternoon. Found primroses in the Amhuin Mhor.

Finlay McQuien started peats today.

Fri. 22nd. (New Spinning Wheel). Everyone off to cut peats. Kate included. Factor left yesterday with the "Hebrides". I forgot to say I got my new spinning wheel from Mr. McKenzie. It is a beauty, made of teakwood.

Sat. 23rd. (Great Day Today). First of all Capt. Walckner came in and also a plain Amazon, "Cornelia". At dinner when another big boat came in – the Norwegian boat and our friend Mr. Herlofson on board. We had a lovely day with him. He had tea and supper with us. We are going to Bunamhuimedor to see him on our return South. A man and his wife from Harris and wife's sister also came as guests to Hugh Gillies' house (to spy out the land and see if the sister would stay as Hugh's wife). The girl wasn't "willin'".

Sun. May 24th. Very wet and stormy. Out to morning church and S.S. Wee Susie and Donny Ferguson there and great fun.

Mon. 25th. (Broken Leg). Great excitement. Little Norman McQuien got his leg broken this morning. His father was throwing down bales of cloth on him from the attic. William MacDonald went off to Boreray with a boat which is from Fleetwood to Capt. Walckner on the "Bannerdale" who is at Boreray. The Captain is taking them away. Norman, the father, and Donald the son (who they say is to speak English!) It is good of Walckner to do what he is doing for them. Alistair Ferguson went to the Dun with John Gillies jnr. and Angus Gillies jnr. for eggs.

Wed. 27th. Boat in today "City of London". Sent us fish.

Sat. May 30th. Two boats away to get eggs and got a good few. Up twice seeing baby Ferguson from Glasgow who is bad with "bronchitis" (I think).

Sun. May 31st. (Norman Left in Aberdeen). Great excitement today. "Bannerdale", Capt. Walckner came in bringing back Finlay Mor and his son Donald. They left poor wee Norman behind in Aberdeen for a few weeks.

JUNE 1908

Mon. June 1st. (A Day to Remember). Lovely day. The "Mercury" only in. Our men went to ask if they would tow them to Stac an Armine and Boreray. So the Capt. said he would. He also persuaded us to go out to dinner and see them trawling – so we agreed. We got as far as Stac an Armine and Boreray when a horrible accident happened on our boat to Neil Ferguson, who got two fingers (the tops of them) crushed OFF between the trawler and the boat. We had to come home at once. Steam yacht came, five ladies and two gentlemen (Hirsts or Hirsch from Huddersfield). A Bishop was there also. Mrs. H. brought me in a lovely bouquet of magnificent Nile lilies and large red lilies with Spirea, lilies of the valley and ferns. Then they invited us out to dinner on the "Monsoon". We went and had a lovely time. Dinner of 8 courses. They were so kind and gave us lots of literature, newspapers, mags etc. and Dunie a 10/- box of baccy! Home and was sea-sick again.

Tues. 2nd. (Sheep Shearing). People started sheep shearing at Glen – in the evening. In the morning at 11.30 the "Monsoon" left and took Neil Ferguson to Stornoway Hospital. Donald Bau went also to help him.

Wed. 4th. No P.M. as everyone was sheep shearing at Glen. Fine weather.

Thurs. 4th. (Chicks Hatch). Four wee chicks out with black and white hen. People sheep shearing again. Lots of boats in.

Fri. 5th. (Two More Whalers). The other two whalers arrived at last with flags flying. Eleasen in his new boat "Sir Samuel Scott" and Paulsen in "Skalligram". The two came in to tea and then went up to see the sheep shearing going on at the back of the village today.

Sat. 6th. (Pet Lamb Returns). Got my cirrie home. She got separated from Rosie by the ruaging. The Gillies' boys found her on the Carn Mor and fleeced her and brought her home. We have put her in the buall with the wee molt lamb. How pleased she was to get home and to get sugar.

Mon, Tues, Wed. (Hens and Chicks Away). Capt. Eleasen and Paulsen in and some boats. Fine weather up to Tuesday. Gave Donald Gillies my black and white hen and 5 chickens. They have been so kind.

Thurs. June 11th. (Away for Holiday). The "Hebrides" came in alright at 10 o'clock, bringing Bain, Contractor and his man. There has been some bungle about the business. Men are coming to begin work on the first "Dunara" in 10 days time, and it will be done before we get back. We got on board the "Heb" alright and I stayed on deck until we got passed Boreray and the Stacs. They are wonderful. The sight of the birds was marvellous. Got very sick and had rather a bad time till Lochmaddy (or Locheport, rather). There was a nice party aboard. One Mr. Moffat from Glasgow was the wit and we had awful fun with him. Bed, in Ladies Cabin, and had a good night. Dunie in Gents. Cabin.

Sun. June 14th. (Wedding Anniversary). Nine years today since we were married!!! Lovely day, feeling nice.

Women busy knitting in the Great Glen. Lawson Collection.

August 1908 – May 1909
EXTRACTS FROM THE DIARY
AUGUST 1908

Aug. 2nd. (Return to St. Kilda). Got here on Thursday morning after a splendid holiday. No diary kept for the last eight weeks. The first 10 days or so we were in Tobermoray resting. Visited Glasgow, Dunvegan and Tarbert. Mr. Herlofson joined us at Rodel and we stayed at Bunamhummedor until Tuesday morning when we got the "Staffa" for Lochmaddy. Stayed Tuesday night with Bain (Contractor's) family and joined "Hebrides" for St. Kilda on Wednesday night. Met Mr. McLennan at Lochmaddy. Also, Mr. McDonald, H.M.S. Inspector from Inverness who was en route for St. Kilda to examine the School. His wife was with him. It was rather rough coming across but neither of us were sick in the least. We got to St. Kilda on Thursday 30th. July.

Fri. July 31st. (Unpacking). Dunie and I busy getting stores put away etc. Had meeting (Mr. McLennan) in evening. The Norwegian Captains came to it but we were not speaking to them.

Sun. Aug 2nd. (Visiting Ministers). Mr. McLennan preaching at all services. The Banns were published between Callum McDonald and Annie Gillies, also between Donald Gillies and Annie McQuien. Donald (og) Ferguson from Ardrossan addressed the S.S. children very nicely and also Mr. McLennan.

Tues. 4th. Ministers, Dunie and Kate all went to the Glen and Cambergh for a picnic. Mr. McLennan went out fishing with the men.

Thurs. 6th. (Visit of Secretary of State). When we were all in church a yacht came in. This turned out to be the Secretary of State for Scotland and Lady Marjorie. Also Mr. Forsyth, the Crofter's Commission. The Capt. of the "Minna", Mr. Murdoch, was also there in charge. They all came in and chatted. When they went off Lady Marjorie Sinclair took her husband's photo

with us. He also took hers with us. It was great excitement. Church at night. Three whalers and two trawlers in the bay.

Fri. 7th. Busy as usual. Three services each day.

Sat. 8th. (Preparing For Communion). Only one service today. Donald Ferguson and Dunie busy making preparations for Communion tomorrow. Mrs. Neil McDonald admitted into membership. Whalers ashore.

Sun. Aug 9th. (Communion). Big day Commissioner. Every member out including Roenig McRommon (McCrimmon) and Beau Angus.

Mon. 10th. Busy preparing for the feasts and marriage tomorrow. Two services.

Tues. 11th. (Two Weddings). Annie Gillies and Annie McQuien married to Malcolm McDonald and Donald Gillies. Great fun in church. Quite a lot of women went to see the ceremony and the men made audible remarks. After 6 o'clock all the wedding party came to the Manse and had tea and stayed to about 10 o'clock. After that Mr. McLennan, Dunie and I went up the village and saw the newly married pairs in bed!!! Such fun. A. Gillies (Beau Donald) looked sweet in her

Visiting Steam Yacht, drawing by R. Jobling.

nightdress and cap. A McDonald did not look so nice, she had a blouse. Callum and Donald just had shirts on. We kissed them all, Mr. McLennan and all and oh, it was fun. I was taken unawares and Norman McKinnon kissed me unawares, greatly to the delight of everybody.

Wed. 12th. (Wedding Feast). Mr. McLennan's last day. He was making the most of it. I know not how many pairs of gloves and socks he got. The men with Donald Ferguson were at Soay and came home drenched and a few sheep. Tonight was the wedding feast in Ewan's house to which Dunie and Mr. McLennan went. Plenty of whales now.

Thurs. 13th. ("Hebrides"). Very misty morning up to 11 am, when we saw the "Hebrides" in the distance. There were such crowds of people. Mr. McLennan had dinner before he went. Our paraffin and other goods came.

Fri. 14th. (Fulmar Harvest). People started fulmar killing at the Cambergh.

Sat. 15th. ("Dunara"). Men busy all day preparing for boat. The "Dunara" came in at 4.15 pm. What a lot of passengers and what a stir.

Sun. Aug 16th. Had a full church and collection of 27/– fully. Nice day.

Mon. 17th. (Dividing Spoil). People dividing the spoil from the "Dunara". Afterwards a fulmar hunt. At night, when at supper, a whaler came in and put out a boat at once. Who had arrived but Miss Moir and a friend (a niece, Miss Winnie Scott).

Tues. 18th. (Ladies Join Fulmar Hunt). The ladies took lunch and went away to the fulmar hunt at the Cambergh. Miss Moir quite brave.

Wed. 19th. They went away today also to the same place. Miss Moir home in great glee. She killed 40 herself, and was down the rope in a fearful place. No P.M.

Thurs. 20th. Miss M. and Miss S. away all day at the Dun. Former down rope again and killing fulmar.

Fri. 21st. Fine day. Miss M. with Neil Ferguson and a few others in the boat to the back of Berenahake (Stac Lang). We went up to watch them killing the birds and saw the boat with Miss M. far below. Very tired tonight and feeling bad.

Sat. 22nd. One whale in the bay, a very large one. "Anon", Capt. Bantock came in. Got lovely plaice and halibut. Miss M. and S. went up Conacher themselves. "Sir Samuel Scott" came in at night, brought letters. Gave Eleasen and his engineer milk.

Sun. Aug 23rd. Out at church twice and S.S. Fine day. Saw lots of boats.

Tues. 25th. "Ornulf" and "Scalligram" came in.

Thurs. 27th. ("Hebrides" Calls). "Hebrides" arrived about 11 am. Box of papers from Lady Marjorie Sinclair and Hon. John Sinclair. Bibles came from Mr. McLennan and a parcel of books from Motherwell's, Airdrie. Very stormy, blowy day.

Fri. 28th. (Xmas Gifts). "Ornulf" only in these last few days. Others must be at the Station. Capt. Ritchie on new boat, the "Chieftain", with engines broken. The mate of "Ornulf" and steward came in. The former brought me a very nice doormat he had made himself for me (in return for eggs). They had tea. Forgot to say got box for Xmas yesterday from George, also Barkmans (dishes), waxcloth and bacon.

Sat. 29th. Capt and mate of the "Ornulf" came in, also the other Capt. Eleason and the two engineers also came and finished the evening.

Sun. Aug 30th. (Visitors To Service). Crew of "Chieftain" (Capt. Ritchie) and crew of "Red Wing", also a lot of the Norwegians, "Ornulf" and "Sir Samuel Scott" went in to the service. Ham and eggs for supper.

Mon. 31st. (Hay Making Starts!). Another blowy day. Men mending Widow McKinnon's byre, which has fallen in. "Skalligram" and "Ornulf" in tonight, "Chieftain". Dunie and Kate started the hay today. They will be in their element now.

SEPTEMBER 1908

Tues. Sept 1st. Three whalers in and the "Chieftain". Poor Capt. Ritchie. It has been a poor trip for him.

Wed. 2nd. All the whalers in. Captains all came in. Capt. Marten of "Ornulf" told the girls to be ready in the morning as the weather looked as if it were going to be fit.

Thurs. 3rd. (Visitors Leave On Whaler). Wakened by loud whistling from "Ornulf" at 4.15 am. Got up at once and got breakfast. They did not get off until 6 o'clock. Had a fine day to myself. Dunie and Kate at the hay. Men went to Soay and brought us a sheep.

Fri. 4th. (Visit of Greenland Whaler). Lovely day. "Sir S. Scott" came in late last night with a whale. "Ornulf" also came in, bringing letters and telegram from Neil Gillies telling about his father. He has undergone operation and is getting on well. Poor Mr. Herlofson's father they tell me is dying and he (Mr. H.) is very much depressed. In afternoon early a very large Greenland whaler came into the bay. The Capt. and son came ashore and had tea. We went out to see the boat with them. They were awfully kind to us and we came home laden with gifts. Tea for Roenig, sweets for the School children and marmalade, preserved fruit, biscuits etc. etc. for ourselves (special gifts to the Dunie of 4lbs tobacco!!!). His name is Capt. Robertson of Dundee. Home at East Newport. They know the McWalters. The marmalade was sold to the natives in 7lb jars for 1/-. Beautiful marmalade, Keiller's. I cannot tell how kind they were to us. "Sir S. Scott" went tonight to Station with a whale (or whales).

Sat. 5th. (Five Whales Away). Awful day. "Skalligram" came in this evening but no whale. The others went to the station it seems with five whales between them. Rough night. Crew of Sk. ashore washing boat at the sands.

Sun. Sept 6th. (Feeling Seedy). Very seedy these days. Sk. went out to fish, but came in about the time that the two came back from Station. "M. A. Dodds" in all day.

Mon. 7th. (Dunie's Birthday). Still very seedy. Got breakfast in bed. This is Dunie's birthday. Dunie and Ceit busy with fiar. "Sir S. Scott" came in with a whale. People all busy with their crops.

Tues. 8th. (Most Awful Day). The whalers going from shelter to shelter, and can't get it in the end.

Wed. 9th. (Hay Into Cleits). Weather still very bad, but the big schoolboys went out and helped Kate in the morning to put in hay which was in danger of being blown into the sea. "Skalligram" sheltering in bay, others dodging. Cruvack allowed into Glebe on tether for first time today. I am so far from well.

Thurs. 10th. (Nasty Accident). Men went out to "Skalligram", three or four of them, and while they were out the "Sir S. Scott" came in and down rushes some more of the men, Donald Gillies, Ewan, Norman McKinnon. Neil Gillies had arrived from Glasgow and letters for us. Got letters posted. While we were reading letters and papers an awful row came to our ears, Ian Ban above everybody else. Norman McKinnon was led in. He had slipped and an iron row-lock had gone into his eye. It was too horrible. Dunie was so good and bathed it for me and helped to bandage. The men came in and by way of encouragement stormed at the poor fellow! The "Skalligram" was just going off to Tarbert, so the Captain took Norman with him to the doctor. It was a horrible business. The excitement was too awful. They were simply off their heads.

Fri. 11th. (Coal From Whalers). Capts. Eleason and Marten ashore by 10 o'clock wanting the men to go out for coals for us. The men are to go out at suitable tide. Got fine lot of coals. Capts. came ashore for tea. Then Aners Anderson came ashore and had tea also.

Sun. Sept 13th. (Norman Improving). "Skalligram" came in tonight bringing Donald McDonald with re-assuring news from Tarbert. Norman's eye is not so bad as supposed, and he is coming with the next boat.

Mon. 14th. (Norwegians Haymaking). Lovely day for all sorts of outdoor work. "Ornulf" came this afternoon bringing Norman McKinnon. His eye is much better but bad enough. Bandaged and dressed it as soon as he arrived. All three Captains were ashore, and were busy at the scythe. Capt. Cristensen managed to break the scythe handle. All stayed to supper.

Tues. 15th. (Men to Boreray). Perfect day. Men set off early for Boreray. We got fine sheep from Angus in the evening.

Fri. 18th. (Sick At Night). Nine or ten trawlers in last night and two whalers. "Ornulf" came in about 12 o'clock. Horribly sick at night again. All three Captains ashore, and three of "Skalligram's" crew were ashore cutting.

Sat. 19th. (Whalers Finished for Season). "Skalligram" left for Station early this morning to see what orders are for stopping this season as the weather is so rough. Came back with orders for the whalers all to leave tonight, which they did at 1.30. They came in and said, "Good-bye" but, or course, I did not see them.

Sun. Sept 20th. Lovely day. Church 3 times. Marvellous for me.

Mon. 21st. (Visitors On "Bannerdale"). Who came in early but Capt. Walckner and "Bannerdale". With them was Alistair Ferguson and Finlay Gillies. The Engineer also came ashore. Got letters and parcels galore.

Thurs. 24th. (Lost Grain Elevator). Great excitement tonight. A large tug, the "Oceana". (Capt. Pickard) came in. They were looking for a grain elevator which they had lost near Tory Island, N.W. Ireland. It had drifted away up north and they called in here on their way outwards. The Capt. and crew were all Irishmen.

Fri. 25th. (Women in Terror). The men were out at the tug last night, but it was no good, the Irishmen wouldn't be "had". We heard, with great amusement, that the women of the village all congregated in one or two houses last night expecting the wild Irishmen from the tug would come ashore and murder them. They consoled themselves that the enemy would begin at the Manse, and they would hear the shrieks up there and could then flee! The boat in question left early and then the women went to bed!!! Very wild day.

Sat. 26th. (Capt. Walkner Gets A Holiday). Lovely day. Capt. Walckner walked with two of his crew over from the Glen. The sea wasn't favourable, but it calmed down. "Bannerdale" left after tea with Capt. Walckner and A. Ferguson and is to lie up for some days while Capt. W. goes to Glasgow for a short holiday. His wife and family went there on Tuesday last to the Ferguson's house.

Sun. Sept 27th. (Sick And Dizzy). Feeling very ill, and fearfully sick and dizzy. Had to go back to bed and stay there all day with vinegar cloths on my head. No one allowed in but Roenig and Meirut.

Wed. 30th. (Elevator Found). Much better but not nearly 'myself'. Towards evening the tug came in. (I'm sure the women are in terror again). The Capt., Mate and Engineer came ashore wanting food, but the men were able to tell them what they heard from a trawler yesterday, namely that this trawler had found the grain elevator and had taken it to Stornoway (to the Custom House Officer).

OCTOBER 1908

Thurs. Oct 1st. (Terrible Weather). No hay dried this week. Angus Gillies, Ian Ban and Donald McDonald down working at Angus' boat. Brought them in and gave them tea and dinner.

Fri. Oct 16th. (Catching Up With Diary). Have been more or less seedy all the time since Oct. 1st and have been lazy about my diary, but will try to put down the most important things. The most outstanding thing certainly was "rain". It has rained almost incessantly from Sat. Sept 26th., now three weeks, with the exception of three half days. The people are in desperation about their grass. Capt. Walckner arrived back here on Oct 8th. Brought me a roast of meat, also goods from Logan. We have been getting molts also. We have had lots of little liners from N. Shields, Aberdeen etc. This evening when we were at tea a liner came in. This turned out to be John McDonald's boat (William's brother). He came ashore with the Capt. also. It seems they brought a terrible amount of stuff for No. 3. Capt. Walckner in the bay for a wee bit. Gave John McD. and his skipper tea.

Sun. Oct 18th. (Visitors In Church). Church and S.S. John McDonald's boat (don't know name yet), came in and went out. Six or seven at church in the evening and the Capt. and crew of the "Star of Hope" came in after church to see me. Such nice men. The Capt. is an elder in the N.F.Ch. (Mr. Murray) Aberdeen.

Wed. 21st. (Dunie and Kate Missing). I as usual went to bed early and slept, as I thought for a long time – wakened and missed Dunie. I called and called and ultimately went in search. He wasn't to be found. Kate was also missing. It was then 12 o'clock. I was cold and concluded Annie was worse and that they had been sent for. However, in they came some time afterward. They had been out with lanterns securing the hay! All St. Kilda was out as the wind had increased so. It was so funny of them. Big gale during the night.

Thurs. 22nd. (Good Day For Hay). Fine windy day. So favourable for hay that Dunie gave the children a holiday. Hear that Capt. Ritchie is in the Glen.

Fri. 23rd. (Onslaught on Hay). Wakened early this morning by the whistle of the "Bannerdale", about 7.30. Brought a Mr. Hay from Aberdeen who wants to stay until Capt. Walckner goes away. He is a very nice quiet fellow. He was helping with the hay most of the day. In the evening Finlay Mor, Donald og, and Don. Gillies (John's son) came and cut while Callum's Donald carried it up and Kate and Dunie made it into

"prabacks". Gave them high tea in the kitchen. Hay practically all cut and we are so glad – especially Dunie.

Sat. 24th. (Spare Room). Very comfortable night in our new quarters. Had a jolly fire and intend to have same every night while there. Lovely day. Mr. Hay working with Dunie and K at drying grass. Two boats in at night.

Sun. Oct 25th. Lovely day. Six boats in the bay, among them Capt. Ritchie, "Chieftain". Very sick at night and hysterical.

Mon. 26th. (Safely Gathered In). Hay finished!!! Not much later than last year, which is splendid work after 3 wet weeks on end. Dunie with Mr. Hay with K all afternoon.

Tues. 27th. (Lifting Potatoes). Perfect day. Dunie started lifting potatoes. Mr. Hay made book-case and went up Conacher.

Fri. 30th. (Spare Room). Finished tidying up the spare room and it is so nice. We are thinking of occupying it all the time, at least in the stormiest weather.

Sat. 31st. (Mr. Hay Departs). We were aroused before 8 o'clock by a big blast from the "Bannerdale's" siren. He blew and blew and had also his flag flying which was the pre-arranged signal that he was ready for Mr. Hay to come out and that they were going back to Aberdeen. Hurried breakfast on and Mr. Hay was out by 8.30 and went off with great noise of sirens. Men went to Dun with sheep. I went up the village and was into every house where they were at home.

NOVEMBER 1908

Sun. Nov 1st. Out to church twice and S.S. as well. The "Star of Hope" in the bay all day. Good day.

Mon. 2nd. (Visiting the Sick). Went up the village to see the host of sick people. Norman McQuien's wife, fainted last night, and is in bed. Callum's wife with the "griem". Neil Ferguson's wife with the "triplitch", Catrione Gillies who was ill with one of these mysterious illnesses yesterday and today. Also old Donald McQuien with bad stomach. It came on very wet as I was finishing my calls. Met Dunie coming to meet me with my coat. The people greatly taken with this mark of "geol mor". Men very busy Saturday and today catching young lambs to send to the Dun. Nice quiet night and did some spinning.

Tues. 3rd. (Men on Dun). Men over at Dun with the lambs. I, of course, busy with cooking and School. Dunie busy these days taking up potatoes..

Wed. 4th. (Spinning). Finished FIRST PIRN of spinning!!! Four weeks.

Thurs. 5th. (Lovely Day). Boat came in whistling, the "Chieftain", Capt, Ritchie. He brought in a lovely dresser affair to Donald Gillies and a box of red herrings to all the St. Kildans (except us!). Capt. Ritchie says the "Bannerdale" is at Boreray tonight.

Fri. 6th. (No Mails). "Bannerdale" came in about 10.45. Great disgust to hear that Capt. W. had not brought mails. Got bread, my Scotch and some fish. It was too bad not to bring mails! "Cornelia" was in at the same time.

Sun. Nov 8th. (Perfect Day). Most perfect day. Lovely moonlight nights these nights. Church in morning and S.S. Had a good read tonight. Glass falling.

Moonlight over Dun. D.A.Q.

Mon. 9th. (Rams from Dun). Very cold. K. and Dunie working at potatoes. Rams brought over from the Dun.

Wed. 11th. Very wet. No boats in but we hear there are five fishing at Borerary and two or three at the South Bank.

Thurs. 12th. (Fleet of Steamers). Very blowy day but fine and fresh. Wind changed to West bringing in a fleet of over 16 steamers.

Fri. 13th. (Too Many Boats). Better day. Busy spinning. Men went out to the boats and out to Capt. Walckner, who they found very cross indeed. He informed the men as there were so many other boats here and so little fish he wasn't coming back any more! We think he will come though. We sent our orders and he took them away.

Sat. 14th. Some boats in at night. "Bannerdale" at Boreray. Leaves for Aberdeen on Sunday.

Sun. Nov 15th. Stormy day. Lots of boats in.

Mon. 16th. Very stormy day. Men out at boats. Had Mary McDonald carding for me.

Tues. 17th. (Men Securing Boats). Another very stormy day. 17 boats in the bay. "Bodach Ruadh" – Wrights and Co. Men down yesterday and today turning their boats upside down. After they were done they went out to "levy Custom". Finished third ball of dluth.

Thurs. 9th. Boats out today. When we came home Angus G. came down with a piece of ancient mutton (killed a week and hanging in smoke since). It was awful. He got what he wished for, a bag of turnips and supper.

Fri. 20th. Lots of boats in. Men out levying toll.

Sat. 21st. Rough wet day. Lots of boats in and men out all day. The "Mercury" called them out for trawl net. Combing wool all day.

Sun. Nov 22nd. Cold wet blustering day. Very rough. "Bannerdale" came in and whistled but, of course, it was impossible for the men to go out.

Mon. 23rd. Very rough. "Bannerdale" and other boats

left the bay. Very big boat came in and everyone thought it was the "Cruiser". It was too rough to go out.

Tues. 24th. (Christmas Presents). Men lucky today. Tide and wind being more favourable. "Bannerdale" came in. Such letters and parcels. Where they all came from I cannot imagine. There was a huge parcel like a bed from Dundee. It turned out to be my Xmas present from Miss Moir, a lovely chair, folding, so that I can lie down on it. The bells came from Mr. McLennan, two of them, one for church and one for school. Box from ladies for School prizes. One from Mrs. Dickson, sweets etc. Box of Scotch from Capt. Walckner. Letters and papers, any amount.

Fri. 27th. Men out levying Custom. "Bodach Ruadh" in Bay.

Sun. Nov 29th. Out at church three times.

DECEMBER 1908

Thurs. Dec 3rd. (Gift of Cruiskeen). Fine day and evening. Dunie and I went up village. Had a long ceilidh with Neil McDonald. Was presented with very old "cruiskeen" which has been in the house for generations.

Fri. 4th. Had Callum's Mary carding for me. Bella McDonald came down with my "cruiskeen" and spun all – Mary carded.

Sun. Dec 6th. William says, "Albert is working at Boreray." Very stormy day.

Mon. 7th. Albert (Walkner) whistled about 9 o'clock. Men out by 10. Eight or nine boats in the bay. Got leg of fresh pork and boiled ham. Capt. W. as kind as ever. Box of oranges from the Managers of Donald Craig. Donald Craig sent me in a carafe of raspberries, vinegar and books.

Wed. 9th. (Reception At Home). Prayer Meeting, after which I held quite a reception. There were Donald Ferguson, Donald McQuien and his wife, Norman McQuien and his two children, and Beau Callum, and Ewan. I got supper and all ended merrily. Old Donald McQuien was too funny. He and D. Ferguson were falling out as to who would say grace after supper.

Fri. 11th. Busy getting letters ready for Capt. Walckner who came into the bay. Dunie went out to see Capt. W. and managed to make peace – he took all the orders as usual and sent me in a lot of lovely home baked bread.

(Felt Seedy – Trawlers Arrested). Have been seedy and lazy since Dec 11th. Could not be bothered with diary. Had two mails between that and Jan 4th or 5th. but Capt. Walckner and "Livingston" Hull, were again arrested a few days before Xmas for trawling at Boreray.

JANUARY 1909

Jan 21st. (Getting Up To Date). It is now Jan 21st and I again start the diary and must try to keep it better. The village people have, in the interval, all had their cardings with the exception of William McDonald, Neil Ferguson (whose wife has been keeping poorly) Finlay mor and Angus. The Finlay Gillies got their carding over first before New Year, they were the only ones, then Callum's people and so on. As I write Kate has been working at my "cur" for a long time. Men all down on Tues. last working at the big black boat. Capt. Walckner left on Friday last (the 15th.) for Aberdeen rather before his time, but the second engineer was very poorly. He has not come back so we are afraid he will not come. Word had come in before he left from the "Minna" that he was to be arrested. Boats in today are the "Cornelia", "Bodach Ruadh" and another. "Dreadnought" in neighbourhood (Capt. Morris).

At New Year I gave Kate a new pink blouse which I had made, and a pretty piece of pink ribbon. Also gave other things "suas". Walckner brought a barrel of apples from Bookless Bros., also 6lbs of tea and 3

Calendars, also Santa Claus Stockings for the children. Have had a lot of letters and cards. Miss Scott's box of toys for the children, came. The children have come off very well this year. They had a splendid entertainment. Today is lovely but we have had some very severe weather. Snow, three of Norman McQuien's sheep, one of Finlay Gillies and one of his son Donald's died in the snow and were washed down in the Amhuinn Mhor. Dunie well and busy and I have started my "layette". Sent £2 to Miss Moir to get me some little things at Brown's sale in February. Hear from her every mail, also from the home folks. I ought to have said that the Pension Officer came with Capt. Murdoch on the "Minna" and the people got the first two installments of their pension, but the money which came is done now; we saw in the paper that the cruiser may bring it across and watch the trawlers at the same time. There is no word of the arrest or anything so we are glad. We got lovely fish today.

Sat. Jan 23rd. (Spectacles for Roenig). Awakened early by Donald Craig's whistle. He did not come ashore with John McDonald as he had hurt himself with the wheel, it seems, before leaving last time. They are just finished carding at Tigh Donald Ferguson. Callum's wife better. Roenig Ferguson still the same. Took Roenig McRommon the spectacles which Mr. McLennan sent her.

Mon. 25th. (First Loom Up). Donald Gillies (MacFinlay) tells us his father's loom is put up today. It is the first. Big combing going on in Tigh William.

Tues. 26th. (Cooking). Donald Craig's boat came in, also Capt. Walckner's. Neil took out letters and parcels. "Fear big" and "Johnnie" came ashore. Made Apple Tart, Jam Tart and Mince Pie. Second loom up today at Callum's. Came on very stormy.

Wed. 27th. (Trouble). Sea very big. William's carding done now, so all are done with the exception of Meirut Ferguson's and Angus' but they won't take long. Fell out with Dunie last night as he stopped me singing under pretences of study, but let Kate make as much noise as she liked. Gave Kate use of my spinning wheel today to see if she can get on quicker.

Fri. 29th. "Donald big" in, also "Concord" and two liners. Hear that Capt. Walckner went home last night. Men out all day for a boat load of coal from "Concord" in return for their help in mending his "rivet" when he was here last.

Sat. 30th. (Cruiser Catches Trawlers). Very cold day. The looms are going up gradually. Donald McDonald was the third. "Donald big" in today. He seems to have a lot of fish. Went up and saw everybody. Lovely day with North wind. Heard up the village that 6 trawlers were caught by Cruiser near Lewis and taken to Stornoway.

Sun. Jan 31st. After church William and his brother went out for "Donald big" – cranky. He and John came ashore for a little.

FEBRUARY 1909

Mon. Feb 1st. (Men to Soay). Beautiful day. The men went to Soay and got home safely with lots of sheep. They say they are very "bochd" owing to the lateness of the season. We got one too. D. Craig went home last night, after a great scare with what he thought was the Cruiser. Afterwards we knew it was the "Dreadnought" – playing tricks to frighten the trawlers at Boreray.

Tues. 2nd. Rain and plenty of wind. Five boats in the bay, among them the "Cornelian" and "Dreadnought".

Thurs. 4th. Lovely day! "Bannerdale" in when we got up, also "Cornelian" and three others. Both Capts. came ashore for Dinner and refreshment!!! which latter they got liberally.

Fri. 5th. (Whalers in Law Suit). Lovely day! Got a few letters and papers. In the latter we were amazed to see a lawsuit between the Herlofson Company (Father and son) and the Harpoon Company. There is a fearful burst up and Herlofson is no longer in their

Company and has severed all connection. The lawsuit is now going on in Norway and Scotland. The "Grecian Empire" in.

Sat. 6th. Another beautiful day. "Donald big" arrived. I was up the village all the afternoon. Met Donald Craig in almost every house and we were great friends!

Sun. Feb 7th. (Gales). Very blowy day, what the St. Kildans call the "Feulach" or Equinox Gales.

Tues. 9th. Kate finishing all my spinning. "Fear big" in loch this afternoon.

Wed. 10th. (Sheep Lost). Men were away looking after their sheep today. They say they have lost a lot. Capt. Walckner came in to rest, he has a lot of fish. He sent me in a cod and a basket of "Trews". Donald Gillies in to supper.

Thurs. 11th. Lovely Spring day. People got the "cratan" among other troubles up, "chloera", "toothache" etc.

Sat. 13th. (Boat Cold Raging). "Cratan" in every house, but old Donald McQuien especially ill. Took him eggs and sent him ground rice and pills for his wife. Gave a lot of toffee away today, and yesterday. Capt. Walckner in the bay all day.

Sun. Feb 14th. Out at church and S.S. Everyone barking, myself included.

Mon. 15th. "Cornelian" arrived. Emmerson came ashore bringing me a 10lb. roast, a lot of spring rhubarb, Jaffa oranges, and Dunie 1lb. of tobacco!!! He brought mate and boy with him. Gave them tea and eggs.

Thurs. 18th. (Fat of the Land!). Very breezy day. Hear the invalids are better. We have been living off the fat of the land, thanks to Emmerson's generosity. Finished two small vests now. They look splendid at a cost of 4d!

Fri. 19th. (Parcels Galore). The "Bannerdale" did not disappoint our expectations because she came in as soon as it was light enough. A big mail bag, a fine box of good things for me from Capt. Walckner, containing two bottles of preserved fruit, a fine cake and a great parcel of finnan haddies. How kind he is! Mackie's

things also came. Also my "layette" from Dundee. It surpasses my expectations. Lovely wee frocks, winsey, nun's veiling, four carries, wee shawls, vests, everything, including powder! The finnans are simply delicious. Lots of letters from everybody, and good news. I broke the "news" of my baby to Kate. She is greatly delighted. Had a most kind letter from Dr. Martine who wishes me to come home and he'll see to me, but I haven't yet made up my mind. All looms up today.

Sun. Feb 21st. Day quite as bad, indeed worse than yesterday (when wind and sea very high).

Wed. 24th. (Visiting Wild Duck). Another lovely day (like Mon. and Tue.), very sunny, very little wind. Went up Berenhake for a walk with Topsy. There has been a wild drake for a week now with ours. We are trying to catch it – for roasting.

Fri. 26th. (Men to Boreray). Walckner ashore all day. Most beautiful day. The men went to Boreray and got a lot of poor sheep.

Sun. Feb 28th. Out at church and S.S. Very cold and stormy. Roenig Ferguson very sick these days and much swollen (dropsy).

MARCH 1909

Mon. 1st. (Question Day). Latha na ceisd. Everybody nearly spoke so the Meeting was long. Dunie suas and while he was up, Donald McDonald came down and ceilidhed. He stayed until Dunie came and had supper and spoke most kindly about my going away. Kate very busy with my cloth bhig which is not to be so bhig after all.

Tues. 2nd. (Snow). Very stormy and a lot of snow, first really this year.

Thurs. 4th. (Cloth Ready). More snow but not much. Donald Gillies came down with my cloth – the wee one, which turns out to be 28½ yards!!! Another piece 35 yds and other 33 yds. They will go in a little, but not

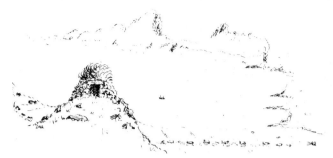

Dun from a Cleit on Conachair.

much. So that is very good out of 3 stones from Connu Morison and 6lbs. from Angus. As well as the molts. It would altogether be less than 90lbs. I got a bundle from Beau Neil Ferguson and Mrs. Gillies, also a little from Meirut, Mairi Bhor and the Bandragh, Liath from the latter five.

Fri. 5th. Deep snow and still falling. More wintry like than ever. Hens doing very badly so far. No village news.

Sun. Mar 14th. Wild day. Only out morning. Seedy. Eight boats in loch all day.

Fri. 19th. Still in bed and still greatly pained. Can neither rise, sit, lie or anything comfortably.

Sat. 20th. Another day in bed. Capt. Walckner in to dinner and ceilidh. Sent me in Castor oil and a large piece of meat, and a loaf, such a big one.

Sun. Mar 21st. Lovely day. "Bannerdale" in and the men were in church. Great visitation today from all and sundry.

Mon. 22nd. (Tragic Drownings). Glorious day. I am still in bed. Think of getting up later in the day. Just like summer and so warm. Two boats left about 10 or a little after for Boreray to see about sheep etc. and Kate told me when she came to tidy my room that five men, Donald McDonald, John Gillies, Neil McKinnon, Norman McQuien and his brother John, went to Dun in William's boat. Kate had gone out of the room and my window was left wide open as the day was so lovely.

All at once I heard the most terrible cries from the Dun and I called to Kate who ran out, and in turn gave the alarm up that something had happend at the Dun. Dunie came from school in time to help old Angus, Finlay Mor and Finlay McQuien, and in a very short time they got over to the scene of whatever happened. The suspense at home was awful; the women were all down and anguished weeping and wailing, I cannot describe. However, the boat came, and our worst fears were realised; worse than we ever imagined. Donald McDonald, Norman and John McQuien were all drowned. Neil McKinnon and John Gillies were rescued in a very exhausted condition. Donald McDonald's body was found floating in the water but poor Norman and John had gone down gripping each other. The scenes are indescribable. Dunie up twice. A beacon was lighted at Berenahake to make the men come home as it seems they proposed staying to kill gannets. Poor Donald og and Ewan McDonald.

Tues. 23rd. (An Awful Place). A little better. I brought in the five who were making Donald McDonald's coffin to tea and dinner. Gave Neil McKinnon coffee also; he will take some time to get right. This is an awful place.

Wed. 24th. Donald McDonald was buried today. Most terribly sad.

Thurs. 25th. Great many visitors myself these days as I am not at all well, though better. No boats.

Fri. 26th. This week is like a month. The bodies have not been recovered. Dunie and Kate up. I was out a wee bit in the sun today, with my big coat on.

Sat. 27th. Out a good while today. Rachel Ferguson very low today. People as sad as ever.

Sun. Mar 28th. (No Sign of Bodies). My Birthday. Up most of the day. Capt. Walckner arrived during the day and was terribly shocked at the news. Went and trawled for the bodies but no signs. Brought me my medicine and also a box of ointment from himself. He had the poorest trip he ever made, only £47. He is wanted to go to Iceland. Services in church terribly pathetic today. I was not allowed to go out.

Mon. 29th. (People Braver Today). Got letters today. People a wee bit braver today. Poor things. It is awfully sad, especially for Beau Toromich. Hens doing fairly well. Very stormy day today and yesterday. The young factor says that Miss Kemble is coming for a fortnight to study the birds.

APRIL 1909

Thurs. April 1st. (Fearful Weather). Dunie at School. I am just taking care of myself. Lots come to ask for me. Weather fearful.

Fri. 2nd. Day just as bad. Then men went over to the Glen and took the letter bag. They spent most of the day with Walckner. They got fish and gannets, 42 between them. Donald Gillies brought us some trews and haddocks and stayed to tea.

Sun. April 4th. This is the second Sunday without lamps. I am not going out to church now. Donald og and the three McDonald boys were at church though I am still a prisoner. Torrents of rain and very high wind.

Wed. 7th. Another glorious day. Capt. Walckner came in the morning for tea, sugar, which he got from Neil, and tobacco which he got from us. He brought in some fish and 6 wee loaves. He is awfully kind. Out all day nearly but awfully tired.

Thurs. 8th. (Clothes for the Baby). Fine wind and glorious sunshine and Kate in the best of humours. I was busy most of the day in the kitchen. Meirut arrived, by invitation, to be shown the "layette". We had great fun over it. Mrs. Finlay Gillies saw it yesterday and they were both awe-struck and never saw anything like it before. Never saw a baby's first long gown! Meirut had tea with us. Busy knitting stockings for myself.

Sun. April 11th. Very bad night. No sleep and much pain everywhere. It wasn't the better for being in church under the breacan and dirty can. The "Roman Empire" in the bay until 5 o'clock. All my chickens came out, ten, so I hope they will all live and thrive.

Wed. 14th. (Feeling So Tired). Lovely day. Out most of the day. So Warm. My chickens in front garden all day and so smart. Kate finished digging the front this afternoon. It feels glorious to be out, but I am so tired. Surely I shall be in luck soon. Poor Donald og down registering his brother's death.

Thurs. 15th. No boats. Feeling miserable just now and bad night.

Fri. 16th. (Baby on the Way). Out part of the day we thought it advisable to have Meirut (Sarah Gamp) down to sleep as I wasn't well during the day. She came accordingly. I turned ill about 11 o'clock but we did not call "Sairy" till about 3 am when I was very ill. Draw the veil over the next seven hours, when a bonny wee girl was born.

Sat. April 17th. (Baby Girl Born). The loveliest wee baby girl was sent to us this morning at 10 o'clock. Kate was just coming in with Beau Neil Ferguson when the wee girl was just coming into the world. She has good lungs at any rate and such long hair, very dark at present but it may all come out. Sairy did well at the event. The house was at once filled with all the women in the place, greatly excited, of course. All had cake and wine – and tea!!! I am as well as can be expected.

Sun. April 18th. (Admirers). Lots of visitors, men and women. Dunie stayed at night and Donald Ferguson preached.

Mon. 19th. William very kindly came last night and put on the iodoform on the "imolac" and is to come till it drops. The girls came two by two to take care of me every night while Sairy sleeps. Mhairi Mhor and Annie Gillies one night, Catharine Gillies and Bellac next night. Time about. They are very kind.

Tues, Wed, Thurs, Fri. All the same, spent in bed with my little darling baby.

Sat. 24th. Lovely day. I'm told. Sat up in bed yesterday and today a little and none worse.

Sun. April 25th. (Visitors). Lots of visitors. Girls have stopped sitting up as waulking starts tomorrow. Baby and I well and sat up long time. "M.A. Dodds" and "Montreal", Johnnie McDonald, in. Four or five at church and Dunie got great praise from the skipper of "M.A. Dodds" for his English sermon. Sent off telegram with the news of the baby to Mother, Flora, Beauty and Miss Moir, but they won't get them till the end of this week.

Mon. 26th. Got my clothes on and up in bedroom for a little. Very shaky. No boats.

Tues. 27th. Up for longer. Wrote some letters. Sairy Gamp left me today. Paid her £1. She was very pleased and is to come back for a morning to wash baby.

Wed. 28th. No news. Getting up and today got for a little into the sitting room.

Thurs. 29th. (Dunie So Good!). Waulking goes on every day. Baby and I improving. Dunie very busy and so good to baby and myself. All through this time he has been such a help and, tired out though he must have been, has never complained.

Fri. 30th. (Russian Trawler Captain). Stormy. One liner in and one trawler. Don't know names. Men went out and got lovely fish, plaice, soles and cod from trawler (Russian Captain). Norman McKinnon came down to tea and see baby. We were out of the bedroom today as it was so cold and I had had castor oil. The corn was sown a fortnight past Thursday last, and is only just appearing.

MAY 1909

Sat. May 1st. Very cold day and not like first day of summer! All of us well.

Sun. 2nd. Better day. Baby and I in the sitting room most of the day and very well. Lots of callers. Baby looks sweet in her clean clothes, and wee "ceanu ruadh"!

Mon. 3rd. Rough stormy day. Question day in church. Lots in to see self and baby.

Tues. 4th. (Potato Planting). Fine day although very blowy. John McDonald and Neil Gillies came and put manure into the "buall" and Dunie and Kate have started to put in the potatoes. Put in 5 drills. The boys put in manure into ¾ of it.

Wed. 5th. (Beasts to the Glen). Another good day. Kate put the beasts, all but Cruvack, to the Glen for the summer. Good riddance as the "fiar" is almost gone.

Thurs. 6th. No news. Baby and I both well. No boats.

Fri. 7th. Kate, Catrione and Annie Gillies washing blankets and doing big washing. Perfect weather.

Sat. 8th. (Men to Boreray and Stac Lee). Men went to Boreray and Stac Lee for gannet's eggs. Got a great many. Men were speaking to trawler at Boreray. Baby out first time today, and so good.

Sun. May 9th. Lovely day. Lots of visitors to see the baby. Colder. No boats. Two boats passed, going different ways, one of them whistled twice. Baby not out. Very good, sleeps well.

Mon. May 10th. (Herring Drifters). Hear the drifters start to work at the herrings today. Beautiful day but very hot. Kate started the cleaning and did store room. Forgot to say that Finlay Gillies did our clothes on Saturday last and we got them all beautifully dried. Baby out a good while today. The men down all day putting up cran and getting ready for the "Dunara". Scraping and tarring their boats etc. Baby a wee cross in the evening and inclined to throw up her food.

This is the last entry. Presumably Dunie, Alice and little Susan left in the next day or so on the "Dunara Castle".

AFTER ST. KILDA

Kate MacDonald (born in 1865, the daughter of John MacDonald), the MacLachlan's servant, in spite of all the advances of her suitors, never married. She left St. Kilda in the 1920's or earlier and became servant to a Minister in Staffin, on the Island of Skye.

In a letter to me in 1987 Susan, writing from Harare in Zimbabwe, commented, "I was an only child. My parents had been ten years married and had given up hope of a family. After St. Kilda they were in Glenelg near Kyle, opposite Skye for about three years. Then they moved to Acharacle on Loch Shiel. That is the part of the world I remember well – a most romantic area. As a child we sailed 20 miles to Glenfinnan where Charles Edward raised his standard and then made our way to Moidart where he landed and planted seven trees. A lovely photograph of my mother with her spinning wheel has gone to the little museum which they have constructed on St. Kilda. My mother developed pneumonia and my father only lived one and a half years after her death. As far as I can make out, from his brother who was a doctor in Beauly, he had a perforated duodenal ulcer, which was possibly neglected. At any rate he was warned not to live far from medical attention which he obviously ignored. I was only 13 years old at boarding school in Edinburgh at the time of his death. My parents are both buried in Acharacle."

MacLachlan family, with Susan at Acharacle. S. MacLachlan Collection.

Susan was writing her letter while attending to African patients in a very busy surgery. She added, "I am a Nursing Sister, Ex-Rhodesian Government, but am called to do a doctor's work. Appears to run in the family – to attend to the ailments of Natives!"

Lachlan MacDonald –
Lachlan's Portrait. Born on St. Kilda – left at the Evacuation.

"Part of the Island of Soer". Showing the Cambir and Soay. Acland.

Lachlan MacDonald was born on St. Kilda in 1906. By the time of the Evacuation, when he was 24 years of age, he had only once been away from the islands and that was for a short holiday with his brother Angus in Glasgow in 1927. He was one of the few younger St. Kildans who stayed on until the bitter end, constrained by the needs of the older inhabitants. When the day eventually came, he was ready to leave. "The older ones were sorry to be leaving . . . there was only half a dozen or so that was able to do the manual work. It was time something was done for the island. I think it was God's blessing the day we left. For me anyhow – I have no regrets I left the island."

During the last ten year I have had the immense pleasure of spending hours talking with Lachlan – chatting about life on St. Kilda. On showing him photographs of the olden days and the present scenery his memory has often been stimulated tremendously with immediate recall of past incidents or customs. There was one occasion when, at 10 o'clock in the evening, he produced a small scruffy brown envelope containing about 70 old snaps – a priceless collection of photographs, many of excellent quality, which I had copied and enlarged. Lachlan was able to name most of the people and explain the background to the occasions. Another interesting addition was when my son Timothy, an archaeologist, obtained permission to survey the byre, the old blackhouse, belonging to house No. 16, Lachlan's old home – his intriguing results and Lachlan's comments are later described. In 1986 Lachlan, and his wife Nancy, came to stay at our home for a week which was an invaluable time for further information gathering! All these conversations I have recorded on tape and have transcribed them and arranged them into a pattern. Lachlan still has a remarkably vivid visual memory and yet is always quick to say whether or not he can recall an incident or an event. He may follow his observation with certain phrases, "I remember that right enough!" or "I'm not so

Portrait of Lachlan MacDonald by David Carter.

sure about that." or "I have a mind of it." He has revisited the island of his birth many times, even in 1987, at a sprightly 81 years of age, on the Jean de la Lune.

In talking to him, not being a Gaelic speaker myself, I have been fascinated by the pronunciations of the St. Kilda place names by a genuine St. Kildan, and by some of the Gaelic words for which he could find no

English equivalents. Here are some examples:-

Place Names	Lachlan's Pronunciation
Cambir	Han Cambelyer
Gob na h-Airde	Gob na Hartcher
Tobar nan Buadh	Tobar na mourg
Stac Biorach	Stac of Biorach
Below the Cambir, Suisle	Soosh-shla
Soay	Soa
Bearradh na cloiche moire	Beren a quasha mora (Lover's Stone)
Bearradh na h-Eige (Ridge or cliff of the gap)	Beren-ee-haykee
Rubha an Uisge	Roo Nischa (Point of the Water)
Oiseval	Oysheval
Geo	Gayo (g hard as in gannet)
Dun	Doon
Boreray	Boyra
Tobar Gille Chille	Tobar Ille Heelee
Tigh an t'sithiche (Earthhouse)	Toy na she-ish (House of Fairies)
Birds	
Gannet	Sular
Puffin	A Bujilla
Guillemot	Warmi

FAMILY BACKGROUND

We can trace Lachlan's family tree with certainty to his great grandfather, Donald MacDonald, who was born on St. Kilda c. 1782 and who died of "inflamations" on 17th. May 1832 about 50 years (Rev. Neil MacKenzie). He had previously married Margaret MacCrimmon, the daughter of Donald MacCrimmon. Donald and Margaret had a family who suffered the traumas of living on a remote and isolated island. Their son, Angus, who appeared as the head of the household in Sharban's map of 1860, was

born in 1816 and was drowned on 14th May 1863, aged 46 years. He was married twice, firstly, on 11th August 1835 to Marion (nee Gillies) who sadly died three months later (9/11/1835) of Green Sickness. He married again on the 6th August 1836 to Christina (nee Morrison) who was 10 years older than himself. They had no children by 1851. She died before 1861 and Angus was drowned on 14th May 1863 at the age of 46. Another son was born to Donald and Margaret, Malcolm, in 1817, he is 5 years old in Dr. John MacDonald's list in 1822, but died on 27th. October 1846 of "cold in addition to boat cold, aged c. 10." In 1820 Donald was born.

This Donald, Lachlan's grandfather, later married Catherine (nee MacKinnon) sometime between 1841 – 45; unfortunately the page is missing from the Marriage Register for 1840 – 45, after the departure of the Rev. Neil MacKenzie from the island. Donald died on the rocks of Carn Mhor on 18th. August 1845, approximately 25 years of age, leaving Catherine to bear a son posthumously in 1845, who was named Donald – Lachlan's father.

The same tragic pattern was again repeated in the experience of Lachlan's father who was married three times. Once between the 1861 – 71 Censuses, probably in Harris, his wife dying before the 1871 census. He was married a second time at the age of 30 on St. Kilda on November 3rd, 1874 to Mary aged 26 (whose father was Donald Gillies and whose mother was Mary, nee MacCrimmon). She had one son, Donald born in 1876 in Harris, who later moved to Glasgow and worked in Cooper's, but she died of an unknown cause on 18th August 1877. Donald MacDonald must have been a highly respected member of the St. Kilda community as he was chosen as Crofter and Fisherman, aged 37, with Angus Gillies, aged 35, to represent the islanders before the Commission of Enquiry (the Napier Commission) on St. Kilda on Saturday, June 2nd 1883. They were examined by

Lord Napier and Ettrick, K. T. Chairman, Sir Kenneth S. McKenzie, Bart., Donald Cameron Esq. of Lochiel, M.P., C. Fraser-MacKintosh, Esq., M.P., Sherriff Nicolson, LL.D., Professor MacKinnon, MA. They arrived unannounced and had a tricky landing. In the verbatim report the following are some of the answers given by Donald:-

"We pay rent separately for the ground that is worked around here, and separately for the hill – £2 for the arable ground and about £3 for the hill. We pay it with the produce the islands gives – feathers, and oil and cloth and also with cattle. 5s. a stone for grey feathers and 6s. a stone for black feathers, puffin feathers, which are finer; 1s. a pint for Fulmar oil, 3s a Scotch yell for cloth. The price varies for the cattle, fixed by the factor. (Another witness adds 'We never got such good prices as under the present factor.') We get £2.10s, and we have got £3 for a stirk from him.

Some people are in arrears of rent but the factor does not press the people at all. Though some were in debt, some were the other way, some people are well off and some are ill off. The laird owes some of us money, anybody that wishes it from him gets it from him in money. The island would not keep us in meal anytime. Some families get 8 – 12 bolls from the mainland in the year (1 boll = 140 lbs), some don't get more than 5 – 6 bolls. Our accounts are made up at the same time for the rent and meal. We got a few bolls from the steamer last year and sold a little cloth to them.

Certainly it would be the better for a pier. If you saw some of the days we have to land here, you would understand then what need we have of it. We need it for ourselves, for the purposes of fishing. Two boats go out to fish now – we are fallen off in able-bodied men. We fish whenever we get the chance. There are many days when we cannot go to the fishing and other days when we have other work to attend to at home and cannot go to fish. We have sometimes been obliged to try and seek shelter in a creek opposite us on the other side of the island when we could not land here. There have been no drownings that I remember but we have lost a boat at Boreray. We catch ling and some cod. We have no herring nets, I believe we would catch them if we had nets, we have spoken about it several times. The herring sometimes come into this loch – and there were Lewis men fishing here and getting herring three years ago.

We catch the birds to get the oil at the beginning (? end) of the summer. We catch the young ones with our hands before they are able to fly away off their nests. We catch the old birds in the spring and at this time of the year with the rod and snare. We descend the rocks on a rope and place the snare over the bird's head and catch it by the neck. I cannot give a guess how many birds, young and old we catch, probably thousands, but I cannot say. One day I remember we were snaring birds at Boreray when we caught at least 1,000 there were twenty men of us.

We catch some solan geese – the young ones for their oil and feathers. We eat them a little and sell them. The number of birds (on the islands) varies, apparently, like the crops, more some years and less other years. It is forbidden to shoot birds when they are hatching, it has been a rule as long as I remember. There is no prohibition the rest of the year.

If we get a pier, bigger boats and nets, if we had to buy the same meal we would be the more able to pay for it.

Sir John MacPherson McLeod made no difference on the rent on account of the improvement of the houses. We had some complaints here about 20 years ago for being made to pay for the rocks on which we caught the birds. We paid at that time £1 for the land and £1 for the rocks. When the complaint was made the laird took £1 off the rocks and laid it upon us for the island of Boreray, for which we had been formerly paying 5s a head.

There is a cross cut about a rock at Boreray, the steep island over there. I have heard of arrow-heads being found and I have heard of little crocks made of clay. I have seen them myself, found where we were digging, of the size of little bowls."

(In the answers given by Angus Gillies he commented, 'We were much worse off last winter and spring than in former years. The crop was bad and we ran out of food. We went in that little boat to the factor at Dunvegan, and he sent *over a vessel with meal for us. We could not bring it in the little boat ourselves. I believe there were very few people in any of the Western Islands that would have undertaken the risk we did.')*

George Murray, the schoolmaster on St. Kilda from 1886 – 87 records a little incident about Lachlan's father in his diary for October 16th. 1886. "On arriving at the other end of the village I was informed that they were spending the day at 'Ruagadh' the lambs and I set out with them, casting my lot in with Donald MacDonald and his lady. The first half of the day we spent after one mischief of a lamb which we at last got hold of. At 5 pm we succeeded in getting other six on Ruaival with the assistance of other two men. Had my dinner in Donald MacDonald's and arrived home at 6 pm to meet, as I expected, an angry face on my landlady. I let the storm go past!" Donald was now 43, and his lady, Rachel aged 24, the daughter of Lachlan MacKinnon; they were to marry on St. Kilda the next year on August 15th, and in due course, were to have a large family.

In his diary George Murray mentions going with Donald MacDonald to collect grass from Oiseval on October 30, 1886, and a visit with him to Boreray to collect gannets by night on April 7th 1887. "On Thursday, 7th, I went with the men to Boreray to kill gannets through the night. We arrived across sometime before dark. When the night began to fall seven went on land and five remained in the boat to cruise round the island to pick up the birds when thrown over the rocks. Donald MacDonald, William MacDonald and I went together and had rare work of it. They (the gannets), be sleeping on the ledges or rocks which to any but a St. Kildian would be quite inaccessible. There is usually on each ledge a sentinel which thinks that he may refresh himself by a short nap occasionally. When he does so the party must pounce upon them, take a hold of as many as possible by the neck and keep them from making a noise lest those in

Gannet ledges on Boreray.

the neighbourhood be scared away. It is merciless slaughter, but as it is one of the means of sustenance on St. Kilda it must be performed. After working for an hour or two, we rested and had family worship. The scene was very impressive. The three of us sat down

113

on the bare rocks with the ropes about our middles, the cloudless sky our canopy, the moon our lamp, and the ocean still and quiet below, and offered praise and prayer to Him who was able to preserve us in such dangerous work, Donald MacDonald leading."

Regarding his schooling, Lachlan made the following comments, "It was during the time of my father that they started on education on the island; it was a Doctor Campbell from Oban who used to come over to the island and stay in a wee tent. I don't know how my father got to know him so well, but he used to talk to him. My father hadn't any English and he was learning words from the Doctor, and my mother hadn't a word of English. Well, it was wonderful the things, the English, my father learnt from him, he could understand the likes of you a little, if you were talking. I don't think he could write anything, but he could understand. He wouldn't have to write very much anyway!"

Returning to Donald MacDonald's family, his third wife was Rachel MacKinnon whom he married on August 16th. 1887 (by the Rev. John MacKay, resident minister). Their first son Ewen, born in 1888, remained a bachelor and stayed on St. Kilda, helping to look after his mother, until the Evacuation, when he moved to Lochaline. He died from a poisoned foot in 1937 while he was working for the Forestry Commission. Catherine was born next in 1890. She was to marry Neil Gillies (son of Finlay and Catherine) in 1917, and had the two boys Donald and Ewen who are still alive. Neil, after considerable suffering, was taken to Oban hospital where he died in December 1928. Catherine died in 1983. Angus was next to be born in 1892. He left St. Kilda just after the war in 1919 or 1920. He left in Alexander Ferguson's boat which was carrying 2 tons of dried fish which he would be selling for the St. Kildans in return for provisions; old Finlay Gillies was also on board after damaging his shoulder in a fall from the rocks near the

Catharine Gillies (Lachlan's sister) and sons, Ewen and Donald (right). L. MacDonald Collection.

Lover's Stone, he was going to hospital in Glasgow for treatment. This was the first time Angus had left the island and half way across to Harris "the wind got up, they entered a gale with the waves coming over the side of the boat and they went into thick mist. Alex was all for turning back, but old Finlay said, 'If you are going to turn back, you can say goodbye to St. Kilda and to everyone else – you would never find it in these conditions.' After a very rough, miserable and anxious time they reached the protection of Pabbay and sheltered there over night and later reached Glasgow.

After this voyage old Finlay became known as Captain Rimo!" (Lachlan). Alex Ferguson got Angus a job at Napier and Millers shipyards. Angus married Alice MacDonald (not a St. Kildan) and had a son Donald Ian who now lives in New Zealand. Angus died in 1980. To Donald and Rachel was born another son Donald in 1895 who left St. Kilda in 1920 going to Stornoway for a short time, then Glasgow for a few years. Later he bought the schoolhouse at Obbe (Leverburgh) in Harris and became a Lay Preacher ministering over a wide area of Harris and Lewis. He married Mary Ferguson from Harris and they had a son, Donald Ian. The fifth child of Donald and Rachel was another daughter, Rachel in 1899, but after a painful illness, probably meningitis, she died on St. Kilda at the age of 22 in December 1921. Lachlan was the youngest of the family, born in 1906.

Lachlan was only two years old when his father died in a drowning accident off Dun at 11am on 22nd of March 1909. An account of that tragic day is to be found recorded in the diary of Alice MacLachlan, the wife of the Missionary from 1906 – 09. Lachlan was, of course, too young to remember the incident but he had been told what had happened. "My father was in the boat, a small skiff, and the men all came off the island of Dun into the boat, and I think they were talking, and they didn't realise there was a rock by the landing place. The boat caught the edge of the rock and it turned and they were all thrown out. My uncle was there and a fellow, Johnny Gillies, but they were able to cling to the boat. My father, and two MacQueen brothers (Norman aged 29 and John aged 17) were all drowned. They said that my father had the oars and if there had been someone when he turned upside down – he had these wooden clogs on and they took his feet up and his head down – he could have been saved. They took him into the boat but they were frightened to pump the water out. Then they brought him to the pier and I think he was still living. If there had been someone to give artificial respiration I think he would still have been alive. That was in March – I was three in April. This was just what I was told."

So ends another sad chapter in the life of the MacDonald's family, but one which they were able to survive and overcome as the family worked and pulled together, supported by the warm community on St. Kilda. Lachlan's mother died at Savary in March 1943, aged 79 years.

In the following pages Lachlan describes his own home and tells his own St. Kilda story.

HOUSE NUMBER 16 – Lachlan's Home

"On the other side of the main street, opposite the house, there was a little wall to break the wind – there used to be an easterly wind on the door – we called it the porch. Ours was about 3 feet high, a few of the other houses had it the same and the washing posts were along the porch. There'd be a gale coming there sometimes alright. Outside the front door was the grinding stone.

As you come in the front door there was a plank there and if you were taking in water there were pails on the plank, ready for the Sabbath. We got our water from a spring just by Number 15 or from the river – we washed our clothes in the river. A door to the right was into the main bedroom, the one to the left into the Kitchen-living room; there was a wee room off the kitchen which we called the closet. It had a double bed in it. The boys would be in there. It had a long cupboard or press the length of the partition with the kitchen and reaching the ceiling, the height of the house, and another cupboard built into the wall. My father made these and we used them for keeping the stores, jams and sugar and things – the mark is still in

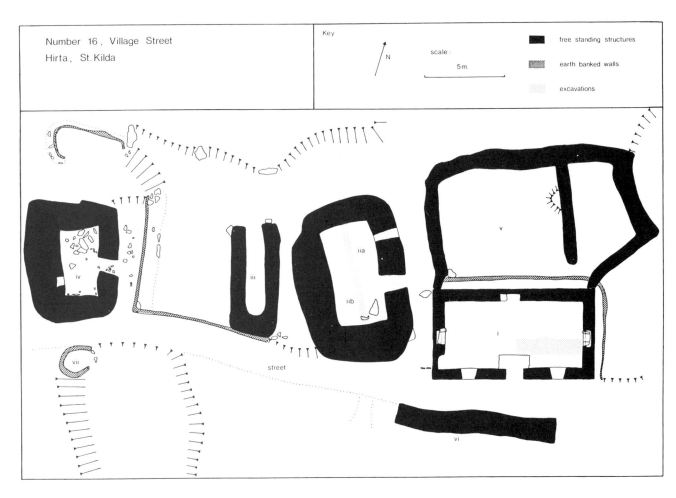

Number 16, Village Street
Hirta, St. Kilda

Key

N

scale:
5m.

free standing structures

earth banked walls

excavations

iv

iii

iia

iib

v

i

vii

street

vi

Plan of No.16.

i) 1860 House
iia) 1834 Dwelling
iib) 1834 Byre
iii) Cleit

iv) Pre 1834 House used for wintering sheep
v) Walled Gardens
vi) Protecting Wall – "Porch"
      (Quine, Dr. T. A. Thesis 1986)

the wall to this day. There was a big box, about 4 feet high and the breadth even greater, with a partition in the middle to separate the flour and the oatmeal. You would put the bags of oatmeal up in the loft and as you were needing it you would bring it down. There would be barrels kept in the corner of the house with oatmeal in.

In the living room the fire was going all the time, summer and winter – you had it for cooking. On either side of the fire you would have a stool and a chair. We had several chests for clothes, under the window and in the corner of the room – they had been bought from the mainland, they fitted very well – it was a good joiner who made them – they kept the mice out – they were the best and polished, and they were lined too. We had a dresser opposite the window, a table just in at the door with the Bible on it, and two spinning wheels pushed into the corners somewhere. My brother liked reading – his books would just be left around anywhere. The loom would be kept in the byre and put up in the living room to the left of the fireplace, between it and the window, when you were using it. You would hardly credit that you could keep all that stuff in such a small space!

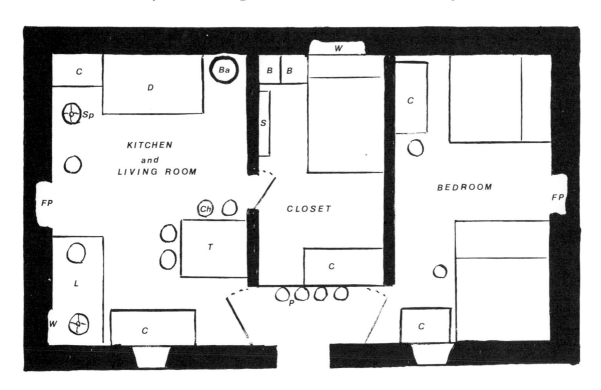

No.16, 1860 House and Contents.

Ba. *Barrel of fulmars*	L. *Loom when in use*	C. *Chest for clothes*	Sp. *Spinning Wheel*
B. *Box for oatmeal*	P. *Pails for water*	D. *Dresser*	T. *Table*
Ch. *Chair*	S. *Shelves*	FP. *Fire Place*	W. *Wall Cupboards (D.A.Q.)*

117

If you turned right as you came in through the front door you would go into the main bedroom. There were two double beds, and a chest for clothes under the window, and another at the foot of the bed and in most of the corners, except where you come in at the door – where you could stand and talk – no furniture other than that. There was a fireplace but it was only used if someone was ill. All the houses were built to the same pattern with the living room on the left and the bedroom on the right, as far as I remember.

Behind the house we had a garden, it wasn't ploughed or used for agriculture in my day, it was just used for storing the stalks of the oats and wheat for winter feed for the cattle. When it was dry we made the sheaves into stacks and kept it there. We grew some potatoes in the walled off area to the right. None of the gardens were used for growing cabbages in my day, some may have grown a little rhubarb.

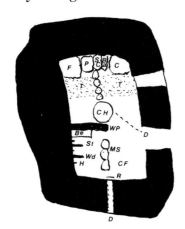

1834 House, later used as Byre and Store.

Ba. *Barley*
Be. *Bedding area for young bullock*
C. *Coal from Trawlers*
CF. *Clay Floor*
CH. *Central Hearth*
D. *Drain*
F. *Fodder for cattle*
H. *Hooks/Pegs in wall for cows*

MS. *Movable Stones*
P. *Potatoes*
R. *Rods covering drain*
SC. *Seed Corn*
St. *Straw for bedding*
T. *Threshing area*
Wd. *Wood separating food for cow*
WP. *Wooden Partition (D.A.Q.)*

Next to the house, to the west, was the byre, the old blackhouse built around 1834. This is the door going into the byre – on the right is a wooden partition, about my height. We had a space for threshing the corn and the barley there – we used a piece of wood with a rope flail on the end. We used to keep some fodder for the beasts in the corner – hay; also potatoes with straw on top of the box before the frost came. We had seed corn (oats) and barley in sacks and coal from the trawlers. Sometimes we kept fulmars in the byre, salted and in barrels, or outside with a lid on. The other end was for the cattle, usually two or three. There were pegs in the wall and a bit of rope from each peg round the cow's horns. Every cow had its own bed and there would be a wee bit of a wooden partition between the head of every cow so that one cow would not get to eat the other cow's grass. The bed was the length of the cow and was made of clay with straw on the top. We had a flat stone at the end of the bed, some of the cows were bigger than the others and taller, you would make the bed according to the length of the cow. You would move this stone up to keep the cow clean, so that they wouldn't get dirt below them. There was a drain through the wall. The dirt you would put into the barrow and this would be wheeled out. We used to keep a corner for the young bullocks. It was made with two running bars of wood and a cross piece so that when it made water it would keep it tidy and clean – very little bedding. He had a box to feed him at the head end – he would be tied there, too. The box was on the ground made from a bit of wood crossed – you put the feed in there so that he wouldn't pull it below himself so that it would be clean for him to eat. In the olden days they had a fire in the living quarters and the cattle was in the other end, but that was no in my day.

(During excavation, my son, Timothy, found the flat stones mentioned above, an underground drain or flue from the living quarters to the door, the hearth, the wooden partition between the dwelling area and the byre, which had

probably been in use until the change of function from dwelling to store c1860 and was buried under earth before Lachlan's time, also the vegetative remains from the bullock's feed and his box). (Quine,T.A., 1986).

Alongside the blackhouse, to the west, we had a cleit with a door to the north – this was for keeping the hay from the croft. Further to the west was another old building – the roof was thatched just as the byre. We used barley because the stalks grew longer than oats or wheat. We kept the hogs, the lambs in here. We let them out during the day – they soon knew where to find food and shelter. We had other cleits on the croft, above and below the house, for hay off the croft.

Above the houses, each croft stretched up to the Head Dyke and below to the wall by the sea. We just called it the high ground and the low ground. Potatoes were planted, maybe down below this year, next year to the side, or above on the high ground. On some crofts the ground was better than others. The east side of the Village was better for growing things. Our side wasn't so good for some reason. You would need to put plenty of manure on to get your potatoes to grow and even grass was not growing so well.

At the end of the summer we cut the hay and that was put into the cleits, but the corn and barley was cut and dried and was all in stacks in the gardens at the back of the house for winter feed. Every crofter had a gate in his own dyke (part of the Head Dyke) and when all the crops were cleared off the crofts, the sheep and cattle were let in to the croft and they were all wintering there until the grass started to grow on the hillside. Then they were put outside the Dyke again and the crofts were closed up.

The cattle would be put in the byres round about October, depending on the weather. Mostly the milking cows we kept in the byres, if you had other beasts you would keep them out, but still, you would take them in during the bad weather in the winter time. Once the cows were in they would stay in until the weather was getting better in the spring. That's the way it was worked.

SCHOOL DAYS

Well, it was in Church, I would be about 5 years old. We were a big family and we would be squeezed in tight on the pew and Rachel MacCrimmon was all on her own on the pew in front. She would turn round to my mother and tell her that we were too crushed and that I could come down under the seat and come up and sit by her. Then I was sat on the seat and when the Minister would start reading the chapter from the Bible I was not to lift my eyes off the Bible on the seat, or if I was to twist, she would be pointing and saying, "You be looking here!" I had to watch it – I wouldn't dare to be looking around! And the praying – it was just the same! People were very kind to us, one would be sharing with the other, whether it was peats or if you were going out fishing.

On St. Kilda they did eat seaweed but not a great deal of it. I have seen me when I was going to school getting a "dulisk" (Gaelic, duileasg, an edible seaweed, Rhodymenia palmata), it sticks onto the rocks; it's long and you tear the leaves off both sides and you've got the centre – it's just like a long twist of tobacco. It was nice and sweet – you would chew the centre bit and eat it – if you were hungry it would soon fill you up. The carragheen – they used to boil it up, it's green, I tried it right enough but it wasn't very tasteful.

I am not saying I enjoyed my school days on St. Kilda. The Missionary's wife was our school teacher – she had plenty to do in the Manse, but she was doing the teaching. Some days the Missionary would come and stand in for her. He wasn't worried too much about our education and if it was a good day at the harvesting he would have the older ones aged 10 or 12 out working at the hay – it was great – we were just enjoying ourselves. We didn't care all that much for school, it was just grand to be outside. It's years after when you look back you'd be missing the education and wished I had done better when I was there. We got on so far, so why worry about these things.

Sometimes the Missionary was interested to go away out with the folk in the islands in the boat to fish or to go for the birds. I mind one night they went over to Stac an Armin or Stac Lee after the gannets.

In school the teacher had a desk and there was a table there. The register was in the desk and she could lock it up. We weren't taught Gaelic in school, not in my day, but my brothers were – there was a school teacher going out there, then.

The Ruagadh – the running after the sheep – I would call it "Ree". Catching up the sheep anywhere in the island. When you were young it was good fun and you were quite excited and you had a dog with you. And climbing too. Maybe you would start when you were about 10 years old, if you were keen you would be wanting to go to the rocks. They would put a rope round you and you would go down, not very far, just a bit. If there was a boy there and he wasn't very keen and he didn't want to go, they would just get a rope round him and say 'You see that bird down there.' He would just go down and he would cope. They would just give him a push and off he would go! You knew you were safe enough – the rope was round you, anyhow. You were soon taught to go. You would practise on something near at hand before going to the steep cliffs. Then you would be gradually getting further and further away, and if it was a very steep place what we used to do, there was a rope round your waist and another one you were taking with you. You were killing the birds as you were going along and you would gather the birds into one place, maybe up to 20 or so, and the other fellow would pull them up on the rope that you were carrying with you. It was a tough job right enough.

Later we had another Missionary. He was good at trying to put something into our heads and his wife was very good too. Three of us, John Ferguson, Finlay John MacDonald and I, he wanted us to take night classes. We went to one or two, but we stopped, and the others stopped going too.

Sometimes we would help to bring the peats down. We would go to the top of the hill to the cleits and we would put the peats in a canvas bag when we were young, we could pull the bag on the snow and ski it down to the house, otherwise we would have to be humping it on our back. So the snow came in handy sometimes!

We used to sell the birds' eggs that they brought back from Stac an Armin and Stac Lee to the visitors. You would get one penny for the gannets' eggs, it was the guillemots' and razorbills' you get more money for, you would get two pence for these shells – they were in great demand. Folks would hardly believe that they weren't artificial – just painted. Some would try to see if some of the blotches and markings would come off! It was great when I think back to these days when I was at school.

THROUGH THE YEAR
SPRING

Birds – The First Arrivals – Gannets, Shearwaters, Puffins.

Gannets

The Gannets are all away during the winter. The first arrivals back would be the gannets – you would see them out over the sea and on the stacs. One night the Missionary went with the men to Stac Lee to take the gannets by night, this was before the gannets started to lay their eggs – you were supposed to go awful quiet out of the boat, no noise, no nothing, and to climb up. If you see one of the gannets – they have one of them like a watchman and you'll have to make for that one quietly and get a hold of that one. This time he made for the one that was on watch, and he got it right enough, but he hadn't the knack to kill it quietly. The gannets started 'Ka-Ka-Ka-Ka' and flying, and some of the stones came rattling down. So the rest was endangering the folk that was climbing. So – supposing he was a Missionary he got some telling off when everything was over! He was a good man though. I didn't care much for the gannet myself, but in the olden days the St. Kildans did. It was coarser, it was more the taste of a fish. Just like everything else you would take to one bird more than the other – someone else would take to the gannet. They're still going out in Lewis yet to get the 'gugas', what they call the young gannet, but that is later in the year. To see the gannets diving for fish – they're great.

Shearwaters

In my day the shearwater would be the first to come on land on the main island on Carn Mor in March or the beginning of April. It was great. A queer noise they make – a lovely musical sound. They would be coming in fresh and it was a nice bird to eat and the eggs, but they were awful difficult to reach – they get amongst the rocks deep underground.

It was at night we used to go on the Carn Mor when it was going dark, you had a dog with you, or maybe two of them, and the dog was trained to catch them. The shearwaters would come in at night, and you would hear them singing underground, and then you would hear the flap of the bird coming in, hitting the rock. If you had a good dog with you he was away as soon as he heard it and he would fetch it. At some times he wouldn't and the shearwater would get in below the stones and rocks and he was away. Then you would hear them singing below. There would be some

coming like a relief, some coming and some going; if you were lucky to get the one that was coming in he was nice and fat, but if you caught the one that was going away he would be lean, he would have been there for two or three days – he wasn't fed. It's a nice bird, too, and it's great to hear them singing – both below you in the ground and above you. The other night, I happened to look out (from my home in Glen Nevis), and I was seeing the lights coming down as the climbers were up on the top of Ben Nevis. I was just away back when I was in St. Kilda when I went to the Carn Mor and you used to take the lanterns and we were there all night – then when you were coming home you would use the lanterns. Some nights, clear and starry nights, you didn't need any light. It just put my mind back when I saw these torches and lights, on one night there was about eight or nine of them coming down from the top of the Ben – I was thinking I was on St. Kilda and coming home from the Carn Mor.

Puffins

The puffins – maybe you were up on the hill or on the rock and you would see two or three of them there – the year's first ones. Then maybe a week after that they would come – thousands of them. If you were out in the boat, maybe you would see them out on the sea – a few out at sea – and then they would come in and sit on the rocks. You would just see a few on one day and then thousands. They were more frightened too when they came in at first. If makes you wonder where they go for the winter – you don't see any then. Some parts of St. Kilda they would start to come – the Dun was a great place for them to start to come at first. They were handy – you could get them through the day, in the burrow or, if you were good with the rod with the loop on it, you could get them like that too. I used to take a dog with me and the dog would point out the hole the puffin was in. There was one time of the year when they were mating and maybe you'd be lucky and get the two of them in the hole at once. You put your arm in and reach them, or maybe it wouldn't reach and you'd have to turn up a bit of the ground to get to them. They can give you a sore nip and catch you on your finger – a sharp beak he has too. You would bring him out and just draw his neck. You had a belt round you and you put his neck in and you collected them until you had so many and then you would go home when you had plenty. I like the puffin. It's funny that the puffin was not so good to eat when it was salted – I don't know why, maybe when it was salted the fat was drawn in. The fulmar when it was plucked and salted was alright through the winter.

It's great when you are thinking of nature – the way the birds go and come back and the way they know their own places. It's great. Hundreds and thousands of Guillemots and Razorbills on the rock there, nesting, and they know their own egg. It's marvellous. And as far as I know the couples don't interbreed.

A Typical Day on St. Kilda – The Books, Parliament, The Cambir.

The Books

First thing in the morning you would be up at about 8 o'clock, 7 in the summer time and you would do your chores with the cattle and the hens and things like that. You would have your breakfast and then you would have "The Books" – Family Worship. It didn't matter what hurry you were in, you would open the Bible and read a few verses and maybe a Psalm and a few more verses. Then a prayer. you were down on your knees before you went to your work. It was the head of the house who led it, my father if he was living, mostly the men who was doing it. And at night, whatever time you were going to bed, the whole family had to be in, and there was a Worship and then you were away to your bed. Even fishing in the boat, in the morning – you'd be away fishing maybe three or four miles away over to Boreray, or you may be away over the other side of the island – you would stay on the end of the line if it was a good night, a dryish night. You would have a wool back, "a Hoostie" and you would lie in the bottom of the boat. If it was a wet night you would come into the islands and go into one of the caves round the islands and sleep there, then away out in the morning to lift the lines again. The same there – you had the Worship in the boat before you lifted the lines.

Parliament

If it was a good day, a very good day, they called the Parliament, you would go over and they would suggest what they were going to do – if they were going out in the boat or going to the rocks or they might decide to "divide the rocks". It was at the time the birds returned that they divided the rocks – they did it by lots. You would put a penny under a stone, or another wee stone or a wee bit of stick. The other guy would be away and he wouldn't see what was going on. He would come back and say, pointing to one of the stones, "He has got that part of the Cambir" or Oiseval or Dun. They knew the district. This was turned every year or every two years. It was all even. The cliffs were shared for the grass and for the birds – you all had a good lot of little bits all round the island. It was all divided, you wouldn't get it your own way to go and cut a wee bit of grass. It was the same if you were killing fulmars and you were counting them and putting them into heaps, you would still cast lots so that it was even and no-one could say that those birds were better because they were in that lot. The same was if you were with the fish

– you cast lots. It was great – so that there would be no argument!

It all depended where you were going what time the Parliament met. If you were going to work together. 'Are we going into the rocks or are we going out in the boat?' If you were going out in the boats – the boats were shared – say may be three or four or maybe two families would have a share in this boat or in the other boat. Everything was worked so that we all worked together. Sometimes we discussed for a long time and sometimes no. This one suggested we go here and this one suggested we go there; like everything else there would be some argy-bardgy between them. There was no chairman. If one was a bit stronger he might say, "I'm off, you go where you like!" The rest would follow then and go away. Maybe you'd have a newspaper and you'd be reading that. If you were going out in the boat, mostly you would be all going together.

The Cambir

We decided to ear-mark our lambs. "We will go to the Cambir this day." they would say. The whole lot would go, it didn't matter if you only had but two or three sheep there, you would go and help the rest. You would go and collect them up in stages, get one batch in and deal with them, you would put them in a fank. You would go near the top of the Cambir, the sheep were right in the rocks there. We called the place "Soosh-shla" (phonetic), I cannot put an English word to it. It was great for growing surrocks – they were sweet, we called them 'Buinyaken' (phonetic). Sometimes if you were lucky, you would start throwing stones from the top, the sheep had a track and sometimes they would come out, but at other times no, they would stick there. Then you would have to walk in and get them out – it was the same all over the island. Sometimes it was that bad maybe two of you would have to go with ropes between you and get the sheep out. They talk about the Lover's Stone, that was a great stone to go out on, not standing on it as the story goes, but you could lie on it and you could see the sheep far below. It was a good look-out post – I was often there. You would take them from the Cambir right along the coast, there would be quite a lot of sheep in the Glen there, and you had a fank in Gob na h'Airde (The Point of the High Ground), down on the rocks. The posts are there to this day, and you had a net from the trawl and you would get the sheep in there. Sometimes it wasn't very easy. We hadn't the dogs trained to gather the sheep – we had the folks to gather them! You had the dogs there, if the sheep were to break out the dogs would catch them – they were trained to catch the sheep and to hold them. Their teeth were filed to half their size so that they wouldn't cut the sheep when they got hold of them. One of our dogs was "Sam", another was "Faithful" – he was a great dog – he would do anything. If you left him on the hill and you went down the rocks – he would still be there. Even if you went home – he would still be there. If they were treated badly some became vicious.

We used to round up the sheep at the time of clipping and earmarking. Others put a blue keel or a bit of blackish cloth and sewed in on. If you put a keel on white wool you would have a job to get it off. To save the wool, if you were making the tweed with white wool you would have to take it all out when you were mixing the colours – that's why we used a piece of rag sewn into the wool.

It was an awful job picking out the lamb to go with the mother. I've seen a wee bit of argument about that! You needed to be very good to spot your lamb and his own mother. You would get them to the fank, if you made a mistake, when you were letting them out, the mother wouldn't take that lamb – she would come back looking for her own. You'd marked that one wrong – then the argument started! Now you would have to catch that lamb and take these marks off and put them on the ear of the right lamb. On the main island itself you could go any day round about, you may see your own lamb and with the dog you may be able to catch it and mark his ears and that was alright. But in some cases you wouldn't get your lamb to mark and then you would have to pick it up in the fank. Our sheep were a cross between Cheviot and Black-face, we didn't like the Black-face as the wool was too strong for carding and spinning. If it was half and half between Black-face and Cheviots, or just Cheviots – that wool was easier worked for making the tweed. The women would bring out a picnic lunch for us. It was a lot of work – hard work! There would be a couple of thousand sheep on the island – it was an awful job getting them out of the rocks and it would take several days. You would be back late for supper, worship and you would be ready for bed.

Other Happenings – Care of Lambs, Crops, German Submarine, Stac Lee for eggs, Sunday Services.

Care of Lambs – enclosures

If there was a sheep that was poor with a lamb, or a lamb that was weak, we would put them in one of the enclosures for a whilee so that she would be well fed. It was more like a nursing home, there was good grass in there and no other beasts could get to eat it. There were a good few enclosures around the island, we called them "Borchin" or "Bowler" (Gaelic – Buailtean, plural, sheep or cattle folds; Buaile, singular, a sheep fold), even away up on An Lag on the way to Bearradh na h-Eige (The Ridge of the Gap), you see them up there, too. The large ones were for the same purpose, one or two families would have shares in the large ones, whereas the smaller ones would be just for one person and the one home. Every enclosure had an owner. The MacDonalds and the MacKinnons shared the smaller enclosure on An Lag, the one to the south west. I couldn't tell you how they came into ownership. I expect it was from the one generation to the other. Maybe that one was built by my grandfather or further back than that, then the next generation would be keeping it up – the same with the dwelling house. Maybe the wife you were getting, her mother was a widow and you would go in with her and the daughter so that you would be looking after the widow that was there. It's great how we agreed – rows sometimes too! That was the way St. Kilda was working. In a way you were waiting until someone would die or go out in order to get into the house.

Crops

The sheep and cattle had all been wintering on the crofts, they could go from one croft to the other. Now with the longer days and better weather the grass was beginning to grow on the hillside above the dyke. The sheep and cattle were put outside and the gates in the Head Dyke were closed up again. That wall going all the way up Oiseval was to keep the cattle from going away over and into the rocks where they would get lost. We didn't like them to go over there – it was steep. If anything were to happen they were right the way down and you would lose them. You had your own croft within the wall stretching from the Head Dyke to the wall by the sea. March was the time for preparing the ground, digging it over, and you had plenty of manure from the beasts – no artificial fertilisers were needed. Then in early April you would be planting your potatoes. You kept some seed potatoes back from the previous year. Sometimes you bought them from the Crofter's Board. At about the same time, before we sowed the oats and barley, we dug the ground with a spade and used a big heavy rake to break it up instead of a harrow. We sowed the seed and used the rake again to cover the ground. We had an acre or two between the oats and barley. We never sowed wheat, we always had to buy the flour through Alex Ferguson in Glasgow, he was a St. Kildan, and it came out on the "Hebrides" or the "Dunara Castle". We didn't plant anything else on the croft.

German Submarine

It was just after we had put out the sheep and the cattle off the croft that German submarine came (May 15, 1918). Before you went to school you had to feed the hens out on the hill. Then the submarine came, everyone was watching it circling round the bay, enjoying the sight of it until it came in very nearly to the pier. This guy, Finlay MacQueen, had a boat which he shared with one or two others and he was going to go out to the submarine – the army folk were there too, and he said, "Ah, I'm getting scarce of tobacco, I think I will go and see if I can get a bit of tobacco." He had the boat loosened to put it on the slip so that he just had to give it a push down. At this time the submarine was away out in the centre of the bay. "Ah!" he says, "it's away too far out, it's a pity!" The next thing the submarine fired a shot. Finlay was up to high doh, and all the Navy boys shouted to everyone to get their own rifles while he crept in among the rocks – it was the best place near the sea by the corner of the pier. The Army huts were right along where the Manse was, right along to where the gun is, but there was no gun then. The submarine was firing for the big house, the Factor's House, they had that for the wireless, and the aerial poles were there and that is what he was aiming for all the time. He never knocked down the pole but he knocked the roof of the big house and damaged it. The operator was there until the shell struck and he cleared out. It's funny that there was nobody killed. I think only one lamb was killed or had its leg broken.

Visiting warship during First World War. L. MacDonald Collection.

He fired 72 shells. I laugh at this, they all went to the hills and he went away in the mist – it was that bad he was afraid that the patrol might get him. However, when the mist cleared the submarine came back again. Between the two hills Oiseval and Conachair, at Bearradh in h-Eige, this old man Donald Ferguson, was there with a stick in his hand, and the submarine was just below the cliffs there. He put up his walking stick and pointing to his dog turned round and said, "Do you think if I were to let off one of these boulders maybe it would hit him!"

The cows were over in the Great Glen at this time and later on that day the women were going over to milk the cows when they saw a man at the back of one of the cleits up on Carn Mor. They thought he was from the German submarine and reported back to the Village. So the officers called on everyone, "The Germans were after landing on the other side of the island." I mind that right enough. All the Navy men that were on the other side of the island were called on to come up, so the whole crowd with rifles and everything went up onto Mullach Sgar with orders to shoot if necessary. Up by the Lover's Stone a face appeared at the back of a cliet as he had a keek out. The poor creature was frightened to come out. Someone suggested, "Is everyone here that was on the island?" Then they put word around to see. They found that this fellow Donald MacDonald is missing and there was no trace of him. "Oh, well, maybe it's him!" someone said. So they started shouting in Gaelic. It was then that he came out and showed himself! He had wandered off by himself to carry out a private watch to see what was going on! It was comic right enough!

I believe it was the same submarine that came back again. One of the Patrol trawlers, they were the big ones fitted with guns, was going back to his depot in Stornoway and stopped to pick up the lines, he was fishing with the long lines. He had his small boat out, the same way we were doing, and the German submarine came on him. He had the gunner, or two of them, on the small boat but he couldn't do anything because the submarine was firing. Anyhow, he would be wanting to get his wee boat in before anything happened. I don't know was it one shot or two shots the submarine got in and hit him just above the water. The fisherman got his boat in, got the gunner and turned on the submarine. He knocked a bit of the conning tower so that he couldn't go under and he knocked the gun out of action on the submarine. I think he killed one or two. He was sinking himself and he had to come into St. Kilda and he beached there on the sand. He was there for a week or so and they patched the boat up and

got her to Stornoway. They got the submarine at Barra Head or somewhere down there.

Stac Lee for Eggs

In early May we used to go from the main island, St. Kilda to Stac Lee or Stac an Armin to collect the gannets' eggs. We would just visit for the day and be back at night. It was a rowing boat we used to go over in, we had a sail but it all depended which way the wind was. There would be half a dozen or more in the boat, you could put six oars on the boat and if the wind wasn't favourable you would just row – it would take about an hour to row across. Sometimes the wind and the tide would be against us. We would land, a couple of us would work together. We had a rope between us and one would go for maybe 50-60 yards or so and the other fellow would come up to there, and we would work it in bits like that right up to the top. You had an empty box on your back and when you got up to the top you would start filling up the box with eggs, mostly gannets' eggs that was there, you might get an odd guillemot egg but no many of them. There might be half a dozen of us, and you would work your way down and you would fill up the boxes as you were coming down. You would get it on your back then and you would carry it down. When you came near the place we would lower them with a rope into the boat. These boxes when full would be anything up to about a half to one cwt, an awful lot of eggs. You would get a wee bit of the nest and put it in the box before putting the lid on to stop them breaking. It was wonderful how they weren't broken – sometimes one or two would be. Then we would take them home. Fortunately, we never got stuck over there. Many a time it was a lovely day when you went out in the morning and many a wild evening you would be coming across, the seas coming on and the wind getting stronger and the waves coming into the boats – but, we always managed to get home! When you got home you would make a hole in the eggs and blow them and sell them to the visitors. What you blew out you could eat as well – they were great for making pancakes and things like that. If you couldn't eat it all you could give it to your beasts.

Sunday Services

On Sunday morning on St. Kilda everybody was going to the Church. You would go in the morning and you would have a short service in English for the sake of the Nurse that was there or for anyone else who hadn't the Gaelic and then they would go home. We were sitting there and then the Missionary would start the Gaelic Service and that would be for another hour and a half – you were there for two and a half hours. At night you were back to Church at 6 o'clock and that would be another hour and a half. The habit on St. Kilda was that you were to go home but you weren't to read a paper or any book – it would need to be the Bible or some other good book."

Interviewed on Songs of Praise in March 1983 Lachlan was asked if the strict upbringing had made his faith very strong? "Aye, it's quite strong, very strong yet, to me. I like to keep the Sabbath day yet. I'm no saying that I wouldn't do things that I wouldn't do on the island, but still, I've got my faith in the Lord, yet. I have chosen Psalm 40, I find the psalms a comfort, especially in Gaelic. It's funny now, but it's true, it gets home to me more in Gaelic than it does in English."

SUMMERTIME – Boats, Visit to Soay, Fishing and Whaling, The Island of Dun, Boreray for the Week, Sheep on Hirta, Cleitean and Corn, Fulmar Harvest, Holidays, St. Kilda Wren.

Boats

"It was in the summertime that we visited the other islands, Soay, Boreray and Dun. We had names for the different boats:-

1. "Fionasach" (Gaelic – Fionnasbhagh) was Gaelic for Finsbay, the name of a village in Harris where it was built. The other MacDonalds had a share in this boat with Ewen Gillies and I think, Finlay Gillies.
2. "Kliosavach" (Gaelic – Greosabhagh), was Gaelic for Grosebay, a village in south Harris where it was built. My brother Ewen and I had shares in this boat with Donald and John Finlay Gillies.
3. "Cruisgean" (Gaelic – Cruisgean) – is really an oil lamp – I don't know how this boat got its name. The Fergusons, John and Donald Gillies had shares in it.
4. "Wachnamatoch" – (Gaelic Loch-nam-Madadh) is Gaelic for Lochmaddy in North Uist, it was built there and was the last to be bought on St. Kilda. We bought it from the Factor. We had shares in it with Finlay MacQueen and the MacKinnons.

When a new boat was bought, usually through the Factor, we had to pay, we all paid our share in the boat. We had shares in Kliosavach and in Wachnamatoch.

Visit to Soay

I was often on Soay. Going to Soay was a bit different from going to Boreray, you could just decide to go, you didn't have to go through Parliament. You would get four or five of you and a boat and you were away. One time John Gillies, Neil Ferguson and John's brother, Ewen and myself went over to catch sheep. You would aim to go when they were in good condition. In the boat we would go through the gap between Dun and the main island if the tide was in, it was a lot shorter that way going to Soay. If the tide was out you would have a job pushing the boat through there. It would be a longer way if you had to go round the Point of Dun, or you would have to go the other way, round the back of the island. Landing on Soay was difficult, it was very steep. You had an old pair of socks that you put on and you would jump onto the rocks – you would grip better if you had socks on. And then, once you got the rest of the party off the boats, you were away, scrambling away up. You were roped between you until you were clear of the bad place, then you put it off and across your shoulders and off you would go. You would be chasing up the sheep, but sometimes you couldn't do that, it was steep, you would try to put them into a rock where there was an end where they couldn't jump away. You would try to put a rope round his neck and pull him to you. You would try to get a fat one – you wouldn't look at a wee lean one – you would leave them!

You took them alive and killed them at home. You would tie them by their legs, put them on your back and carry them. Very rarely you would get one that would walk. They were very different from the Black-face sheep on the main island, you could get them to walk with a rope round their horns. Not the Soay Sheep – they were wild! You would tie the four legs and you would put the head between your oxters and the feet up in the air and a rope to hold them. Sometimes you would have two live sheep, one on your back with the legs tied, and one on your front, and a rope over your shoulder. In places where it was steep some folk would put their heads up to their legs and make a kind of bundle and you would have one arm free, or maybe two if you were in a bad place. It was kind of tricky. You didn't have much time to admire the view! You were keeping your eye on the sheep and scrambling away in the rocks and trying to take care of yourself and no bothering about views! It was a hard

day's work. And you had to pay the Factor for your sheep, whatever you caught, they were counted. If you went together, suppose you caught a sheep, you wouldn't get it to yourself; it would be brought back to St. Kilda, it would have to be skinned and cut. There would be some poor and some good and they used to cut them and share them out and then cast lots for them. One person wouldn't get all the skinny ones. The Factor didn't mind how many you took so long as you paid for them, but they were not easy to get. If you took too many you would soon be told! You would be lucky if you got half a dozen to a dozen in a day, and that would be with half a dozen folk trying to catch the sheep. The sheep we killed we had to salt that meat for the winter.

Fishing and Whaling

We sometimes went into the caves to fish, you would get a good few bream in there. Some of the caves were a quarter of a mile long, the birds were all about the mouth of the caves, but never far in. In some of them you would get frightened – it gets dark as you go along, the sea is coming in, washing in, there's a movement, it doesn't matter how calm it is – it's very eerie. If you were to go in on a day when there was a swell outside it wouldn't be safe to go far in then, the sea would be going in and dashing against the sides and maybe coming back at you. There were seals about, especially round about Boreray, not in the caves but lying on the rocks outside, or popping their heads up out of the water if you disturbed them. We would see the young seal calves on the rocks too, then once they were away you'd see them popping out.

When we were fishing with the long lines we would use the caves all round the island, we might be round the back of the island or away over to Boreray or beyond. It was ling you would mostly go for with the long lines baited with conger eel. We used to set the lines and leave them until daybreak. If it was a good night you would stay on the end of the line; you had one of those wool bags for putting a lot of wool in – they were awful good, you would get in and put it over you in the bottom of the boat and you would stay there, it didn't matter if it was cold as long as it was dry. If it was a wet night, we used to come with the boat into one of the caves at night and you were dry and sheltered there and then you would be out in the morning to lift your lines. I am not saying that they were that religious but this was the way there too, before you went out of the cave you would have a worship and then you would go out to lift the lines. Then you would return to the main island, take the fish ashore, split it and clean it, take the big bones out of it and salt it and put it out on the stones to dry in the sun. Oh, it used to be lovely fish right enough. Then you would make it up in them days into 1 cwt (50kg) packets and sent it to Glasgow, to Alex Ferguson the Merchant – he was taking it all and then he would be giving you groceries or anything you were wanting.

Whale in Village Bay, Lachlan on the fin, the boat is 22ft long. L. MacDonald Collection.

The whalers, Norwegians, used to come in at any time, they had a base in Harris. When they started coming here at first there were a lot of whales round about the islands. They used to come round the islands and kill the whales, huge big whales, then they would come in with their catch of one or two whales and tie them on to the buoy in the bay. When they had been lying there for two days or so the whale came up like a huge great balloon – if it burst the smell was terrible – the stink was terrible – but usually they took them away. Then they would go out and see if they could get more, if they were lucky they would have four attached to the buoy and they would go out and get a couple more. Then they would come in, pick up the ones they had there and go with them to Tarbert in Harris. Many a time I have seen them towing six back to Harris. That's the way we got so familiar with the Harris folk, you would get across with the whalers and they wouldn't charge you anything; then you would be able to pick one of them coming back – that is if they were kind hearted! They would come straight back into the bay, they would drop you and then they would be off in search of whales round the islands. Even when they were coming from Harris to the landing, if they were to meet a whale they would harpoon it. They were going out of their way, doing a good turn for us. We were well off then, at that time, right enough. The other time we were well off was when the 1914 war was on when the boats were coming in, warships and destroyers at first, later trawlers with guns.

The Island of Dun

Sometimes we would go to the Dun for birds – for puffins – the Dun is full of puffins. It wasn't very often, it was more to look after the sheep. We didn't grow crops there but there are lazy beds there, more than on St. Kilda, there were a few near the Factor's House and the Manse wall. We would go over by boat to Dun. Or when the tide was out you could jump from one rock to another in Dun passage, it's easy enough. Then there is the chain hanging down and you would get onto the

Oiseval from Dun Passage.

end of the chain and pull yourself up. To catch the puffins I would take a dog with me and the dog would point out the hole where the puffin was. You would put your arm in and reach him and bring him out and just draw his neck. You had a belt round you and you put his neck in and you collected them until you had plenty. I liked the puffin. Anytime you were feeling hungry, instead of putting a pot on the nice peat fire, the puffin was cleaned and split open and you would just put it standing propped up by the fire on a brick or a stone. If you put it too close it would get blackened and he burnt, it wouldn't take long to cook, just slowly – it would be lovely – that's if you were wanting a wee snack!

Later in the season, round about October, when the grass stops growing and gets scarcer we would take the lambs over by boat and put them on the Dun. Before we took them over we sometimes put them in some of the enclosures above the Manse, but everyone of them had an owner and you couldn't go on another man's croft.

Boreray for the week

We would go over to Boreray for a week or so to clip the sheep and to take the wool. It was no bother for us to go over there in the boat, most of it would be rowing, but if the wind was favourable we would put up the sail. We stayed in the little stone houses, you had your bed at one end and the cooking place at the other with a wee chimney. There may be four of you, you all shared there too – say you were all related you would go in your own house; there would be three or four houses. We had our own fire and we cut our own peats when we were there and put them in the cleit ready for the next year when we would go over again. The puffins would make an awful mess of the houses, but that's the way we were working then. We would take little sticks for kindling the fires and straw for bedding. You'd be lying on straw and you'd have a blanket put over you. You would be quite warm in those houses – there would be some dampness in them when you first went over there. That was no bother in them days. The cleit village was for putting your turfs in, the peats. You would only be living there for the

The wild sheep on Boreray. T. A. Quine.

130

season. I haven't heard of anyone living there all the year round.

We went over to clip the sheep and to take the wool, and to mark the lambs. We never looked after them. They were the real breed when we were there. Everyone had his own sheep and they were all marked. It was a job, when you got over there you would go round first and spot the lamb to your own sheep. Then they were rounded up. It was an awful job to catch them. There wasn't a proper fank on Boreray, you had to corner them against the cliff and maybe you would have a wee bit of fencing and a little bit of trawl to keep them together and close so that they wouldn't run their way out. They were cornered into a rock, the best place we could get. It was a job to get the lamb of your own sheep when they were in a heap, when all the lambs were in one – Oh aye! After you had marked them you would be letting them out and you maintained it was your lamb that you had and you let it away with your sheep. Then when you let her out the lamb wouldn't follow, and she would be coming back looking for her own lamb! Then the noise would start! The lamb would start applying to his mother, and the mother would be 'maying' away and one of the other fellows would say, "Oh, that's her lamb, now." Then you would make a bee-line to get hold of him – you would put a mark in his ears – then you would be alright – you'd got it. Maybe you'd go back again and get the other lamb and put the right mark on it. Many a time there would be a few words too, "You need to watch what you're doing!" – and such like!

There was one year, this fellow when we went over from the main island of St. Kilda to Boreray, took his food and his clothes and his stuff, his straw bedding. I don't know how it happened to be but – here was a mouse! Well they chased this mouse and it went into one of these cleits and they lost it. They knocked down this cleit until they got it! From this day, I don't believe there is a mouse on that island!

Map – Showing method of rounding up the sheep on Hirta into temporary fanks.

Rounding up the Sheep on Hirta

From the Cambir and the Great Glen.

Our route to Gleann Mor was to leave the Main Street by No. 16 and cross the river and go up to the Head Dyke – the path then followed the present road. There would be half a dozen of us working together to round up the sheep for the clipping time and the marking of the lambs. My friend was Neil Ferguson, the younger one, we were great pals, and one of the MacKinnons went with us. We would collect them in groups, bringing them from the Cambir and the Great Glen to Gob na h-Airde, to a sheep fank there. There's a slope down there and a rock up against it which the sheep couldn't climb. Where the sheep might climb we put up bits of iron and sticks, and used some netting from the fishing trawlers to make the fank.

From Carn Mor, Ruaival, Conachair and Oiseval.

We used to dip the sheep once a year. Before collecting them we made a temporary fank with trawl netting at the back of the Village. Above the cemetery there was the croft, then through the wall – to the west of the Tobar Childa – the fank was there. We used the water from the Tobar Childa – this had to be kept clean – and we had a portable wooden dip, like a large wooden box, tarred to keep the water in. It had a ramp inside with wooden ridges for the sheep to walk up and

View of the Village from the slopes of Conachair. A,B,C: marks the temporary sheep fank, G: Graveyard, H: Bull House, HD: Head Dyke, MH: Medieval House.

a holding pen at the top for the sheep to wait for about five minutes while the dip dripped back into the pool – nothing was wasted. The dip would come from Glasgow, brought out on the 'Hebrides'. The wooden dipper was kept there all the year round.

When the fank was up we went to collect the sheep from Carn Mor and Ruaival as well as Conachair and Oiseval. Sometimes if you were going for the sheep they were difficult to get out from the rocks; if you were to frighten them too much they would run for shelter into the rock and Och! You would have an awful job to get them out and maybe you would have to get someone else to help you. You'd get a rope round you to help you to take them out – there may be just one or two that would go like that. As long as you were to take it easy and you no start chasing them with a dog, they were trained and they would come out by themselves. Even throwing a stone would frighten them and put them away. You would take them on until you would get them out near Ruaival and then you were alright – you could bring them to the fank at the back of the Village.

Then we would gather them from the other side, from Conachair and Oiseval. They would be away in the rocks there too, and you had to get them out and bring them right round Oiseval and then into the same fank – that was the one main fank there for shearing and for dipping. Once in the fank, it was closed up. Inside the men would be catching the sheep one at a time and carrying them to the man at the dipper. He would grab hold of them and heave them over the side into the dip – it was really hard work and we would take it in turns. He would drop the sheep in on its back to get it completely covered. The sheep would quickly turn over – sometimes we had to help it – it would walk up the ramp with the help of the wooden ridges through a narrow gap into the holding area. Here the sheep, up to about a half a dozen, would wait for about five minutes to let the water and the dip run back off

them into the main dipping pool – the dip was expensive. After about five minutes they were let out through a gate into the fank. They would be kept within the fank until they were united with their lambs and all the sheep were dipped. Then the fence was taken down and the sheep usually made their own way back to Ruaival and Carn Mor – finding their own way home. That's how we did it on St. Kilda. A couple of policemen used to come there to see that they were dipped. The sheep were that wild they couldn't do anything about it if you missed some. They would quite enjoy being on the island for a week or so – a grand holiday. The rules and regulations were that there had to be a policeman and he had to sign the papers.

If there was just one sheep you had missed, suppose you were up on Carn Mor, you might catch it with the dog and get it out by Bearradh na cloiche moire (the Lover's Stone), but you would have to be on the Glen side where there would be plenty of chance for you to catch it. Sometimes in the Carn Mor you think you might be able to catch it with a dog, but it was very seldom you would manage it. You would clip the odd one there with a pen-knife and bring back the fleece, you'd leave the sheep there. If it was a sheep with a lamb you would try to get hold of the lamb, and put a mark in his ears. Once you had caught the mother it wasn't difficult to get the lamb. The lamb would come to her if you kept the mother tied there a bit – you would catch her with a dog.

The fleece you would bring back home and leave it until you had a lot and then you would wash them and dry them. You would leave them like that until the winter came.

During the summer there were some places which we kept the sheep out. We kept them from Carn Mor by putting a fence up at the top of the ridge in the dip between Claigeann an Tigh Faire and the steep rocks going up to Mullach Bi. There is also an earth dyke up on Uachdarachd to keep the sheep from going down onto the slopes of Conachair. This was to stop the sheep from disturbing and spoiling the nesting birds.

Cleitean and Corn

Cleitean – Uses and Building

Some of the cleits were for hay and some were for peat. The ones inside the Head Dyke were for hay off the croft. We also carried the hay and put it in those cleits near the wall on Oiseval, it would be dry in there. There's one cleit out on the point of Aird Uachdarachd, below the summit of Conachair (high above Mina Stac). This was one of our own cleits. There's a green bit there, we used to go out and cut the grass. If you were cutting grass in the Village you would use a scythe, but on the hill you would use a hook (= sickle).

Medieval House with the Bee-hive Annexe.

134

For grass anyone could go anywhere. If you were lucky you would carry it in a canvas or a rope - you would take it up to the cleit. What you couldn't take home you put in that cleit, you would go and collect it in the wnter when you had your beasts down on the croft, to feed them and to keep them going. In my day not many bothered to cut grass away from the Village, but if you had several beasts you would need to.

Up away on the hills the cleits were built for peat, wherever it was handy. One of the ones I built, I saw it there in the photograph, it was between Mullach Mor and Mullach Conachair. That was for the peat, you had your own bit of ground up there, and you cut your peat any time when there was good weather in May or later. You would leave it there until it was dry and then you would put it into the cleits. There on the top of the hill you would get deep peat, a black peat that would be like coal, you would put that in. Then in the winter time you would take it home just as you were needing it. The cleits on Oiseval were for turf - everyone had seveal cleits there. The row of cleits to the Gap - everyone had his own cleits for turf - everyone knew which was his - you knew and trusted everyone else. In Gleann Mor we used to cut peat down by the river - on the other side - it was the real McCoy down there. We would cut it, stack it to dry and then we brought it up to the row of cleits at the head of the Glen - where the path leads down. Beyond the Lover's Stone on the high ground every family had a cleit here for peats - you left them there and collected them when you needed them in the winter. Everyone had his own hag and trusted everyone else. You would never go on anyone else's - they were very good folk - they would never steal from one another.

Within the Head Dyke - the House of Fairies (the Earth-house) was not used in my day. The Medieval House with the Beehive annexe was just used for hay in my day - we didn't have a name for it - we just looked on it as a cleit. It would belong to the croft house - within the Head Dyke. The croft extended above the Head Dyke so that the enclosures and cleits belonged to the croft below.

When you were going to build a cleit - mostly they were built from old ones - first of all you would gather the stones wherever you build it, then your friends would come and give you a hand. There were no proper foundations of cement or gravel, just soil raked and levelled. You would start the foundation, the lower layers, and as you were building it, the one stone had to catch on the other stone to secure it against the wind. As you were building it up you were taking it in, drawing it in until the top would come as narrow as 2-3 feet. Then you would get some biggish flat stones, about 6 feet in length and put them right across. Then you would put straw on the top, soil and rubble, then you would cut turf and put that on top to keep it dry, keeping it to a slope so that the water would run off.

Corn

Cutting the Corn. When it comes to cutting the corn you do it with the scythe and bundle it into sheaves and stick it up until it is dry. The barley grew higher - you would pull it up by the roots - and you put a bit of string round near the top and set it up to dry off. Then you would cut off the heads and put them into the byre. The stalks you kept in the byre or stored up outside in the garden until you required them for thatching the byres - the old houses. When the corn is dry enough you would take it into the garden at the back of the house and put it up in stacks there for the winter. As you need it you take it in, maybe a stack at a time and put it into the byre. Then you can thresh the corn off it at any time - it doesn't matter if it is wet outside or no. You keep the seed and give the rest to the cattle to eat.

For threshing we had a stick, like the handle of a brush, and a big thick rope, maybe 10 inches long, with a piece of leather attached to the handle. This was so that when you were threshing you weren't hitting the corn with something hard. You would do this in the byre on the hard earth floor, and the cattle would be up at the other end. If it was a good day you could do it outside and thresh it there so that you could get the corn and the other stuff would be away with the wind. The barley is awful bad for sticking in you when you're threshing – like thistles. We would keep the rest for thatching, and we would get the netting from the trawlers and put that over the thatch and it would do for a year and keep like that.

The Missionary had a cow and what we would call a "follower", a calf, and he would be getting milk to keep him going. If the cow would be dry then he would get milk from the crofters – he would go down the village and they would give it to him. His cow was at the far end of the Glebe beyond the Store – the MacKinnons and the Camerons had cows on there. They didn't take their cow over to Gleann Mor for the summer. They didn't have any sheep. At this near end of the Glebe was what he kept for hay, and he would cut it and store it up in some of the cleits there. The crofters sometimes used to cut his hay for him, it was just like everything else, the one would be helping the other. If he was a youngish Missionary he was working it just the same as we were ourselves. He had a good byre at the back of the Manse.

Fulmar Harvest

If it was a good day you would go to the Parliament and if it was the time for killing the fulmars they would just decide that they were going to the rocks. Everyone on the island would have their sections of cliff to go on to kill the fulmars. They divided the cliffs by lots and you would have shares all over the island. There may be three or four of you going together but you wouldn't dare to go off your part of the rocks. There's one point when you're at the top of the Cambir and looking down below you, we called it "Soosh-shla" (Gaelic – Suisle), it's full of fulmars. We used to kill them and carry them out of there on our backs. It was a long way to carry them back home, but it was good. Conachair was good, it was steep but you were going down. Och, I was quite often down there and at Bearradh na h-Eige (the Cliff or Ridge of the Gap) – there are a few fulmars there too – that was good, and Oiseval too. All these places we had names for but I am forgetting, and you had your share on Conachair and on the Cambir and all over. We used to change them by casting lots every year or every second year. Sometimes you would be near home and sometimes far away from home.

You would be away down on the cliff on a rope and the other fellow was up at the top and you were going along killing the young fulmars. You had to catch them and you had no to pass any time. Before they spit the oil you had to get hold of them and kill them – just give a wee shake and the neck would be broken. Maybe you would have 50 or 60 and sometimes if you hadn't plenty of rope you would be swinging them over your shoulder and climbing up on the rope – the other fellow was above – you would climb up so far. Then he would draw up the slack and you would climb up. At some other times if it was a very steep place you would make a bundle of 20 or 30 and he would lower down another rope, you would tie it on and he would pull it up. If it was a steep place it was easier to pull up – there wasn't any difficulty where they would catch on the rocks. When we had them at the top of the rocks, maybe there would be 100 or so, and if there was an oldish man there he would get hold of them and squeeze the oil into a drum. Or you might do it yourself; you would squeeze the clear oil out and when you would see that the oil was getting a little bit dirty you would scoop the dirt somewhere out onto the ground – you would just put the pure oil into the drum. Maybe you wouldn't carry it down the same day, you would come back another day and bring it back home. In the old days they used to sell this oil and put it to the Factor to pay the rent, and the feathers they used to keep to give to him. But in my days we never bothered much about that – we put the feathers away but it was more making the tweed and sending the fish. They used the oil in the lamp, the cruisgean, I used it myself with fulmar oil – you would hang it on a nail in the byre. It was there and you just had to put a match to it when you were going to milk the cows.

That was going on for days and you would come home again at night and pluck them and clean them. There was a barrel there and you salted them – put them in a pickle – the ones you were going to keep for the winter. They were awful nice to eat when they were killed fresh; you put them in the frying pan and they would be nice and tender, just like roast pork. On St. Kilda they liked the fulmar more than anything else. They also liked the puffin and the guillemot too, but we never salted them – they were very nice tasted fresh. The puffin, it was great for making soup – puffin soup, or roasted by the fire, it tasted beautiful.

The young fulmar you don't need to singe, they were quite bare when you had plucked them. The old ones, when you had plucked them, you would need to singe them. The young ones are very tasty. The best method for me to cook one would be in the frying pan and I would let it fry slowly in its own fat – they're lovely, smashing! At the St. Kilda Club dinner we had duckling and it was lovely but I was saying to them, "Why don't you take some young fulmars with you from St. Kilda – I'm sure you could put them in the freezer and keep them?!" I was just joking – we hadn't a freezer in those days on St. Kilda right enough! The Army have the freezers there now.

On the whole, not many lost their lives falling on the cliffs. There were two, they were together in the cliff killing the young fulmars, away down on the rocks on the Mulloch Mor, the two of them were killed. I expect the ropes were between them and they were not careful enough – it was not a bad place. They must have been walking and killing the birds, and one would slip and he pulled the other. A good while after they got the body of one of them, it was jammed in the rock; the rock would be sharp and it would cut the rope, and the other body went into the sea. One of them was John MacDonald and the other one was Ewen Gillies, that's his daughter, Mary Anne Gillies, her mother comes from Harris. Some of the St. Kildans would go for wives to Harris or somewhere else.

Holiday – 1927

(It was strange that Gladstone recorded in his diary for Monday July 25th 1927 that Lachlan MacDonald was one of three St. Kildans leaving the island on the "Dunara Castle". It was, in fact, the one and only time Lachlan left the island for a holiday).

It was the only time I was off the island, I was going to stay with my brother, Angus, in Glasgow for two weeks. I was not bothered by trams or trains or cars – we had seen pictures of them. The thing that frightened me out of my life was a fellow on a bicycle. When we pulled in at Tobermoray I was standing on the quay when this fellow comes down the hill on his bicycle – flying down the hill and suddenly turned off the road and onto the quay – he suddenly stops – just by me! I couldn't understand how he was able to stand upright on two wheels! When I came to ride a bicycle I found it took me weeks to learn. I couldn't get over that fellow on his bicycle!

It was my brothers who took me out to Glasgow, I enjoyed being with them and being taken round in buses, I thought it was great there. Och, I didn't settle after I got back to St. Kilda.

St. Kilda Wren

The wee wren, he was nice, we always tried to save them. It was great seeing him going from one stone to another and going into the holes in the cleits. They nested in the dyke and in the holes in the cleits. If you would see the nest you wouldn't disturb it, you would just leave it there. They were all over the place, away over to the Carn Mor you would hear them singing from one rock or the cleits. In the Carn Mor they were down there, early in the morning and during the day they would be singing, especially when they were mating, the one singing to the other. It's a funny thing now, there on St. Kilda you would hardly see them during the winter, just the odd one, but they must have been there, they wouldn't be able to fly to anywhere else. It is great – nature – when you think about it there on St. Kilda when you would see all the birds coming and they would be there for the summer, and when the summer was coming to the end they would all be disappearing, and then they would all be away!

WINTER-TIME
On the Croft, Bull and the Bull-House, Saw-Dock, Making the Tweed, St. Kilda Mouse, Visiting Trawlers
On the Croft

You were as busy in the winter-time as you were in the summer-time. When the winter comes and the short days, as long as it was daylight you would be working among your beasts, bringing down the hay from the cleits on the hills and taking the peats home for the winter. Before the beasts could be let onto the croft, everything had to be cleared. Sometimes other folk would be complaining that you hadn't got your tatties (potatoes) lifted and the cows would be spoiling them and eating them. So you had to wait until everything was inside. When the potatoes were lifted and the oats and barley were all in, the gates in the Head Dyke were opened and the sheep and cattle were let into the crofts and they were all wintering there until the grass started to grow on the hillside. Then they were put outside the dyke again and the place was closed up. The milking cows we put into the byres round about October, depending on the weather, once they were in they would stay in until the weather was getting better. If you had any other beasts you would have them out on the crofts but you would take them into the byre in a bad winter.

For food there was the hay off the croft in the cleits and on the hill. In the garden at the back of the house you had the corn in stacks for the winter. As you needed it you would take it in, put it in the byre, and then thresh the corn off it anytime; you would keep the seed and give the rest to the cattle to eat. In the byre some had the paraffin lantern, others had the cruisgean hanging – the oval oil lamp with a point on it – you would use the oil from the fulmar. It's great but it's a wee bit smoky to have in the house, but in the byre it was quite alright. It gives a good light but it all depends on the wick – if it's thick it will give you more light. The habit was, with an oldish person, in the winter-time when you go out in the byre to feed the beasts, when you feed them he would get down on his knees and put up a prayer. Do you know this, it was lovely if you were outside and listened to the prayer – it was all in Gaelic.

We used to put most of the hoggs on the Dun for the winter. Everyone had a share over there – we would have to pay the Factor for each one. We also put a few on Stac Langa – below the Gap. In good weather we would go round in the boat with twelve or so sheep. In bad weather we lowered them down on a rope. One man was at the top and one was lowered down first on a rope to untie the sheep when they reached the bottom. There was some good grass down there to the left as you look down from the Gap – we called it Calanguin (phonetic).

Bull and the Bull-House

On St. Kilda we had a red Highland bull with good horns. It would have come across in the "Hebrides". To get him ashore you tied a rope around the roots of its horns, when the side of the boat was lowered he would be pushed out into the water and towed by the rowing boat as he swam to the island. It was not a pleasant introduction to St. Kilda. The bull was kept out grazing with the cattle but in the winter-time we had a place for him outside the Head Dyke. The bull-house was bigger than the ordinary cleit, built higher, its roof wasn't turf but wood and straw, the same as the old byres in the olden days (it is in fact the pre 1834 house near the Tobar Childa, DAQ). There may be a bit of the roof, some bits of wood lying about there now. I should imagine the dung we cleaned out and just threw outside in a heap would still be there. The crofters would feed him for a fortnight each, doing the round. We were cutting the hay and every crofter had to put so much to feed the bull in the winter. There wasn't a weighing machine in St. Kilda so you used a long piece of rope and you put the hay in a bundle; with this rope you measured it so that it was the same size both ways. When the next fellow put his hay in he used the same measure – it was the same for the sixteen crofters. They never quarrelled about it! My nephew Donald Gillies remembers it, after his father died, he remembers being told by his grandfather, Finlay Gillies, to go and feed the bull. Finlay would be at the back of the house and he would be watching Donald feeding the bull outside the bull-house.

Saw-Dock

Just above the path from the Store to the Village, about 25 yards up from the Store, before you get to the first cleit, on the side of the hill was a saw-dock or saw-pit. It had two sides like walls built into the hillside, but you could walk into it, maybe 6 feet or more in height. One man would stand at the top and one below with a huge big long saw between them and you worked it up

Bull House, a pre-1834 House.

Saw Dock near the Store.

and down. You made planks of whatever size you wanted out of the logs. I was only young at the time but I mind of them doing it. You could use drift wood if a boat had been sunk and it came in. Otherwise you could buy the logs, it was cheaper in bulk. If you had it already cut it would be a lot dearer. So they did it that way so that they could do a bit of joinery themselves. The boats were coming out from Glasgow in the summer, the "Hebrides" and the "Dunara Castle", anything you ordered they would pick up and bring it for you.

Making the Tweed

After clipping the sheep in the summer you would bring the fleece back home, you would leave it until you had a lot then you would wash them and dry them. They were like that until the winter came. We did a lot of dyeing the wool, taking the crotal (lichens) off the stones. You had an old spoon or a bit of tin and you had an apron on you, you would scrape the crotal into your apron until you had a big bag full of it. You would collect the grey ones, not the yellow, but they were a different colour when you had boiled them. You boiled it up in water, some of the folks used a docken as well and it would keep the dye better – then the dye wouldn't come out, it would make it fast. The same with the indigo blue they used to put a docken or two in it. You would use the roots of the docken, not the leaves, take the soil off, boil it up and that would make it fast. The grey crotal would turn the wool a darkish red and then we mixed white with that and made colours of it – all the colours I cannot remember. The soot in the chimney made a good colour too, put that in and boil it and dry it. It came out not black, but brownish – they're great in Harris for all that, we weren't doing much of it ourselves. They had great ideas in the olden days, the things they used to do. There was nothing going to waste on St. Kilda!

Then you would be teasing that wool and spinning it. We used to make the warp white and it was made a bit stronger for the loom. The other ones you mixed whatever colours you were wanting – black or blue or whatever. You would go with your friends, from one house to the other. If you would go to his, he would come back to you again – it was a big night – the carding and the mixing of the wool. While you were in other people's houses you were sitting there on a chair and you got a pair of cards there for mixing the wool and you'd be talking away. You'd be chatting away and sometimes making fun, jokes but mostly talking about what you were doing through the day, and what the sheep were doing, the other fellow would ask you if you had seen his sheep that had gone missing and if they were alright. There would be no sing song there in my day, we had not a word of music, no fiddles and no instruments, but they were great nights. You had two or three nights working at that, you would start in the winter time it would be dark round about 5 o'clock when you would have your tea, or sometimes your dinner and you would be there all night, until midnight or one or two in the morning, when you would be getting another dinner! It was meat and potatoes boiled in a biggish pot and one person would be cutting the meat in chunks at the end of the table. You would be having a good feed. Then you would go home in the early hours of the morning, and there would be girls you would be giving a hand to, maybe you would see one to her home first and then you would go to your own home.

When all the carding and the mixing of the wool was done you made the thread – you were spinning the wool. You would set up the loom, you would bring it in from the byre, after the New Year, sometimes before and you would be working at that for weeks. While you were working at the loom, the spinning wheel and the carding would be going on at the same time too. Odd time jobs you'd be doing too, and the women were working like the men, bringing down the peats, and you had to be looking after your beasts when you were doing the carding and the weaving as well.

After the weaving they had two or three days for waulking the tweed. In my day we didn't bother to waulk it, we washed it and cleaned it – that was hard work. If we were making blankets for ourselves we would waulk it, but not the tweed they were selling unless they were making a suit or some tweed for somebody special. In the old days, at the waulking, they would first be trampling on it, then they washed it in a tub and then they had a big long washboard so that half a dozen could sit on one side and half a dozen on the other. It all depended how many you had, but there needed to be four or an equal number and they would go at it. It was great how thick it would get – they would have ribs on the board and you were rubbing it backwards and forwards, the one to the other, but it was a dirty job. When you were hammering away there would be splats on your face and you had soapy water over everything. Sometimes they would have a kind of a waulking song. It was a big day – that day!

After waulking you would wash it. You would take it to the burn and you would be trampling it out until it was perfectly clean. In those days they had a stick like a bat and they would be hammering it to get all the soapy water out of it and some would be trampling it in the pool. After you'd washed it you spread it out on the walls to dry – on the dyke, there was no hanging it on the clothes line, it was quite a good job – hard work. When you had finished with the loom it was put away in the byre until next season. That's the way you had to get a living on St. Kilda.

Some of the tweed we sold to the visitors, but most of it we sold through Alexander Ferguson, he was from St. Kilda and was a tweed merchant in Glasgow. During the war we got a very good price from the Navy people who came, a high price, much better than ever before. Some St. Kildans were working at the looms night and day to sell all they could to get money. But those who sold to Alex Ferguson were able to get what money could not buy – white flour and sugar! How he got it I don't know. Others could only get black flour with their money!

St. Kilda Mouse

The St. Kilda Mouse, we tried to get rid of him more than feed him. He used to do an awful lot of damage especially if he got into the house. He would get in among the oatmeal – he would make a hole in the pack and spoil it. It was not what he would eat but the mess he would make. Oh, we would chase him alright! We had a wooden trap with a spring and we put oatmeal on the four holes and the spring would get him. We never thought of poisoning them then, there was no such thing. In them days there were a lot of them about, mostly in the grass, but they would get into the house. There was the home mice and the field mice.

Visiting Trawlers

We'd often see trawlers in the bay in the winter-time, not so often in the summer-time – they would be outside. Some would be from Fleetwood and some from Aberdeen. The Aberdeen drifters fished with the long lines for ling, halibut and anything. We were fishing with the long lines too, with the boat. We used to get halibut but we didn't care for them much, we never salted them, we would only eat what was fresh. If we were lucky and we had a couple of halibut or a big one, if the drifters were in they would be glad to get it. If he had ling he would give us a few ling instead of the halibut – swap them like that.

A skipper from Aberdeen, Donald Craig was very good to us taking mails and bringing provisions for us. This day Rachel MacCrimmon was giving him a wee bit of a telling off for going away and working on the

Rachel MacCrimmon's 1834 House near the Factor's House.

Sabbath Day. As he was passing her home she knew perfectly well that he was going to fish, she would say, "Well, where are you going today?" And he would say, "Well, you mind that this is the Sabbath Day." She would lay on that he should not be working today and then she would say, "And where would your soul be today. May the Lord be with you. Above all, mind your Saviour."

One winter night there was an awful gale and it was misty and there were several trawlers sheltering in Glen Bay. This fellow comes in, he was a great friend of ours from Fleetwood, he used to take the mails to the island and the groceries we wanted. I think what was the matter, he knew the place that well, he just came in right passed the other trawlers, right into the bay, and he went into this cave, Geo nan Ron, Seal's Cave, and he sank there. It's awful deep – it shows you the depth there, it was quite a big size of trawler too, and you would only see the top of one mast at low tide. Eight of the fishermen were lost. You could jump onto the rock there, but it must all have happened so quickly that they didn't know where they were. It was a sad tragedy day, right enough.

A few times we were out in the boat and a storm got up, night came and with a south wind we couldn't get into the bay and we had to go into a cave at the back of the island. Many a fright we got and the wives wondering where we were or when we were coming. They couldn't sleep at night and they couldn't go to bed, wondering what had happened and waiting to see if the wind changed.

THE EVACUATION

Life had become pretty well impossible, it was just the one helping the other all the time. They were trying to get off the island before 1930, I was told. A few years before there was the 'flu – there was a few who died, some of them were up in years right enough, but that put the finishing touch – the islanders were trying to get off. The last winter was bad right enough on St. Kilda. Then Mary Gillies was ill, they took her to Glasgow and she died there. The island was left to only

Ewen (Lachlan's brother) with Nurse Barclay. L. MacDonald Collection.

a few who could do normal hard work and working the boats. To my knowledge it was the Mackinnons that started it. They were a big family, ten or eleven of them, and it was just with a struggle that he was bringing them up, it was always difficult to make a living on the island, so he thought that he would get away, which was a good thing – so I was thinking myself with a few more. Well, he was talking to Nurse Barclay, about it. We decided, with the Nurse and the Missionary, Mr. Munro, that we would get clear of the island, they were doing the writing to the Government and putting the finishing touches to it. The older people agreed to leave but when the case came to the push and they knew they were going, well, they would rather stay, but they had signed the petition and what was the good of them staying anyhow; there would need to be some young ones there to do the jobs and to help, and they couldn't do it, especially the widows and the old folk. Ah, I think it was God's blessing the day we left, for me anyhow, I have no regrets I left the island.

They were not taking it to heart at first, but when it came to be the desperate way, then some would rather be the way they were. The sheep had to be rounded up and the cattle sold. They took two or three shepherds out there and their dogs, we didn't use the roundsmen, the whole lot of us would go out to round up the sheep. It was a help, but the sheep were that wild the way we trained them, we knew our own sheep and you had your dog trained to catch one sheep at a time. Our dogs were no use for rounding up the sheep the way the shepherd does here on the mainland and bring them back. So the shepherds were not getting on very well, they were a help right enough, but the sheep were here and there, and scattered round about. It was a bit of a job right enough. We brought them down to the crofts and on the Manse, we fenced them in and kept them there to such a time as the boats came in and took them out. They took them to the auction mart in Oban. Some died, it wasn't very good ground for them. Och,

The Evacuation – Lachlan on the Harebell. L. MacDonald Collection.

aye, it was wonderful how we got on, packing everything up and carrying it on your back to the boat. All the stores and cattle and sheep came off in the "Hebrides" and the "Dunara Castle".

All the St. Kildans came off on the "Harebell", the Fisheries Protection Vessel. The day we left – it was a good day with a smooth crossing. There's a photograph on the Harebell after leaving St. Kilda, there's my mother and me there – wondering where I was coming to and how things were going to be. It turned out not too bad anyhow. We came into the Sound of Mull, but we had to be shifted into a smaller boat, the "Princess Louise" that took us from the "Harebell" to Lochaline pier.

I don't suppose ever before or ever after there was as much crowd on Lochaline pier! Och, there was hundreds of them and the reporters and all that, and there was two taxis there at the time. We got quite a good reception. At Savary they had put the house in good order and they had the fire ready for us. It turned out to be for the best.

POST EVACUATION – New Home, New Jobs, New Partner, Postscript.

A New Home

Archie Hendry was next door to us but, oh, what was in the papers about the St. Kildans! He took it in and believed it. It was himself that was telling me this story. The shepherds would go to some place miles away, it was the clipping time and they wouldn't normally come in that night. He made sure he would come back that night we came off the boat and he bought locks, and put locks on all the outside sheds. It was like that for maybe a few weeks. We got on talking and so forth – it was great the way folk believed the way they had it in the papers. So he wasn't long to find out that we weren't thieves – he took off all the locks off the doors – you see, we hadn't a lock on anything back on St. Kilda, and he did just the same and took all the locks off all the doors. I must say they were very good neighbours, he was a shepherd. The Forestry bought the ground from the owners and the Forestry kept the sheep for a good whiley and he was

the shepherd. One of his sons, Sammy, was shepherd, (father was getting up in years in the wartime), he came home to shepherd for his father. They were a great family and very good right enough. The MacDonald family were all in one house, there was my mother, my brother Ewan and me, my sister Catharine, her husband, Neil Gillies, had died before the evacuation, with her two boys Donald and Ewen. Finlay Gillies, the boy's grandfather came in too. He wasn't feeling very happy sometimes and then he went away to Tiree to his sister there. He was coming backward and forward. At the hinter end the MacKinnons left and went to the Black Isle, he went and stayed with them, he was there when he died.

New Jobs

At first I was working for the Forestry in the nursery at Savary with my brother and some other St. Kildans. The trees have been cut down there again and the place is wide open. I was there for 15 years and left at the end of the war in 1945. During the War I joined the Home Guard at first, but it was unpaid, so I decided to be a despatch rider, on a motor bike and joined the Royal Observor Corps, we were paid then!

By this time Ewen had died in 1937 of a poisoned foot, and my mother had died in 1943, and my sister and the two boys were there. I didn't know what to do. So I decided to leave and landed down in Dundee and worked in the sawmills there. I wasn't very happy there because of the noise from a whole lot of saws. A builder from Forfar, gave me a job as a driver. In the past I drove a motorbike, but I never drove a car or a lorry. He told me his nephew would go with me and tell me what to do. So he took me over to the garage to his nephew and he said, "There's the lorry, get it out of the garage." I said, "Do you want me to knock the garage and everything down?" Well, he jumped in beside me and he told me what to do, but the sweat for

Lachlan and Ewen hoeing in the Forestry Nursery at Morvern. L. MacDonald Collection.

no reason was pouring off me and I felt terrible. He gave me a hand, we loaded the lorry and off we went to Laurencekirk. I hadn't a clue, I hadn't a map or anything, but we got there. Then I had to take the men home. I was saying to myself, "you boys, if you knew the guy that was at the wheel – oh, my!" That was my first day and my worst day! I had some experiences right enough. The boss was very good to me, and to this day his daughter's still living and comes up to see me. They were very friendly. I was two or three years in the building work.

Then I came back to Fort William and tried to get a job. Eventually, I got one in a shop in Fort William, so that was alright. Then this job was advertised for the Forestry.

A New Partner – Nancy Cameron

I first met Nancy back around 1935, I was living at Savary at the time and Nancy and her family had their holidays in the area and we met at Church and local

happenings. Nancy's sister Isobel married Donald Gillies (Lachlan's nephew) on 28th March 1952 in Glasgow in her home Church and then returned to Savary. Nancy used to go to Lochaline on visits to see her cousins and friends. I met up with her again.

We were married in Glasgow on 29th April 1955 in the John Knox Church in the Gorbals by the Rev. John MacKay. He was a native of Carloway on Lewis and came to take Communion on St. Kilda. He was in Portree on Skye before going to Glasgow. He also officiated at the last wedding on St. Kilda between Neil Ferguson junior and Mary Annie MacQueen. It was just about the time I was leaving school that he first came to St. Kilda. There was the famous well, the Well of Virtues, and the Minister was keen to go there for a walk over the hill. I was put with him. As we came back at the end of the Village, I said, "There's the Manse down there you can manage by yourself now, this is my house here." He put his hand in his pocket and he gave me half-a-crown, in these days I was thinking it was a lot of money. When I was getting married, I heard who he was, I was not very sure that he was the same Minister that was on St. Kilda. When I saw him I knew that he was the very man I had taken to the Well

Lachlan in trouble on the road to Mallaig – the exhaust fell off, the ladies returned late! L. MacDonald Collection.

Lachlan and Nancy on St. Kilda in 1980 for the 50th Anniversary of the Evacuation. Photo R. A. Hebrides.

of Virtues. When the wedding was over we were talking and I asked him, "Did you have a mind of that?". "No" he says, "I may have been over to the Well of Virtues but I cannot remember." "Well, I says, this is the wee fellow that took you – I still mind the tip you

gave me! I thought it was great." He gave us a Bible and we've got the Bible now.

We came to Glen Nevis after we married and are now 32 years here. At work we were shifted from one gang to another, sometimes 10 or so, sometimes 6 or 7, it depended where we were working or what we were doing – planting, draining, thinning – all kinds of jobs. Many a time at night we had to fight fires all over the place."

Postscript

In October 1986 Lachlan and Nancy stayed with my wife and I in the Langdale Valley in the Lake District. On the Saturday morning they decided to go on their own, by bus, into Ambleside. They had a long wait at the bus stop and while they were standing there, a car drew up and a man with a strong Scottish accent said, "You'll have a long wait here for a bus to Fort William!" Friends who were down for the week-end to run in the Fell Race were quick to recognise Lachlan and Nancy!

On their last evening we went out to supper with some friends, Dr. John and Mary Halpin. As usual Lachlan was in great form and had been fascinating us with his reminiscences most of the evening. As we said "Goodbye" to our hosts, Lachlan retorted, "When I am six to eight foot underground that tongue of mine will still be wagging!"

Calum MacDonald, Portrait of a St. Kildian-Londoner

House No. 3 had been the home of a remarkable family of MacDonalds who could trace their ancestry on St. Kilda back to 1753 – the years just after the terrible outbreak of small-pox. After the 1st. World War William MacDonald was the first to evacuate his whole family in 1924. One of his sons, Calum, became Valet/Butler to Lord Dumfries and went on to work at the Grosvenor House Hotel in Park Lane. Before his death in 1979 he wrote his autobiography, which his widow, Marie, has very kindly allowed me to quote at length. It is a fascinating story which well deserves to be told.

Talking to Marie, in March 1987, she described

Sgarbstac with Stac Lee behind and Boreray to right. Acland.

Calum as "a shy man, a perfectionist in all that he did, a real Christian who never held bitterness to anyone, and a very good father to his children. He had a tremendous love for the Island – I always said that I married St. Kilda. not a St. Kildan!"

LIFE ON ST. KILDA (1908 – 1924)

Family Background

"This story spans 68 years from my early remembrances as a youth on Hirta, as St. Kilda was called in my Gaelic mother tongue, until yesterday, the 30th March 1976; the day of my retirement in the Great City of London, where I have worked for the last 26 years as a valet in the Grosvenor House, Park Lane. There I met many people of different creeds and cultures. Some I came to know as friends, whom I shall always remember as real fellow men. Many were rich and famous, two categories I never belonged to, simply because I was born poor, nevertheless I have been happy by birth and by nature.

My family tree dates back to 1753. My great-great-grandmother came from Lochinver, a Miss Betty Scott, born in 1816, died in 1863. When she came to the island as a servant maid to the Minister she married my great-great-grandfather after whom I was christened, 'Calum'.

My father's name was William, my mother was Mary Ann (MacQueen). They had married in 1895 when my father was twenty and my mother was four years older. Eleven children came from the marriage, of which eight are still alive, the oldest living is my brother, 79 years old, the youngest is my sister who is 56 years old. These are Finlay, Annabella, Mary, Finlay-John, Calum (self), Rachel, Marion, Mae, and the three of the family who died were John, Mary-Betsey, and Kirsty. I was born in 1908. It was quite a

MacDonald family Group. Calum's mother standing with hand on his shoulder, Finlay John against the wall, seated probably Mrs MacKinnon. M. MacDonald Collection.

large family to be raised under such circumstances, as it would be, even today. My father had little money coming in, but with the proceeds that the tweed which we made brought in, we were able to live quite well. Our diet consisted of birds' eggs, salted seabirds, sometimes fish we caught. It was good staple food and we never went hungry.

Naturally we went short of some items at times which we could not grow ourselves such as sugar, tea, oatmeal and flour. We never went hungry, though, and father always bought flour and oatmeal in bulk. Mother and sisters did all the baking; flour-scones and oatcakes, as long as we had this in the home, we were always full.

Our supplies in the summer came from Glasgow but in the winter we depended upon the fishing trawlers which often sheltered in St. Kilda Bay or called on their way to and from the fishing grounds. These boats came from Fleetwood, Hull and Aberdeen, many of them were great friends. In the winter they would bring us anything we were short of. They also acted as mailman and would take and bring us any letters that needed delivering. To us young boys there was always great excitement when the trawlers came into the bay for a short stay, on occasions there were as many as twenty boats at anchor. We used to go from one boat to another and received many a titbit from the cooks; large mugs of tea, sometimes a slice of cake which was really a treat. Cake was unheard of on the island and so were most sweet things. The fishermen were real friends and would give us anything that they could spare, sometimes we would exchange their kindness by taking them fresh eggs or a pair of knitted socks.

On the island we all lived by the same standards and education. Our English education was limited, as we only spoke in Gaelic most of the time. English was taught in a small school by the Missionary's wife who was a Gaelic/English teacher.

All my life I have been very fortunate because I was born among a small community of Christian belief, who lived and shared their lives as a whole, not as separate units. Our closeness was partly due to kinship and also isolation from the outside world.

Birth and Early Recollections

Most of the villagers were up in the hills with only a couple of elderly women left behind at home. My mother did not feel too well and after mid-day she went to lie down for a while. Soon after, my mother started in labour and called to my sister Annie, who was 8 years old, to go for help. Annie did not realise what was taking place as she ran out of the house and spotted Uncle Finlay (MacQueen) in the field below. She ran to him and told him mother was ill and wanted help right away. When he got up to the house and into the bedroom he heard a baby cry. He never faced such an urgent situation in his life before. He rolled up his sleeves and told my sister to get hot water, then he took out his pocket knife, dipped it in the boiling water, then proceeded the operation to sever the umbilical cord, he knotted it at both ends, mother's and mine. The operation completed, he told my sister to go and inform one of the old women to come at once and finish the necessary part of nature, then he walked out of the room. Today, I can look down and say, "Well done, Uncle, you did a mighty good job, and I am sorry for any embarrassment I might have caused you, when coming into this world."

My earliest recollection as a boy is a very happy one, having a very religious upbringing in a very happy home atmosphere, as Christianity was the basic standard of family life. The first thing in the morning was family worship and prayer, and the last thing at night before retiring to bed. Sundays were strictly observed as the Lord's Day. A morning service at 11am, Sunday School at 3pm. followed by an evening service at 6pm. No work of any kind was done on

Sunday, except cooking meals. Even the water was drawn up from the wells on Saturday and stored in pails to last all the Sabbath day. One was allowed to roam the hills and glens in between services and we, the youth of the village, would climb the hills, looking over the cliffs watching the numerous birds which nest in the cliffs and the rocks in their thousands, far down below, but we were not allowed any kind of play.

The village nestles at the foot of the hills, the highest and my favourite was called Conachair. The cliff side, which is a sheer drop of 1397 ft., was covered with nesting birds. As you watch the Atlantic rolling waves dashing against the cliffs, it can be very exciting. One can get a panoramic view of the island, and smaller islets like Boreray, Stac Lee and Stac an Armin; on the other side Soay, Levenish, and on a clear day the Outer Hebrides of Lewis, Harris and Benbecula. Clinging to the side of each hill and glen, like limpets to a rock on the seashore, are hundreds of cleits where our stores of peats were kept. Around the village there are also cleits where hay was kept for cattle. There are stone dykes around the village to keep sheep out, also stone built gardens where poorer sheep were put for better grazing.

The houses of the village were elongated along the main street, overlooking a large natural bay. All the houses were built to conform – 1 large kitchen, 1 large bedroom and a smaller bedroom. In between the two was a small lobby as you entered. These were called "Crofters' Houses". There was not a lot of space for a large family, and when all our family were at home, some of us had to sleep in the byre.

My father was religious, as was my mother. On Sundays it was his duty to ring the church bell, calling the villagers to the church services and he was called the "Precentor" who led the congregation singing in Gaelic. My father was always last to leave the church, and in the winter he had to light the paraffin lamps before the service and extinguish them when the service was over. After the rest of the congregation had gone home, I sat in our pew till all the lights were put out and my father had lit the storm lamp. My father would tell me to kneel down beside him while he prayed, then he would ask me to say the Lord's Prayer in Gaelic. After, we would walk hand in hand home.

As a boy I never wore boots or shoes, only the elderly people wore any, except in winter time, so that as a result our feet were tough like leather. We were allowed one pair of tackety boots a year, sometimes they had to last for two years, and even the young women in their teens had to go barefoot throughout the summer months.

Each family had sheep of its own, and each, its special marking, made in the ears of each lamb when it was born and at a distance one could tell who the owner was. Also, naturally, each had at least one cow, and in the case of a large family, two cows to provide enough milk, butter and our own special kind of cheese. If a family should not have enough milk the neighbours provided a pint free each day. Our main staple food, or course, was 'salt mutton', fulmars, gannets and potatoes. In the spring when the puffins, guillemots and razorbills arrived from their emigration we slaughtered them in their hundreds, for fresh food and for their feathers. They were fat and nutritious, and their eggs were also collected, which added to our food variety – they were enjoyable to eat, either boiled or fried and made into a kind of omelette. The puffin's eggs looked and tasted very much like chicken's eggs, but they were very difficult to get as the puffin lays its eggs in burrows under the ground. We would often get nasty nips and cuts by putting our hand in a puffin's burrow, for he guarded his eggs so well.

The main industry of the island was the making of the famous St. Kilda Tweed. It was all done by hand, from the shearing of the sheep till the finished produced tweed. It was a long, monotonous process, the long winter months were occupied by the making of the tweed. Long after the younger members of the family had gone to bed, the parents and the older members of the family worked till two in the morning, and started again at seven the following morning.

Some of the women were as strong as the men, and they had to carry just as heavy a load, in this sense they truly had their "equal rights". The difference between the men and the women was that the women were never allowed to scale the cliffs in order to collect the birds' eggs, nor were they allowed to go out in the rowing boats. However, I can remember that on a certain occasion when the wildfowlers were visiting the smaller islands some of the young girls were allowed to accompany the men. I have seen two of my sisters and a female cousin on such a trip but this was a very rare occasion.

It was every boy's ambition to visit the islands around St. Kilda collecting the eggs in early spring. All the men and boys took part in this operation, we visited all the Stacs, even though some were very difficult and dangerous to land on. Although it was considered hazardous, it was our way of life from generation to generation. On one such occasion I lost an uncle over one of the cliffs, and also a friend who was with him. On this occasion, the cliffs, which were known by name, had been divided up among the community; this meant systematic coverage of the nesting places. The men would be lowered down the cliff by rope, they would catch the young fulmars which were killed and salted and as such provided the islanders with a year round diet. The cliffs had been allocated by pulling a piece of paper from a cap which had the name of part of the cliff on it – the head of the family would take the draw. Where it was a one man family or where a man's family were not yet old enough to go down the cliffs he would team up with another family and together they would share their parts of the cliff. It was in this matter that my uncle

joined with his friend to work as partners. No one will ever know what happened. My uncle's friend's body was recovered between the rocks far below the cliffs, and my uncle's body was never found. As we believed, the rope must have snapped between them and my uncle fell to the sea below. The whole island was shocked and grieved for many a day.

The men visited all the sea Stacs around the main island as these precipitous pillars often provided excellent pickings of gannets and guillemots. At dark they would approach the stacs and from rowing boats, spring onto the steep rocks. Then, gripping the rock with finger holds and by digging their toes into the narrow cracks, they ascended to the top of the cliff or the ledge the birds were nesting on. At their approach most of the birds would take to the air. The men would then take up their positions and wait for the birds to return. When dusk had passed and darkness approached, the birds would return for the night. At first the birds approached the nesting place and circled three times, before having assured themselves that all was clear, then finally settled down. First one would land, then groups would follow, until the ledge was crammed with birds. One bird would take over as guard while the other birds slept, their heads tucked under a wing. The first job was to catch the sentry on guard. If he let out his piercing cry to warn the other birds, then the whole night's work would have been wasted. One of the men would creep up behind the look-out bird while holding his breath, so as not to alert the bird. When near enough, the wildfowler would make his move to grab the bird's beak with one hand and his neck with the other. A sudden twist backwards and the neck was broken. It was easy then to catch the sleeping birds and then kill them. They were then collected by the boatman and the wildfowlers would make their descent.

On one occasion I nearly lost my young life. I was about five years old when I asked my brother to lower me down a cliff to catch a fulmar on its nest. It was during the time of the year we call the fulmar harvest and the whole family was present. My father and brother were after killing all the birds they could carry home for that day and were getting ready to leave. My brother was none too keen to oblige my request but I persisted by asking my father to tell John to lower me down. Finally he relented and said, "Come on, I will lower you down, but you'd better catch a fulmar." The rope was tied in a lasso around my waist and I was lowered down. It was difficult to get a foothold with my bare feet. The cliff was almost perpendicular, I dug my toes into small grooves in the face of the rock and clung on with my small fingers. As I descended opposite to the nest, the young fulmar watching my descent became restless, it hissed and spumed all over my face. I drew back, for I did not like the oily spume which had been squirted all over me. I tried several times but the bird defended itself admirably. Everyone above kept shouting, "Go on, catch it." My brother, meanwhile was becoming impatient at my antics; he gave a sharp tug of the rope and before I could retrieve my position I was hanging upside down. From my upright position I was looking down onto the bottom rocks and the foaming sea. Everyone was shouting and bawling at my brother to stop pulling me up as I now began slipping through the noose. The rope slipped round my knees, I held on with my hands for dear life; but it was becoming a terrific strain. I was being banged against the cliff and getting caught on the jagged rocks which protruded from the rockface. The noose had tightened round my ankles and I was doubled up, before I finally felt my brother's strong hands pull me clear of danger. When he had pulled me to safety, he said, "That is the last time I will ever lower you down." He then walked off on his own, I can only imagine what his thoughts must have been at that moment.

The War Years – 1914 Onwards

My first contact with strangers took place after the 1914 war had broken out. A warship arrived in our bay, we were told that the government was putting a naval base on the island for the duration of the war. The sailors came ashore with their equipment and set up huts close to the beach, on the land belonging to the missionary. This land and some grazing pasture was requisitioned and no one dared to object to this. Some of the islanders were engaged in the labour force, they were not paid very much but it helped the economy of the island. We also knew that the ships would call more regularly and this would bring more contact with the outside world and hopefully ensuring trade. At first the sailors kept very much to themselves and rarely communicated with the natives. However, among these strangers we found two sailors who could speak Gaelic, having originated from the island of Lewis. This was wonderful news to the old men and women, for they came to church and took part in the Gaelic service. They were invited into our homes and allowed to visit us any time they wished. In the end we were all the best of friends and strangers no longer. From then on the ships called more frequently, usually to bring mail and supplies to the sailors.

People on the island were now able to travel to the mainland and the isles of Lewis and Harris with trips provided by the visiting ships. My father often travelled to Lewis and Harris and sometimes as far as Aberdeen and Glasgow. It was an entirely different world to them, and as children we would listen in awe at the tales they told on their return.

John Joins the Army

In 1913 my eldest brother, John, left home for Glasgow to take up employment in the city. My family and the islanders gathered to say goodbye, we were all sad. My father did not object as there was no work on the island and it was plain to see that his future lay elsewere. My youngest sister had not been born at the time and it was an especially sad occasion as this was the first break in the family, although one sister had died before I was born.

When World War 1 broke out in 1914, we had a letter from my brother in Glasgow saying that he was joining the army. The news upset my parents very much. They had fears for his life as any parent would. The word soon passed round the village, all our neighbours came to our house sympathising and offering encouragement. I was about six years old at the time and could not grasp what all the fuss was about, neither could I grasp the fact that in the outside world a nation was fighting another nation. To me, St. Kilda was my world. No other land was in view, only a great expanse of water, the Atlantic, as far as the eye could see.

I can still remember the first army leave my brother John ever received. He had been stationed in France during the war and was given a week's leave. It took him nearly three days journey to St. Kilda, with the result that he only had eight hours to spend with his family, before he had to leave the island to return to his unit before his furlough ran out. My father was away visiting one of the small islands with the rest of the able bodied men.

When we realised that father was not present and he would not know of the homecoming of his son there was a bit of a commotion. No one knew how to get word to him. An old man left the party and began to walk up the hill. He walked the whole length of the island to where the island of Soay juts out from the furthermost part of St. Kilda. Soay itself is separated from the main island by a narrow sound which can only be crossed by a small boat. The man scaled down the cliff to where some men were manning a rowing boat as a ferry. He shouted to the men what was happening, those in turn passed the message to my father. My father left the men on the island in the boat and was put ashore to hear the news first hand from the old man. Finally, the old man told my father, "You go on, I shall follow." It was a long walk over moorland and hills. When he was in view of the village side of the hills, my mother told John to go and meet his father. Everyone was watching their encounter; the distance between them narrowed until they finally embraced. We watched as they knelt down and prayed in thanksgiving. John had one more leave the following year; however, on this occasion he was able to spend

Soay Sound with Stac Biorach and Soay Stac.

four days with his family. He was always remembered in all our prayers both in the church and in every home in the island. He joined the army at the outbreak of the war and until he was demobilised in 1919 at the age of twenty-three, I am glad to say he was never wounded. Our prayers were truly answered.

We did not have any sort of music on the island and no one ever learned to dance until the navy station was installed in 1914. The navy men would give a party for the young women and children at Christmas time. It was a great occasion. Their huts where the party was to be held were gaily decorated with flags about the walls and bunting. New games were taught to the children and we were given chocolate, sweets, and Christmas stockings. Everyone had a wonderful time singing and dancing.

The towering cliffs of St. Kilda were very important to the Navy during the four years of the war as they provided excellent positions for keeping track of shipping and enemy submarines. The two strategic lookout posts were on hills called Oiseval and Mullach Mor. Oiseval was manned by the Navy and Mullach Mor by the St. Kildans. The view from these two vantage points extended for miles out to sea. Any movements were notified by telephone to the Naval Station and noted in a log-book by the men on duty up the hill. Many merchant ships passed the island plying to and from America and sometimes German submarines were spotted. In the vicinity of St. Kilda numerous ships were sunk by these submarines' torpedoes or deck guns. The crews of the unfortunate ships came to our islands in their lifeboats and were taken care of by the Navy until a ship was sent from the Mainland to transport them back to Scotland. The caves around the island were full of flotsam and wreckage from the doomed merchant ships. The natives went around all the accessible caves and salvaged everything of value. Barrels of oil, crates of candles, boxes of cigarettes and planks of wood would be towed ashore to supplement the St. Kildians' spartan mode of life. The Naval personnel did not intervene or claim any find so we were at liberty to sell the oil to merchants on the Mainland and use the candles in our homes.

Our best find was a cask of rum. It was shared out among all the heads of each family and stored in every bottle or utensil one could find. When we ran out of bottles the remainder was left in charge of the Postmaster and locked in his byre. Alcohol was only used on the island for medicinal purposes like treating colds and 'flu. In the end most of the rum was used to entertain tourists or strangers who visited the island long after the war ended.

Fishing Expedition at Night

As a boy on St. Kilda, I think my greatest thrill occured in 1916 when I was eight years old. My father asked me if I would like to go fishing with him and the other men of the island. One condition that I would have to accept if I went, was that I would still go to school as usual the following morning at 9.30am. This I readily agreed to.

Fishing on these occasions would last all night and we would return to the village the next morning. Every family on the island possessed a deep fishing line which was anything up to 200 yards in length. At intervals of about one yard there extended a string, attached to which was a 4 inch hook. Every fourth family shared one of the four rowing boats that the community as a whole owned.

We set out one evening six men rowing and one man steering, the rowers alternating with the steerer in order to have a spell of rest. At last when we were about four miles out to sea we stopped and began setting our fishing lines down. To each end of the fishing lines was attached a buoy with a red flag protruding from the top of it. When all the lines had been attached we rowed back to Dun. It has several small caves eaten into it by the constant battering of the Atlantic rollers. There is one cave, however, which is cavernous inside. The sea inside this cave was very calm only if the wind was from the east or north-east. This was to be our home and shelter for the night. We arrived about 10pm and anchored in the centre of the cave; I looked around in awe at its walls of sheer rock. On the ledges just above the waterline there had been resting some seals, but on our arrival they tumbled into the water and disappeared from sight. In the numerous cracks and crevices there were thousands of seabirds. The noise they made was deafening as they flew in and out all night. Though it was still quite bright outside, the inside of the cave was fairly dark. After anchoring, the men took their food parcels. Before supper, however, grace was said. Conversation then resolved around what we might catch the following morning.

I did not take part in this conversation. I was more interested in the life going all around me and the thrill of it all. After supper was ended and packed away, the Bible was taken out. We all started to sing a Psalm, it reminded me of the church as the sound echoed throughout the cave. Most of the birds took fright and abandoned their nests, not to return until the service was over. After a chapter from the New Testament was read, we all knelt on the bottom of the boat and my father said evening prayers. Afterwards we rose up and climbed into our sleeping bags. We were packed like sardines, head to feet. Our day clothes were kept on and a blanket covered each of us. My father made me comfortable and asked me if I would like to be at home in my own bed. "Oh, No!" I said, "this night I shall never forget." During the night I could not sleep one wink, I could hear snoring from the others in the boat and the din from the birds was indescribable. The sea was lapping against our boat as we circled around our anchor and with my general excitement sleep was an impossibility. At that time of the summer the nights

that far north are very short only lasting two or three hours. At 4am everyone was awake but feeling rather stiff and sore as a result of the crammed conditions on board. Everyone was concerned as to how I slept. "Not a wink," I said. They all laughed and said they thought that the music of the birds would have put me to sleep. The sleeping bags were soon put away. The Bible was taken out and service started the same as the night before. After this, the box of food left over was brought out and we had breakfast, which was washed down with cold tea. When this was completed we weighed anchor and rowed out of the cave. My father told me to row with him to warm myself up and to get my blood circulating, which I did. After an hour's hard rowing we reached the place where the markers were bobbing about on the ocean. I looked over the side of the boat in order to catch the first glimpse of the catch as it came into view from the darkness below. Suddenly I saw a voluminous shape approaching the bottom of the boat. It was spiralling around and around when it broke the surface, it was a halibut, the largest I had ever seen. It was over five feet in length and nearly as broad. The men had great difficulty in getting the fish aboard and it was not until it was finally gaffed near the tail and a rope was tied around its body, did we finally succeed. We now had such a heavy catch that the gunwhale of the boat was nearly level with the sea. We packed away the fishing lines and rowed back to St. Kilda Bay. On reaching the island all the fish was salted and preserved for a later occasion. All, that is, except the halibut, for that was too large to salt. Instead, it was cut up and divided among the families on the island.

When the boat had touched shore I left the fishermen and made my way home for I would have to be at school by 9.30am. My mother was waiting for me and she embraced me, asking "How did the trip go? Did you managed to sleep?" "No." was my reply. "But I must get ready for school." "Not today," she said firmly, "it's straight to bed for you." I shall never forget the thrill and the experiences of that one night spent on the sea.

St. Kilda Shelled by a German Submarine

One recollection that will always stay in my mind occured one morning as I was preparing for school. It was about 8am when word came from the Naval Station that a submarine had been sighted by the watchman on Oiseval heading towards the bay. As no British submarines were known to be in the area we were advised to take to the hills. We did as we were bid and I followed my aunt until we reached halfway up the hill behind the village. We stopped to watch the submarine as it slowly entered the mouth of the harbour. She stopped her engines at this point and did not enter any further. We had never seen a submarine before and wondered at its strange shape as compared to the trawlers and other vessels with which we were familiar. All of a sudden we heard the boom of her guns followed by a splash as the shell exploded close to the shore. "Oh! the Devils" my aunt exclaimed. "They are trying to kill us. Run, run for your lives. Put the hills between us" someone shouted. We had never heard such a terrible noise as those guns made, and we were terrified. We kept running up the hills until we thought we were safe. Other families arrived, most were frightened out of their wits. Still the submarine kept up the barrage, the cattle were going mad. They were running all over the hills in a stampede. The old folks were praying and the young women huddled together. Then after what seemed an eternity the firing stopped and a great silence followed. The submarine began to slither away but the men thought she might return so we were told to stay where we were. The submarine had now moved out of St. Kilda Bay, keeping close to the shore around the island. An old man standing on the cliff edge waved his walking stick in a futile gesture. "I wish this were a gun," he shouted, "I would shoot you right now, you devils." We watched her moving out to sea far below. Our gaze returned to some of the crew on the conning tower, who could see us on the majestic cliffs far above them. When she was far out to sea, most of the spritely of the men and women took courage to return to the village. The old people and the young were not allowed to leave the sanctuary of the hills at that time.

In all the Germans had fired seventy-two rounds of ammunition (shells) into the village. The only casualty, though, was a two-day-old lamb which had been killed. My father had gone to the village with Annie and Finlay to see the damage and to get provisions to take up the hills just in case the enemy returned. They found the Naval personnel back in the station taking stock of the damage. The wireless station had been damaged. One shell went right through the church, another landed 10 yards in front of our house and another blew a crater behind our house. My uncle's house, which was next to ours, was half demolished and next to his the whole house lay in ruins.

After my father surveyed the damage he returned to our home and prepared a meal to take up to the hills, as we were not allowed to return until the following day. During the night the wireless station was repaired and a message was sent out to Naval Headquarters at Stornoway, Isle of Lewis. Armoured trawlers were dispatched at once to our aid. After they arrived we returned to our normal way of life.

Gradually from that day on our way of life was changed. Ships called upon us more frequently and strangers walked our streets in increasing numbers. We invited these strangers into our houses and through their conversations we learned about the outside world. Some of the islanders were given free

157

passage to the other islands and mainland of Scotland. My father would make annual visits to Stornoway and visit the families of the two Lewis Naval men who were stationed on Hirta. My father would take some tweed with him and barter for the goods we required. The families he visited also gave him gifts of dresses for my sisters, shirts with stiff "school-collars" for us lads; dishes of all kinds, tea-sets and dinner-sets for mother. In fact, our home began to look very modern indeed. The delight and happiness in my sisters' lives being dressed in modern clothes must have given great pleasure to my parents. All the sewing that was done, even women's dresses, were undertaken by the men. The women folk knitted all the socks and gloves.

Taxidermy for Manchester Museum

My father had a unique hobby on the island. This was catching wild birds and stuffing them in the tradition of a taxidermist. He sold the finished product to the Manchester Museum in return for cash which helped to pay for the little extras that most families enjoyed. I used to watch him at this job, it took about one hour to complete one bird. He made an incision under one wing then carefully worked out the insides of the bird. The body was then cut at the leg and wing joints and eventually the head. The eyes and brains were then scooped out. The skin of the bird was then cleaned up with a poisonous liquid which was kept in a bottle. Alum was then rubbed into the skin to prevent decay. After this my father stuffed wool into the bird until eventually it had resumed its original shape. The incisions were then sewn up. The wings were tied to the bird's side, it was now ready to despatch by mail to Manchester Museum.

I was always told not to touch the poisonous liquid bottle which was kept in the cupboard in my father's bedroom. Also in this cupboard was kept a bottle of vinegar. The vinegar was supposed to be a remedy for sore heads, if your head ached or you had a cold. The two medicines in every home were vinegar for sore heads and Epsom salts for any other ailment. Many a time I was given both if I was ill, just to be on the safe side. If you can imagine any place where you cannot get lemonade or mineral water you can easily acquire a taste for our thirst-quenching drink. This was a glass of water with one or two drops of vinegar in it to give the drink a tang.

As we had no shops on the island we had to make our own sweets. Sugar was not plentiful but most families had a hundred weight bag of sugar to last out the whole year. In the winter nights when we went out to play, we often pinched a cupful of sugar, if we had the chance. A group of us about the same age would go away up the field where there was an underground cave. It was called the Temple. We took a candle to light up the inside and some dry sticks and old paper, a couple of peats and would light a fire. Someone would produce an empty syrup tin. We put the sugar we had pinched from home altogether into the tin. The tin was placed on the fire till the sugar became a brown, running liquid, we then added a knob of butter. When it boiled and all the sugar grains were melted, we took it off the fire, outside to a small stream. We put a flat stone in the bottom of the stream and then poured the liquified sugar on to this slab of stone to cool, and "Hey Presto", there was our sweet shop. The toffee was then divided into equal shares and put into a newspaper or a piece of cloth. We doused the fire and made for home.

Carding the Wool and Waulking the Tweed

One winter event I always looked forward to was known as the night of the "Big Carding". This was a special occasion. All the tweeds made on St. Kilda were one of three shades, light blue, light grey and brown.

Rolls of cloth ready for export. Three generations of MacDonalds. Adults Left to Right:- Grandfather Neil MacDonald, his son William, Unknown visitor, Finlay MacQueen and the boy, Calum MacDonald. Photo R. C. MacLeod of MacLeod, 1912.

The brown is a colour derived from boiling the stone moss; the resulting mixture was used as a dye, into which the wool was dipped until the tweed was the required reddish brown.

The kitchen in the house would be cleared of everything except chairs which were set out in a circle.

One person from each of the other families on the island would come and take his or her place in a chair. There would be anything up to twenty-five persons present, including the grown up children of the family concerned, seated in the kitchen. The procedure involved went something like this. Each person was given a bundle of plain wool which was set beside him. Then he was given some dyed wool. The "cards" were pieces of wood with short wire teeth like a brush, onto this you placed the white wool with some of the dyed wool. These were stroked between two cards until the required tone and colour of wool was derived. It took about five minutes to complete one cardful of wool. The finished mixture was thrown in a heap on to the floor until a small hillock amassed in the centre which eventually would reach up to the ceiling. Carding would start around midday by the family themselves. Around 6 o'clock the neighbours would start to appear one by one and carding would then go on till the early hours.

We children who were too young to card could only look on from the back and listen to the conversations, jokes and stories that were being told. Some of the stories had been handed down from ancient times, some concerned life on the Mainland. At 1am everybody stopped work for the night. The wool was stacked into canvas bags. The tables were brought back into the kitchen and laid out with a meal for all those who had taken part in the work. The highlight of the meal was the huge dumpling set in the middle of the table. Grace was said and the feasting went on until around 2am.

Another occasion I liked very much and which you might think very funny occured when the tweed had to be taken down from the loft and washed. The tweed had to be washed because, in order to weave the wool, it had to be oiled in order for the fibres to hold together during the weaving process. As everyone knows the oil is very difficult to wash off anything and it requires tremendous washing to extract it from the thick tweed. The way the Islanders overcame this difficulty was carried out by the women. Half a dozen wooden tubs were placed in the middle of the kitchen floor. A huge boiling pot was suspended over a fire by a hook and chain hanging from the chimney. Into this pot was placed the next best thing to ammonia that the Islanders could obtain. The pots under the beds were emptied each morning into a large barrel placed for strategic reasons behind the house. This fermenting liquid which was up to a year old was used to act as the detergent to shift the oil from the tweed. It was placed in the pot over the fire and brought to the boil. The boiling mixture was placed by the women, for this was women's work, into the tubs. Washing soda and soft soap were added and the whole lot allowed to cool to a certain temperature. The smell was horrendous.

The women then tucked up their dresses to knee length and stepped into the tubs. They put as much tweed in as they required and began treading it very much in the grape treading fashion. All the time they danced, they chanted some Gaelic rhythm, which I could never make out. Under the circumstances I never stayed around long enough to try to understand. They kept this activity going for ages, sweating, laughing and shouting until all the tweed had been through the tub.

When they had finished dancing in the tub the tweed was then spread across a long wooden table. Two women would get each side of the table and pound the tweed for all they were worth. It was then thrown into the air to fall back on to the table. As this process was carried out, the tweed began to get thicker in texture. This action was called "waulking" the tweed and was very arduous as the tweed was soaking wet. It was a great body exercise.

The tweed was then taken out to a running stream by my father and we boys went through the same process but with a certain relief that we were out in the open. Finally, when the water was running clean and clear, the tweed was taken to a stone dyke. Here it was spread out and left to dry. When dried it was measured, rolled up and was now ready for selling.

View from the Summit of Boreray – in the distance Dun, Hirta and Soay. David Miller.

Summer Visit to Boreray

To visit the islets around St. Kilda was every boy's dream, especially the Isle of Boreray – it had a magnetism of its own. This probably arose due to the abundance of bird life to be found inhabiting the most perpendicular rocks. Every year the St. Kildian men would send a party to shear the wild sheep which roamed freely over the craggy surface of Boreray. While there, the men would live for about 14 days in underground houses which had been dug into the steep, sloping top of the islet. These had been built many years past in the bygone ages when the islanders had first visited the place and used it as a pasture for their sheep. On the occasion of every yearly visit the thick undergrowth around the cleit-like houses had to be cleared away and the insides cleaned out to make them habitable.

I often visited Boreray on such an occasion. The puffins which covered the face of the island would come out of their burrows and stand at the entrance to their own underground homes. They would only fly off when you were so close that you felt you would be able to bend down and touch them. The birds took up their own hierachy in their nesting habits. The gannets were on the high cliff tops and the fulmars on the cliffs below them. Guillemots and razorbills were situated on the ledges, and the kittiwakes screeching in and out of their caves produced the kind of music I loved to hear.

During their stay the men lived off rations brought with them and a sheep or two killed to supplement their diet. Of course, there were always seabirds in abundance to provide a square meal. The Sabbath was still observed as a day of rest and worship. All the men would gather in the largest of the underground houses and service was held exactly the same as in the church on St. Kilda. Meanwhile the mothers took over the normal family worship each morning and night when the menfolk were away.

The End of The War

When Armistice Day, 11th. November 1918, arrived I was sitting in class. My teacher came in and told us to stand up and say a prayer. She told us the great news and led us in thanksgiving for our great deliverance. We were given the rest of the day off. We ran home in jubilation, as much for having the time off as for the exciting news. The villagers were out celebrating and chatting excitedly. My parents were particularly excited, as probably all parents would be, at the news which meant their sons would return. Sadness was intermixed with all the jubilation for the news meant that our friends, the Naval men and officers, would now leave the island for good. It was truly a mixed blessing that the war had come to an end, although we never regretted the fact for one moment. In the four years they had been stationed on Hirta we had come to learn of the wondrous outside world, now we were once more going to return to our isolation. These men had been wonderful to us children, teaching us to speak the English language, expanding our knowledge with stories of faraway places and giving us a wider perspective of the opportunities open to us elsewhere in the world. They had shown us such kindness as bringing presents on their return from leave, holding parties for us at Christmas and generally showing great friendship. The older people, however, could not communicate with them very well because the aged St. Kildians could only speak Gaelic which was like a foreign language to all the Naval men, except the two Lewismen. These latter two were, as a result, made especially welcome; even so these two friends would now be returning to their own families.

The news of the Armistice, however, brought one matter to a head. Dick MacLean, one of the naval ratings, was married before he left to Mary MacDonald, one of the native girls.

My brother arrived home six months after the war ended. He was made a "Hero" having fought the Germans as a gunner in France and Gallipoli. He came through it without a scratch. Many a tale he told us of the war and his comrades that were killed in battle. John only stayed home for one year. He saw no future for him on the Island and he took a passage on a fishing trawler and went to Glasgow. My second brother, Finlay, followed him the next year, and also went to Glasgow. Now there were only eight of the family left at home.

Death of Christina in 1920, Aged Nine

In 1920, my sister Christina, who was only nine years old died. She was a very religious child and grew up different from the rest of the family. She had a beautiful voice and was always singing religious hymns. Her favourite was "Jesus loves me". One Sunday night my mother stayed home to look after five of us who were too young to go to church. We all sat round the fireside while mother took a Gaelic Bible and read to us. As she read about the birth of baby Jesus and His life and why He was crucified, Christina burst into tears. My mother asked her why she was crying, "Oh! because I love Him so much." was her reply. I said, "You are a softy." she turned to my mother and said, "I am not a softy, I love Him more than anything else in the world." She was more delicate than any of us, but yet full of the joy of life, and played with us in and outside the house. She caught a chill one day and was confined to bed. It was winter time and our busy time of the year when the spinning and weaving was in progress, work went on till one or two in the morning.

We children went to bed at 10 o'clock, because of school the next day. My father was weaving, my mother and the two older sisters were spinning when they heard my sister, Christina, singing in the small bedroom off the kitchen. Mother told father to listen. "Do you hear Christina singing? She must be feeling better as she was feverish earlier on in the night." Father stopped to listen, and so did my sisters who were spinning, they thought it a bit strange. So mother got up and looked in the room, which was in semi-darkness. The singing stopped as she entered. Mother thought Christina must have gone to sleep so she returned to her spinning wheel and the work continued. Then the singing started again, so everyone stopped and listened. Mother felt a strange feeling come over her so she got up and went in, turned up the paraffin lamp and looked down on the bed. She gave a loud cry, shouting, "Christina is dead, she looks so cold and serene, and very pale."

The wailing and crying woke us up. Mother walked in and told us to get up, that our sister was dead. My brother and I could not believe it at first, but we got up and ran into the bedroom where she lay, so very quiet. We bent over her and kissed her forehead, which was very cold and then we all burst into tears, it all seemed so unreal. This was the first time I looked down on death, it was a fearful experience. When morning came and the village heard the sad news they came one after the other, and joined in our bereavement. Earlier in the morning whilst standing outside I saw my father coming out of the house ringing his hands, tears running down his face, crying, "Christina, Christina." He walked passed me and I saw him going into the byre, I followed him and listened. I heard him praying for strength and comfort - so I crept away quietly. I waited about till he came out, he seemed so much calmer, then he went back into the house.

When death came to anyone on the island, nobody did any kind of work for a whole week, everybody seemed to be sharing the same grief. Time is a great healer, and as the days and weeks went by we began to resume our normal way of life. Now there were only seven of the family at home.

Visiting Whalers

More trawlers from Fleetwood, Hull and Aberdeen began calling on us, also the Norwegian whalers began to call, bringing in and anchoring whales they killed in the bay. The whaling factory was on West Loch Tarbert, owned by a Norwegian called Hallesen. We used to visit those whalers when they came in but the crew could only speak broken English, so we were at a disadvantage to carry on any conversation with them. Sometimes when they brought in a freshly killed whale, they would cut out a large chunk of whale meat and say, "Very good, very good, you eat." We would shake our heads signifying. "No, thank you." When they killed as many as six or seven whales they would lash them to the side of the ships and sail off to the factory. After they killed the first one or two whales they would leave them anchored in the bay. Sometimes a whole week would pass before they came back with the next two or three. They would go away and hunt for more. If the weather was very warm the whales would inflate to an enormous size, their skin peeling off and hundreds of birds, gulls, fulmars and others, swarming all over them. They also attracted many kinds of fish which fed off the peeling skin. Their stomachs inflated out to look like a large red balloon. When this was pierced by a bird's beak the stench was vile and lingered over the whole bay for a long time. People in the village street often went around holding their noses after such an occurrence. Eventually a ship would come and tow the whales to the processing plants at Tarbert.

Calum's Brothers and Sisters

My two eldest brothers left home and went to work in the shipyards of Glasgow. They had met two Stornoway women and were married the same year. Work in Glasgow, though, was very difficult to come by in those days and eventually they had to return to the Isle of Lewis to try their luck in Stornoway itself. John found work in the herring processing industry which was of considerable importance to the island economy. Finlay, my second brother, found a steady job in the Gas Works. A job he stayed in for a further six years.

My father would visit them every year, getting free passage on a trawler or whaler visiting St. Kilda. On one occasion my father took time off to visit one of the naval men who had been stationed on our island during the war. The man was Kenneth MacLeod, he had since retired from the Navy to look after his croft. My father was made very welcome during his visit but his greatest surprise lay in store when, after a few days, Kenneth took him aside. Kenneth told my father he

was in love with my sister Annie, and if he had no objections he would ask for her hand in marriage. My father was flabbergasted as he had no idea that such a love affair had been going on, although he knew Annie was receiving letters quite regularly. He told Kenneth that he had no objection provided they were really in love. My father would ask Annie on his return whether she would like to marry this man. If Annie said yes, then my father would give them his blessings for he knew Kenneth to be straight and honest, and a God-fearing man, who was able to support her.

When father returned home he took Annie aside and with my mother present he put the question to her. "Yes," she said, "I am in love with Kenneth but I will not marry him if either of you object." They both agreed he was a good man and that they had no objection. When the family were told there were a few tears but also great joy. The following year my father took Annie away on a whaler to get married in Stornoway. My mother could not go on such a long journey with all the rest of the children, so we remained at home. My two brothers were now able to represent Annie's relatives at the wedding.

On his return my father began to have thoughts about life on Hirta. There were now only five of us left at home and the family was getting smaller and smaller. He wondered whether to take all the family away and leave the Island for good, but for the moment anyway, it was only a dream.

My father was very friendly with a young engineer on one of the trawlers out of Fleetwood. This particular trawler often called into the bay on its way to and from the fishing grounds around Rockall. The man was a Scot from Aberdeen, and he always visited our house when ashore and he almost became one of the family. One day he asked whether he could give Finlay John a treat and take him on a trip to Fleetwood. Although wary about letting their son go they eventually relented when told they would return the very next trip. My brother, who was the toughest of all the boys – "Determination" seemed to be his motto all his life – agreed to go. In fact, he was thrilled to get away to see the world outside. The trawler was expected to return at the end of the week. By the end of the third week there was still no sign of her, eventually we found she was fishing different grounds. After a month my father was told Finlay John was aboard another trawler, the Caldew, which was supposed to have returned him to St. Kilda. A week later the Caldew put into the harbour, Finlay John was not on board. The Captain assured my father that Finlay John was quite safe and that he had indeed been fishing with him not long since but, as he himself had to fish in the Minch, Finlay John was put ashore in Fleetwood to arrange a lift with another trawler who was due to fish near our island. Father decided to go to Fleetwood on board the "Lilly Melling" which was returning with her catch. At last we found out that Finlay John had been taken on as a member of a crew of a small fishing boat which was not due to return until the following week.

When the ship finally pulled into port my father was standing on the quay waiting. He walked back to where the boat had tied up to unload. There was Finlay John oblivious to all the worry he had caused. At first he did not want to return as he rather liked life at sea. Father on the other hand would have none of this and told him he was too young to be left behind. Finlay John was paid off, the princely sum of £2 plus a percentage of the catch. The two of them made a few purchases to take home and found a trawler which was going to St. Kilda and which would take them home.

Years later Finlay John did return to sea when he became a Merchant Seaman. His ship was torpedoed in the Atlantic by a German submarine on the first day after the Second World War was declared, and he spent the duration as a prisoner of the war.

LEAVING THE ISLAND 1924 – 1947
Opportunity and Departure

In 1924 my father decided he would leave the Island for good. He suffered from asthma for many years and only seemed to find relief from it when he was on trips away from St. Kilda. My brothers who lived in Stornoway told him that he would be able to work without the hardship and stress that living on Hirta entailed.

At that time Lord Leverhulme, the founder of Sunlight, owned the Islands of Lewis and Harris. He was a millionaire industrialist and had plans to develop the Islands. This plan engaged the building of houses for the workers and the expansion of the town of Stornoway. The Port facilities of Stornoway were developed so that it could cater for a large fishing industry, and act as a fishing terminal for factories, which provide employment for the natives of the Islands. The whole scheme was a token of gratitude from Leverhulme for the contributions and sacrifices the Scots had made in helping to defeat the Germans in the 1914-18 War. However, the returning soldiers and sailors did not want or approve the scheme. All they required was a piece of land of their own on which they could build a home, keep cattle and develop it as they wished. Lord Leverhulme, realising he could not pacify the Islanders, transferred the scheme to Obbe in Harris. On the whole the new site was less favourable to develop. The name of part of Obbe was eventually changed to Leverburgh.

Lord Leverhulme was living in Stornoway Castle which was within a mile of my brother's house. During one of my father's annual visits to Stornoway he was persuaded to seek an interview with this great industrialist. He got in touch with Lord Leverhulme's secretary and an interview was arranged. The meeting took place in the Castle. His Lordship listened to my father's reason for wanting to leave the Island. Lord

The Village Street beginning with House No.1.

Leverhulme was especially interested in the fact that my father's asthma attacks improved when he left the Island. Lord Leverhulme explained that he too suffered from illness and told my father he had his sympathy. "Yes, I will be able to help you." he said. "You bring your wife and four children and anyone else who wishes to leave the Island. I personally guarantee you all work and eventually a real home. In the meantime, until such houses can be provided, you can live in a large temporary house. I shall get in touch with my manager in Leverburgh and arrange everything for your arrival." The interview ended.

My father now made up his mind that he would leave the Island the following autumn. On his arrival back to St. Kilda he told the family of his intention. We were highly delighted that we would all leave as one family. The islanders, though, were rather sad that here was one house that would close its doors for ever. Some of the younger people already knew that our way of life in St. Kilda was doomed. Their future lay outside those shore. Since the war six men and two women had left for other lands and without young people life was bound to come to a standstill. Now,

three more young men said that they would also come away with us and seek work in Leverburgh.

In the spring of 1924 my father left to take up employment as a labourer in Leverburgh. He was going to work a preliminary three months to earn enough money before evacuating us from the island. He returned in August to collect us and pack our household belongings. There was not much in the way of packing to be done though, as we possessed little in this line. Most of our furniture was home made and only suitable for our spartan way of life. My father arranged with some friends who lived in Tarbert, Harris, that some of the family would travel there in advance. The rest of the family would follow in one of the Whalers a week later. The first party consisted of my sister Mary, one of the other Islanders and myself. On the morning of our departure most of the Islanders gathered on the small quay. Some were weeping and looking rather sad. At that time I was only sixteen years old. My uncle, who had delivered me into the world, pressed four shillings into my hand as he bade me goodbye. My aunt gave me five shillings and my father ten shillings. This money was to be used to provide for my keep until we met up again in one week's time.

The young lads with whom I had grown up told me to be sure and ask the Whaler's Captain to let me pull on the ship's siren. When we had said our last goodbye we put on board. Four dead whales were lashed to the side of the ship with two being towed astern as we made our undramatic exit from St. Kilda Bay. I went to see the Captain and found that he could not speak any English. So I made a sign and simulated pulling the ship's siren. He nodded his head in agreement. I pulled and pulled for 10 minutes until we were out of sight of the bay. The Captain made a sign, as much as to say, "Enough." I left the bridge. As we slowly sailed on, the coastline of St. Kilda and the other islets became hazy in the distance astern. There was a heavy swell and the sea haze hung over the waters. Eventually we lost sight of our Island home and we were alone in miles and miles of ocean. All we could hear was the throbbing of the ship's engines as it cut laboriously through the waves. Most of the crew had gone to sleep in their cabins. We were invited to use the dining room if we required to lie down. This invitation was accepted by my sister who was feeling a bit sea sick.

I stayed on deck for a little while, not feeling very happy and wishing I had never left home. Still some of my friends, the gulls and fulmars, were escorting us. I watched their aerial ballet. Every now and again they would land on the towed carcasses and peck at the skins. I envied their wings and the freedom they had to return to my beloved Island. It took ten hours to arrive at the Isle of Harris. As we drew near my sister and my friend Donald came up from below deck. We were offered food but none of us felt hungry. It was the first time we had ever been on such a journey by sea. The smell of the ship and the rotting whales did not help our appetites. As we sailed into West Loch Tarbert, towards the whaling station the stench became unbearable. Men were everywhere busy cutting huge strips off the dead whales. Steam and smoke rose high in the air from the oil extraction processes. The harbour was a hubbub of activity. The whales that we had towed were anchored near the pier. The ship itself was then tied up to the pier. We bid the Captain and crew goodbye.

A native of Harris stepped forward. He greeted us and said he had expected us. We were to stay at his house, as had been arranged. He took us to his home and made us very welcome. After tea, which we enjoyed, we felt a little more cheerful. Before retiring this man and his family held worship, in which we joined. We were then taken to our separate rooms. We did not have much baggage. My sister had a small case, Donald had a small bag, and I had all that I was standing in.

The following day we went by bus to Tarbert and, for the first time in our lives, we did some shopping. We were amazed to see how men travelled on a two wheel bicycle and could not understand how they did not fall off. The fare on the bus was one shilling for four miles. We began to realise that we could not get very far without money. This resulted in us taking great care of the little pocket money we did have. Instead of taking the bus back to our friend's home, we walked. Looking back now I think the wear on our shoes was probably just as costly as the shilling we saved.

The next day we were to separate. My sister was to go to Stornoway and my friend Donald MacDonald (Lachlan MacDonald's brother, D.A.Q.) was to leave for Leverburgh to look for employment with Lord Leverhulme. I was supposed to stay till the following week when my father would arrive with the rest of the family. The separation was too much for me and to be left with strangers was unbearable. My sister boarded the bus and set off on her journey to our brother's house in Stornoway. I made up my mind to stick with my friend Donald and told our Harris friend of my decision. "Well," he said, "I cannot hold you against your will, but your father will be annoyed."

That evening we boarded the mail boat which took us to Rodel. After a short journey we disembarked and set off on foot on the four mile walk to Leverburgh. It was getting quite dark and night was fast descending when a lorry pulled up along side of us. The driver asked where we were headed. I told him, Leverburgh. "Right, jump in the back and I will take you." he said. This we did and were soon travelling up the glen towards our destination. The road climbed steeply until finally we began to descend a very steep road indeed. Suddenly there was a thud. The lorry hit a car which was coming up the road in the opposite direction. As the lorry jerked to a halt we jumped out, rather shaken but none the worse for wear. Both drivers were arguing heatedly. We made sure no one was hurt. My friend turned to me and whispered, "Let's away from here, otherwise the police will come and we will have to go to court." This was rather a frightening experience and a prospect we wanted to avoid at all costs. We were unduly frightened of being questioned by the police. We left the bickering drivers and walked the rest of the way to Leverburgh.

We were to look for a building called "Bridge House" which was situated near the river. This house had been used by many St. Kildians who had been visiting the area. They had always been made very welcome and the lodgings were clean and comfortable. We found the house, knocked and went in. The house was owned by an old woman who resided there with her married son. The son had been married less than two years and, apart from his wife, the other occupants on the house were a set of twins in a cradle. Conversation revolved around the various St. Kildians who had stayed from time to time in their abode. They knew my father well as he had lodged with them during the summer. I explained why I was there instead of stopping in Tarbert. They said that they understood and I was not to worry. They would take care of me until my father arrived.

In the meantime I was to help the yong mother by looking after the twins while she went to milk the cows. I would also have to draw the water from the well and generally make myself useful round the house. I agreed to do this as I did not have too much money to otherwise pay my way. We were then shown up to our rooms in the attic which were small but comfortable.

Next morning Donald went off to look for work. He succeeded and was employed as a labourer in the quarry, working for a rate of 4 pence an hour. The hours were from 8am. to 5.30pm. Saturday work finished at noon. He would begin the following Monday.

Towards the end of the week I received a letter from my father. He would be arriving early Monday morning. I was delighted. They were due to arrive on the "Dunara Castle" at Leverburgh. The ship had not called at Tarbert before coming to Leverburgh so no passengers had been picked up. I felt very disappointed as I walked back to the house. I arrived about lunchtime and was met by Donald. "Has your family arrived?" he said. "No," I said, "they must be coming by road." Well I don't know what will happen to you in the meantime." he said. I enquired what he meant. "The lady of the house is very annoyed at you for not staying to look after the children. She told me that you need not come back as she will not give you a meal." I was flabbergasted and by now thoroughly depressed. There was nothing left for me to do but to turn around and return to the pier. I asked the boatman if he could take me to the "Dunara Castle" so that I could return to Tarbert. There I hoped to find a whaler that would take me home to St. Kilda. The boatman agreed to take me to the ship lying out in the sound and I bade Donald farewell.

I paid four shillings and sixpence (23 pence) to the Purser for the single fare to Tarbert. On board I met another young St. Kildian who was going to Glasgow where his brother was working. It was a great surprise to both of us to meet in this way. I had not eaten all day and was famished. We went to see the Steward who in turn gave us a mug of tea and some sandwiches, for which he charged us 10 pence. It took us two hours to make the trip from Leverburgh to Tarbert.

We pulled into the quay where I was very fortunate indeed. Who should be standing there but my father and brother. "Where on earth are you going?" he shouted. I could hardly believe my ears. I told him I was on my way back to St. Kilda. Donald Hugh, whom I had met up with on board, said, "Are you going to Glasgow?" to which I replied, "No." "Did you get my letter saying I would be in Leverburgh on Monday?" My father asked. " Yes, but seeing the "Dunara Castle" did not call in here to pick up passengers. I thought you had not left St. Kilda yet." I answered . "No," he said, "we came over on a whaler earlier than we expected but the ship never called in to pick us up. I have hired a lorry and everything is piled up on it. Your mother and sisters are waiting beside it. It's lucky for you that we stopped a few minutes to watch the "Dunara Castle" dock, otherwise we could have been on our way and you would have missed us." My father then turned to Donald Hugh and said to him, "What about you joining us? There is plenty of employment in Leverburgh. Besides, your uncle Donald is here with us and he is going to stay with us when we reach Leverburgh."

I met my mother and the rest of the family and then told them what had happened. My father was very annoyed that I had been treated so unkindly, still we ceased to worry about that as we all piled into the lorry. Off we went on our overland journey.

It was well after midnight when we reached the hut that was to be our home for the next two years. There was no electricity, so light was provided by candles. We were unable to light the paraffin lamps we brought from St. Kilda because we had not taken any paraffin on such a journey. We unpacked our bedding and took some food out and mother prepared a meal. After we had eaten we gathered round and in the dim candle light we said our thanksgiving. Prayers that night were kept short as everyone was thoroughly tired from the arduous journey.

New Home and Work in Harris

The rest of the week was spent in organising our new home. Our furniture consisted of four bunk beds, a double bed and one single bed; there was a long table and three long seats made of wood; last but not least there was a stove. Outside in another hut there was the toilet and washroom. The interior of our hut was divided into separate rooms by hanging sheets from wall to wall. This provided scant but extra privacy. Our living conditions were now less favourable than those we had left on St. Kilda but this we hoped would soon be corrected after we had settled into the run of things. Mother took my younger sisters along to enrol at the local school and my father, brothers and myself went along to the employment office to sign on for work. We were not kept waiting long. The following Monday morning at 8 o'clock sharp we were to report to different quarries. There we were to work as navvy labourers. So we returned home for the short while until our employment was to begin.

Monday came and we reported as told to the various quarries. I remember the picture of utter confusion that first struck me. There were hundreds of men scattered far and wide, drilling, digging, blasting, levelling and pushing barrows. This particular area was to be the site for houses that would eventually be built, another quarry was preparing the site for a factory and so the jigsaw was forming. Our wages were 4 pence an hour and for that we sweated and laboured all day. We were happy, though, because this was our first employment and we were glad of it. The whole project was, as I said, to make Leverburgh into a fishing port. New piers were being erected on the water's edge to accomodate the ships and fishing boats that were expected. I found the life very tough and some of the navvies even tougher. I was introduced to language I had never heard before in my life.

Luck was to come my way, I changed my employment to that of shop assistant in a general merchandise shop to a local shopkeeper named Lowe. My wages were 1-15s (£1.75) per week. I worked from 9am till 8pm when the shop closed for the night. After this it was my job to take the "Post" which had been left in the shop the 1½ miles to the Post Office, a round trip of three miles, before I was allowed to return home. This was accepted as being all part of a day's work.

My parents found it hard to make ends meet with such a large and young family as we required a lot of feeding and clothing. I handed over my pay packet each Saturday and was given five shillings (25p) back as pocket money. After a year we were all feeling disillusioned with the way things had turned out and we realised we were better off living on our own Island. My brother and Donald Hugh made up their minds that they would go to Glasgow to work in the shipyards. They expected to earn more money there than in the quarries of Leverburgh. My father took on an extra job as part-time nightwatchman to make a little extra money to add to that he got for working all day. Eventually, though, his health began to suffer. This is how we carried on until the following summer. It was at that time that we heard that Lord Leverhulme was dying and rumours began to spread that the whole Leverburgh project would cease. My father was very worried about the consequences to our family if this was to occur. We would probably have to return to St. Kilda.

We were told of the tragic news of Lord Leverhulme's death soon afterwards. Work came to a standstill and all the men were paid off. It was a disaster for many families. One could hardly believe the hardship which this created. The place looked desolate, you would never believe that only a few months before it had been a hive of activity. My family were forced to pack up and leave for Stornoway. There we hoped to live with my brother's family and Annie and her husband until my father and I could find some work. Our hopes and aspirations were dashed when the life left Lord Leverhulme's body.

My eldest brother, John, was living at that time in a one room flat with his wife and three children. Finlay, my second eldest brother, had a three bedroom house but, as well as his own twin children, he had his mother-in-law and brother-in-law living in the house. Annie lived out in the country with her husband and his parents. They were in the process of building their own croft. We therefore had to stay at Finlay's. We slept like sardines the first two nights. After that my parents took my three younger sisters to the country to stay with Annie. I stayed on at Finlay's in case I could find work in the town.

Soon after my father arrived at Annie's he became ill. His health was very run down. My sister's mother-in-law who lived near Annie wondered why my father went down every day to the seashore. She had known my father many years now and thought this strange. One day she followed him very quietly and hid herself behind a boulder. Then she heard him praying. She was amazed and only now realised that this was the vigil he kept every day. She listened as he prayed to God for the comfort and strength for the Island of St. Kilda and its people. She felt ashamed of eavesdropping on such a good living man in his hour of agony. My father died a few days later. This story only came to light after my father's death, when the old lady told my sister.

My mother was now in a dreadful state with three young girls to support and I was still without work. She received a widow's pension of fifteen shillings (75p) and this was all the money coming into the family. My brothers helped as much as they could even though they had families to support of their own. I used to go to the gas works where Finlay was fireman. The gas works was situated near a kippering shed where herrings were smoked. The air round this area always had a strange odour but was bearable. My brother told the boss of the kippering shed our family situation and how I was unable to find work since arriving in Stornoway. This man made a fine gesture and said I could start work with his nightshift men starting the following nightshift and the wages were £2 per week.

My first job since we left Leverburgh, even though it was only seasonal work; still it was great to get some work to help mother and my sisters. Then when the season was over the Manager of the Gas Works noticed how I was always helping my brother firing the retorts which produced the gas. He asked me if I cared for a job, painting the windows of his house and doing odd jobs in the Gas House, I said, "Yes, I do not mind that kind of work as long as I have a job." He engaged me on the spot.

My brother and another man were the firemen. One undertook the nightshift and the other the dayshift. These roles were reversed each week. The hours were 8am to 6pm. When you started the nightshift the change took place on Sunday. From 8am Sunday morning, you had a whole day's rest. The wages were ten shillings (50p) a shift. It so happened my brother's mate was taken seriously ill and I was asked to take over as fireman. It was a hard, hot life. One needed a lot of stamina to cope with the heat of the furnaces, you sweated most of the time, especially in the winter, for the town of Stornoway completely depended on gas for heat and light. The furnaces were fired twice in the shift, which meant twenty-eight times a week. Besides firing the furnaces I had to go underground and clean the furnaces, which in turn fired the retorts. It was also part of my job to clean out the purifiers once a week. One had to work very hard to maintain the plant and keep it running to its full capacity in order to keep the town well supplied with gas.

Life seemed to be improving for the family now. I had a steady job and we had a council home of our own for the first time. In 1928 my sister Mary met Alex MacLeod who had been a Naval Officer on our Island during the war. He was home on leave from the sea. They fell in love and married in Inverness. He returned to sea a year later when their first child had been born. He was sailing out to Australia and soon sent for his wife and child to come to settle in Melbourne. This was another break in the family and a sad departure when she emigrated. It was forty years before I was to see her again.

During this time mother and my eldest brother would be dead and her first husband would have passed on. She married again, this time to an Australian by the name of Joe Hill. They both came over again in 1974 for a two month visit. It was a great get together occasion for the family. She was 72 years old and still had her St. Kilda accent and still had the same charm she had when she lived on the island.

In 1929 I made a return visit to St. Kilda. It was my first visit to my Island home since I left in 1924. I still had uncles and aunts living there, but life was changing and dying. Most of the young men were after leaving the island. The elderly realised that without the young the old could not maintain their ancient traditional way of living.

After a dispute with the Manager of the Gas works I left his employ and was engaged in building the first Power Station in the town. My first work was helping with the laying of electric cables underground throughout the town. This did not last long. Once all the cables had been installed and the electric power initiated, I was paid off and joined the unemployed queues for the first time. I received 75p per week.

Visit to St. Kilda to Transfer Soay Sheep in 1932, Also the Visits in 1933, 1936.

My prospects had taken a turn for the worst. Two months of being on the dole passed and still no work was forthcoming. I was beginnning to get very apprehenisve, when I received a letter from A. G. Ferguson, the St. Kildian tweed merchant in Glasgow. He asked me if I would care to join him in a visit to St. Kilda. The purpose of this visit was to catch wild sheep on the island of Soay, these would be transferred to the island of Hirta. The ownership of the islands had now passed from MacLeod of MacLeod, who had owned the Islands until the evacuation, to Lord Dumfries who now instigated the trip.

I grasped at this opportunity and replied by return of post my acceptance of the kind offer. So in June 1932 I joined the "S.S. Hebrides" which was lying at anchor in the Sound of Harris. This ship made annual voyages to the Western Isles. On board was A. G. Ferguson, his brother Neil and his wife Annie, who in turn was my aunt. Their son John was with them, as was Finlay MacQueen (my uncle), Finlay Gillies, Donald MacDonald, John and his brother Neil Gillies and their sister-in-law, Kirsty Gillies. It was quite a meeting, for we had not seen each other for many years. We were all terribly excited to be going back to our dear island for the duration of that summer. We headed out of the Sound of Harris at 2pm and arrived in St. Kilda at 7pm the same evening. There was great activity getting our stores ashore via the ship's small boat. This task was not finally completed until well after midnight. The ship anchored in the bay until the following noon. In the meantime the passengers who had landed with us the previous night embarked early

Lord Dumfries' Party after the Evacuation. Left to Right:- Kate Ferguson (Alex's wife), John Gillies, (father of Norman John), Christine Gillies (mother of Rachel and Cathy), Possibly Lord Dumfries' brother, Finlay Gillies, Donald MacDonald, Lord Dumfries, Neil Ferguson, Unknown, Unknown, Alex Ferguson, Neil Gillies, Lord Dumfries' Party, Donald Ferguson. E. Ogilvie Collection.

in the morning.

All through the night my aunt and myself cleaned out the old homestead and unpacked the stores. When the ship had left we gathered together to plan our stay. A. G. Ferguson, who had a boat stowed away on the Island, suggested we got her ready to visit the islets. It was like old times with everybody so happy to be back. We caught a hundred wild Soay sheep and transferred them to the main island, and killed three or four for our own use. In our spare time we wove tweed for A. G. Ferguson who had brought the yarn ready for the loom. This was the first time I ever sat on a loom weaving and I was going to be paid for this trip. All my free time was spent weaving. We feasted on puffins and fulmars like the olden days. Everyone slept in their own homes except me, as my aunt would not let me sleep in my father's home, I had to sleep in her home. She told me on several occasions during these days, "I wish I had never left here. Today I feel so happy, as if I had never left here."

At last our stay was near an end, the last ship was due to arrive. We packed to leave, with each of us to go our separate ways. We went to the church for the last service together, the sermon was taken over by my aunt's brother, Neil, who was an elder of the church. It was said in Gaelic. Neil talked of the past and of the Christians lying at rest in the quiet burial ground behind the village. Knowing that none of us present would ever lie beside them, it was a sad service but so very true of the people who had lived from generation to generation in a world of their own making.

The "S.S. Hebrides" arrived and the passengers came ashore. They walked up and down the village before returning to the ship. We also went on board with them. I landed in Harris and made my way to Stornoway, the rest of the party carried on to Glasgow before separating. For my part of the expedition and working on the islands, I received a cheque for £20 from A. G. Ferguson with all expenses paid.

The rest of the year I did any sort of work that came to hand, such as discharging boats of coal and fishing drifters; also taking patients out to the Inverness psychiatric hospital. These were not very pleasant jobs, but jobs which needed to be done.

In 1933 A. G. Ferguson wrote to be again asking if I would join a party to St. Kilda. This time Lord Dumfries and his party were going to visit his newly acquired possession, which was to be a bird sanctuary. A. G. Ferguson pointed out that I would be a great asset being young and able to show them around the Island. The "S.S. Dunara Castle" picked me up in the Sound of Harris, like the year before. On board were Lord and Lady Dumfries, the Honourable Bob and Willie Stirling from Keir House, Stirling, Lord David Crichton Stuart and Mr. John Drummond. They went to some of the other islands where, in the Caithmor at night, we caught two shearwaters, ringed them and let them fly away again, we also ringed some puffins and fulmars. They were much impressed with the whole trip and in 1936 made another trip. We, the natives, stayed on for a month roaming about the island, lobster fishing and sea fishing, feeling much at home like the old days.

Employment with Lord Dumfries

Soon after returning to Stornoway I received another letter from A. G. Ferguson, this time asking me if I cared to join Lord Dumfries' staff at Dumfries, Old Cummock. His Lordship was very much impressed with me while on St. Kilda. He said he would like to help me, if I was still unemployed, as an odd job man while I would be gaining experience for a better situation in the household staff. My wages were to be £1 all found after takings. After talking it over with my mother and family I decided I would give it a try and wrote accepting the situation. I duly arrived a week later at Dumfries House and was introduced to the housekeeper, butler and the rest of the staff. The following day I was confronted with his Lordship and her Ladyship who heartily welcomed me as a member of the staff. This, my first introduction to the elite, was quite an occasion. The butler informed me of the duties I was required to carry out. My day started at 6.30am; stoke the domestic boilers, sweep the whole corridors (scrub and wash on my knees said corridors once a week) and carry coals in buckets to the rooms, some three flights up, as well as to give a hand washing up in the pantry after meals, also the servants' dishes, look after a small aviary outside and brush down the front steps every day. There was a break from 2pm till 6pm every day and work continued till 11pm after the dinner dishes had been washed. There was also one day off a week. For the large sum of £1 a week, there was an allowance of 17p for laundry and 2p a day for beer. I was allowed one suit made to measure, valued at not more than £12 a year, plus a pair of dungarees for working in. After a week I began to wonder if I had taken leave of my senses, but gradually as I came to know the rest of the staff I began to enjoy the life.

There was much entertaining of the Gentry and Houseparties were held frequently. The staff consisted of a butler, footman, pantryman (oddman), head housekeeper, three maids, one chef, three kitchen hands, nanny, maid and two grooms for her Ladyship, who did a lot of horse-riding. We, the staff, made our own entertainment and amusements which were playing cards, gramophone records and an occasional flutter on the horse races. This was my first initiation into gambling.

At the end of two years' service I decided to leave private service and go to Glasgow to see if I could find a better paying job. I asked the butler to inform his Lordship I was giving a month's notice. Later in the evening his Lordship called me to the drawing room. He said, "MacDonald, will you tell me why you are not happy here?" "Oh; yes, my Lord," I said, "but I find I cannot support myself, my mother and two sisters on my wage here, I therefore decided to go and look for a job where I can earn more and be able to support them." His Lordship replied, "MacDonald, I don't want to lose you and especially since you are a St. Kildian, for I intend to visit your Island again from time to time and I would like to take you with me. Would you think it over if I made you my personal valet and footman? I feel I need a second footman, as we entertain a lot. Besides, you will be looking after some of my guests, unpacking when they arrive. I will raise your wages to £1.25 a week, plus you will be receiving tips from the guests you look after, that would greatly increase your wages from what you are earning now." I considered his Lordship's offer there and then, replied, "I will accept your Lordship's offer, but I have no experience in valeting." His Lordship smiled and said, "Don't worry, I will get the butler to teach you, I am sure you will find it easy and I am pleased you will stay with me. I shall tell my butler to get you measured for a footman's uniform. He will teach you how to lay out my clothes in the morning and for the evening meal."

This for me was a step up the ladder upon which I would come into contact with the nobility through offering them my personal service. My job now included laying out the dining table, serving meals and pouring out various wines.

The Lord and Countess of Dumfries had twin sons about one year old when I joined the staff. One was Lord John, the other Lord David, they were lovely boys. I became very fond of them, and sometimes I used to go up and watch their nanny getting them ready for bed. They were very natural boys of their age and full of fun. After, Lord James was born and later Lady Fiona, who was my favourite as she was so beautiful and sweet.

I stayed with the family for four years, in that time I

Calum (the taller) as Footman to Lord Dumfries. M. MacDonald Collection.

met many of the nobility who came to the grouse and pheasant shootings. I used to travel with his Lordship as his "gun-loader", out on the moors. It was a great life and experience for me. Our shooting parties often consisted of such gentry as the Duke of Montrose, Lord Mansfield, the Hon. Drummond-Hay, the Hon. Boland, Bill Stirling, Lord Robert David Rheadian, brother of Lord Dumfries, and Lord Forbes as well as many other rich and famous people. Yet, however much one mixed with them and spoke with them, one was aware he was only a servant. There is always a barrier between the rich and the poor which, to my way of thinking, is quite wrong, for without the poor they would never be rich and I believe that on this earth we are all equal in the sight of God.

In 1937, if my memory serves me correctly, his Lordship told me he was going to take a party to my Island home and he would take me and one of his kitchen hands to look after his party. I was delighted with the news and the thought of a visit to my beloved Hirta once again. Also on the trip were to be some of my fellow St. Kildians. It was arranged I should first take my annual holidays home at Stornoway. The party was travelling from Glasgow on the "S.S. Hebrides", I was to travel from Stornoway to Leverburgh and pick up the ship in the Sound of Harris.

I spent a fortnight's holiday with my family in Stornoway and returned from there to Leverburgh by bus to await the "S.S. Hebrides". I stayed with friends I had come to know when I first left St. Kilda to work for Lord Leverhulme in 1924. They lived in a Black House (or thatched roof cottage) close to the shore. Nearby was a waterfall. I received a telegram from Lochmaddy, saying the "S.S. Hebrides" would stop in the Sound of Harris the following day and pick me up.

Unfortunately for me, everyone in the house slept so sound that night that none of us heard the ship's siren sounding for hours, as the waterfall drowned the sound. When I eventually woke up and looked out of the window, she was after heaving anchor and passing through the channel into the Atlantic on the way to St. Kilda.

I was flabbergasted knowing his Lordship depended on me to look after the party and now there was no way to get to the Island. I felt dismal and thought this will mean the sack and discharge from his Lordship's service. I got a bus to Stornoway where all the family wondered what had happened to me. When I told them, they were very sympathetic. They also could not see how I was to get to the Island till I met my eldest brother, John. He said he thought there was a fishing trawler from Aberdeen taking on fresh water at the pier, so I went down to see if they were fishing near St. Kilda.

We met the Captain and explained my predicament to him. "Yes," he said, "I am going to Rockall and will gladly call at St. Kilda, but if I cannot land you will have to stay on board till the end of the trip. It's up to you to take a chance, I will be sailing in an hour's time." This was an opportunity I could not miss and I was only a day behind schedule. We set off round the Butt of Lewis, passed the Flannan Isles, on to St. Kilda. The wind rose during the night and we hove to at the back of Dun till 8am when we sailed into the bay.

The Captain blew the trawler's siren, but no one seemed to make an effort to come out to us. We could see the party on the Island, but they did not realise why we were hooting the siren. Eventually, as we persisted blowing the ship's siren, we saw them launching a boat out. On board was his Lordship, he just looked at me and said nothing. He got into conversation with the Captain. Only my native islanders spoke to me and asked how did I miss the "Hebrides" the day before. They thought it was quite amusing. Only when we got ashore did his Lordship ask what had happened. I explained as best I could. "Well, MacDonald, I really intended to sack you when I got home, but when I saw your face on the trawler I thought differently. I could see you had a rough passage and I am glad you are here now," he said, "I don't know how I could have fared without you." So the incident was forgotten and I was reprieved.

We all had a wonderful time, lobster fishing, shooting seals, catching puffins and ringing them, roaming all over the hills of the Island. Lord and Lady Dumfries' party consisted of the Marchioness of Bute, Miss Howie, the Hon. Bill Stirling, Mr. Drummond, Father MacQueen (a priest from Barra), a cook named Carruthers and myself. Also on the Island was A. G. Ferguson, Finlay MacQueen and Neil Gillies who helped look after the party. Unfortunately, after a week's stay, our cook met with an accident and broke his collar-bone while trying to shoot a seal out in the bay. He was sent back to the mainland on the first ship that called for a doctor's attention, and did not return. I was then solely left in charge to look after the whole party. We all got on well together while on the island and we were reluctant to leave when the time of our departure came. Life was so blissful and peaceful compared with the hurlyburly of city and town life.

Wider Experiences – In Service and in the War (1939 – 45)

After four years in private service with his Lordship I decided to leave and find service in another private establishment for more experience, in the hope that one day I could become a butler. I applied to domestic agencies in Glasgow and was put in touch with Major Parson, Ford Bank, Johnstone, Paisely and was employed by him as Footman. It was a much smaller homestead than Dumfries House. They kept a smaller staff and did not entertain on the same scale as the Dumfries'. I received a bigger weekly wage of £2 a week plus allowances for laundry etc. The butler was a very experienced man and he taught me quite a lot. The Major had another estate at Southend, Argyle. His wife was one of the "Glencoats" of Paisely, a very famous name in Scotland. They had two sons and they spent each summer at Southend where they had a small yacht, and we sometimes sailed up the Clyde, round the Island of Arran. Myself and another employee on his estate were the only members of the crew. I thoroughly enjoyed these sails.

When the war broke out in 1939, Major Parson informed us we were to be dismissed from his services as he would not be requiring our service and he would only be keeping on the elderly butler, cook and maid.

I then returned to my home in Stornoway and started work with my brother as barman in my brother-in-law's pub. I did not like this very much, so I left and got a job in Tweedmill. I did not care for this either. I met an Aberdonian, married to a Stornoway girl there, and we became friends. He said, "I'm going back to Stornoway, where are you making for?" I said, "Glasgow."

After a few days in Glasgow I was employed in the Rolls Royce factory in Hillington, as a trainee, making parts of aircraft engines. It was a fascinating experience seeing a whole Rolls Royce engine being made and put together. It was a job I kept till the end of the war.

While I was in the factory I received a letter from home that my brother, John, was seriously ill with a brain tumour. We took him to Edinburgh Royal Infirmary, but there was nothing the doctor could do for him. We brought him back to Stornoway where he died two days later without regaining consciousness. It was a sad blow to all our family and our hopes.

Shortly after one of the German raids on Glasgow, I visited my old Uncle, Finlay MacQueen, and my Auntie Annie Ferguson in Kincardine, Fife. As I walked up the garden path he was sitting in a chair in front of their home. His greeting to me was, "And how is your navel, son?" He then said, "You won't be seeing your old uncle much longer. I am getting old but you will always remember me when you undress and look at your tummy and don't you forget it." "No," I said, "but how are you?" He was getting old by this time, his great black beard was now snowy white. "Well," he said, "I sit here day after day, just thinking of the days long ago of our dear Island. Today I have no one to speak to, except the family living in the house with me. People pass by and wave to me, but I cannot converse with them as I have only the Gaelic, but I am old and will soon be at rest." "Oh," I said, "you must not be so morbid, you have many more years yet to come." He was not really listening to me and said, "These Devils (meaning the German planes) passing over at night to bomb Glasgow worry me a lot. It's a sad world we are living in." He carried on, "Do you see that hand?" Putting out his right hand. "That hand shook hands with the King of Great Britain." I said, "When did you shake hands with the King?" He said, "At the Empire Exhibition in Glasgow, in 1938. I was introduced to him." He was very, very proud that he, Finlay MacQueen from Hirta, shook hands with the King of Great Britain. He died a year after I visited him.

On that day I visited them, there were five of my relations living in that house, but today they are all gone. The last, Neil Ferguson, died on the 28th June, 1976, and he was the last Ferguson born on St. Kilda before it was evacuated in 1930. There are several alive, born descendents of the Ferguson clan, scattered about Scotland.

At the end of the war I was made redundant and returned to Stornoway after three months' holiday. I saw an advertisement for a Footman with a Miss Campbell in Ayr. I wrote for the situation and was taken on.

Lord Dumfries, Kames Castle and Courtship

While with Miss Campbell I received a letter from Lord Dumfries' Secretary asking if I cared to take over as Butler-Valet with his Lordship at Kames Castle, Rothesay, at a salary of £4 per week, which I duly accepted. When I arrived I was much greeted by the family and made welcome. Lady Fiona was an addition to the family since I first left, and was still at home. The boys, however, were now grown up and attending college. The staff were mostly strangers to me, but we soon got to know each other. Food was still rationed but we had our home farm and garden which was a great asset to the French chef. The Lord and Lady did not entertain on the same lavish scale as before the war but the chef could still produce a very tasty dish for the dining room table. Instead of a footman to help me in the butler's pantry, one of the maids was my helper. Later on she became my wife, but it was not love at first sight, in fact, it was quite the reverse, as she thought I was too strict in carrying out my duties. His Lordship decided he needed a footman and asked if I knew anyone for the job. I recommended my nephew, William, who was discharged from the army. (William had been a Drummer in the Seaforth Highlanders. He was a twin with Andrew, the sons of Finlay MacDonald). He duly arrived and I taught him his duties as footman which he soon picked up and carried out most efficiently.

Her Ladyship kept two nanny goats as pets, which roamed around the Castle grounds. They were the most mischievous, playful animals I ever came across. If they found any door open, they would run about the passages and it was quite a job to get them to return outside. I usually set the dining room table for dinner in the afternoons. It was a long, highly polished oak table, and after laying out the silverware, table mats, napkins etc, one afternoon I finished the table by putting two vases of flowers on it and it looked extremely beautiful. I then went back to the butler's pantry, just off the dining room, to attend to other necessary jobs. Suddenly I heard a commotion in the dining room, looked in and there on top of my laid table were the two nanny goats and everything topsy-turvy. The wine glasses smashed on the floor, the silverware scattered everywhere, the vases on their sides and the two friends munching away the fresh flowers.

My dear mother died in 1946, soon after I rejoined Lord Dumfries, I went to the funeral. This then was my last tie with a promise I made to myself that I would never marry while she was still alive. I was thirty eight years of age now, and still a bachelor. I became more friendly with the Irish maid, named Marie Doyle, the maid who used to help me in the pantry and who certainly did not like me in those days. Yet, we had a lot in common, as our backgrounds were very similar in many ways. Her parents came of a country background in Eire. We both liked the outdoor life and often went cycling round the Isle of Bute. Our temperaments sometimes clashed, but never seriously, which of course was natural, with her being Irish and me a Scot.

She was a good few years younger than me and gradually our friendship developed to the courting stage; whereby man and woman by instinct learn they are meant for each other, and always want to be in each other's company. Yet at no time did we talk of marriage, but we did decide to leave Scotland and go to London.

My wife-to-be gave in her notice of leave and left for London in May. Our understanding between us was that, if she found a suitable job, I would follow and we would get married. She phoned me regularly and one day she said she had good news for me. If I gave his Lordship a month's notice and came to London, we could get married as she had found a nice situation from an agency. A Mr. and Mrs. Goldburgh, 4, Manor

Davies Street, needed a married couple to look after their flat, and would also give us a bedsitter of our own. This was the kind of opportunity we were seeking. Without further delay I handed in to his Lordship my month's notice of resignation. By now he had become the Marquis of Bute on the death of his father the year before. He rang for me to come to see him in the dining room and enquired as to why I wanted to resign. I explained my reasons and he accepted gracefully. He wished us "happiness and prosperity" and added, "MacDonald, I have come to like you a lot and I regret that you are leaving me. If I had a cottage to offer you both, would you consider staying with me?" I replied, "Thank you, my Lord, but it is our wish to start a new life for ourselves, and London seems a good place to start. My nephew William, the footman, is a good chap and he will look after you as I tried." And so he did, he was promoted to Butler as soon as I left and he served his Lordship for eight years longer.

LIFE BEGINS AGAIN IN LONDON (1947 – 1979)

Marriage and a New Home

At the end of my month's notice I left Kames Castle and came down to London. We got married in the Catholic Church on July 5th, 1947, at St. Dunstans, Chiswick. It was a very quiet affair, for neither of us knew many friends in London. Our honeymoon was taken up exploring round London and visiting the museums and parks. On July 15th, we started our married life working for the Goldburghs. They were charming employers who had two daughters and who did not entertain a lot so we had plenty of leisure hours to see the sights. The following summer we went to Ireland, it was my first visit to the "Emerald Isle" and I fell in love with it and with my in-laws. My wife's home was in Bray, Co. Wicklow, close to the coast. The first

day we climbed Brayhead up to the cross which stands on the top and you can see for miles around. The view is wonderful from up there, as far away as Howth; Dublin and the Sugar Loaf Mountains in the opposite direction and the beautiful green valleys thereabouts. Sitting on the top of Brayhead reminded me so much of my native Isle, St. Kilda, and I just felt I wanted to live there always. We have been over there every other year since and have travelled most of the country since then. We have never travelled abroad, it's been one year in Ireland and the other year, Scotland. In 1949 we had to look for another situation as my wife had become pregnant and No. 4 The Manor was not suitable for a child.

I had an interview with a Mr. and Mrs. Coriat who wanted a Butler; a free cottage was part of any agreement settled. They lived at Twaddley in Malmsbury. We decided to try it and see how things worked out. On the 7th. of May my son was born. My wife and I were so happy and so was my wife's mother as she was now a granny for the first time. We had our son christened John Patrick David, and afterwards we held a party in our cottage. Later we left the Coriat's, we travelled back to London, to my sister who lived near the Oval. That evening my wife, son and mother-in-law went to Ireland while I stayed behind to look for a job in the city. After a few days I got a temporary situation as houseman with a Mrs. Mills, South Street, off Park Lane. Her husband owned "Les Amabassadors" Club near Hyde Park Corner. She had met with an accident while skiing in Switzerland and sprained her ankle and needed a temporary man in the house while she recuperated, for she entertained guests of the club, while confined to the house. During the fortnight I was with her she entertained the film stars, Tyrone Power and his wife who were newly married, also Michael Wilding and Stewart Grainger. They were all friends of the Mills' and were regularly at their club. Cooked meals were sent in from the club and I had to act as waiter and butler to these famous stars of their day.

I found Mrs. Mills a very friendly individual, but at the end of the fortnight she was well enough to dispense with my services. She asked if she could do anything to help me. I said, "No. I would look round on my own for something different from private service." It was not easy so I signed on at the Labour Exchange at Brixton.

Grosvenor House, Park Lane

After a week the Labour Exchange advised me, with my kind of experience, to try the hotels and gave me a list to go for an interview. Of the many I tried, only Grosvenor House had a vacancy for a relief valet. I was taken to the Manager's Office, where I was asked about my past employment and if I had any reference I could show. I produced the only one I had. It was from the Lord Bute, and it read as follows:-

Mount Stuart
Rothesay,
Isle of Bute.
9th November 1948

To whom it may concern,

Malcolm MacDonald was for several years in my employ as valet, footman and loader, and for a considerable period was in sole charge of plate and silver. In all the time he was with me he carried out his duties most efficiently. He is clean, sober and honest in every way, and I can personally vouch for his absolute integrity of character.

He has travelled with me a good deal and from experience I can say that he packs extraordinarily well, and looks after everything on the journey in such a way that his employer has nothing at all to worry about. Never have I known anything to go wrong either by land, sea or air, when MacDonald was with me.

He is extraordinarily good with children and was a great favourite with my sons and daughter.

He looked after my shooting dogs on many occasions, and did so extremely efficiently. In fact, animals appeared to take a ready liking to him.

He left, much to my regret, when he got married, because at that time I had not a single vacant house on my estate to offer him.

Should any further information be required I shall be only too pleased to furnish it.

Signed – Bute.

When the Manager read it, he was much impressed. He offered me the job as valet, which I accepted, and followed up with the question, "What wages do you expect starting in the Hotel?" I said, "I don't know, about seven or eight pounds a week." "Tut, tut," he said, "you will be earning far more than that." This was great news to me and I was exceedingly excited at the prospect of informing my wife in Ireland, that at last, I had found a very good job, and that they would be able to return very soon to London. I was told to go and see the head valet, a Mr. Smith, and if satisfied with me I could start the following Monday, which I did.

My first wages were about £14, plus tips, which brought them up to about seventeen pounds. Nowadays, or course, wages are much higher and a valet can earn up to £60 a week and sometimes £70 with overtime, but it was only since I retired that this happened. Still I was very satisfied when I first started and I liked the job and meeting all kinds of people. I was able to give each individual whatever kind of service was required by each guest; and one only worked eight hour shifts, instead of all day long as in private service. The staff were provided with a uniform and their meals while on duty.

My wife and son and I stayed with my sister at the Oval while we looked round for a home of our own. In a local paper we saw an advert, "A flat in an old Victorian house on Wandsworth Road, with a large garden at the back; present occupier going to Australia." The lady wanted £100 for the key and furnishings and seventeen shillings weekly rent to be paid to her old father who was living in the basement flat below. We accepted her offer and handed over our little nest egg of £100 we had struggled to save. It was a good investment in the end, for when the council knocked down the old building years afterwards, we got a council flat across the road, where we are living at the present time. As the family came along, in the old house, besides John, there was Charles, Elizabeth and Marion born there.

When all the children were attending school and able to go and come home on their own my wife suggested she should take a part time job to help rear the children and also to pass the time. We were now living in our new council flat. She took on part time domestic work for various people in the city. It was a great asset to the family budget and holidays each year. She then took on a steady job at 40, Queen's Gate, a block of flats, as a maid from 10am till 4pm. After a year she was asked to run the place as manageress. I told her to go ahead, that she had enough brains and common sense to give it a try, which she did, and I am proud to say she never looked back. She developed a wonderful personality and has a brilliant alert mind and a photographic memory, which amazes me at times, and not only me, but her employers too. The place has prospered from the day she took over, and most of her guests are very rich Arabs from the Middle East. She is known as Mrs. Mac to them all, including the Arabian Embassy in London. Some of her guests include very prominent people from the Middle East and across America and throughout the world. Each and all her guests receive the same courtesy and attention, her Irish sense of humour outrides any diplomacy expected to be given; a prince or a rich sheik, they all receive the same treatment.

Working in a hotel brings one in contact with many cross sections of fellow beings, creeds and colours. In my lowly capacity as a valet I have met very famous names: America's Cardinal Spellman, Rev. Billy Graham the evangelist, Margaret Lockwood, Doris Day, Shirley MacLaine, Ray Milland, Rock Hudson, Tony Curtis and Peter Falk. His Highness Sultan of Brunei, His Highness Sultan and family of Johore, George Formby, Captain Townsend, Sir Oswald Mosley, Sir Gerald Nabarro, Commander E. H. Walker, Enoch Powell my favourite politician, Jackie Stewart and many more famous names. All very charming, sincere people. I have also met some others who were the opposite.

Last Trip to St. Kilda – 1967

In 1967 I made my last trip to St. Kilda and took my eldest son, John, with me. We joined the party from the National Trust for Scotland. It was my son's first visit to his ancestral Island and it meant great excitement to look forward to. The party was in great spirits when we left Mallaig, where we all joined the boat that would take us there. It was not the most comfortable boat to make such a journey. We all sat on deck until we reached Lochmaddy, where we stayed for the night. In the early morning we left Lochmaddy and came on deck, where we all sat for the next eight hours till we reached St. Kilda. It was cold and uncomfortable with sea mist most of the way. Once we had gone through the Sound of Harris and headed into the Atlantic we drifted a bit off course because of the running tide. A straight course would have brought us in between Levenish and Boreray and the Stacs of Armin and Lee to get our bearings. We could not see much ahead for a while, the mist was all around us, but we knew we were in the vicinity of the Islands for we could smell the guano of the gannets and the other birds which nest there. Gradually we could see all the islands. We started our engines again and sailed close to Boreray. How familiar they all were to me, and happy I was as I tried to explain to my son the different islets and rocks as we passed by the main island and bay. It was 2pm when we came in the bay and, to everyone's relief, the boat finally stopped rolling from side to side in the Atlantic waves.

It was a nostalgic visit for me, even though the party was very cheerful and my son was with me. As I walked on my own one day through the village street and stepped into every ruined house, I had vivid memories of each and every family who occupied each house in my youth and recalled their greetings, and now only ghosts remained. As I walked into the cemetery where rested my two sisters and forefathers, it was a sad experience which I tried to hide from the rest of the party.

The Army added to our excitement by taking us up to Mullach Sgar by jeep to wait for a plane coming in from Benbecula, which dropped the mail from about a hundred feet up. It made a circle overhead and flew back to Benbecula after the drop. The Army Captain kept up conversation with the pilot by radio all the time. Such a thing to have happened in my forefather's day would have been a miracle, and, if they had been told it would happen one day, they would have called you a "crank". On another occasion they entertained us at the station by first giving us a drink at their special bar and then showing us a film, an evening well spent. I even had the pleasure of phoning London and spent a few minutes talking to my family, who were surprised and excited, so that they could hardly believe it was from Hirta I was speaking to them. On Sunday the Army Chaplain held a service in the old familiar church. The preacher's pulpit is still there, also the smaller box pulpit where my father, as Precentor, used to lead the singing in Gaelic, but there are only a few of the congregation's pews to be seen. The trip was

wonderful and exciting for my son, he enjoyed every day. It was all too brief, but it gave him an inward sight of my kind of life as a boy, compared to his in the city of London. Here Nature led you by the hand through the four seasons of the year, one was born free and Mother Nature took charge of you.

On returning to London, my son John took part in the Duke of Edinburgh's Gold Award by climbing Mount Snowdon in Wales. He was presented with the Medal at Buckingham Palace, a very proud moment for him and us. He joined the Police Cadets at Hendon, where he passed out as a Police Officer, he is now attached to Willesden Police Station. He played rugby for the metropolitan Police for a couple of years and he also plays for London Scottish and toured the U.S.A. in 1976 with them and won the silver cup. He married in 1971 a Miss Haley Waterworth, who represented London in the Rose of Tralee competition in the same year. They have a son named Stuart who was born in 1973 and looks as if he is going to be another born rugby player for the future. He is five years younger than my youngest son born in 1968

My second eldest son, Charles, married in 1973 a Miss Susanne Gouldsmith, a policeman's daughter. He is a qualified chartered accountant and they now live in Australia, after emigrating in 1976.

My eldest daughter, Elizabeth, is a hairdresser, and Marion a staff nurse at Westminster Hospital. Neil is an apprentice plasterer, and Andrew is still at school.

In 1971, Tom Steel, the author of "The Life and Death of St. Kilda" phoned me for an interview, informing me that he was making a film of the Island and would like some information about my life there. I agreed to the interview. A few days later, to my surprise and unprepared, he came with his crew and television cameras and set them up in my home. Tom Steel interviewed me while his crew filmed it. A remark I made in my sitting room, saying, "It was a far better place" became the title of the programme. It was the first time I had ever sat in front of the television camera and it was quite an ordeal. I am very glad to have contributed a small part in the film, which was a great success in this country and Australia where it was shown. His book gave an insight into the life of the island long before I was born and contains many picturesque accounts of the natives and Island.

Reflection Over the Past

At this stage in my life I feel I have a lot to be thankful for, as I look back over the years, since I started out on life's journey till my retirement in 1976. Most of the credit is due to my cool-headed wife, her devotion as a wife and mother, in rearing a happy family and who, through her own initiative and without scholarship, has achieved a great success in life.

I have time to reflect on my past life, of the many kinds of jobs I was employed in, since I left my native Hirta, and to be thankful to my Creator for his goodness to me throughout my life, for good health, an excellent wife and a happy family; to be able to give them an opportunity and start in life which I did not have at their age. I trust they will be proud of their ancestry on both sides of the family and know that all men are equal in the sight of God. Riches and wealth, or an exciting life was never my ambition; for by nature I love all that is natural – the hills and glens, the country and the sea. As each day passes, I still traverse in dreams my native home, its shores, its caves, the way of life that once was, and wish I could return and spend a few more years in the quiet solitude of its embrace, away from the turmoil of city life – but I seem to live in memories."

Calum MacDonald died on St. Mary's Hospital, Paddington on the 22nd July 1979, of a heart attack, after two years of a very painful illness. The National Trust for Scotland and the British Army kindly allowed Calum's ashes to be taken back to his native home, which he loved so much. They were buried in the cemetery on St. Kilda.

UPDATE 1987, CALUM'S BROTHERS, SISTERS AND FAMILY
Calum's Brothers and Sisters

JOHN (1896 – 1942) Married Kirsty Campbell from Stornoway and had 11 children, Bella, Murdo, Norman, Christina, Malcolm, William, Ina, William John and three children who died in infancy.

FINLAY (1897 – 1982) Married Mary Nicolson from Stornoway and had two sets of twins, William and Andrew, Katherine Mary and John, and Finlay.

ANNABELLA (1900 – 1985) Married Kenneth Macleod of Stornoway and had four sons and one daughter, Donald, Roderick, William. Kenneth John and Christina.

MARY (1902 – 1985) Married Alex MacLeod from Stornoway and had four daughters, Chrissie Anne, Norma, Nancy and Mary. After the death of Alex she married Joe Hill, an Australian.

MARY-BETSEY (1904 – baby).

FINLAY-JOHN (1906 – Still alive) Married Kate Graham of Stornoway who had two children, Catherine and William John. Finlay-John was a prisoner of war and now lives in London, during last 7 years he has had nine operations, including a leg amputation. The Nurses call him "Bionic Man!"

CALUM (1908 – 1979) Married Marie Doyle and had four boys and two girls, John, Charles, Elizabeth, Marion, Neil and Andrew.

KIRSTY (1900 – 1920) Probably died of diphteria, aged nine.

RACHEL (1912 – 1985) Married Alex MacLeod of Stornoway but had no children.

MARION/MORAG (1916 – 1988) Married William MacDonald and had three daughters, Mairi,

Anne Christine and Wilma.

MARY/MAE (1917 – alive) Married Angus MacLeod and had four boys, Neil, Angus-John, Lewis and Murdo.

Four of the MacDonalds married MacLeods, none of whom were related, and one married a MacDonald who was not related.

Calum and Marie MacDonald's Family

JOHN, born in 1949, married Hayley Waterworth in 1971 and have one son, Stuart born in 1973.

CHARLES, born in 1950, married Susanne Gouldsmith in 1973 and have one son, Duncan Calum Charles born in 1987.

ELIZABETH, born in 1952 married Andrew Gibbon in 1982 and have twin boys, John and Alexander.

MARION, born in 1954 married Alex Petschi in 1986.

NEIL, born in 1959 married June Chalk in 1982 and they have a daughter Kirsty born in 1984.

ANDREW, born in 1968 is an apprentice electrical engineer.

Mary Cameron –
The Manse, 1919 – 26.
A Childhood Portrait

Sea cliffs of Dun. Acland.

BEFORE ST. KILDA
IN THE BEGINNING, 1919
EXACTING CONDITIONS
OVER THE MOON
SUMMER MONTHS
MAKING THE TWEED
IN THE END . . . 1926
AFTER ST. KILDA

The contents of this Chapter were produced in a booklet, "Childhood Days on St. Kilda" being the reminiscences of Miss Mary Cameron, who as a young girl lived for many years on St. Kilda. The booklet was designed, compiled and produced by the late S. Barker Johnson (Bee Jay), partly from material which Mary had written earlier as articles in the Oban Times. Sadly the booklet is now out of print but his widow has kindly given me permission to reproduce this portrait of St. Kilda by Mary Cameron, who herself has recently died.

BEFORE ST. KILDA

Mary Cameron and her sister Christina comprised the family of the Rev. and Mrs. Donald Cameron. He was a lay missionary of the United Free Church of Scotland, and from 1919 – 1926 went to St. Kilda to preach the Gospel there for two terms of office; generally a missionary who could be found to accept the St. Kilda call was only supposed to stay three years at the most. He and his family stayed seven years; and were loathe to leave even then.

Mary was born in 1913. Christina was fifteen months her junior. Their mother was born and bred in North Uist; their father was a native of Argyll (brought up in Ballachulish) but had spent some years in North Uist where he met and married the lady of his choice. They lived in Stornoway for two years and Mary was born there shortly before the outbreak of the First World War. They were then sent to the mission station at Callernish (Lewis), where Christina was born. They arrived in St. Kilda in the early summer of 1919 on the steamer "Hebrides" from Lochmaddy.

IN THE BEGINNING, 1919

"When, at the early age of five and a bit, I arrived at St. Kilda with my parents and my younger sister, on a

Some of the Girls. Cameron Collection.

summer day in 1919, the tide was out: and the rowing boat which conveyed us ashore from the steamer 'Hebrides' landed us on the rocks thickly covered with slippery seaweed, as the little jetty was high and dry. My very first recollection then, is of being carried up to the house which was to be my home for the next seven years, by a tall comely woman of the island – Mary Gillies. My sister was similarly transported by another young woman and remembers being frightened by the strangeness of it all. Mary Gillies entered domestic service in Glasgow some years after this and became Mrs. Wright. The only other thing I remember of that momentous day is that my mother wore a black velvet hat, with a bunch of cherries on the brim!

The Manse was a long low building, substantially stone built, with very thick walls. There were six rooms on the ground floor. Some of the windows were fitted with shutters on the inside. My mother found the window recesses very useful for the cultivation of her beloved geraniums.

Above the living-room fireplace was a portrait of Queen Victoria at her most forbidding. On another wall hung a picture entitled "The Squire's Daughter", depicting a young lady in a riding habit, holding a horse's bridle. Some of the rooms were lined with wood, painted or varnished, but two had plaster and wallpaper, and I faintly remember that the living-room paper had roses on it.

The kitchen was a small room at the back of the house, with a sink and a cold water tap in the recess. There was a small coal range and beside it the press where my mother kept all her china. All the best things were there, taken out on special occasions. There were shelves, too, on the walls of the kitchen, and crockery was kept there too.

Off the kitchen there opened a roomy pantry – a most fascinating place. There were no shops on St. Kilda, and each household laid in its own supply of everything necessary for a year or so. This meant several sacks of flour and oatmeal: a hundredweight bag of sugar; tea by the stone; dozens of tins of syrup, treacle, meat and milk; butter in large tins prepared for export; whole cheeses; hams and bladders of lard; tins of biscuits and quantities of dried fruit, jam and so on. We grew our own potatoes and some vegetables, but onions we must have stored. There were also delightful surprises tucked away. On a wet day, my mother might produce a surprise treat in the shape of a bar of chocolate or a handful of sugared carvies, which we munched as we pored over books.

My mother was an excellent baker, and in St. Kilda she had plenty of opportunity to practice the art. Bread was treated as a luxury, and kept for making toast. The rest of the time, we ate my mother's good scones and oatcakes, pancakes and home-baked cakes. Most of the trawler crews made their own bread, and they occasionally brought a loaf or two ashore, and some fresh fish, when they called. Often, too, they would

St. Kilda Field Mouse outside the Factor's House.

187

bring from their home ports a small order or any groceries which might be running short.

Of course, a sharp lookout was kept for mice in the food store, and some traps were always kept handy.

Our parents each had their jobs to do. It was a dual appointment. My father was responsible for the spiritual welfare of the people, while my mother, who had been a teacher before her marriage, had children's education in her charge. When we went to St. Kilda first, there were 72 people on the island – 36 of each sex – and there were 17 on the school roll, including our widowed nurse's two boys (Ian and Alex MacKenzie), my sister and myself. Before we left the number had dwindled to eight, and the total population was, if I remember rightly, 49. As has happened in so many other Highland and Island townships, some less remotely situated than St. Kilda, the younger folk left to seek their fortune elsewhere, and it became mainly a community of older people.

Evacuation became necessary when there were not enough able-bodied men to man the boats, without which contact could not be maintained with the other islands in the group (all uninhabited); and to carry out the fowling and bird-nesting expeditions so necessary for the maintenance of the islander's natural food supply.

EXACTING CONDITIONS

The church was connected with the schoolroom by a door, and sometimes my father took a class by themselves in the church. When we arrived, part of it was in ruins as a result of bombardment by a German submarine shortly before the end of the First World War. Miraculously the dwelling-house and school escaped without serious damage.

The ferocity of the gales on St. Kilda had to be felt to be believed. You could hear the rush of a squall as it came down the steep hillsides of Connachair and Mullach Mor, and if you were wise, you got hold of something substantial before it reached you. Everything, even in summer, had to be fastened down, because, out there in the Atlantic, we never knew when the wind might get up. The rowing boats, so essential to the life of the community, besides being drawn up, high and dry, were anchored to the ground with heavy boulders. I remember, once, a particularly severe storm lifted one boat bodily and hurled it down on the rocky shore.

In addition to a well stocked-larder, a well stocked-coal cellar was necesaary; and casks of paraffins were stored in another outhouse, for that, together with a supply of candles, was of course, our means of lighting and it meant that matches had to be stocked as well. Power cuts did not worry us.

Yet another of the little outhouses was our meat store, where now and again the carcase of a fat wedder was hung, part of it to be salted in a barrel for future use. There would also be a half-barrel of herring stowed away somewhere – the Highlander's mainstay.

The running water in the manse came from a well a few yards from the house. It was clear, cold, spring water from an unknown source, and we never knew it to run dry.

Our potatoes and vegetables grew well enough, but high wind was always a bogey, especially at the crucial stage of flowering in the case of potatoes. We must have been plagued by birds, because my father once set up a scarescrow in the garden, and Mrs. Ferguson, the postmaster's wife, spent a whole day wondering what on earth he was doing there standing still in the one spot. We grew rhubarb, with which my mother made quite a lot of jam. We also kept hens and a cow.

The byre, like all the other buildings, was a substantial, slated one, with a little house built on at the end, in which Annie's calf was quartered until it could be shipped to the mainland.

OVER THE MOON

During the First World War, St. Kilda was a naval lookout post, transmitting reports on enemy submarines and shipping by means of a wireless installation. There were two immensely tall aerial masts, both of which were still there when we arrived on the island. It was not until 1918 that the Germans took steps to silence the St. Kilda wireless station.

One summer day, that year, a submarine appeared in the bay, and, after warning the inhabitants by loud hailer (the captain must have been a humane person), proceeded with the bombardment, first of a large store near the shore. The next shell hit the church, and demolished the byre, in which, incidently, Annie (the cow we later owned) was buried. She belonged at that time to my father's predecessor there. Fortunately, the poor creature was unharmed, and was later rescued, in a very bad state of nerves.

All this had happened before our time, but we always noticed that Annie visibly started if she heard a shot. She never forgot her alarming experience. A newspaper published a report of the incident under the caption, "The cow jumped over the moon".

The next shell practically demolished the nurse's cottage, which had an upstairs flat used by the factor on his annual visit. One of the village houses was also demolished.

In all, I believe over 70 shells were fired, after which the submarine withdrew, and the people came back from the deep gulley in which they had taken shelter, and surveyed the damage. The commander of the submarine could have easily rendered them all homeless. But only No.1 was demolished. The wireless station was out of action for only a few hours, and no lives were lost.

I remember that the glebe was pitted with shell holes, into which we children used to creep when playing hide-and-seek. The whole place was littered

Church Shell damaged by the German Submarine. Cameron Collection.

with cruel looking pieces of shrapnel. We held church services in the part of the building which remained intact, but I remember it was dark, with some of the windows and the broken walls covered with sacking. One glorious Sunday we had morning service out of doors. The district nurse, Mrs. Mackenzie, and her two boys had to live in one of the naval huts, left after the war, until the cottage was repaired. In due course, the village house which had been hit was also repaired.

The wireless installation was removed after the war. Had there been some means of direct communication with the outside world left to them, it is possible that the younger people of St. Kilda might not so soon have left for the mainland, and so hastened the evacuation of the island. That, and a regular (even if monthly) mail services all the year round, might have made all the difference. As it was we were dependant for our mails on the visits and kind offices of English trawlers from August until the end of May, and during these months our mails were directed "via Fleetwood". During the summer we got them addressed "via Glasgow".

189

Sometimes, if the trawlers had to go further afield for their catch – say to Rockall or the Flannans, or even further – we might not see them for many weeks on end. Once, I remember, we were 11 weeks without mails, and were opening our Christmas cards in March.

In a newspaper which arrived by that mail, there was a sensational report of the hardship inflicted on the people of London, who had, owing to a printing dispute, been obliged to go without their morning papers for (I think) three days. My father was so struck by the humour of it that he wrote to the paper concerned, telling of the length of time which his Majesty's subjects on St. Kilda had had to wait for their Christmas mail. The paper published the letter, and the next mail which reached St. Kilda brought such a shoal of periodicals of all kinds that not one sack, but several, had to be used to cope with it! People from all over the country sent reading matter; and one gentleman sent my father the Manchester Guardian regularly from then on, for quite a long time.

The church was a very simple place, rather austere, which matched the simple, robust faith of the folk who filled it each Sunday. There was no heating, but I don't remember that we ever complained of the cold. The St. Kilda folk were grand churchgoers. Even babies of a few weeks old were taken to church; nobody stayed away unless they were ill.

The manse pew was at the side of the pulpit, at right angles to the other pews, and from it we could see everyone who was there. The men and boys sat at the inner end of the pews, and the female members of the family on the outside; and when the service was over, the menfolk remained seated until the women and girls had left the church.

In the winter, each family was lighted to church by a hurricane lantern, or a ship's lantern; and these were carefully placed on the floor, with the flame turned down, until the service was over, when they were turned up for the homeward journey. There was something very comforting about the string of twinkling lights which pierced the darkness as the congregation walked home.

I have never heard such hearty singing anywhere as in the church at St. Kilda, and we had two excellent precentors in William MacDonald and Norman MacKinnon, both of whom have, alas, long since passed on.

School inspections were carried out by the Inverness County Education Authority, and I can remember a visit paid by the then Director of Education for the county, Mr. Murdo Morrison. One inspection was carried out in the wee sma' oors. It happened this way. The steamer arrived on Sunday, and the St. Kildans, being strict Sabbath observers, would handle none of her cargo until after midnight. A school inspection on the Sabbath was, of course, out of the question. The ship's captain was very anxious to sail as soon as the cargo was landed, so we children were mustered out of our beds soon after midnight, in order that His Majesty's Inspector of Schools might comply with the regulations. I am quite sure we did not give a very impressive performance – what child would?

A doctor from the Board of Health also used to pay an annual visit. We always had a resident nurse on the island, and she had a supply of medicines, but my mother always kept simple remedies in the house and was able to cope with most situations. We had a very nasty epidemic of whooping-cough once, brought to the island by a young man home from Glasgow, and practically every man, woman and child took it. I can remember having mumps there, too, but at so early an age that I took it again after coming to the mainland.

SUMMER MONTHS

I am sure my mother was appalled to see the cliffs were not fenced! We were put on our honour not to go too near the edges, and we never met with an accident, although the potential was practically at our door.

I suppose everyone has heard of the St. Kilda Parliament. I have often seen it in session, outside the postmaster's house. It was simply a gathering of the menfolk of the village to discuss plans for the day's work – very necessary where so much of the labour was of a communal nature.

Another very clear recollection I have is of the scene after a day's bird-nesting, when the men sat on the grass with the boxes of eggs - gannet, guillemot and fulmar – which they had culled from the cliffs, and shared them out.

Innumerable sparrows, starlings, wrens and other small birds nested in the crevices of the many stone walls, and we were taught to respect them and not to pry too much lest they deserted their eggs.

Like ourselves, practically every household kept a cow (perhaps two), and all the winter's supply of hay was grown on the island. Linseed meal, and poultry

The Village, An Lag, the Gap and Boreray from Mullach Sgar.

food, we did import, like the other food stuffs, but we never had to buy any hay. Grass grew in abundance on the glebe, which was walled in and divided into two parts – for grazing and hay respectively.

I have more than once referred to the strong winds which we experienced. One particularly severe storm left us deaf for a week – incredible but true. The noise of the wind, the pounding of the heavy seas, were indescribable. This storm was accompanied by thunder and lightning, but we could not hear the thunder for the other sounds. Our windows were often white with salt spray, and it was awe-inspiring to watch the billows and the spindrift.

The glen ended in a steep cliff, called Bearradh na h-Eige, and there, dropping plumb to the sea many hundreds of feet below, was the nesting place of many fulmar petrels. The narrow ledges were full of them; and just before a certain date in August, the men of St. Kilda secured the young birds to augment the food supply. After that date it was too late – they were on the wing.

The rope was fastened round the fowler's waist, the other end being secured to a companion, who paid it out as the fowler made his careful way, barefooted down the cliff face. It was dangerous work, calling for a steady head, strong hands, a stout heart (and rope); fatal accidents were not unknown, although none, happily, occured in our time.

I have seen a boy of ten years taking his turn with the grown-ups, and proudly bringing up his quota of young fulmars from the cliff. The women folk did not go down the cliff to catch the birds, but they were always in attendance, ready to help carry them home; and I have seen them run, barefoot, to meet the bird-catchers, in places where ordinary people like ourselves simply closed our eyes, shuddering! The rod ('slat-riobaidh) used for fowling was a long cane-like fishing rod, with a horse hair noose at the tip.

The women were adept at carrying heavy loads on their backs, and thought nothing of carrying a full-sized sheep thus in a piece of sacking, its legs tied together. This they had in common with many other Island and Highland women. I am thinking of the heavy creels of peats so often carried long distances by the women of Lewis. I cannot remember having seen creels in use in St. Kilda, but we were often amazed by the way in which bolls of flour and oatmeal were carried with apparent ease, with a rope tied round the middle and passed over the shoulders and across the chest of the bearer, just as a creel is carried.

MAKING THE TWEED

In stormy weather, in autumn, winter and spring, the Village Bay was a haven for trawlers sheltering from westerly and north-westerly gales. I have counted 47 trawlers at once, and they were all a long way from the shore. At night, all their bright lights gave the impression of a town, and we felt less remote when we saw them.

Our parents used to hang a lamp as a guiding light in one window of the house which directly faced the mouth of the bay. There was, and still is, as far as I know, no light or beacon on the St. Kilda group.

Some of the trawlers' names, and the names of the skippers, I can still recollect – City of London, City of Selby, Imelda, Lunida, Wyre, Philip Godby, Rose Valley; the variety was tremendous. These were all Fleetwood, Hull or Grimsby trawlers. Sometimes several members of the same family skippered boats. There were the Wright brothers, the Brewsters (of whom I think there were three), and two Sandhams (James and Tom), Captain Hargreaves, Captain Pennington, and many others. When the wind blew from the south or south-east, the vessels sheltered on the uninhabited side of the island. In the summer months, line fishing vessels from Aberdeen and other east coast ports frequently anchored in the bay at weekends. As is well known, the east coast fishermen were extremely devout, and great singers. They observed Sunday as a day of rest, and the strains of Moody and Sankey hymn tunes were often wafted across to us.

We were sometimes taken, of an evening, with our parents when they went visiting in the village. There were no electric torches, so we took a paraffin lantern, which cast the most exciting shadows as we walked along. The dogs at each house hailed us with loud barking, and when we were ushered inside, there would be quite a scene of industry round the fire. There would be the purr of the spinning wheel, operated by the woman of the house. The men and the boys, and older girls, might be teasing wool ('cireadh'), picking out rough bits and pieces of grass, and preparing the wool for its next stage, the carding; or else working oil into it to make it easier to handle ('armadh'). There might be someone else wielding a pair of cards – flat wooden brushes with steel teeth, which comb out the wool. The worker then, with a deft movement, would fashion the combed wool into a soft roll ready for spinning; or he might lay it aside in a flat pad ('peard') to be blended later with another shade ('colmadh').

Before New Year, what was known as the 'cardadh mor' (the big carding) took place. It was communal work and the people gathered in each other's houses in turn. Each had a pair of cards and a quantity of wool. They sat round the room, and as each 'peard' or pad came off the cards, it was thrown into the middle of the floor. The pile gradually got higher, and the work was lightened by many a tale and a merry jest.

After the 'cardadh mor', the wool had to be carded again, more thoroughly, blended as to colour, and fashioned into rolls ('rollagan') for spinning ('Sniomh'). Then the women got busy with their spinning wheels, and I can hear the drone and rattle of them still.

About February, or perhaps a little earlier, the looms were taken down from the lofts and assembled, and the men got down to the business of weaving (figheadh'). I have so far omitted to mention the dyeing of the wool before it was processed, or the warping (deilbh) which had to be done on a frame on the wall before it was ready for the loom. They were handlooms, with treadles operated by the feet, for the changing of the warp. I remember, one night, seeing a man weaving by the light of cruisie ('cruisgean') because of a shortage of paraffin. It was fed with fulmar oil, if I remember rightly, and looked rather like a large candle as it burned with a smoky flame.

The dyes used were 'crotal' or lichen, from the rocks, which gave a reddish brown shade when the wool was boiled in water with it; and indigo blue ('guirmean'), which was imported from the south. Black sheep were cherished for their wool as they were scarce.

When the weaving was finished, the looms were packed away again on the lofts; and, with the coming of the spring, the tweeds were waulked (that is, shrunk by hand, the process known as 'luadhadh'), washed, dried out of doors on the many stone walls, and neatly rolled up.

Visitors, landing from the Glasgow steamers during the summer, when they paid their monthly calls, bought lengths of the tweed, and also socks and gloves knitted by the women folk, as well as the beautifully marked shells of the seabirds' eggs.

It frequently happened, if the sea were choppy, that passengers being ferried ashore in the small boats (the steamers were unable to berth at St. Kilda) were drenched with spray; and my mother would have to come to the rescue with dry clothes. On one occasion, an elderly lady appeared at the door, very wet, and my mother took her in and lent her garments until her own were dried. It had been a rough crossing, she said. She had got into conversation with the captain, who had enquired if she were a good sailor. She had answered, airily, that she had sailed round the world. 'Ah, yes, madam', he had remarked, 'but you haven't been to St. Kilda yet!'

We did have some rough crossings, but only one comes to mind. We took nine hours that day from Tarbert, Harris to make the crossing to St. Kilda. It normally took five. The weather worsened as we plunged westwards. There was a south-westerly gale. The seas were mountainous, and the little 'Hebrides' took the billows one by one, rolling and pitching. Sometimes her side rails were in the water, and we wondered if she would ever right herself. We were so miserably sea-sick that we felt it might not matter very much if she didn't! I think practically everyone on board was ill. Even Finlay MacQueen, a hardy St. Kildan, who had been on holiday on the mainland fell victim to the malady; and that was unheard of as far as the men folk on St. Kilda were concerned.

When things were at their worst, my mother, who was sitting on the deck in the shelter at the top of one of the companionways, holding on for dear life, saw Mr. George Blair, the purser, approaching, immaculate as always in his neat uniform, and with his pointed white beard. 'Oh, Mr. Blair', she moaned, 'isn't it terrible'; to receive the rather disconcerting reply: "Well, what do you expect in the middle of the Atlantic?"

That was one day we were truly thankful when our island home hove in sight! We heard afterwards that it would have been impossible for the captain to turn back.

IN THE END . . . 1926

While on the subject of ships, I must mention one especially eventful day. It was towards the end of May, one bright Sunday morning, and we were awaiting the arrival or the 'Hebrides' on her first call of the season. A boy had gone round the promontory known as Gob Choll to see if she were in sight. Presently he reappeared, waving his arms excitedly and suddenly we saw, not the little ship we expected, but the enormous black hull of an ocean liner. She was the T.S.S. 'Sarpedon' of the Blue Funnel Line, Liverpool, on her maiden voyage – a cruise of the Western Isles. The owners, the Holt brothers, were on board, and with them a large company of business friends, including titled people, and Japanese and Chinese business men and their wives. Messrs MacBrayne's had lent, as pilot, the late Captain MacArthur, who served on so many West Highland and Island ships, among them the Clydesdale, Loch Ness and the Loch Seaforth.

The 'Sarpedon' did not venture into the bay, but her motor tenders soon brought her passengers ashore in relays. The owners were very anxious to give the islanders a supply of provisions, and said that their own crew would do all that was necessary, which they did. Our larders, which were becoming a bit bare, were very amply replenished that day! We children must have forgotten our manners, and stared open mouthed at the visitors for one Japanese gentleman asked us, smilingly, if we had ever seen Japanese before. We hadn't, of course, except in pictures, and we were greatly fascinated by them.

During the afternoon the 'Hebrides' came on the scene, and looked like a toy ship beside the giant 'Sarpedon', the level of whose bridge was just reached by the tops of her masts. A few hours later the 'Sarpedon' steamed majestically away to continue her cruise.

In May of our last year (1926) on St. Kilda, the island was visited by a very severe epidemic of influenza. The germ was brought by a trawler. The weather was hot and beautiful, but it was a deserted village one saw when one looked out, as practically every soul was prostrate. Our district nurse at that time, was the late Miss Katherine Littlejohn from

Banchory, Aberdeenshire. She had been stationed on Fair Isle before coming to us, so she was admirably fitted for the St. Kilda post! Nurse herself fell ill, and was only just able to crawl through her daily rounds. Her medicines were almost exhausted. Not a ship was in sight.

It was 1926, and there was a general strike on, although we knew nothing about it. Four of the older folk died in one week – a devastating blow in such a small community. One night, Nurse and a few young men dragged themselves to a hilltop with material for a bonfire, hoping to attract the attention of passing shipping. It was a vain hope, but mercifully, on the evening of the day on which the fourth funeral took place, the 'Hebrides' put in on her first call of the summer from Glasgow, and help was at hand.

We left St. Kilda that summer. Annie, the cow had still one adventure to meet. She swam out to the 'Hebrides', behind the boat, one of the men holding her head above the water. On arrival at the ship a sling was passed under her in the water (a very difficult operation) and she was hauled aloft by the ship's crane. To our horror, the sling slipped, and poor Annie plunged headfirst into the ocean! Needless to say, we thought that that was the end of her, but no. Up she came, and another attempt was made to get the sling on, the ship listing heavily meantime as everyone on board crowded to watch the operation. It was successful, and a very 'drookit' Annie was safely stowed on board; where by and by my father went below and milked her for the last time. She was old, and we had to part with her.

These then are some of the memories which my sister and I cherish of our sojourn on the (then) loneliest outpost of Britain. We shall always count it a privilege to have spent some of our earlier years there".

AFTER ST. KILDA

After leaving St. Kilda the Cameron family settled in Glenelg where Mr. Cameron was ordained. Later they moved to Easdale, Lochaline where they once again met up with some of their St. Kilda friends. Having served next in Shawbost in the Isle of Lewis, Mr. Cameron retired in 1944 and settled in the Kyle of Lochalsh. He died in 1950 and his wife a year later. Both Mary and Christine studied at the Inverness Royal Academy and both became outstanding school teachers.

John MacLeod –
A Missionary's Portrait

BERNERAY BACKGROUND
FIRST MARRIAGE AND FAMILY, 1912.
NEW START AFTER TRAGEDY, Second
Marriage.
INTERESTS AND INFLUENCES

LIFE ON ST. KILDA – 1926 – 29 First
Impression, Church Life, School Days,
Visiting Trawlers, Keeping in Touch.
ST. KILDA TRIBUTE
AFTER ST. KILDA – John MacLeod and
Family.

John MacLeod was the Missionary and Teacher on St. Kilda from 1926 – 29 with his second wife, Bessie,

Oiseval through to Boreray and the Stacs. Acland.

School at St. Kilda in 1927. Photo by Cockburn. Schoolmaster and Missionary, John MacLeod, together with:- Back Row – Finlay MacKinnon, Donald Ewen MacKinnon. Middle – Donald Gillies, Cathy Gillies, Flora Gillies, Mary Ann Gillies, Rachel MacKinnon, Alick MacLeod. Front – Ewen Gillies, Kenneth MacLeod.

and his two sons, Alexander and Kenneth. I first met Alexander camping on St. Kilda in 1979; he had just retired as the Gaelic teacher in Tarbert, Harris. I was about to take a service in the Kirk when he walked passed the cottage where I was staying with a National Trust Work Party. I explained what I was about to do,

invited him to join us and gave him details so that he could find his way to the Kirk. Quietly spoken he graciously replied, "I do know the way, I used to live here!" He then disclosed who he was!

I asked if he would like to write a portrait. He answered, "When the initial dismay had subsided

Alick arriving in the Golden Chance which later sank in Village Bay.

John MacLeod's birthplace on Berneray.

somewhat and the ever hungry ego had time to respond to the appeal made to it, it occured to me that I might have something to contribute after all." The following is Alexander's portrait of his father, John.

"We have in Gaelic a rather beautiful concept enshrined in a vivid expression, "Clach air a charn" (a stone on his cairn). It conjures up a picture of a monument built of stone as a memorial to someone held in high esteem, each stone symbolising a personal tribute from an admirer. I should like to place such a stone on my father's cairn.

BERNERAY BACKGROUND

My father was born in 1885 on the island of Berneray, in the Sound of Harris: he was the eldest of a family of seven. The family home was a small black-house (or thatched cottage), one end of which was sure to be washed by the waves when the wind was from the south-east and a spring tide flowing. The space within was limited and the fare on the home-made table was frugal but wholesome. The head of the house, my beloved grandfather, lived a life of unremitting toil in which his faithful help-meet fully

shared. He was a lobster-fisherman, owning his own boat – a sailing boat classed as a "Zulu", and even in a community of superb seamen he was renowned for his skill and courage. It is almost impossible today to imagine what it was like to navigate a small sailing boat through the innumerable shoals and rocks and reefs and skerries of the treacherous Sound of Harris; to outwit the tides and the hidden currents, the dangerous winds, the sinister fogs and the ominous calms – and then to station and manoeuvre the vessel close to a rocky shore while creels were set or hauled.

It was a hard and dangerous occupation and my father was early apprenticed to it. As the eldest in the family he had, even before leaving school at the age of fourteen, to play his part in the breadwinning. In addition to helping on his father's boat and all the grim toil that entailed, he had to share the rigorous labour involved in cultivating such plots of ground as were made available to "cottars" or "squatters" by the goodwill of the more fortunate "crofters". The principal crop was potatoes and the cultivation of these entailed the back-breaking labour of harvesting seaweed as a fertiliser, transporting it to the assigned ground, and spreading it prior to digging. One is tempted to elaborate on the sheer physical toil necessary to ekeing out an existence on the island of Berneray in those days; not just the basic task of "earning a living" but the unending concomitant chores associated with the maintenance of property and the running of the household. Boats had to be hauled ashore periodically, scraped and repainted; sails had to be repaired, creels had to be made, bait had to be procured: houses had to be thatched; water and fuel had to be fetched. The list is endless!

How, one may well ask, did a Berneray boy, fully involved in all this, ever manage to attend school at all – far less have any time to learn anything there? What chance was there for "homework" or study or even the simplest reading, in the small, smoky, dark crowded home? Yet, out of that home, typical of homes all over the Western Isles – came, in addition to my father, an accomplished mariner with a First Mate's ticket who served in ships and yachts world-wide; a lady telephonist with whose attractive voice the governor of a Lothian institution fell in love and whom he subsequently married; a Postmistress, held in the highest regard by at least two communities; a graduate schoolmaster with a long and honourable career; and an Insurance agent whose career included a period as company-representative in Africa.

My father's first paid job was labouring at the new road which was being constructed about the time that he left school. The wage was a mere pittance but all grist to the family mill. My father left Berneray at a very early age and found his way into "domestic service", a career which he followed in various forms until he eventually entered the service of the Church. He was employed in Finsbay Lodge where he learnt the rudiments of stewarding, and in subsequent years followed this career in such establishments as "Barr and Strouds" in Glasgow, and in military messes during his war service, but mostly in ships and yachts – these being the great love of his life.

FIRST MARRIAGE AND FAMILY

On the 12th. November 1912, at the age of 27, my father married my mother Katie MacDonald from Leverburgh (Obbe, at that time), Harris. He was then employed as a Ship Steward on the S.S. "Medway" of Glasgow, while my mother was in domestic service as a cook in the same city. My eldest brother, Donald John, ("Donnie", as we think of him) was born on the 7th of March 1914. My father was still stewarding at the time, but when I appeared on the 21st of April 1917, he was a private in the 2/4th Battalion of the Cameron Highlanders. As he had a flat foot he played an unheroic role during the war years, and seems to have been mostly employed in Officers' and Sergeants' Messes. After the War he returned to his former occupation mostly in ships such as the "George Ward" (which I think was a cable ship), the "Osprey" a steam yacht, and passenger/cargo vessels such as the S.S. "Hebrides". The family home was in Glasgow and on the 20th January 1919 my sister, Chrissie was born and on the 12th of September 1920 the youngest member of our family, my brother Kenneth. The language of the home was Gaelic, and the atmosphere lovingly Christian. We were nurtured from our tenderest years on the Psalms of David in metre and on the Shorter Catechism. An amusing story comes to mind in this context. My brother Donnie, for some misdemeanor, was banished from the room on one occasion and made to stand in the passage outside. After he had languished there for few minutes, the tearful chant was heard in Gaelic by those listening inside, "O set ye open unto me, The gates of righteousness." Needless to say, this opportune prayer received a favourable answer.

During his years in Glasgow my father seized every

opportunity to further his education. He had been converted as a young man and had a consuming interest in religion; thus, perhaps sub-consciously, he sought education as a means of extending his knowledge and understanding of Christian doctrine and theology. The local Church of Scotland minister, in Berneray, the Rev. M. Morrison, seems to have been a kind of "patron" of my father. One of his sons was contemporary with my father and the two lads were great friends. In Glasgow he associated with educated Christian people, ministers and teachers, and was closely connected with the Church. He was an avid reader in both languages and had a very retentive memory. He had a methodical, logical mind, and was adept at forming his own opinions and defending them when necessary. At some stage he attended the Bible Training Institute in Glasgow.

Sadly, when my brother, Kennie, was only about seven months old, my mother died and the happy Glasgow era came to an end. We three boys were lodged with our dear old grandparents in Berneray and our little sister with a grand-aunt and her husband, a lovely couple who took Chrissie to their hearts and lavished on her all the love and care which a cruel fate had prevented them from expending on their own daughter who died in infancy.

NEW START AFTER TRAGEDY –
Second Marriage

After this shattering experience, my father had to face the world once more and wrest from it a living sufficient to provide for his motherless bairns. He went back to sea and for the next three and a half years he pursued his calling as a steward. Between voyages he took employment ashore and visited his family in Berneray. In 1924, while serving on the S.Y. "Osprey", he met an attractive widow who was employed on the

Bessie, John MacLeod's wife. A. MacLeod Collection.

yacht as a lady's maid to Lady Liddell the owner, or the owner's lady. They were married in Glasgow on the 26th of August 1924. So began a new phase in my father's life.

My stepmother was Mrs. Elizabeth Gamble. Her father, Charles Gilman Hill, had been a hair-pin manufacturer in Malvern and her mother was Elizabeth Clayfield – both deceased at the time of her marriage to my father. At the time of Elizabeth's marriage to my father she still had a pet parrot, reputedly from Australia, where she had lived for some time with her first husband. She also had a lovely "Old English Sheepdog" – quite irresistible to boys of my age. She was, of course, very much higher up the social scale than our people, both by virtue of her family background and her subsequent employment among the "gentry". I think, as a girl, she had trained as a dress-maker or seamstress; she excelled at cooking and baking; she had a cultured English accent and was a beautiful speaker: she was very musical and was a lovely singer. It is not surprising that she was so often employed as a lady's-maid or lady's-companion, in which capacity she travelled the world in private yachts and cruise liners. She was several years older than my father, their respective ages at the time of their marriage being 45 and 39.

As I try to recall what I know of her background, I wonder anew at the equanimity with which she adapted to such a totally alien environment as our Hebridean islands – in particular, how she settled down to live happily in St. Kilda for three years! Naturally, there was friction from time to time; misconceptions and misunderstandings were inevitable. But over-all, Bessie is as deserving of "a stone on her cairn" from me as my father. She was indeed one of the many wonders of St. Kilda! But I am anticipating my story!

Shortly after my father re-married, he took his new bride back to Berneray and they lodged for some six weeks with his aunt Chirsty and her husband – the couple who were caring for my sister, Chrissie. During this period, an area of land in North Uist – Howbeg, Cheesebay, and Lochportan – was being broken up into crofts and allocated to returning Servicemen. My father was fortunate to be given the tenancy of one of these crofts in Lochportan, and had arranged for a house to be built on the land. In the latter part of 1924 he and Bessie moved on from Berneray to take up residence in Lochportan, and early in 1925 my brother Donnie and I joined them. At the risk of being accused of littering the landscape with cairns, I can never be grateful enough to our aunts and uncles, grandparents and other relatives in Berneray for the warm-hearted love with which they welcomed us "Glasgow waifs"

into the bosom of the family; my brothers and sister would joyfully echo these sentiments.

INTERESTS AND INFLUENCES

My father's domicile in Lochportan was a short one but appears to have been one of concentrated effort. People with any pretension to a reasonable standard of education were in very short supply and in no time at all my father was operating a shop and a Post Office. At the same time he was in constant demand for writing letters and filling in forms for neighbours. Right from the start he was "bull-dozed" into holding religious services in the district as there was no resident minister or missionary. He found himself involved in the movement to persuade the Church authorities to build a Church at Lochportan, and largely as a result of his efforts, so I have been told, a Church had been built and a missionary appointed by the United Free Church of Scotland by the time we left Lochportan in 1926. By that time also a new school was in the process of being built.

Amongst my father's many interests was a fondness for music. He had a pleasant tenor voice and from the time that he was converted as a young man, he had been accustomed to leading the singing at Gaelic church services in Berneray and subsequently in Glasgow and in other places. Prior to that he was in popular demand as a singer of Gaelic songs, and somewhere along the line he had taught himself to play the bagpipes. In Lochportan he organised and taught Psalmody classes. One of my clearest memories of our Lochportan days is of accompanying my father and stepmother on a dark winter's evening to the class. It is not so much the actual activities of the class I recall but the thrill of being out in the dark with a lantern. It was a first experience and the memory of it is a vivid one. The aim of the class was three fold: to teach new tunes, to teach members to read the sol-fah notations for themselves, and to train incipient "Precentors".

My father also had an artistic talent. He was fond of drawing and painting in water colour and he had a special interest in lettering. His own handwriting was beautiful and stylish – basically copper-plate with minor embellishments; but he had also learned the old Gothic style of lettering and could produce very pleasing work executed in blue and red ink. In consequence, his services were in frequent demand for painting the names and registration numbers on the local boats in Berneray.

This then was my father, as he was in Lochportan in 1926, the springboard for his new career as a Missionary with the United Free Church of Scotland. As he himself was proud to acknowledge, he owed much to the example, influence, and persuasiveness of several good friends both in Berneray and Glasgow. In particular he had a special affection (albeit tinged with not a little awe!) for his old Minister, the Rev. Murdo Morrison, under whose preaching he had been converted. The Minister's son, later to become Dr. A. J. Morrison, a leading preacher and outstanding scholar of his day, was contemporary with my father and exerted a great influence on him. There were many other men and women, whom he frequently mentioned, but perhaps the one whom he held in the most affectionate regard was the beloved Highland evangelist, the Rev. Lachlan MacLeod, one of Bereray's greatest sons. They had grown up together and they had both been in the Camerons during the War. Lachie, had in fact been a piper in that regiment; perhaps their mutual love of piping was a further bond between the two friends! After the War Lachie went to University and after graduation trained as a teacher; but he subsequently found his true vocation in the Ministry, and it was the bond of Christian fellowship that was the strongest link between the two friends. The Rev. Lachie was a son-in-law of the Rev. Murdo Morrison, thus strengthening my father's ties with the Manse.

By dint of persuasion and encouragement these three stalwarts of the Church had pointed my father in the direction of further committing himself to the Lord's service. He was not really cut out to be a business man and Lochportan seems to have had a particular significance in his life as the "Valley of Decision". Here he received the conviction that his experience in life up to this point had been a preparation for such commitment. It was impractical for him to enter the Ministry by the normal gateways of University and the Divinity Hall, but the humbler sphere of Lay-missionary service was open to him. He applied for admission to the Lay-missionary service of the United Free Church of Scotland and was accepted on the recommendation of his own Minister and of the local Presbytery of Uist and Harris. After the Church Union of 1929, the United Free Church joined the Parish Church (or the National Church of Scotland) to become the Church of Scotland, the Home Board being responsible for the Lay-missionary service.

LIFE ON ST. KILDA

My father was thrown in at the deep end! The station he was offered was St. Kilda, and the appointment involved the Headship of the local Public School as well as the spiritual oversight of the island. No doubt with some misgivings he accepted the appointment; but once the die was cast, I am sure he was too busy planning and preparing to worry unduly. Arrangements had to be made to sell the house in Lochportan and for the disposal of the shop and Post Office. Provision had to be made for a year's existence on St. Kilda, and one can only guess at the meticulous care with which goods had to be ordered. All this turmoil seems to have passed unnoticed over my carefree nine-year old head! But it occurs to me now that as well as thinking of the needs of the home – coal, flour, clothing, medicines etc, my father must have had to arrange for the needs of the School and the Church.

First Impressions

Sometime in the summer of 1926 we sailed for St. Kilda from Lochmaddy. I have somewhat hazy memories of being lodged in the Lochmaddy Hotel, in an upstairs room, whilst awaiting the sailing of the "Hebrides" for St. Kilda. My clearest memory is of my father, looking even smaller than usual from our upstairs window – signalling to my stepmother the hour at which the boat was due. He, of course, was on the roadway below the window, looking up, and the signalling consisted of simplistic gesticulations involving the fingers; the obvious method of calling up to Bessie might have disturbed the other Hotel guests – and after all, pater had been a steward! But I thought it was all wonderfully clever, this silent means of communication, and that, no doubt, is why I remember it. Reference to my father's stature reminds me to mention that he was not very tall, about five foot six, but he was broad and muscular and physically strong.

Sometime in the early hours of the morning the

Evening Light, view from the Gap over the enclosures to Dun.

"Hebrides" sailed with us "adventurers" on board, my father, stepmother and myself and my younger brother Kennie, who would then have been approximately 5½ yeas old. I myself would have been approximately 9 years old. Landing on St. Kilda entailed transferring to a large rowing boat and being ferried to the concrete landing slip to the accompaniment of an infinity of clamorous sound. Intermingled with the yelling of Gaelic voices was the ferocious barking, yapping and snarling of dogs racing to and fro above the jetty. It was no doubt an enthusiastic welcome but to our tender ears a frightening one! On subsequent occasions, happily, our reactions were quite different and we shared more as it were the excitement of a home-coming.

So began our three-year stay on this fascinating and fantastic island. My own first impression was of the incredible lushness of the Manse Glebe grass. Berneray had been close-cropped green, lawn-like grass while Lochportan seemed to be mostly heather. But here was a veritable jungle of knee-high growth such as we had not experienced before, with a gentle brook flowing shorewards through it, and across this brook a plank-bridge destined to feature largely in our future play. I recall squatting on this bridge doing something boyish with a pocket-knife when one of the girls in my class bumped into me with the result that I gashed my leg above the knee – I carry the scar to this day! But what highlighted this incident was not the pain nor the annoyance at my playmate or anything like that but my father's wrath when he discovered us trying to clean up the mess with water from the stream. I could not understand at the time but I suppose the poor man had ghastly visions of his son dying of tetanus on an isolated island and he being helpless to avert the tragedy! Fortunately, this dire eventuality did not occur. Indeed, during our stay on the island our family were remarkably free of illness or accident except that I suffered nasty bouts of asthma from time to time; but St. Kilda was not initially responsible for that.

In his dual role as pastor and schoolmaster my father had a very busy life, but he somehow found time to help in the domestic scene and he saw to it that his two sons did their share of the daily chores as well. Thus it is that I am really handy in the house! The only thing I never dared attempt was carry an armful of loaded dinner plates the way my father did! Before leaving Berneray I had learnt the rudiments of knitting and my stepmother continued my education in this fascinating hobby so that even today I think I could still turn a heel with the best of them. She was fond of cooking and baking and I learned a lot at her elbow, including the inner mysteries of the English Christmas, especially the "Christmas pud".

Church Life

My father had two services every Sunday, one prayer-meeting each week, and an additional prayer-meeting at the beginning of each month. Regarding the Sunday morning service, it was really two services in one, as the Nurse and my stepmother had to be catered for in English. The "main" service was in Gaelic, but when he had completed his Gaelic address, the preacher switched over to English and gave a resumé of what he had been saying. This was followed by a prayer in English. All the singing was normally in Gaelic and was led by a "precentor" in the traditional Gaelic style. The Sunday evening service was all in Gaelic, and between the two services came the Sunday School. My clearest and fondest memory of Sunday School is of the period when it was conducted by the geologist, Alick Cockburn – in English, of course, as Mr. Cockburn had no Gaelic. He was a delightful young man, very devout, and we worshipped him. He was equally popular with the adults; a remarkable young man, who sadly, died while still comparatively young.

At the prayer-meeting, prayers were offered up by the male communicant members of the congregation, at the invitation of the presiding minister, missionary or elder. My father would begin the meeting by announcing and reading a metrical psalm. The "precentor" would then lead the singing of the prescribed stanzas and after this my father would either pray himself or invite someone else to do so. There would follow another singing and a second person would be asked to lead in prayer. At one stage my father would read a passage of scripture and base a short address on the passage read. In all there would be four to six prayers with singing in between.

In St. Kilda it was the custom to "intone" the prayers. The man praying would start off in a normal, devout manner but as he warmed to his theme and his fervour grew, so he slipped (unconsciously, I believe) into a sing-song tone of voice gradually increasing the volume till he was almost singing. The effect was rather mesmeric; or perhaps from a small boy's point of view, "soporific" would be a more apt description! The prayers were entirely spontaneous and unrehearsed and remarkable for the elegance and the facility of language used as well as for the profound knowledge of scripture and the depth of spiritual understanding shown. I have to confess that my father's own prayers (at that stage of his ministry) were inordinately long – anything up to half an hour – and as we always stood for the prayers, Ken and I found them wearisome.

In common with the rest of the Gaelic speaking area at that time, it was considered somewhat improper to accede too readily to a request to lead in prayer; any undue alacrity to do so was deemed immodest and lacking in the Christian virtue of humility. Inevitably, this in some cases led to the other extreme when the missionary had to plead with and coax an individual to lead in prayer. My father came up against this when he first went to St. Kilda, and someone whom we shall call

"Q" proved to be a veritable "thorn in the flesh". Every time "Q" was called upon to pray, he buried his head in his hands, and sighed and groaned and muttered about his unworthiness and pleaded to be excused, and generally carried on until the whole situation became quite farcical. My father stood it for so long but at last in exasperation and in desperation he decided to teach "Q" a lesson. At the next meeting when it came to "Q's" turn to pray my father addressed him – warmly and respectfully as usual, "My friend, "Q", would you be kind enough to lead us in prayer" or words to that effect, in Gaelic. There followed the usual pantomime ending with the specious plea, "Excuse me for now, please, and ask somebody else." Without further ado, my father turned to "Q's" neighbour and invited him to pray which he did without any fuss.

The next day my father went visiting up the village and entered "Q's" house. The latter was standing in the middle of the floor, in a somewhat belligerent attitude, when my father entered, and instead of the usual courteous greeting in Gaelic, the hurt and querulous exclamation, "Weren't you abrupt last night?!" My father understood at once. "Yes, Q," he countered, and went on to explain how demoralising he had found his conduct to be, and how un-Christian such conduct really was. "At the next prayer meeting," he warned "Q", "I shall ask you to pray, and if you don't get up at the first word, I shall never ask you again." At the next prayer meeting and whenever he was subsequently asked to pray, "Q" responded immediately, and without fuss!

The same man had another infuriating habit which led to another "confrontation" between himself and the missionary. He had a large silver-plated pocket watch which he consulted frequently in the course of a sermon. This would have been harmless enough in itself but in order to show the time the watch had to be opened and closed again. This closing could be accompanied only at the expense of a very loud "click" which reverberated all round the little church and the effect on the preacher was devastating! My father was not at all the extrovert that people imagined him to be; he was self-conscious and very sensitive about addressing an audience. One can imagine how trying he must have found "Q's" clicks to be! He remonstrated with the offender with little effect. "If you don't stop," he told him, "I'll break that turnip of yours to smithereens." Cheap, paltry watches were often referred to derogatively in Gaelic as "turnips". Once again my father went visiting and upon entering "Q's" kitchen found the latter standing rather aggresively in the middle of the floor. The greeting this time took the poor missionary rather aback, "Seadh, tha no bustraichean agaibh!" "Yes, you have the power of witchcraft!" "What makes you think that?" my father asked. "Stad an t-uaireadair," was the reply. "The watch has stopped!" When my father looked around he saw the offending time-piece in bits on the table having evidently defied "Q's" efforts to resuscitate it!

My father and "Q" had the quaintest of relationships. They were as the former would say, "forever at loggerheads" and yet they had the greatest respect for each other and my father was really very fond of "the old vagabond" as my stepmother sometimes disrespectfully called him. Again, she too, considered "Q" "rather a pet" and I think that he, a widower, rather enjoyed visiting the Manse to exchange English with her! On one such occasion there was a washing hanging out on the line in the Manse garden and "Q" must have had a good look at the garments on display. Subsequently he accosted my father outside somewhere and questioned him, "What kind of trousers were those that I saw on your clothes-line the other day? I never see you wearing them." My father laughed. "That's not surprising," he said, "those are my pyjama trousers and I wear them only in bed!" "Q" was aghast. "Do you mean to tell me that you allow anything to come between you and the flesh of the dear wife that the Lord had given you!"

My father was a very sociable person by nature so his visiting of his flock, although required of him as part of his duties, was a labour of love rather than the performance of a duty. He prayed in every home he visited and he had some very close friends amongst the St. Kildans. One of these was Ewan MacDonald, a brother of Lachie. A sister was married to Neil Gilies and, during our time on St. Kilda, Neil took ill and was transferred to hospital in Oban. After he had been there for some months word arrived via a trawler that Neil had died and according to the usual custom the missionary attended the home that evening to conduct the family worship and to commiserate with the widow, children and other relatives. All knelt for the concluding prayer. The prayer came to a rather abrupt conclusion, with my father getting up off his knees and announcing, "If I have understood the Lord's message aright, the news we have received is in error, and Neil is still alive and as well as can be expected." Two or three weeks later a subsequent message from Oban confirmed that Neil was still surviving. In fact, he lived for some time after that, although he finally succumbed in hospital. I have heard my father refer to this incident, but had forgotten it until reminded recently by Lachie MacDonald who is very clear in his mind and very positive about the authenticity of it.

School Days

As my father was also the Schoolmaster perhaps it was rather appropriate that the school also served as the vestry for the church! The school was built onto the church and there was a connecting door between the two buildings. One of the duties entrusted to Kennie and myself was the sweeping and dusting of these buildings each week. Two things about cleaning the church remain imprinted on my memory – the awful asthma caused by the dust, and the compensating thrill of "preaching" from a real pulpit. Ken and I took turn about at "preaching" and "precenting". No doubt "precenting" would have been reasonaly tolerable for we were both good singers in those days, but the less said about "preaching" the better! Ken later matured into a first rate singer and after some years in the RAF during the War, eventually became a Minister in the Church of Scotland. So the practice we had in the St. Kilda pulpit may not have been wasted after all! In my own case, however, my musical talents developed in another direction, and my preaching practice in the St. Kilda pulpit must at least have served the purpose of convincing me that I was not cut out to be a St. Paul!

If it is true that the best judge of a teacher's ability is his pupil, then I am in as good a position as anyone to pass judgement on my father in his capacity as a schoolmaster. Allowing for the limitations of his professional training. I would say that he was as competent as could reasonably be expected in the circumstances. He was conscientious in passing on his knowledge to his pupils and he was careful to seek the advice of the "professionals" whenever he could. As it happened, his youngest brother Norman, was newly out of college as a graduate (MA Aberdeen) teacher and was thoroughly versed in all the latest trends and methods of training. His friend, the Rev. Lachlan MacLeod, had also been a professional teacher; and there were others too, from whom my father sought counsel.

I recall one incident which serves to show how this professional guidance operated. From time to time my father used to forward some of our written work in different subjects to Norman to assess. On one occassion Norman pointed out that the method I had used on "Proportion" was no longer encouraged and he forwarded worked examples of the more recent method. From then on we were as up-to-date as any other school in our method of solving problems on "Proportion".

There were ten of us on the school-roll during our stay on St. Kilda, including Ken and myself, and our ages ranged from five years to fourteen or fifteen, so that the schoolmaster had to cater for the whole Primary range of subjects. We studied English and Gaelic, History and Geography, and Arithmetic (written and mental). We had Religious Instruction, Drawing and Painting, Singing and a little Physical Training. English included Reading and Writing, the latter included Penmanship. We used Copy-books, and the style of writing was cursive or copper-plate. We used slates for most of our "rough work" but pen and ink for competitions, transcriptions and other written work. There was no problem of discipline, naturally! We were all one happy family and the classroom atmosphere was quite informal. For example on cold winter days we took it in turns to sit in a corner beside the fire – the master's desk was also near the fire!

Talking of informality, we used our native Gaelic except where English was deemed necessary. To "ask out" did not necessitate an alien tongue but even here there were pitfalls. One day a boy who shall remain nameless stood up and when asked what he wanted replied, as he thought , "I am thirsty". What he, in fact, said was, "I am drunk!" He had got his Gaelic idiom somewhat out of focus! In Gaelic a statement such as, "I am sleepy" is expressed as, "the sleep is upon me". Similarly we have, "The hunger is on me. The cold is on me. The measles is on me. The anger is on me." Thus, "I am thirsty" becomes, "The thirst is on me" which in Gaelic is "Tha am pathadh orm". The cure for thirst is, of course, a drink – in Gaelic "deoch" and that is what our young friend needed, so he said, "Tha an deoch orm" – i.e. "The drink is on me". Unfortunately, this, as in English means, "I am drunk". The incident, needless to say, made our day, especially my father's!

"Silent reading" was one of the areas of private study. The books for this exercise were provided by the school library which was very well stocked indeed.

I understand that this, in common with school libraries throughout the Highlands, was provided through the generosity of the Coates family in the first instance. However, additional gifts of books from well-wishers had led to a well stocked library in the Manse as well. Consequently, once I had mastered the art of reading, my nose was never out of a book! I can recall some of the titles with nostalgia even today; Masterman Ready, Mr. Midshipman Easy, Robinson Crusoe, The Swiss Family Robinson, Treasure Island, With Cochrane the Dauntless; even the authors stuck; G. A. Henty. Captain Marriat. I even recall the words under an illustration of an old pioneer Scots woman pouring scalding porridge over attacking "Redskins" in one of these stories – "Yer brithers hae gotten the rest of the kale and ye can cla the the pot". I didn't know much "Braid Scots", but the meaning could not have been clearer!

Perhaps it is trite to remark that children learn a lot from each other, but I certainly learned a lot from my compeers in St. Kilda school. Amongst other things I learned Semaphore, an art in which I later attained a considerable proficiency in the Boy Scouts in Portree Secondary School. I believe the St. Kildan's knowledge of Semaphore stemmed from the time when the Naval Detachment was stationed there during the First World War. My chief instructor was Finlay MacKinnon who was about my own age, perhaps a little older. The natives used this method of signalling to communicate with the trawlers in the bay, and in no time at all I could signal, "Did you get any fish today?" Poor Finlay, he did not long survive the evacuation from his native island.

Just the other side of the wall enclosing the Manse and other church buildings, the St. Kilda men used to lay up their boats for the winter and Kennie and I spent many a happy hour, in imagination restoring these vessels to their proper position in the sea, investing them with all the imposing accoutrements of Cunard liners and captaining them into wild and stormy waters off Cape Horn or some other equally romantic location. When we tired of that there was this marvellous "cannon" a few hundred yards away – a relic of the Great War, and possibly the result of the great British penchant for locking the stable door after the horse has gone – pointing Village wards in those days, and just at the ideal height for little boys to play on at a distinct danger to life and limb. Towering above the "cannon" the almost precipitous sides of Oiseval frequently provided the setting for the grim spectacle of a sheep desperately fleeing from the pursuing dogs, racing down the hillside and unable to stop plunging hundreds of feet into the sea. Sometimes the poor creature was rescued, and it is possible that a hardier animal than most sometimes managed to swim across to Dun, but usually the outcome was death for the unfortunate victim.

School was not "all work and no play" by any means, and the Christmas season in particular allowed

Christmas Party around 1927 in the boat. A. MacLeod Collection. Back Row – Mrs. MacLeod, Donald Gillies, Ewen Gillies, Donald Ewen MacKinnon, Kenneth MacLeod (striped hat), Finlay MacKinnon, Alick MacLeod, Mr. John MacLeod. Front – Unknown, Unknown, Unknown, Mary Ann Gillies, Flora Gillies, Rachel MacKinnon.

plenty of scope for relaxation. No doubt my stepmother, aided and abetted by the Nurse, provided the main impetus for our festivities, but it must be said that the missionary's Calvinistic prejudices did not precluded him joining in the fun! In fact, considering his upbringing, and his orthodoxy and his deep religious convictions, my father was remarkably tolerant although he did not always give that impression. So Christmas was a happy time with us on St. Kilda, and even the dark months of winter in retrospect evoke pleasant memories.

Visiting Trawlers

The trawlers, mainly from Fleetwood, frequently sheltered in Village Bay transforming it at night into a twinkling Fairyland of lights. How indebted we were to those intrepid mariners. They ferried our mails to and fro, they gave us generous gifts of fish and they gave us their time and company by coming ashore and visiting in our houses. To us boys who knew only MacKinnons, MacQueens, MacDonalds, Gillies and Fergusons, the names of our gallant visitors were tinged with romance and adventure – Captain Tonner, Captain Carter, Captain Bruce and many, many more – we idolised them. Amongst the other favours that we owed to the trawlermen there is one that remains uppermost in my memory because of the uniqueness of it: my stepmother began her annual holiday one year by boarding a trawler in St. Kilda and sailing all the way down to Fleetwood in it! It did, of course, attract the attention of the press at the time. The Daily Mail for 28th. May 1928 carried the following report:-

GIRL FROM LONE ST. KILDA
First Glimpse of Motor Car
Thrills of a taxicab ride

Miss Rachael Gillies, a 17 year old girl, who has never seen a motor-car, train, horse, or a cinema picture, was one of three residents from the lonely

Mrs. MacLeod and Rachel Gillies on St. Kilda. Gladstone Collection.

island of St. Kilda, in the Outer Hebrides, who landed at Fleetwood yesterday.

Captain Reginald Carter, skipper of the Fleetwood fishing steamer Loughrigg, brought Mrs. MacLeod, wife of the Missioner on the island, Miss Gillies and Mr. John MacDonald, an islander. Mrs MacLeod and Mr. MacDonald are on holiday, but Miss Gillies has found work in Fleetwood. This is the first time three inhabitants of the island have ever left it together.

When they left the trawler at Fleetwood they were taken to the home of the captain in a taxicab, a ride which thrilled and amazed Miss Gillies. Fleetwood streets amazed her with wonder.

News By Wireless

Mrs. MacLeod told the Daily Mail representative:-
There are 11 families on St. Kilda, a total population of 42. I have a two valve wireless set at the parsonage, and get Daventry and sometimes Continental stations. As we get no newspapers I never know what to expect, but when I hear anything interesting I write it out and distribute it among the islanders as a news bulletin, which is highly appreciated, for it is sometimes the only news we get for months.

Our greatest difficulty on the island is the lack of fresh vegetables and meat, for we cannot grow anything on the island. Sometimes we have vegetables almost ready for digging when a gale comes, bringing sea spray across the island and turning everything black.

We live mostly on scones made of flour and baking powder, and have to bake often as food soon goes rancid. There is a happy spirit among the islanders, and what one family lacks in food is made up from the stock of another family.

There are many young men on the island who have nothing to do except weaving tweeds from the wool of the sheep, which they dye with herbs gathered on the mountains.

If a trawler or whaler had a consignment or mail for St. Kilda on board, it would indicate that fact to the waiting populace by blowing long and exuberantly on its siren as it rounded the point into the bay. What a "joyful sound" it was! And what excitement in the Manse as we later emptied our own mail bag and examined the accumulated mail of weeks and sometimes months. The variety of mail was as cosmopolitan and intriguing as the volume of it and I am tempted to elaborate on this theme. However, I shall limit myself to one item. Whether it was a book of pipe music or a catalogue, or an article in a magazine or what I cannot remember, but there was printed pipe-music and a picture of a kilted piper involved and these it was that inspired my imagination and kindled a flame of love of the great Highland bagpipe and its music that has never diminished. How thwarted I felt, looking at that music and not being able to comprehend it! No doubt my reading about heroic derring-do involving gallant pipers and brave Highlanders had whetted my musical appetite in the first instance. At any rate my performances on my mouth-organ must have redoubled in intensity with a swing of emphasis from the sacred to the martial!

This leads me to wonder how I had attained such a proficiency with the mouth organ at that time – where had I acquired such a repertoire of tunes? The source of the sacred music, mainly jaunty Sankey tunes was obvious enough – my father was a great "Sankey" man and never wearied off regaling us with excerpts from the "Sankey" hymn-book. But what about the other tunes I could play – Gaelic songs (including "puirt-a-beul", the Gaelic so-called "mouth-music" used for dancing, or waulking tweed amongst other things), and pipe-tunes-marches, strathspeys, reels etc? The answer came to me after a bit of mental struggle – my Uncle Ian! Not only was he a piper himself but he had brought back to Berneray on one occasion a gramophone and a wide selection of records. That is how I was able to play so much music in St. Kilda! I had picked up the tunes from Uncle Ian's gramophone, and have loved them ever since. To complete the story, I may add that later on, while at school in Portree, I did learn to play the the bag-pipes and amongst my teachers was the great P/M Willie Ross MBE. How appropriate that this occured in Skye – the land of the McCrimmons! As in St. Kilda all these years ago with my little mouth-organ, so today I pass many happy hours and derive great enjoyment from playing the great Highland bagpipe. No longer thwarted by any inability to read pipe-music, I delight in learning new tunes, and find it so sad to hear young people today continually complaining about being bored and having nothing to do!

My thoughts go back to my father who himself played the pipes and never lost his love of pipe-music. In my earliest memories of him he sported a "Kaiser" moustache, ends liberally waxed and bristling challengingly upwards and forwards as if to ward off criticism. However, before going to St. Kilda he had shaved off this adornment.

Keeping in Touch

One other memory I should mention is that of listening to broadcast services on the radio, or the "Wireless" as we called it. Apart from the weather forecast and the news my father was not much addicted to the wireless, so it is associated in my mind mostly with my stepmother. Either there were two sets of earphones, or one earphone could be detached from the pair. I cannot recall the precise details but my stepmother and I usually shared the Sunday services and I became as familiar with the name of "St. Martin-in-the-field" as that of any church in the islands.

We all had a holiday from St. Kilda each year that we were there: my father, Kenny and I went to Berneray while my stepmother visited friends and relatives in England. One of the things that I recall very vividly about my first holiday back to Berneray was the disconcerting discovery that everything there seemed to have shrunk since we left! The Berneray "mountains" had been flattened to hillocks, and the "loch" and the "river" adjacent to the old home had dwindled to a wee pond with a burn flowing through it. I had no profound feelings about it at the time but no doubt, subconsciously, my perspective had been profoundly affected by the grandeur and the immensity of the St. Kilda topography, and nothing could ever be the same again.

My sister Chrissie salvaged a letter which I had written from St. Kilda to my brother Donnie in 1927:-

Manse, St. Kilda
9/10/27

Dear Brother,

I hope you are all well, the same as we are. Daddy and I are going to send you some books and I hope you will like them. I got your letter last Monday and I was quite pleased with it. I also got a letter from Nurse Little-John, and some photographs that she took at Christmas. Mother brought home some balloons and she had one the other day when we were out for a walk with nurse. Nurse has got a little darling pigeon and we saw it the other day. Mother took it up a few peas, and when Nurse came down the next day she said that it had placed them round in a funny fashion. Kennie and I were playing at a boat on a sea-saw today.

We've got a new map in the school and St. Kilda is on it, for a wonder, and I suppose it's through Mr. Matheson. Mr. Cockburn put a big pole on one of the mountains and we saw it through Mr. Mathesons big telescope. Mr. Cockburn and Nurse is coming to stay here when Mr. Matheson goes away, as Mr. Cockburn wont be finished his work when Matheson is.

Give my love to everybody,

With love from your loving brother,
Alick.
Send Kennie some letters for he's longing for one.

In an earlier letter to Donnie dated 3/9/27 I had commented:-

"Our potatoes were all spoilt by the gale, and I expect yours are the same. We had a minister come named Mr. Fraeser to the commion, and he went away by a whaler. The Nurse comes down each day to see us. We've still got the lamb, its getting very fat. We got new pens and pencils in the school. That's all I can tell you just now . . ."

While Mr. Fraser, the Minister from Rosehall, was on St. Kilda for the Communion the weather broke and he was stranded on the island for quite a while – much to our delight, for he was that kind of man – he eventually "escaped" on a whaler!

ST. KILDA TRIBUTE

Like ourselves, their counterparts on the mainland of Harris, the St. Kildans were mostly very poor in the material things of life. Even so they were in at least one area, better-off than the majority of people in Harris at that time – they had "modern" cottages, with timbered roofs covered with tarred felt! But if they were poor materially, they were abundantly rich in the moral and spiritual virtues that constitute real wealth. Wresting as they did a living from their environment, they were rich in their knowledge and understanding, and appreciation of that environment. They treated with deserved respect the crags that they climbed and on which so much of their livelihood depended; and with equal wisdom they did not presume on the sea but accorded it the cautious approach which it merited – they recognised and accepted its dual role in the pattern of their lives, cutting them off from the rest of mankind, yet providing the means of communication with the outside world; lavishly producing the fish to feed the myriad birds that frequented the island and so indirectly benefitting the human populace as well, while also pounding mercilessly at beach and shore and crag-base with demonic ferocity.

The St. Kildans were rich in Christian faith and were rich in the graces that stem from that faith. Thus they lived together in unity, and their differences were of a minor nature incidental to living in such close proximity to each other. They were open and honest, mutually helpful, and generous to a degree, as we in the Manse were privileged to know. They were affectionate by nature and quickly endeared themselves to all those with whom they came in contact. Even their censure was kindly and courteous as a story about a dear old gentleman called Finlay Gillies illustrates. Finlay was once travelling on one of the passenger steamers during a somewhat severe, typical Sound of Harris storm. He came across a man of the cloth whom he knew, travelling on the same boat, a minister of the more austere sects indigenous to the islands. This man was incautious enough to reveal to Finlay that he was terrified of the storm, to which Finlay, himself as unconcerned as his Master on the Lake of Galilee, gently responded with the words, "Now, now, Minister, "He that feareth is not made perfect in love." (1 John 4 v 18).

The St. Kildans were rich in manual skills, in initiative and in adaptability. Their whole way of life, and the way in which they adapted their environment to their own use, coupled with the expedition with which they adapted themselves subsequently to a new environment, is proof of this.

People who had heard that I had some connection with St. Kilda have often asked if I were a St. Kildan. I have frequently been tempted to claim that privilege, and it has always been with a tinge of regret that I have had to answer in the negative.

Let me in conclusion describe an incident which moves me profoundly whenever I think of it. I went out to Inverness to attend the funeral of my Uncle Norman, headmaster of Culcabock School, to whom I have already referred. While standing at the graveside, I sensed someone approaching me and when I looked up there was Norman MacKinnon (Junior), from the Black Isle. I greeted him warmly when I had got over the shock of my surprise, and then asked him how he came to know Norman. "I didn't know your uncle at all," was the reply, "but I knew your father."

I think that expresses very adequately the type of people who lived on St. Kilda, and our relationship with them.

AFTER ST. KILDA – John MacLeod and Family

John MacLeod and his wife Bessie

After leaving St. Kilda in 1929, John was posted to Staffin in the north end of Skye. As already explained, he refused ordination to minister status and continued to serve as a missionary (or lay-preacher). The head church of the Parish was in Kilmuir where the minister had his manse. The minister at the time was a Dr. MacDonald, a venerable old man, due to retire at any time. Once a month or so the minister would come to Staffin to take the Sunday services and the missionary would go to Kilmuir to take Dr. MacDonald's services and on such occasions the missionary blessed his luck and relaxed in the pulpit while his "boss" preached. A favourite anecdote of my father's refers to such an occasion – with a difference. Dr. MacDonald conducted the service as usual and reached the stage where he gave out the text. But instead of beginning his sermon, he continued with the shattering announcement, "Now, Mr. MacLeod will preach on that text." And without preparation or any previous warning, Mr. MacLeod had to do just that!

When Dr. MacDonald duly retired, he was succeeded in Kilmuir by a Lewisman, Rev. Murdo MacLeod, and he and my father became the closest of friends – so much so that the missionary became the unofficial barber to the minister! This was somewhat of a joke with the joint families as Murdo was practically bald – but he was an ex-serviceman (Navy) from the Great War and liked to feel trim and tidy about the head and the back of the neck!

A missionary was expected to remain in a station for three years but this was not a strictly enforced rule and my father remained in Staffin for about five years. In 1934 he was sent to Lochaline, in Morvern, Argyllshire. Here he was re-united with many of his former St. Kilda congregation; some of them were by now settled in Lochaline itself and some were at Larachbeg a few miles from Lochaline. In Staffin the missionary lived in a "Mission House" – an ordinary West Highland cottage, but in Lochaline the missionary had the privilege of residing in the Manse! This was one result of the union in 1929 of the United Free Church and the Established Church to form the Church of Scotland. There was a Manse to spare and at that time it was used to house the Missionary.

We were in Lochaline for less than three years. About 1936 or 37 my father was sent to Elphin, in Assynt, Sutherlandshire (where he reverted to "Mission House" status!). I was at home on holiday in Elphin when war was declared in September 1939, but as from then on, I was "out of the nest". I am not too sure about the actual dates on which my father moved from place to place. I think it was in 1941 that he left Elphin and went to Cross, in the Isle of Lewis (where he was again in the Manse!). Cross is in the Parish of Ness, up in the north of Lewis. From there, about 1944, he was posted to Sollas in North Uist. He retired to Tarbert, Harris in 1951 and was promptly recruited by the Rev. Murdo MacLeod – now minister at Tarbert – as his "assistant". When Rev. Murdo retired through ill-health, he was succeeded by Rev. D. A. Macrae – our present minister here. My father continued his role as assistant to Mr. Macrae until shortly before his death of cancer on June 4th. 1964.

John's wife Bessie, died in Cross, Ness in November 1943 and is buried in Berneray, North Uist. I was in the Army at the time. Shortly afterwards my father moved to Sollas in North Uist and got married for the third time to a widow from Ness – Mary MacLeod, nee Campbell, who survived him for several years.

John MacLeod's Children
Donnie

In due course Donnie went to Kingussie Secondary School and then returned home to Staffin. Here he contracted T.B., a fatal disease in those days and very rife in Skye. He died in Robroyston Hospital in Glasgow on 24th. August 1933 at the age of 19½. I was very attached to him and still recall the grief I experienced at that tragic time.

Donnie was the apple of my father's eye and this second tragedy in his life was a shattering one – especially as Donnie suffered terribly. But we did have the consolation that a few months before his death, Donnie experienced a very profound conversion and became a very bright, born again Christian.

Alex

From St. Kilda I went straight to Portree Secondary School in 1929, my home being in Staffin. I took my "Highers" in 1935 and was Dux boy of the school in that year. I went on to Aberdeen University and graduated M.A. in 1938. After that I did a year and a term at Aberdeen Teachers' Training College and

Alick during the Second War. A. MacLeod Collection.

emerged in December 1939 as a fully fledged probationer teacher! I also got married! My fiancee was Dolina MacPhail from Bragar, Lewis and she had just graduated B.Sc in Chemistry at Aberdeen University.

I was called up in the following July and saw service in North Africa, Sicily and France being finally discharged in 1945.

I taught at Daliburgh Junior Secondary School, South Uist and from there went to be headmaster of Knockbreck Primary School in Skye and at Berneray, Harris. When a better post as Gaelic teacher in Sir E. Scott J.S. School Tarbert became available I took it. When I retired in 1979 I was Principal teacher in Gaelic and Deputy Headmaster of the school which by then was a 4 year Secondary offering S.C.E. "O" grade subjects. For my loyalty to the E.J.S. during my teaching career, I was made a life member on retirement!

We had five children but sadly the last one, a girl, survived for only a day – the result of the rigours of Berneray and the main reason why we decided to leave. So, essentially, we have a family of four. Catherine obtained her M.A. degree at Aberdeen University, then Teacher Training College and into teaching. She married Hamish Anderson, the youngest son of the Rev. George Anderson and they have one son, Alasdair. Effie MacPhail followed in Katie's footsteps except that she went to the Nicolson Institute, Stornoway and is now teaching Gaelic in Sir E. Scott Sec. School Tarbert. She married John MacSween from Scarista, Harris and they have two children, Dorothy and Iain Alasdair. Donald John chose medicine instead of Arts obtaining his medical degrees at Aberdeen University – M.B., ChB., D.Obst., R.C.O.G., M.R.C.G.P. He married Marjory Burnett from Aberdeen and they have two boys Andrew and Neil. John, our youngest went to Inverness Royal Academy, then to Glasgow University to study for a B.Sc in Mathematics. He has a Computing job in Manchester, unmarried but shares his home with a huge friendly dog with a terrifying bark – and a cat!

Chrissie

Chrissie married John MacKillop, a crofter fisherman from Berneray. She could have followed an academic career but, as so often happened with girls at that time, she was kept at home to look after ageing relatives. They have two daughters, Chrisetta and Kathleen.

Kenny

After he left St. Kilda he went back to live with grannie in Berneray, found a job in Lochmaddy where, seemingly, he became an expert telegraphist. He was called up for War service in the R.A.F. and did a stint in India in Chittagong and later in Saigon. He was converted while in the R.A.F. and after "demob" he was accepted for training for the Ministry of the Church of Scotland. He studied at New College Edinburgh and after being licenced he held charges at Dundonald (Ross-shire), Kilmartin (Argyll-shire), Daliburgh (South Uist) and Portlethen (Kincardineshire). He is now retired and lives in Stonehaven, Kincardineshire. His wife, Georgie Colquhoun comes from West Lothian and they have four children, Alick, Mary, Catherine and Ian."

Postscript – Kenny told me (D.A.Q.), being younger than his brother Alick, that he didn't recall much about St. Kilda. However, he remembered vividly his first impression on landing. It was the imposing, black-bearded figure of Finlay MacQueen standing over him on the quayside. "I was absolutely terrified and screamed my head off as I was carried bodily up to the manse – later we became good friends."

John Gladstone –
Portraits within a Portrait
Visited St. Kilda in 1927

SETON GORDON – NATURALIST
JOHN MATHIESON – SURVEYOR
ALEX COCKBURN – GEOLOGIST
JOHN GLADSTONE – BOTANIST

"North End of Borera". Acland.

John Gladstone (1908 – 77) visited St. Kilda for three weeks in 1927. He was studying History at Magdalene College Cambridge at the time and noted that Geological and Topographical Surveys were to be carried out on the islands by John Mathieson and A. M. Cockburn during the summer. He took the opportunity of offering his services as a botanist. He was accepted and, like so many others, came under the spell of St. Kilda. From his three weeks' stay he produced three volumes of diaries, letters and press cuttings. Few could have amassed a greater wealth of material after such a short period – perhaps he was only surpassed by George Seton who was on St. Kilda for only four hours but managed to develop his observations and research into his book, "St. Kilda Past and Present" with no less than 346 pages, published in 1876. James Ritchie, Professor of Natural History at Aberdeen University read Gladstone's diaries and in his letter returning them he commented, "It is a most interesting record and I thoroughly enjoyed the reading of it. Its records, gathered from so many sources, will become more and more valuable as the years pass." (dated 21.9.31) This has indeed been the case.

The year 1927 was a particularly fascinating time to be visiting St. Kilda. It was suffering from a dramatic decline in the population from 73 in 1924 to 42 in 1927; many of the inhabitants had left in search of a less arduous way of life in Glasgow and elsewhere; six people died in the terrible influenza outbreak of 1926, and several lost their lives in one type of accident or another. This was putting a great strain on the few able-bodied men who were having to look after their own crofts and those of the older widows. It was also the year in which the island came up for sale and a period when St. Kilda had an invasion of eminent visitors.

SETON GORDON – NATURALIST

Seton Gordon, the famous Scottish naturalist, author and traveller, whose homes was at Duntulm House of the Isle of Skye was visiting St. Kilda for the first time with John Mackenzie, the factor. He resided in the attic of the Factor's House and took the opportunity to visit the islands of Soay and Boreray. Following his visit he wrote an article on St. Kilda which appeared in the Scotsman of 25th. July 1927. He had a remarkably smooth crossing from Uig Bay. In his article he described the indelible impression made by his first day on St. Kilda.

"Even before we had passed abreast of Shillay we could see faint and ethereal the cone of St. Kilda on the western horizon and, a little later, the peak of Boreray, its attendant isle . . . As we steamed knot after knot across the Atlantic plains it was difficult to realise that this could ever be a country of storm and great crested seas – and all the time St. Kilda and her neighbouring isles appeared to be advancing to meet us, and to greet us with smiles.

Cleit Village on Boreray and Stac Lee.

Some four miles to the north of the main island is Boreray, with a cliff 1200 feet high on its northern face. Near it are two great "stacks" where solan geese in their thousands nest – Stac an Armin and Stac Lii. The Skipper of the "Dunara Castle" courteously altered the course somewhat so that we should pass close to these stacks and see the solans. As we neared the smooth, grim faces of the rocks, an incredible flock of solan geese launched themselves into the northerly breeze that blew keen and invigorating. They flew out to meet us, then, at a height of a full five hundred feet above our decks, sailed in circles. Each bird, as in its aerial course it swung round and faced the sun, was suddenly lit up, and as each solan in turn caught the sun's rays the effect was as though many lamps were suddenly flashing out from the blue deeps of the quiet sky.

As we rounded Stac an Armin and steered southwards with the long northerly swell lifting us gently, we passed Stac Lii, which is another nesting haunt of the sulair (as the solan is known in Gaelic). Upon the summit of Stac Lii the solans were crowded so closely that at a distance they gave the illusion of barnacles clustering to a rock. The previous week a boat load from St. Kilda had gathered a harvest of eggs from this stack. The share of each man was 100 eggs, and the crew consisted of 12 men. It is said on St. Kilda that the solan when she is robbed lays again in 19 days.

Passing the rocky point . . . we sailed into a calm bay, where the sunlit waters showed pale green above the sand that gleamed dazzlingly. The shore sloped gently to the water. In a crescent the houses of St. Kilda stood, a little removed from the tide, with the tiny fields of potatoes and oats green and quickly springing in the strong June sunlight. In the bay a trawler was anchored. It was curious to see that she was of Belgian nationality – "Prevoyance Sociale" of Ostende. A far cry, surely, from Ostende to St. Kilda!

Late that afternoon a friend and I climbed Conacher, for the visibility was such that we hoped to see far-distant hills. One climbs a grassy slope where rock pipits twitter and wheatears call and suddenly, near the hilltop, emerges at a ridge and looks over a great precipice to where the Atlantic swell breaks in pale foam upon the cliff-foot, 1000 feet below. Here seals thrust faces through the surf, and solans in a tireless company dive for their prey under wave. Fulmar petrels in their hundreds brood their eggs on the giddy ledges of the cliff. Today they were soaring in the north breeze that sent an uprushing current beyond the cliff, and it was a delight to watch them, and to marvel at the grace and poetry of their flight.

From the hilltop that evening was a view such as the west alone can give – westward there was the sun and shade on the lonely Atlantic plains that stretched away and away toward the setting sun. North-east rose the Flannan Isles, so clear that the lighthouse showed distinctly. Beyond them was Lewis, and Harris of the peaks. Then in turn all the Outer Isles lay clear – North Uist, Benbecula, South Uist, Heavel off Barra. Haskeir seemed close: the lighthouse upon the Monach Isles showed needle-like. On Baleshare of North Uist, and upon the low shore of Benbecula the houses were distinct. A hundred miles distant on the far horizon eastwards, rose the Cuillin hills in Skye. Each member of that storm harried range was clear cut, even at that distance. Some of the old people of St. Kilda had seen the Cuillin hills, but it is only on days of great clearness, and at intervals of many weeks and even months, that they can be viewed. On the summit of Conacher – this peak of St. Kilda – the north wind blew as though straight from distant ice fields, but out of the breeze the sun was warm, and we sat there awhile, looking across the rugged coast of Hirta on to the near island of Soay and seeing the village clustered twelve hundred feet below us. In the bay the "Dunara Castle" lay at anchor, a thin whisp of smoke trailing from her funnel.

That evening, at the service in the small church, there was thankfulness in more than one heart that the boat had crossed safely. As one sat with the simple worshippers one's eyes rested on the deep blue of the sea, and faintly on the fitful breeze came the hollow suck of the waves on the shore, and the deeptoned music of the tireless swell upon outpost cliffs – music that blended in harmony with the cadences of Gaelic psalms and earnest prayer." Seton Gordon

JOHN MATHIESON – SURVEVOR

John Mathieson, FRGS, of Edinburgh University was spending several months on St. Kilda in 1927 engaged in Survey work. He was an adventurer at heart having been on the Scott Antarctic Expedition a few years earlier and in 1926 he was in the far Arctic regions surveying the Spitsbergen archipelago. Having retired recently from the Scottish Ordnance Survey he was free to apply himself to his greatest ambition which was to survey the St. Kilda Group of islands, the only corner of the British Isles which had not been officially mapped. In a report to the Times (20.4.27) he outlined his plans and that of his colleague, Mr. A. M. Cockburn. "We are going to make the first topographical survey of the island on a scale of 6 inches to the mile giving place names, antiquities and topographical features. It is intended to make a contour map of 100 ft. so that physical features will be clearly traced . . . The geological survey is being done by Mr. Cockburn and we hope a botanist will join us later, so that the geological, topographical and botanical survey will be complete." The botanist was John Gladstone. Mathieson made the point that the surveys were being made purely for scientific purposes and at their own personal expense. The article continued, "Mathieson and Cockburn left Fleetwood for St. Kilda in the afternoon of Tuesday 19th of April 1927 in the fishery steamer "Robert Murray" together with a month's accumulation of mails and parcels from Fleetwood post office and plentiful supplies of tinned provisions." Gladstone was to follow later and in the meantime received a letter dated 15.6.27 from Mathieson, "Today we are experiencing the worst storm we have had since we came here and if the steamer comes it will be impossible to land either stores or passengers . . . I am making good progress with the survey of the islands and I can give you a tracing on which to mark your botanical finds."

Mathieson had taken up residence in the attic room of the Factor's House, where Norman Heathcote and his sister had stayed during their summer visits in 1898 and 99. Gladstone first met Mathieson, soon after reaching St. Kilda, when he visited the island of Boreray for the afternoon. Climbing up about 600 feet he saw one of the old houses, built into the hillside, used by generations of St. Kildans. This was where both Mathieson and Cockburn were sleeping. Back on Hirta Gladstone visited Mathieson. "I went in and saw for the first time the little attic above the Nurse's house . . . We then went out to take the records for the day. Besides the barometer and temperature gauge there is a rain gauge, which has never been moistened this last week, a sun gauge, and a ground thermometer. The instruments were lent by the Ministry of the Air; they would gladly leave them on the island where there anyone who would regularly take records. I think that Mrs. MacLeod would find time to do it, but Mr. Mathieson does not agree with me, and has decided to take the instruments with him when he leaves the island."

Mathieson looked in to see Gladstone who was staying with Mrs. MacLeod at the Manse, "and came in with the pressing paper which Kew had sent him and a tracing of the island." On another occasion he showed us, "Kilda's well, the underground house, his excavations on the site of Christ Church, his hut and his instruments."

Mathieson and Cockburn stayed on the islands after the last tourist steamer had called as they both wanted to press on with their work. Mathieson eventually managed to escape (leaving Cockburn behind), on one of the Norwegian whalers from Harris in mid-September, his departure being delayed by some of the worst gales that even some of the oldest St. Kildans could remember and which ruined the potato crop.

For his painstaking work, ably assisted by Cockburn, John Mathieson was awarded the Gold Medal of the Royal Scottish Geographical Society. The Scotsman for 21.10.27 carried a full report of the proceedings of which some extracts follow. The Medal was presented by Viscount Novar in the Usher Hall in Edinburgh in the presence of 2000 persons.

"Lord Novar, who was accompanied on the platform by Lord Salvesen and Mr. A. M. Cockburn, said they were all grateful to Mr. Mathieson for what he had done to investigate and record those Gaelic place-names which so accurately and poetically revealed every feature in a landscape. Nor were his services in Spitsbergen with the Bruce Expeditions less well known. He had shown that professional drudgery and hardship could not dim his zeal and enthusiasm for the work he had taken in hand. This year he had, on his own initiative, carried through a survey of St. Kilda, thus giving an exhibition of personal energy and enterprise unusual in these days when the ubiquitous official investigator and inspector invaded and occupied so many fields of activity at a cost sometimes of inadequate results. As Scots people mindful of the bawbees, and as members of this Society interested in all pioneer work, they did well to honour men like Mr. Mathieson. (Applause)

Following the presentation of the Gold Medal Mathieson gave his lecture on St. Kilda. He introduced the subject, "The lonely island, situated far out into the Atlantic Ocean . . . was without lighthouse or postal arrangement of any kind, and only visited once a year until within the last forty years. Could one wonder that the inhabitants had not kept pace with the advancing civilisation on the mainland?" He then discussed the Name, ownership and tragedies of the island before describing life on the island and its possible future.

"The present population was 43. Formerly about 50 acres of land were cultivated; today only about 2 acres, and for the present season the crop had been almost entirely destroyed by a gale on 27th. August. The stock consisted of about 16 head of cattle and about 1200 sheep.

During the summer the men had little to do beyond four or five days' sowing their crops and the same period cutting turf for fuel. There was plenty of peat on the island, but they preferred to cut good green turf, depriving their sheep and cattle of patches of the best pasture. They also spent a few days killing puffins in the spring and fulmars in the autumn.

During the winter both men and women were busy making the St. Kilda tweed, of which they exported 1000 to 1200 yards annually. That was practically the only commodity they could give in exchange for the various articles of commerce they required.

The St. Kilda men were about average height and build, but were clumsy in their movements. The women were very pleasant and hard working. They always dressed with a shawl on their head – a pretty coloured one on Sunday – and their frocks of blue generally reached within a few inches of the ground. He felt sure they would please Lady Astor. (Laughter) The climate was too humid to be invigorating. They kept a complete meteorological record for the months of May, June, July and August – the first ever kept on the island. The total sunshine was 627 hours, against 644 hours in Edinburgh, and a total rainfall 11½ inches, against 14 inches in Edinburgh; while the average warm days was 63 degs. F., compared with 67 degs. in Edinburgh.

The area of the group was 2117 acres, and the hills were all green pasture to their summits. There were no trees and scarcely any heather. The inhabitants had no horses, pigs or goats, and there were no rabbits, hares, frogs, toads, serpents, lizards or rats on the island, but two kinds of mice. The chief flesh food was mutton and fulmars.

The island was not self supporting, and for their spiritual enlightenment, elementary education, and the services of a trained nurse a sum of between £500 and £600 was spent on the 43 inhabitants annually. If some profitable industry such as a whaling station, quarrying granite, or improving their tweed could be started, St. Kilda might have a prosperous future." Otherwise, he thought it would be much better to encourage those between the ages of 16 and 40, and in good health, to seek employment in the Colonies. He believed that many of them would be glad to go if the financial requirements could be met, and if that were done St. Kilda would in a few years join with Rona, Flannan Isles and the Shiant Isles and become uninhabited".

In an excellent article written by Mathieson and carried in the Edinburgh Evening News for 26.11.27 he underlined the decline in the animal and human populations of the island and again cast doubts on its future viability. Following are two short extracts. "When Martin visited the island in 1697 the population was 180, and they had 18 horses, 98 head of cattle, and 2000 sheep. Today the population is 43, with 16 head of cattle, no horses and 1200 sheep. Formerly the islanders cultivated the land to the extent of 50 acres; today they cultivate about two acres of potatoes and barley, and this year's crop has been almost completely destroyed by a gale on August 27. During this southwest gale the waves rose to 200 and 300 feet, and the wind carried the spray over the whole island . .

. It would, of course, be regrettable that a group of islands with over 2000 acres should become uninhabited but economic facts must be faced and unless the bay could be used . . . it is difficult to give a reason why the inhabitants should be encouraged to remain on the island. It seems strange that no attempt has been made to establish a meteorological station here, where it would be most useful, being in the track of the S.W. gales, and it is equally strange that no lighthouse has been erected, seeing that trawlers are constantly sheltering in the bay. The attempts made hitherto to assist the natives have generally been of the wrong kind. They have often been supplied with material they did not know how to use. What they want is a strong-minded and well-informed person who will live amongst them and, by example, teach them how to get the most out of the land, sea and rocks."

ALEX COCKBURN, FSE – GEOLOGIST

Cockburn was a young man of about 25 when he went out to St. Kilda. He was to assist Mathieson in his survey work but he was also to study the geology of the group of islands for his thesis for his B.Sc. degree at Edinburgh University. He pitched his tent behind the Factor's House and managed to survive there for over five months through several terrible summer storms. He returned in 1928 to finish his task. He offered to share his tent with Gladstone as there was no room available in the Factor's house.

During his stay on the island Cockburn found a good friend in Ewen MacDonald of House 16 who also acted as his assistant. His cragsman skills enabled him to descend the cliffs and slide into crevices and along ledges to collect rock samples which Cockburn would have found quite impossible. In later years, after his marriage, Cockburn called his son Ewen as a tribute to his St. Kilda friend. Cockburn's brother Stanley joined him for a few weeks' holiday on the island during the summer of 1927.

While Gladstone was on St. Kilda Cockburn called in to tell him about his expedition to Levenish, "He said that the men who had been out with him had wanted to set fire to the long grass on top of the island. This grass had grown long for no sheep are put on Levenish and men very seldom land on the island." On another occasion they had a long talk together when Gladstone found him chipping away pieces of rock in a cave to the east of the Factor's House, Cockburn commented that he had already consumed 1000 cigarettes. They explored Oiseval together, Cockburn collected rock samples and Gladstone his plants, although it was Cockburn who found some honey-suckle. Gladstone brought the trophy back as a present for Mrs. MacLeod who was delighted with it.

In Gladstone's "Who's who" he says of Cockburn that, "He took an interest in everything on the island and collected all that he could lay his hands on." He was also a very accomplished photographer, most of the very best photographs of this period were taken by him and illustrate many books.

On his return to the mainland in October he passed on a message from the St. Kildans to the Sunday Post reporter for their readers. "One thing the St. Kildans were anxious that I should tell the people of the mainland when I got home was that a very bad storm, following the wet summer, had completely ruined their potato crop.

For the study of geology the island is a very interesting piece of ground. It is interesting because of its isolation. It is also excellent in that it affords splendid climbing facilities. The high ways of the tremendous storms sweep the ledges to an altitude of a hundred feet and more, clearing them of all boulders and loose material. The storm which finished the St. Kildans' potato crop was tremendous. I saw spray six hundred feet high coming over the island – a sight one could never forget.

My work entailed a great deal of climbing, but I was under the care of the St. Kildans all the time. They are magnificent climbers. It is a sight to see them moving about on the face of the rocks. All their climbing is done in bare feet. The highest of their rocks is the precipice to the northern face of Conacher, which is about 1300 feet high. It is not absolutely sheer, precipices being slightly broken, but no man has ever gone down it at any one point from the top to the bottom. There were many thrilling minutes, but we had no accidents. The St. Kildans are very cautious. Although they go into very dangerous places they don't do reckless things. One man, for instance, would never go into a dangerous place without another man and a rope between them.

Climbing is a necessity for them. It means a large part of their food supply – to get both eggs and birds they have to be adept at it. The fulmar petrel, which along with the puffin, forms an important item in the menu, they take from their nests before the fledglings can fly. I had a good many of these while I was there, and found them quite good, although many people cannot even smell them far less eat them. They are extremely oily. I didn't care for the puffin, however. It is allowed to reach maturity before it is taken. The flavour of their flesh was far too strong for my taste.

The island is not quite so isolated as it once was. The missionary's wife, for instance, has a two valve set with which she gets Daventry very well, and she keeps the people informed of the news. There is also a wireless set at the Post Office, and the trawlers have sets which the islanders make use of occasionally. They are not at all excited over the wireless, although they would ask any of the manse people they met what the day's news was

As to the practical results of my survey, I did not find a gold seam or any precious metal. But I have brought back specimens that are scientifically very interesting. The geological formation consists entirely of igneous rocks, and about one third of the island – the northern third – is of granite. It is not like the granite of Aberdeen or Peterhead. It is neither red nor black, but, a sort of cream to white colour." (Sunday Post. Oct. 1927)

The pressure of work was felt by Cockburn as soon as he returned to the University as he explained in a letter to Gladstone dated 15.12.27. "I have had an extremely busy time since I came home in the middle of October. On top of my geological work connected with St. Kilda, and just when your first letter arrived, I was writing and illustrating a magazine article on St. Kilda, correcting proofs of an article for a friend, and preparing lectures and demonstrations for the University classes and night classes of the Heriot-Watt College." He also made some other interesting comments, "Neil Gillies informed me he had two sheep actually living on Stac an Armin! . . . After six months residence on St. Kilda I cannot point to a single example of glacial striation, of 'roches moutonnees', hanging valleys etc. This you will realise is negative evidence . . . I am hoping to return next year to do several more months' work. I hope soon to give you some copies of my St. Kilda photographs, many of which are really good. Even they are not all printed yet."

Cockburn did return in 1928 to complete the practical work for his thesis. The Transactions of the Royal Society of Edinburgh carried his work, "The Geology of St. Kilda" in their publication of 1934-5. It was a major contribution to the geology of what had been the least known of Scotland's ancient volcanoes.

Cockburn obtained his degree of PhD of Edinburgh in 1929 and was elected a Fellow of the Royal Society of Edinburgh in 1936. In the University Geological Department he served as Senior Lecturer and Director of Studies from 1951 onwards. He died on 28th February 1959, Professor Arthur Holmes commented, "All who knew him will remember with gratitude and affection the help and advice he gave so readily, and his unfailing kindness, wisdom and good humour. As a lecturer he was unusually inspiring. Last year's lectures were never good enough to be repeated. Every recent advance had to be assimilated and incorporated into an orderly system, so that his lectures kept pace with the progress of the subject. Thoughtless of self-advancement and never seeking geological fame, yet his beneficent influence has already spread far and wide across the world, wherever geologists trained in Edinburgh are to be found." (Scotsman, 6/3/59)

JOHN GLADSTONE – BOTANIST

ARRIVAL AND LIFE AT THE MANSE
DAY BY DAY – Extracts from Gladstone's Diary
STRAINS AND STRESSES – Extracts from the Empire Review

ARRIVAL AND LIFE AT THE MANSE

John Gladstone arrived at St. Kilda on Sunday July 3rd on the "Dunara Castle" with his two friends. "The day was dull, soon turning to rain and fog; thus the sight of the base of the Oiseval cliff was very sudden. We anchored in a bay protected on the north by the hills of Oiseval and Conacher, and on the south by the long island of Dun. We looked on to the village, a long line of 16 two-roomed cottages stretching in an arc of a wide circle about 200 yards from the sandy beach. At the eastern end stood the factor's house, larger than the rest. Close down by the sea near the pier was a group of buildings, the manse, the mission church and the school. Further to the east was the store, roofless and ruinous, and close beside it a machine gun. Behind were grassy slopes rising steeply, but whose tops were covered with mist. These clouds hid from view the summit of the island, and gave one a feeling that there was a vast stretch of unknown land behind. For ten minutes we saw no sign of life on the island; then the doors of the church opened; four women came out and walked in single file along the top of the bank which overlooks the shore. They were wearing bright red shawls over their heads and black dresses. Later another line of men and women went from the church up the village to their houses. After about an hour they had finished their meal, and were ready to bring a boat out. I and my two friends, Tom Steuart Fothringham and Ian Lindsay, were taken ashore with our luggage. We were met and given tea by Mrs. MacLeod, the Missionary's wife, who said that her husband was away on holiday. After six o'clock the boat went out three times to take ashore our fellow tourists from the "Dunara Castle".

Mrs. MacLeod was to look after Gladstone and his friends during their sojourn on St. Kilda. "She was the daughter of a Gloucestershire coachbuilder – she married a chauffeur who took her out to Australia where they lived for about 8 years. He died out there and she came back." Her second husband was John MacLeod, whose story is the subject of another chapter. Before coming out to St. Kilda Gladstone was briefed that Mrs. MacLeod would be able to supply all the food he and his two friends would need apart from tinned meats and fruit which they should bring with them. They put in an order at Coopers in Glasgow to cover all possible contingencies. 22.6.1927

5 x ½lb pkts of tea at 2/8	13s	4d
1 jar apple jelly	1	2
5 jars Scotch Marmalade	6	0½
1 stone Jonathan apples	9	
1 piece streaky bacon 10lb	15	
6 tins pineapple at 1/–	6	
6 tins peaches at 11½	5	9
6 tins fruit salad at 1/1	6	6
1 Bot. Bovril	3	9
2 pkts of 500 Toilet Paper	1	7
Half ham, 6lb at 1/7½	9	9
5 1oz Murrays Mellow Mixt.	5	2½
3lbs Bulls eyes	2	6
Total £3 – 18 – 1		
My Share £1 – 6 – 0		

(Coopers reckoning seems to be a little out!)

While her husband was away Mrs. MacLeod had the help of Rachel Annie, whose father Donald Gillies had died of appendicitis on Boreray. She later visited Fleetwood and Blackpool hoping to get employment there but she was not happy away from St. Kilda and returned before long.

In his diary Gladstone comments, "Mrs. MacLeod is extremely fond of the islanders. They give her milk every night and mutton whenever they kill a sheep . . . One evening little Donald Gillies (Neil Gillies' son), came and brought her a sheep's liver; they know and remember, so kind they are, that she is especially fond of liver . . . As vegetables, apart from potatoes, were non existent she grew her own watercress having six pots on the go at a time . . . It was reckoned that (on Hirta) there were more cats and dogs, which numbered 27, and these had nearly exterminated the little St. Kilda House mouse. Mrs. MacLeod didn't keep a cat and so occasionally sees them in the Manse and was able to trap two this year."

On one occasion Mrs. MacLeod showed Gladstone a plan of the Manse and how the rooms had been arranged in the days of the Rev. John MacKay, 1865-89.

1. School, Foundation laid by Miss Heathcote in 1899.

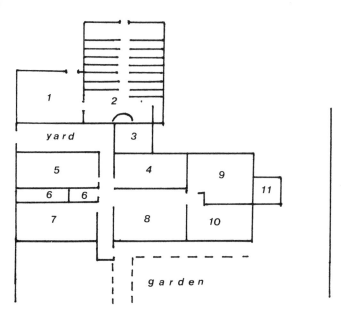

Plan of the Manse.

2. Church.
3. Room (now coal-cellar) where John MacDonald slept.
4. Rev. John MacKay's bedroom.
5. Kitchen (a servant girl used to sleep in, top right hand corner; there was a screen between her bed and the door).
6. Now divided off into two cupboards, one opening into the passage and the other into the kitchen. (Elizabeth MacKay, the Minister's sister used to sleep in the long and narrow room, which had no ventilation nor light. Her tombstone – she died at the age of 44 – is one of the only three in the churchyard with an inscription on it.
7. Now bathroom, used to be spare bedroom for any minister or guest who happened to come.

8. Sitting room and dining room as in John Mackay's time.
9, 10, 11. Rooms added during the last 20 years.
9. Mrs. MacLeod's bedroom.
10. The children's bedroom where we slept.
11. Shed.

Part of Gladstone's diary, the pages covering July 20 – 21 are missing, having been torn out by Mrs. MacLeod! Some of his entries included petty rows between individuals which she must have felt were better forgotten, it must have been a critical point in Gladstone's stay on the island as in the next day's report he announces that he is going to leave early – three weeks before he had originally planned.

DAY BY DAY – Extracts from Gladstone's Diary

Sunday, July 3rd. – The Departure of the "Dunara Castle"

"We walked up Conacher and were astonished at the view of the birds obtained at the top of the cliff. One looks down a sheer drop of 1350 feet and sees nothing but a vast expanse of sea with Borera and its attendant stacs four miles out. Then we watched the passengers being taken on board for the boat again. This was done with difficulty for the wind was in the east, and a heavy swell was coming into the bay. We had a meal at ten o'clock; St. Kilda mutton and cheese. At eleven o'clock the "Dunara Castle" sounded her horn; everyone on the island saw that it was becoming unsafe for her to ride at anchor any longer, for a S.E. wind was blowing; and anchorage is unsafe in the bay when the wind is from this quarter. So the islanders, in face of the prospect of obtaining no provisions unless they went out to her at once, launched a boat. The stores were taken ashore and unloaded with difficulty. We carried up Cooper's boxes to the Manse. Then another boat went out, to take on board Neil Ferguson senr, and Finlay Gillies who was going to see his daughter in Tiree. It was an extraordinary sight to see the old man embrace and kiss all the women of the island, who kept on crooning and wailing as if he were going away never to come back. All the St. Kildans were down on the pier. Their dogs had followed them down; there must have been 25 there, all barking for no reason. The little boat after five minutes hard rowing reached the "Dunara Castle", and deposited its passengers on board. The "Dunara Castle" sailed at midnight; everyone watched it disappearing round the cliff. They would not see that boat again for over six weeks. We went in and unpacked my bed.

Monday, July 4th. Exploring the Island

We tidied our room till lunch . . . We had some lunch at two o'clock and started off for a walk of discovery round the island. We went to the south east corner and photographed Dun with the sun streaming on it; I had never seen any scenery so grand. Below our feet the carpet of thrift and sea plantain made the ground a lovely blue-green colour. Far to the south, two trawlers were fishing. On the far eastern horizon

Clearing Cloud over Soay.

we imagined we saw the hills of South Uist. We walked along the south shore and down "the glen" to the North Bay in which two trawlers were anchored. Then seeing the clouds rising to pass over the cliffs on the south shore we went up there and spent an hour looking down at the sea 1000 feet below and at the cloud capped island of Soa. Home again, arrived back at seven. For supper we had two of the "meally puddings" which my friends had brought from Iona. Afterwards Mrs. MacLeod came and talked to us about the islanders. She told us that Finlay MacQuien was still alive . . . and that the nurse made a daily inspection of the houses."

Tuesday, July 5th. Visiting in the Village

A very wet morning, clear later. Mist all day on Conacher whose top I have not yet seen . . . I went and helped two little boys to chase sheep out of the glebe . .

I met two friends with Mrs. Mathieson, Nurse Flett and her friend Miss Vidler; we walked up the village street. We first of all went in to see John MacDonald (who looks and talks remarkably like an old English groom) and his wife. Then passing "Ivy Cottage" we came to No. 11 where lives Mrs. MacQuien whose husband was drowned in the bay when the boat in which he was crossing to Dun was overturned. She instructed us in the arts of spinning and carding . . . After a long time in her house, we walked back down the street, not daring to go any farther, for one seemed to have to stay at least half an hour in any house one went into . . . In the cottages there are no carpets or pictures but advertisements from magazines are hung up on the walls. After lunch at 2 o'clock I went out, clouds being on Conacher, to the point of Dun. While I was very lazy sitting doing nothing in the glorious sun I saw Neil Gillies on his way to catch sheep. He said that rams were now feeding on Dun and that lambs were put there later. MacLeod made a charge of 1/- a lamb grazing there. Back to supper about 8 o'clock.

Wednesday, July 6th. Visiting Donald Gillies

A dull day turning to rain. Fine in the evening but little sun. When we woke up a boat bearing the mark F.D. 26, was in the bay. Mrs. MacLeod tells me that, if these Fleetwood trawlers ceased to call at St. Kilda the islanders would get no more coal. They beg coals from the Fleetwood boats – for the Aberdeen, Grimsby and Norwegian boats coming into the bay refuse to give it to them.

I had promised to call to see some plants which Donald Gillies had brought for me. So I walked up to his house with 6 apples and 3 bars of chocolate in my vasculum. Donald met me and took me in, and we talked about the German bombardment, about cloth and about the problems of St. Kilda. Finally, he asked me to buy some cloth and I promised to get 10 yds from him. I liked Donald and his family so much that I gave away the 6 apples and the chocolate I had brought for our lunch . . . Went out to the east point of the island . . . watching the puffins . . . back about 7.30 and a good supper. Afterwards busy doing my plants and did not go to bed till 11.30. Two trawlers (one

Aberdeen, one Fleetwood) were in the North Bay today. Saw the top of Conacher for the first time.

Thursday, July 7th. Parliament and Visit to Borera

A brighter day, eight hours sunshine. Woke up 8.45. Grimsby trawler G.Y. 1198 in the bay. I looked out and saw the "Parliament" of the island assembled outside Ferguson's house. One man was waving a white handkerchief to the boat, another was viewing it with his telescope while the rest were talking as hard as they could. I crept up the street, said a word to Norman MacKinnon and managed to get a photograph of them. It was not until midday that they decided to take two boats to Borera. They both set out about an hour later, our boat going on ahead while the second made for the trawler in the bay. She having nothing to do kindly towed it along and picked me up half way. The landing on Borera is difficult. The man who is most expert as a rock climber lands first carrying a rope with him and takes up his position in a secure place on the rock. You have to stand in the boat, a rope round your waist, and wait till the boat is washed near the

Visiting Grimsby Trawler. Gladstone Collection.

Landing on Boreray. Gladstone Collection.

rock; then you jump and clamber up, the man on the top holding onto your rope. The island rises up steeply to a height of 1220 feet. From about half way up the south slope to the top grows very good grass which feeds 200 sheep all the year round. Donald Gillies, his brother John Gillies and the oldest MacKinnon and us three went off to see the sights of the island. On the way up we met Mr. Mathieson and Mr. Cockburn . . . we saw the huts in which they had been sleeping; Donald Gillies caught a puffin and put it in a noose which was found lying there for Tom to photograph. We went up a natural path along the west of the island, seeing Gannets and Fulmars nesting, and looking down on Stac Lii and Stac an Armin, white with Gannets. Climbing all the time with bare feet, we reached the top of the island after a nasty little climb up a wet chimney. After munching a little food we came down to the landing place, got into the boat and rowed back to the trawler. There we were taken on board. I went up to the bridge where I encountered the skipper, a bulky man, with three pairs of trousers on . . . When the boat was anchored in St. Kilda bay we were taken to see the fish in the hold. There were fish of all sorts and kinds; salmon, halibut, plaice, cod and ling. They very

Puffin Noose given by Donald Gillies.

kindly gave three baskets to the St. Kildans, and the Missionary's wife got her share. We had a good supper on fish and the puddings which my friends had brought and went to bed late. I have to work hard to identify my plants in the evening.

Friday, July 8th. The Great River – Collecting plants

Misty morning, but later very warm. I went out to explore the "Great River", as they call the stream which comes down from Conacher in a rocky glen. I collected a lot of plants and got to the top of the hill (1,396 feet) where I found my friends . . . soon after lunch I walked to the top of Oiseval taking with me Cobbet's Rural Rides. Read there in the brilliant sun for a long time and came back about 6 o'clock. Dinner off a queer fish, which had come off the trawler, tinned peaches and three of Mrs. MacLeod's oat cakes.

Saturday, July 9th. Ruiaval, and selling wares

A very hot day, 8½ hours sunshine. In the morning walked over towards Ruaival and up the little glen that comes down from Mullach Sgar. Found there Silene acaulis and the gentian . . . I decided to bathe at 4 o'clock, my friends refusing to accompany me. The water was cold and I was very happy when it was all over. At 6 o'clock there was great excitement when a small yacht was seen rounding the point of Dun; all telescopes were fixed on her while she sailed into the bay and it was at length decided she was the Quest III. A small boat containing six men came ashore and were met on the pier by all the islanders and dogs, in a state of frenzied excitement. The men carried down great rolls of tweed, the women had the socks and stockings they had knitted, and the boys brought boxes of wild bird's eggs. The crew came ashore and gave newspapers, magazines, and Chambers' Journals to all, and a packet of tobacco to Finlay MacQuien. They went up the village street never saying a word to us or to Mrs. MacLeod and stopped at the Post Office where they were closeted for about 10 minutes with Mary-Ann Ferguson. Great was the disappointment of the island when it became known that they had bought a length of cloth from the Fergusons; "the Fergusons" all said, "get everything". So they do – but I told the islanders that it was impossible that the men could buy cloth from them all . . . They soon went off, and the dogs barked as if they wanted to go with them . . . Then we went into No 2 and listened while Mathieson talked Gaelic to Finlay MacQuien, who tried to persuade us to buy a white puffin which he had caught. Soon home and to bed after sitting up till midnight pressing plants.

Sunday, July 10th. Sunday Service

A nice cool breezy morning; no rain, a little sun from 4 – 6. Woke late and started breakfast about 10.30. The service was at 1 o'clock (new time), and we did not go out till then. At 1 o'clock people were seen coming from their houses (which had seemed deserted before) and making their way in the direction of the church . . . As a mere formality Norman MacKinnon, the precentor, gave six pulls at the bell rope, although everyone on the island had collected. We went in, putting our money in a little box on a pedestal. We sat down in the back left pew (Ferguson's) and discovered old "blind" Calum in the precentor's seat, for no-one occupied the pulpit. Calum began to read through the metrical psalm which the congregation was to sing. This being over Norman stood up and "led the praise", singing each line first, the congregation repeating it after him. The psalm ended, Calum read a chapter of 40 verses from St. John. After he had finished reading the New Testament he put up his hands and prayed. The women sprawled over the desk in front of them and the men stood up; for this is the custom of St. Kilda. Another psalm was then sung; and the Old Testament

lesson, the last chapter of Ecclesiastes, was read. Old Malcolm's address followed. One would never think that the old man was capable of preaching with such inspiration. We then sung the 23rd psalm to the tune Covenanters. Finally, Calum called on John Gillies to pray. John said his prayer – for every man in St. Kilda prays in turn – with beautiful rhythmical lowerings and risings of the voice, and we were struck by the beauty of the sound. We did not venture to say a word to any but went back and had lunch. At 4 o'clock we went away for a walk, climbing Conacher from behind. From the top of the hill, I had the privilege of seeing the congregation disperse after the 6 o'clock service. A late tea at 9 o'clock and to work on my plants afterwards. I did not go to bed tonight until half past twelve.

Monday, July 11th. A Visit to Dun

A lovely day, bright sun and no wind. Soon after breakfast we went up the village to see whether they were going to Soa, and talked to Norman MacKinnon and Finlay MacQuien about it. We were surprised to find that a charge (of 5/– the boat and 5/– each man in the boat) was made for all expeditions to the neighbouring islands. This practice has probably been adopted for the first time this year.

In the afternoon Norman MacQuien and I landed and climbed about from one end of Dun to the other; if I had had my camera I could have photographed a young fulmar which tried to squirt oil at me, a young gull and a razorbill which Norman caught by putting his hand into the rocks. We went passed a cave where they used to sleep when they went to catch razorbills. We also saw the ledge on which the razorbill catcher used to stand. His method of operation was as follows: he held in his hand a piece of white cloth, which, in the darkness of the night, the birds mistook for a ledge of rock. When a bird came and settled on his hand, he killed it and threw it up to the rocks above, and stood

Puffin catching on Dun. Drawing by Sands.

ready waiting for the next victim. At the extreme east end of the island stands the "old castle" from which the island takes its name; it is simply a wall of stones cutting off the east point from the rest of the island. We sat down and soon discovered that Norman was covered with puffin ticks. Norman filled in the time by telling me how he had left the island to try to get work in a ship-building yard in Glasgow; how he had worked there about a year, but, because of the depression of trade, was sacked . . . At about 7 o'clock we saw the boat coming – we climbed along a little farther to the entrance of the natural arch which goes right through the island. I got down the rock preparatory for landing. When the boat came up Finlay seized me by the feet and pulled me into the boat. We came alongside the trawler and Norman MacQuien went aboard and got sacks and sacks of coal; he is said to be a past master in the art of begging from trawlers. While we were watching the coal being put into sacks, a whaler (the Southern Seas, Capetown) slipped into the bay from the north towing a whale on either side. These whalers come from Bunavoneader in the island of Harris; this whaling station is the only part of Lord Leverhulme's scheme which has been profitable; for whales' fat is used to make Port Sunlight soap; there is only one other whaling station in the British Isles, that is in the Shetlands. All the Bunavoneader whalers are manned by Norwegians . . . A lovely night, brilliant sky, but the midges have been terrible today and I foretell rain.

Whales in Village Bay with accompanying Fulmars. Gladstone Collection.

Tuesday, July 12th. The Well of Virtues and Mullach Mor

A lovely morning again! We took our lunch and ate it at the Well of Virtues. We slept, talked and read till about 5 o'clock, when we went down to see the cave under the mouth of the stream in the glen. It was absolutely impossible for us to see how far in the sea goes. We climbed Mullach Mor on our way home. Just before supper Cockburn came in to tell us about his expedition to Levenish. After supper we read the articles that a reporter had written on St. Kilda last winter. There was a bad epidemic of 'flu in the early spring; the trawlers had ceased to call and there was no way of getting help. Nurse Littejohn had walked up to the top of Conacher carrying wood and a tin of paraffin which she lit to show that help was needed. However, help did not come until the first "Hebrides" called. The whales still lie in the bay covered by gulls, and are beginning to swell and smell. My friends expect to go tomorrow on the whaler.

Wednesday, July 13th. Settling Debts – Whales Burst

A dull day with no wind. Tom and Ian packing and settling up their affairs in the morning. About midday we went up the village street, and paid Mrs. MacQuien for stockings and Ewen MacDonald for eggs. The two whales left last night in the bay have swelled out enormously and have completely changed their shape. Every moment we expect them to burst and to send out an awful smell. This happened about 7 o'clock just as the island was coming from its prayer meeting (for besides the three services on the Sabbath a prayer meeting is held every week on Wednesday evenings, and regularly attended). After supper I talked to Donald Gillies and paid him for the trip to Borera. I went up with old Finlay Gillies to Donald Gillies to get my 10 yards of tweed and sat for about half an hour talking and smoking with him, his brother John and their wives. I am very fond of Donald, a kind, simple man who had inherited all the old St. Kilda virtues. He has a family, he proudly told me, of two girls, three dogs, two white cats without tails, one hen and chickens and a wife. I walked back and found my friends had not arranged with Donald-John about the boat which was to take them out to the whaler, whenever it happened to come in. So we walked up again to see what John MacDonald was going to do about getting out, for he was going by the whaler to take one of Widow Annie's little girls to have her tonsils removed by the doctor at Tarbert (Harris), but had made no arrangements. My friends were determined not to be left behind at the last moment . . . So we went back to John Gillies and asked him to get four men . . . Here we are then at one o'clock reading Calum MacFheargus to pass away the time against the arrival of the whaler. This may not be till next morning; we do not even know definitely whether a boat will go out to it.

Thursday, July 14th. Tom and Ian leave on the Whaler – Island illnesses

At 6.30 the whaler came into the bay. We all went down to the pier with John and Donald Gillies, the two MacKinnons and Donald-John Ferguson. John MacDonald and his little girl went over to the boat with my friends. The whaler had got two more whales and the six were going back to Bunavoneader. How they will smell during the voyage and how slow the boat will go towing those enormous things alongside! I afterwards heard from my friends that they did not enjoy the trip on the whaler – the smell was much too intense. It was a fine day, but very little sun; there was a little more wind and mist and it was generally more unsettled. I had lunch on the west of the glen and watched a man catching sheep on the opposite side of the hill. I went on to the Cambir and found the ordinary vetch growing among the short grass as mentioned by Gibson. Back about 5.30 and had dinner with Mrs. MacLeod. She says they have not had Communion on St. Kilda for two years and it seems it will be a very great event.

About 8 o'clock Nurse and Miss Vidler came and talked for an hour or so. Nurse says the islanders are always getting skin diseases, boils, sores, abscesses and blisters; she thinks it is caused by the food they eat – always meat and no vegetables. She talked about old "blind" Calum's illness last Saturday, how he fainted and looked blue all over . . . They love pretending

they are ill, she says, but they won't do what she tells them or listen to her advice.

Writing letters and a little more work. From my window I can see the gannets diving straight down into the sea; every 10 seconds or so one sees a splash in the calm water and a moment later hears the "plop". There must be at least a hundred fishing in the bay tonight.

Friday, July 15th. Stitches, Surveyors and Sundials

Very little rain last night – a lovely day again, glass rising. 13½ hours sunshine. Got up late in the morning and took my grey flannel trousers to Norman MacKinnon to be mended; he soon put a piece of St. Kilda cloth into the hole. Stayed all the morning reading in the garden; went out with my lunch about 12 o'clock to the cliff below Oiseval. There, meeting Cockburn who had found a clump of honey-suckle, I had my lunch and stayed a long time talking to him. He said that an ordnance survey of the St. Kilda group would cost £4000. Four men, a surveyor, an assistant surveyor with two men to carry their instruments would have to come if the survey were to be carried out in accordance with the official regulations. After supper I went over about 9 o'clock to Mr. Mathieson to show him a plan for a sundial which a Mr. Hamer (who had come by the June 30th "Dunara") had asked me to give to Mr. MacLeod; this Hamer had told me on the boat that he had heard that there used to be a sundial on the island; but that lately, it had fallen down and that the inhabitants were no longer able to tell the time. He had taken the trouble to find out the exact latitude and longitude of the island, and had made all the necessary calculations. All that was now needed was a flat stone and someone capable of carving on it. Mr. Mathieson said he had not the time to do the work; he will give it to Mr. MacLeod, who will probably light the kitchen fire with it the next morning!

We saw a boat about 30 miles out at sea giving off

curious flashes from the deck-level. We could not understand what was the matter and we were inclined to believe with Mrs. Mathieson that she was on fire. The boat soon disappeared behind Dun still emitting these curious lights and thick black smoke from her funnel.

Saturday, July 16th. Plants on Oiseval, Men on Borera

The glass higher, Mathieson says, than it has been this year; but not quite such a brilliant day as yesterday – high clouds – 6½ hours sunshine. As arranged last

Hauling up the boat on the slipway. Gladstone Collection.

night, Cockburn, Norman MacKinnon and I set out at 10 o'clock to explore the Oiseval cliffs. We thoroughly explored all the country round that part of the island, I picked up all the plants I could find, and Cockburn cut off samples of rocks. I had found enough down there to keep me occupied a long time, so after lunch, Norman and I went off again in search of plants on the rocks above. Two whales were again in the bay; the whaler must have come in last night unheard. Norman MacKinnon said that the buoys in the bay are leased to the Bunavoneader company by MacLeod; it must be MacLeod's only definite source of income from the island.

After dinner to work and to wait the return of a boat-load of men (Norman and Donald MacQuien, Donald-John, Neil Ferguson and Neil Gillies) who had gone to catch sheep on Borera. About 8 o'clock they came back with five sheep. They were carried up the pier, but when they got on the path they were untied and led up the street. Some were to be killed tonight and some kept till tomorrow.

Sunday, July 17th. Aberdeen Liner in Bay, Climb Conacher

A nice day, cloudy, but very warm with a warm wind. Got up at 10 o'clock and had breakfast; worked in the morning; service at one. "Blind" Calum again held forth; Norman MacKinnon "led the praise" and made the prayers with John Gillies.

Lunch at 3 o'clock. Soon after 4 o'clock an Aberdeen liner came into the bay and sounded her horn. We were afterwards told by Donald-John that the boat had on board a crew of Plymouth Bretheren who refused to work on Sunday. They wanted, he said, to come ashore and give an English Service. Donald-John says that, before the war when piety was more in fashion, there used to be as many as ten of these Aberdeen boats anchoring in the bay on Sundays.

Had some tea and did a little work. After supper I

climbed Conacher (1396 feet) without a stop. Mist was coming in from the north and I had a wonderful view of Borera with the sun shining only on the bottom of it and on Stac Lii and Stac-an-armin.

Monday, July 18th. Excitement – Visit of the "Hebrides"

A nice day again. Got up at 8.30. Great excitement eveywhere about the "Hebrides" calling. It was finally decided "in Parliament" that she would not be in till the afternoon. I sat for a few minutes on the seat outside the Manse with John Gillies who was darning my stockings. I found out how many dogs there were on the island, the relation of everyone to everyone else, and the marks of sheep.

number of dogs	name	sheep markings			house
		head	back	tail	
3	Norman MacKinnon	red	red	black	1
2	Finlay MacQuien	black			2
5	Neil Ferguson			black	4 most sheep
4	Neil Gillies	red	black		7 next most sheep
1	Calum MacDonald	black	black	red	8
3	John MacDonald	red			9
	Mrs. MacQuien			red	11 least sheep
3	Donald Gillies	black		red	13
	"Widow Annie"	red	red		14
3	John Gillies			black	15
3	Ewen MacDonald	Rag			16

Total 27

John has just been called away to launch the boat while the tide is high.

(6 p.m.) All the excitement is over. Everyone has retired to talk over the astounding events of the day; for there are only 8 days like it a year in St. Kilda. Even I was feverish with excitement and Mrs. MacLeod had a headache after it all. When I was writing letters indoors, at 12.30 the dogs began to bark. I went outside and saw the "Hebrides" slowly rounding the Oiseval cliffs. At once the two boats were launched. The boats were a long time alongside, but eventually came back full of trippers. One of the men, a school inspector, went up to the Manse, where he was met by Mrs. MacLeod. He had expected to find her husband at home since he was not on the boat. When Mrs, MacLeod realised that her husband had not come and that she could not go for her holiday she was furious. She told the inspector that she would never come back to the island. He had to inspect the school children in the time the "Hebrides" allowed him ashore (1 to 4 p.m.); the school bell was rung and the children collected in school with difficulty. But such was their excitement that they were unable to begin singing, one of the tests, and Mrs. MacLeod had to go and start it off. Meanwhile the trippers came ashore and gave their impressions of the place to their friends. I was surprised that my letters had been forwarded to me. I had many to answer but before I could do this I had to go to the "Hebrides" to get some butter and bread to replenish Mrs. MacLeod's scanty supplies.

I went over in a boat which was taking a small load of wool sacks on board. (The St. Kildans this year are not trying to make tweed which they cannot sell, but are sending away their wool to Edniburgh for any money that they can get). Norman MacKinnon was bailing out the boat all the time we were rowing across. The boat contained Donald Gillies in great form, Neil Gillies, Norman MacQuien and Donald MacKinnon. When we got on board the boat I got a parcel my friends promised to send from Tarbert (Harris) and went to get the butter and bread from the steward. There were many pigs on the boat going out to islands at which the boat calls on her return journey; many of the St. Kildans have never seen such a sight before –

they stood round touching, poking and talking about them. Back again and helped them to land the stores. Then I had to write some letters in answer to my post; for the letters had to leave by the "Hebrides". At 3.30 the passengers had to be taken on board again; the tide was so low that they had to embark from a rock, before the pier was built, the old landing place which appears in Norman Heathcote's pictures.

At 4.10 p.m. the boat weighed anchor and slipped quietly out of the bay. All is quiet again and it is a lovely sunny evening. The gannets are fishing in the bay and I sit in the garden looking out to see Rachel-Annie has just called; she has brought me some money which I had lent her when a tripper bought two yards of cloth from her mother (widow Donald Gillies). The island had done well out of the "Hebrides" call; except for the inspector, they surely enjoyed themselves. For paint-boxes, sweets, knives and beads have all come to them; one man had brought Punches for the Missionary, another Bulletins for the Nurse; another a bag of sweets for the whole island.

All day many had carried bundles of tweed which they either took out to the boat or showed when the trippers came ashore. Old Finlay MacQuien had carried a big length of grey cloth all day. I felt sorry to see him wandering about with such a large bundle under his arm. I am not amused when I see the most venerable looking man on the island, who had hardly a word of English, being pushed aside; but I hate far more to think of what is passing through his mind. He remembers the time when these things were not done; when it was counted an honour to have caught more puffins than the rest; to have climbed to places among the rocks into which others had never penetrated.

Tuesday, July 19th. An Uneventful Day

A wonderful fine day again. Boiling sun, no clouds but a good little breeze. An uneventful day. I worked all the morning at plants and took out my lunch and ate it on Ruaival. Came back, collected grasses on the way and painted. Mrs. MacLeod and I went up at 4.30 to the Factor's House and had tea with Nurse Flett and Miss Vidler. We talked about everything . . . I had brought a lot of plants in, so came back at 6 o'clock and worked at them till 8 p.m. Mr. Mathieson called and said that if the weather kept fine we would go to Soa tomorrow starting at 8.30 a.m. Let us hope all will go well.

Wednesday, Thursday July 20,21. Missing.

Torn out by Mrs. MacLeod.

Friday, July 22nd. Decide to leave early

Like the last few days very gusty and trying to rain the whole time. I have been taking the opportunity of doing some work, especially as I have decided to leave by the "Dunara Castle" which comes on Sunday or Tuesday. I am trying to get all my work done by then. Three weeks with nothing to do here can thus be avoided and I shall be able to explore the Long Island south of North Uist and compare its flora with that of St. Kilda.

Tonight a whaler came into the bay . . . the boat went out . . . and they soon came off with John MacDonald and his girls who had left for Tarbert on Wednesday the 13th. The doctor had told her she had to wait another three weeks. She landed at 11 o'clock. Back to my plants and to bed at midnight.

Saturday, July 23rd. Plants and Presents

A nice warm day. Got up at 10 o'clock and went to do Conacher.

Working all evening. I am afraid I have failed to find one or two rarities and, or course, I now wish I had a week more on the island. About 7 o'clock Donald Gillies came in and took off his cap. It contained six guillemot eggs which he offered to me. I reluctantly took them, protesting that they would be sure to break on the journey. He asked me to let him know whether they had hatched by the time I arrived home; which I did, he being overjoyed that I had remembered his little joke. Donald seemed rather offended when I offered him a tin of peaches; although I tried to point out that it was a present and not a payment for the eggs.

Sunday, July 24th. Last search for Plants: "Dunara Castle" arrives

A showery day, clearing later. Up early at 9 o'clock and about saying good-bye to Mathiesons and others.

Donald Gillies and family. Gladstone Collection.

I took a long walk over Conacher to make a last attempt to find some badly needed plants. Back at 2 o'clock as the islanders were coming out of church. Went in to Donald Gillies to ask whether I could photograph him and his family. He offered me a cup of tea, some suet pudding, scones and cheese; the first food I had eaten in an islander's house. While I was struggling with the stringy suet, the "Dunara Castle" came in. I photographed Donald, his wife and family and set off down the village street saying good-bye to all en route. Saw the boat come off the "Dunara" with John MacLeod, his boys and a Mr. Duncan, a minister from the island of Taransay (Harris) on board. I had a meal with Mr. Duncan and his son. The meal finished, I went out and saw the boats with the first load of Glasgow trippers. I talked to a group of them until the English service was announced by Donald-John. There was "a great crowd" as they say in Glasgow, in the church listening to a sermon by a man who had come off the "Dunara". Mr. Duncan, the Taransay minister, was with him in the pulpit, and John MacLeod was in the precentor's seat. Kenneth and Archie MacLeod were looking exemplary in the Manse pew. After a good sermon we sung the 103rd Psalm to an excellent tune; this ended the service.

After the service I had a long talk with dear Donald who asked me to buy him a packet of Ever-ready razor blades, and with Finlay, to whom I was eventually forced to give the remains of my last packet of tobacco. I went back to the Manse, Mr. and Mrs. MacLeod were sitting in the kitchen. They gave me a cup of coffee and we talked away. Mr. MacLeod is an exceptionally charming man, who takes a great interest in the island and is very fond of its people. We decided that Mrs. MacLeod should stay the night at Tarbert, Harris, and catch the mail boat there. After a long talk about plans, we retired to bed about midnight, I, having packed my bed had to sleep in the same room as Kenneth and Alec, who both snore disgracefully.

Tonight there are four boats in the bay; an Aberdeen liner, a Fleetwood trawler, a Bonavoneader whaler and a Glasgow "steam packet".

Monday, July 25th. Loading and Unloading. Farewell St. Kilda

About 5 o'clock I was woken up by the steam hooter

Loading a calf for shipment to Tiree. Gladstone Collection.

of the "Dunara Castle" and got up immediately. I dressed and went out and saw the boat launched. They begun unloading and the good work went on and on. Everyone was rushing about down at the pier. There were three calves to go to Tiree, for if they are sent to Lochmaddy they get very little money for them for it is known they are coming; in Tiree they are kept for a short space of time by Finlay Gillies' son-in-law who fattens them and sells them in his island. Two were tied to the Manse wall; the other belonged to widow Donald Gillies and was in a fank behind the coffin cleit. I helped her to catch it, and she asked me to accept a pair of gloves as a present from her. It was extremely kind of her to give away 5/– worth of goods; it means far more than one imagines to a woman like her. She has not the monetary instinct if I may so call it; she only thinks of making people happy.

At last we went off by the last boat, Mrs. MacLeod and I together with Lachlan MacDonald (No.16), Donald MacKinnon (No.1) and Finlay MacQuien's brother (No.2) – who had come on the "Hebrides" last Monday to pass a week on the island. Then there began the job of saying goodbye to St. Kildans who had now to leave the boat. When I shook hands with the men it was the saddest part of my stay on St. Kilda. I have been fond of the people and I only hope they have been fond of me."

Having returned home Gladstone sent a box of onions to Mrs. MacLeod and he received this reply which epitomises the day to day living conditions on this remote outpost in the winter. Written – 25/11/27, Postmarked Barra 19/12/27, reached Gladstone 21/12/27 "Dear Mr. Gladstone,

I received the box of onions yesterday (Nov.24), your letter is dated September 25th. so you can tell how long it was on the road, however, the onions arrived quite sound.

We have only had three mails since the last boat in

August, two via Fleetwood and one via Aberdeen but Aberdeen is not our recognised winter depot, and it is the only time we have had letters that way since I have been in St. Kilda.

Poor little Fleetwood has had a severe doing, I heard over the wireless on Sunday evening, some of the trawler skippers lost heavily, their houses being totally destroyed. We get the winds at times but so far no damage has been done . . . the sea drift certainly spoilt everything and although our potato tops were shrivelled up we got a good many potatoes, but of poor quality and flavour.

Mr. Cockburn, as you know, left us early in October, we have not heard from him since he left.

We are hoping to get a small bag away tomorrow, there are about a dozen trawlers sheltering in the bay, and if still there tomorrow, and a small boat can get out, they will send a bag.

The village still stands and everybody is just as you left them except Norman MacQueen who is away and I hear has either joined the Navy or the Naval Reserve, however, he is at Devonport, and poor old "blind" Malcolm has had a stroke of paralysis, but is bucking up under Nurse's skillful hands, although he cannot speak.

We do not expect another mail until February, although I sincerely hope someone will bring our Christmas one before that. I have a box of pears on the road somewhere between here and Malvern, the letter got through but the pears did not. I am now busy making Xmas puddings. Nurse and I intend to go a little bit mad for the season, things have been so terribly dead and miserable lately.

I will finish by wishing you the compliments of the season,

      Yours respectfully,
        B. MacLeod."

STRAINS AND STRESSES ON ST. KILDA

Extracts from an article written by Gladstone and published in the Empire Review for May 1928. It gives a realistic assessment of the pressures which were tightening their grip on St. Kilda in 1927.

The Urge to Escape

"I am confident that there is not a young man on the island who would refuse a passage to Glasgow or Canada were he sure that there were work to be obtained or if he were able to leave his old father or mother. These words could not have been written in 1900 when Heathcote found that none of them wished to leave. But he says very truly, "Probably as they become more educated many of them will become discontented with their primitive life and wish to take a more active part in the progress of the world. All I may say is I do not believe it will add to their happiness." Here I concur. For increasing contact with liners, traders, whalers and tourist boats and the consequent better communication have instilled ambition into the average St. Kildan. His relatives who have left the island describe their new home as paradise. As William Cobbett said of the emigrations of 1830, "It is the letters written across the Atlantic that do the business". They make him want to get away and see the world, and he is usually so fascinated by the world that he stays in it.

The Changing Economy

The chief occupation of the islanders used to be fowling; they caught literally thousands of puffins by throwing a noose over their necks from behind or above, plucked them and sold their feathers. They used to catch razorbills at night by standing on the ledge of a cliff and holding out a white rag which the birds imagined to be a piece of rock; solan geese too used to fall victims to an ingenious trick of theirs. They still catch fulmar petrels, no longer for their oil, which they used to and send away in barrels, but for salting down as a reserve food against the winter. They say it no longer pays to sell puffin or guillemot feathers; they take their eggs now, however, together with the eggs of rarer birds, such as the fork-tailed petrel which they have nearly made extinct – and sell them to tourists or send them away to collectors.

The sale of calves nowadays forms a large part of a crofter's income, £13 or £14 being the usual price in N.Uist, The St. Kildans, however, have been unable to benefit from the good prices; they have to send away their cows in summer when the steamers call; they arrive in Lochmaddy perhaps at a difficult time and get a little money for them.

There is one industry that has increased since the war: for now everyone on the island makes cloth; spinning, carding, fulling, dyeing and weaving are all done at home. The greater part of the cloth used to be sold to the brother of one of the islanders at about 2/6 a yard; but he has not been able, owing to the slump in demand for homespuns of recent years, to take so much as the islanders like. They count, therefore, on selling at 4/6 and 5/– a yard, a certain amount of cloth to the trippers from the "Dunara Castle" and the "Hebrides", but all on the island realise that this is a very unsatisfactory way of earning their living . . . The St. Kildans, too, take no pleasure in accosting trippers who declaim against them for "cadging" and "pushing their wares". This year they have been extremely unfortunate. The "Dunara Castle" has twice called on a Sunday; on the Sabbath, it is agreed by all, no goods shall be sold, no cargo unloaded . . . The islanders have large quantities of last year's cloth unsold, and this year they are sending away their wool to fetch what it can. It is difficult to see how the tweed problem can be solved. The manager of the crofter's agency in Tarbert says he cannot give a remunerative price to the islanders and at the same time compete with the merchant in Glasgow who buys the cloth. And no matter what were done to ensure a regular sale, it is probable that the islanders would prefer to continue to send away their cloth to their own relative – for all are related to all – for whatever price he could give them.

The Taste For A Wider Diet

The St. Kildans are no longer contented with the food which has nourished their fathers for countless generations. Presents of food are now sent by "well wishers" and a fund exists to supply them with flour; men who have left the island come back for their holidays and tell of the delicious things they have eaten in Glasgow. But many of the St. Kildans have not the money to buy the food. They do not make as much money as they did, and they still have to pay their rent; thus they are sometimes compelled to beg the food and coal from trawlers. We can hardly blame them for asking the necessaries or life which they have not the money to buy . . . The men find it very difficult to do without tobacco: when their tobacco runs out they smoke tea!

The Problems Over Communications

We must remember that awful uncertainty exists about the stores which the St. Kildans have ordered. They cannot get everything by the last "Hebrides". Eight months have to pass before the tourist season reopens. Their only method of obtaining food in the winter is to order by trawler and hope to get it when the boat happens to came back. But, of course, the trawler skippers never know when they will be calling again at St. Kilda. Some skippers, on account of the coal they have been pursuaded to give away, have been instructed not to let the St. Kildans come aboard their boats. I have just seen in the Daily Mail that the purser of the "Hebrides", which has made her final call of the season at St. Kilda, has sent a wireless message to say that, "until Whitsuntide of next year the islanders will have to depend for communication with the mainland on chance fishing craft seeking shelter in the bay." Many think it impossible that men can endure life in these conditions. The privations their forefathers have suffered alone can have accustomed them to it; but every year they are getting less hardy. It seems to us incredible that in the year of grace 1927 there can be any part of the British Isles without regular communication during eight months of the year. It is impossible for us to imagine the isolation of St. Kilda during the 8 months they call their "winter"; and strange to say, it is not always a voluntary isolation; to go out to a trawler, and to be unable to persuade the skipper to take orders must be sufficiently terrible.

But talking of this strain, it is only too easy to exaggerate and to paint a worse picture of St. Kilda today than in 1900 when boats rarely called at the island at all in the winter. We say that St. Kildans were born to suffer: the older men, one may confidently say, find little difficulty in facing the winter. What the nurse and the missionary call suffering, they call discomfort.

One stormy night last July I saw in the bay an Aberdeen liner, a whaler from Lord Leverhulme's whaling station in Harris with, of course, a Norwegian crew, one Grimsby and two Fleetwood boats in the bay; and I am informed that as many as forty boats have been seen in the bay on a stormy winter's night.

What Future Has St. Kilda?

St. Kilda cannot go on as it has done in the past. Industry has ceased to be profitable; Land is annually out of cultivation; the cutting of turf, instead of peat, for fuel, is slowly robbing the land of its grazing; rates have to be born by an owner who can get little return for his money; the government must spend quite £400 a year on the school and the nurse. St. Kilda has failed to fit into the modern world. It has become a mere curiosity and a very charming curiosity at that; for it contains – I speak from personal experience – the kindest and most affectionate people I have ever met. "One happy family" their missionary has been pleased to call them. Every morning the family meets together outside No.4 (for all the houses in Main Street are numbered and one is even called Ivy Cottage) to discuss what is to be done during the day. Here questions, such as whether potatoes are to be weeded or sheep caught, occupy perhaps two hours; here one has to wait if one wants to know whether a boat is going to Borera or whether sheep are to be sheared; here perhaps one hears arguements in favour of collecting crotel (to dye wool brown) or mending the boat, or of catching fulmars, if it be after the 12th of August. But this delightful communal spirit alone, sad to say, cannot carry them through the 20th century: virtues which count for much in a primitive society are of little use nowadays.

And so we wonder, as the books of the 1880's have wondered, what will be the future of St. Kilda. Mr. Heathcote, in 1900, expected great changes in the future. When he was on St. Kilda the islanders exchanged their produce with the factor for stores. But the government refused to help the owner to repair the bombarded store and it has been left as the Germans left it. The islanders now attempt to conduct their own business; each orders his own stores. Mr. Heathcote wanted this to happen; he thought the islanders would become more self reliant and would "develop the resources of the island of their own accord". But this has not been the case and none of his recommendations – burning peat – fishing – cultivation of their ground better – have been carried out. It is difficult to see how anything can be done for St. Kilda, which will cost money never to be returned. Its unique position, 45 odd miles out in the Atlantic, makes communication both precarious and costly. This is the difficulty which faces all who talk of St. Kilda as a fishing depot, a whaling station, or a tourist resort

(I shudder to write it). The world in general has no use for St. Kilda. Men like to see her, make lists of her birds and flowers, write books about her and photograph her. St. Kilda is, however, of great interest to the individual. And so I divulge my secret – St. Kilda is up for sale. She has remained for centuries under the protection of a MacLeod, great chiefs of a great clan; the present owner finds that he cannot afford to go on losing money year by year on St. Kilda; but I do not see why someone, who has a little money to spare, should not buy it. If you know anyone in that enviable state of life, tell him; tell him that if he were to take no rents and to ensure, for a boat to call once a month at St. Kilda, he would be doing an enormous service to the island. It would cost money; but a kind-hearted millionaire would do it were he to realise the enormous good he would be doing."

The price for St. Kilda was £3,000, which included the brown sheep on Soay and everything else.

Gladstone's work as a botanist was recognised. The Royal Botanical Gardens at Kew wrote to him acknowledging the receipt of 145 Herbarium specimens of plants collected by him. Dr. David Lack paid his own tribute having visited St. Kilda with a team of Scientists in 1931. He wrote to Gladstone, "Our botanist was very annoyed that you had done your work so thoroughly!"

The MacKinnons –
An Unfinished Portrait

FAMILY BACKGROUND
LIFE ON ST. KILDA
EVACUATION AND AFTER

Anthony Troloppe called in at St. Kilda on his way to the Faeroe Islands and Iceland in 1878. In his book, "How the Mastiffs went to Iceland", he included his own description of the islands and the people and concluded that, "St. Kilda is a most picturesque point in the ocean at which to land and at which to marvel at the freaks of nature. But it is an atom of land hardly

Stac Lee and Borera. Acland.

intended by nature as a habitation for man . . . (the inhabitants) existence cannot be good for them and certainly not for their posterity – as far as we can judge a time will come when that posterity must die out, unless the people be removed." These words of prophecy were fulfilled in August 1930 when St. Kilda was evacuated. In the end, after a dreadful winter and near starvation, felt perhaps even more painfully by the MacKinnon family than by others, as they were the largest on the island, they made the commitment to leave in the summer of 1930 whatever happened. They approached, with others, Nurse Barclay and the missionary, Dugald Munro, to ask them to write letters to the Government pleading for them to have them removed and resettled somewhere on the mainland.

St. Kilda Parliament of 1927. Photo by Cockburn. Left to Right:- Ewan Gillies, Norman MacKinnon (Senior), John Gillies, Ewan MacDonald (above the head of Ewan Gillies), Donald Gillies (standing), Norman MacQueen (standing), Neil Ferguson (Junior), Finlay MacKinnon, Neil Gillies (standing), Lachlan MacDonald, Donald MacDonald, Norman MacKinnon (Junior), Finlay Gillies, Neil Ferguson (Senior), Donald Ewan MacKinnon, Malcolm (blind Callum) MacDonald.

FAMILY BACKGROUND

"MacKinnons are plentiful in both Harris and Skye but the Christian names in use in the families suggest the latter origin." (Lawson, 1981). Dr. John MacDonald in his list of the inhabitants made on his visit in 1822 mentions two families:-

No. 4. Ewen aged 63 and his wife Christian, with Donald 17, Lachlan 14, Norman 5, Mary 8 and Catharine 2.

No. 15. Neil MacKinnon aged 37 with his wife Christian MacDonald and their children Malcolm 8 and Christian 5.

Lawson comments, "It is tempting to place Neil as a son of Ewen by a prior marriage but if Mitchell is correct in his statements as to relationships this cannot be so and Neil could at the closest be a nephew of Ewen, perhaps by a brother Malcolm. Neil had only one surviving son, Malcolm and he had no surviving family and so all the MacKinnons latterly on St. KIlda were descendants of Ewen. He had two sons; Donald (who was sent by MacDonald of Ferintosh for training on the mainland as a catechist-teacher, and after a brief spell on the island married Isabella, daughter of Armiger Nicholson, catechist on the island of Berneray, Harris, and settled at Obbe, Harris, where there are still descendants), and Lachlan, who was the grandfather of Norman MacKinnon whose decision to leave the island with his large family in 1930 finally precipitated the evacuation." (Lawson, 1981).

Lachlan (1808-95) was married three times, first in 1832 to Ann MacQueen. Their first son Ewen died in infancy, they named their second son Ewen, he died in a fall from a rock precipice into the sea, only one year after marrying Mary Ferguson. Their third son Donald died on the ill fated Dargavel in April 1863, when all seven men and one woman were lost on their way to Harris. Lachlan's second wife was Rachel Gillies and they had two sons, Norman and Neil. Neil married Kirsty Gillies and through their first son Norman, who married Ann Gillies, they produced the large family who lived at No. 1 at the time of the evacuation. They had five other children who died in infancy and lastly Lachlan who died before the evacuation.

Lachlan's third wife, Rachel MacDonald had three daughters, Catharine who married John Gillies in 1881, but she died two years later; Rachel married Donald MacDonald (Lachlan MacDonald's parents) in 1887; and Kirsty who married Norman MacLeod MacQueen in 1900.

LIFE ON ST. KILDA

The few references to the MacKinnon family in books and diaries seem to be caught up in recording the misfortunes of the different members of the family.

George Murray

Schoolmaster George Murray in his diary for December 1886 recorded the traumas due to infant tetanus and the terrible disappointment and suffering involved.

"Dec. 14th. Cold and dry. A shower of hail. Today at 03.30am was born . . . MacKinnon. Parents Neil and Mrs. M. MacKinnon. Child large and very promising. Mother doing well.

Dec. 20th. Today still hard frost with showers of snow. St. Kilda looks very well when covered with snow. The people in single file carrying home peats over the white hills present a curious spectacle.

Dec. 22nd. the child that was born a week ago took ill, the jaws fell last night, and it is not expected to live long. It got all the attendance that could be bestowed upon it.

Dec. 27th. Last night at 10.30 the child, after six days'

intense suffering, departed this life. Everyone expressed great wonder how it lived so long after being seized with illness, as they generally succomb at the end of a week after they are born. This one was thirteen days less 1½ hours. It had a frequent cry since it was born; but the first sign of it being dangerously ill was at the end of a week, when it ceased to suck the breast, but still sucked the bottle. The following day 'thuit na gialan', (the jaws fell), when all hope of its recovery was given up. From that time till its death it occasionally took a little milk in a spoon or out of the bottle. The last two days a little wine in water was given it once or twice. It very often yawned and looked very hard at you.

It was pitiful to see the poor little thing in the pangs of death. May God prepare us all for the same end. In the grave which was opened I saw the coffins of its two little brothers that died the same way. I sympathise with the parents in their bereavement. I think something should be done to lessen the plague. Want of attendance and care at the time of birth was lately held out as a cause. This, in its turn, like all other supposed causes, must be abandoned, for I can honestly say that both the nurse and the parents did all in their power to keep at bay the 'dreaded plague'. It is not for me to say what the long sought cause is, but, as one without skill whatever, I would attribute it to the work of the women, and partly, perhaps, to their too frequent exposure to the cold owing to their being barefoot, more than to anything else." (Murray, 1886-87)

Norman Heathcote

A happier occasion occured when Norman Heathcote and his sister visited St. Kilda in 1898 in which Norman MacKinnon took an important part. They had climbed Stac Lee and explored Boreray but, attempting to return to Hirta, they were caught up in a storm and were forced to return to Boreray. "We rounded the south east point of Boreray and found ourselves in absolute quiet under the sheltering archway of a cave. We had visions of landing and spending the night in a hut with a bright fire and roast puffins for dinner, but no such luxuries were in store for us. The men said that, if the wind were to shift to the south, the cave would be unsafe, and they would have to leave at a moment's notice; and as to reach the hut would entail a difficult climb of about 800 feet in thick mist, there was nothing for it but to make the best of it in the boat . . . We had not comtemplated being out late, and all that remained from our luncheon was a piece of cake, a few biscuits and some chocolate, while the men had some cheese and cold tea. I have seldom enjoyed a smoke more than my after-dinner pipe that night. Presently Norman MacKinnon, the only English speaking member of our crew, told us that they were going to "make worship", and then followed one of the most impressive services I have ever attended. I could not understand a word, but the earnestness of the men, the intoning of their prayers, the weirdness of the Gaelic tune to which they sang the psalm, and the solemn grandeur of the place, combined to make it a most interesting and impressive ceremony. We were anchored in a sort of triangular cave about sixty yards wide at the mouth, with deep water right up to the end, and plenty of head-room. It was perfect shelter from the wind and rain; but in spite of being "rocked in the cradle of the deep" we none of us succeeded in getting much rest. Several times I was nearly asleep, but either I slipped down into a pool of fishy water and bumped my head against an oar, or the boat drifted too near the rocks and had to be shoved off; at any rate, something always happened to prevent sleep, and so there was plenty of time for observing the natural phenomena of our night's quarters . . . Gannets, fulmars, kittiwakes, guillemots and shags were sleeping either in our cave or just outside it . . .

Later we landed in St. Kilda, after an absence of about twenty four hours." (Heathcote, 1900)

Alice MacLachlan

1906-09. During this period Alice MacLachlan, the wife of the schoolmaster, kept a daily diary. The name of MacKinnon is mentioned frequently as she recorded their kindness and the troubles that faced their family.

Soon after the MacLachlans arrived in September 1906 Alice recorded that Neil MacKinnon brought two lovely red mullet. The MacKinnons also provided one of the sheep, part of their winter rations, which Norman brought alive and promptly despatched in the back lobby! Norman was entertained to supper afterwards. On another occasion Norman came with Lachlan and brought a nice piece of mutton. Then, before school one morning, Christina came in with two bits of mutton. One evening Lachlan dropped in to say that his mother was going to make cheese and invited Alice and Duine to call in for a lesson.

Alice was very kind and caring to the MacKinnons, as indeed she was to all the St. Kildans. She often visited them in times of illness and recorded taking ½lb of tea to Rachel MacKinnon when she was rather low. She treated poor Rachel for shock and dressed her thumb, time and time again, after she fell down part of Conachair's steep side. Her thumb was badly broken with the bone protruding through the skin. Alice persuaded a doctor from the visiting steamer to have a look at it, but he could only advise amputation, which was impracticable on the island. She treated Christina's sore throat and Neil's crushed finger. One day Alice noted that the men were roofing Widow MacKinnon's byre after if had fallen in, and that Neil often called in to ceilidh in the evening and stayed to supper.

One of the worst incidents Alice had to deal with

was when poor Norman slipped on an iron row-lock which went right into his eye. The sight was horrible. Duine came to the rescue and bathed the eye and Alice bandaged him up. Fortunately, the Captain of the whaling vessel, "the Skalligram" was just about to return to Tarbet, Harris, and he kindly took Norman to see the doctor there. On his return she dressed his eye daily for a considerable time. She reported that he was not a good patient! In appreciation he sharpened their scythe for them.

Alice also recorded the events of the terrible drowning accident in March 1909 when Donald MacDonald, Norman and John MaQueen all lost their lives off Dun. She noted "Neil MacKinnon and John Gillies were rescued in a very exhausted condition." (The full account may be found in the MacLachlan chapter of this book).

First World War

The First World War was no less cruel on the MacKinnons – more trouble was to come their way again. By some quirk of fate their house happened to be the only one damaged by shells from the German submarine in May 1918. The shells struck the Store, the Factor's House, the Wireless aerials – House No. 1., the MacKinnon's, was the only one of the Village Street to be badly damaged by the German shells. The roof was blown off and most of the walls were demolished.

THE EVACUATION AND AFTER

Towards the end of their time on St. Kilda life became one tremendous struggle to survive. Norman was a very fine man, gentle, kind and courteous – he was the 'chief' precentor in the Kirk, taking on the task after William MacDonald left in 1924. With his wife

Annie, a daughter of Finlay Gillies, and their large family of eight children, Norman, Donald Ewen, Finlay, Rachel, John, Christine, Mary and Neil – life became little more than an existence, just scraping for a living. Needless to say, Annie was hard working, but she was also very friendly and clever. From time to time she would help out at the school taking care of the children in times of emergency. If she had been given the chance she would probably have become a school teacher. Norman had the reputation of being the most skilful tailor on the island.

This was the family which was the feel the effects of

View between Boreray (left) and Stac an Armin with Stac Lee, behind, Dun, Hirta and Soay.

the hard and prolonged winter of 1929-30, it was the worst that the St. Kildans could remember, having been without mails from August 1929 until March 1930, and with food running short. The islanders persuaded the Missionary, Dugald Munro, to write to the Prime Minister, Ramsay MacDonald, "We are now twelve weeks without news or relief supplies, for weeks all of us have been without sugar and potatoes. Paraffin oil is running short when we most need it for light to work our looms in the making of the Highland Tweed."

The tiny population struggled on against impossible conditions until they reached the point of capitulation when on May 10th. they wrote to the Rt. Hon. W. Adamson, Assistant Secretary of State for Scotland.

"We the undersigned, the natives of St. Kilda, hereby respectfully pray and petition H.M. Government to assist us to leave the island this year, and to find homes and occupations for us on the mainland . . . Several men out of this number have definitely made up our minds to go away this year and to seek employment on the mainland, this will really cause a crisis as the present number are hardly sufficient to carry on the necessary work of the place. These men are the mainstay of the island at present, as they tend the sheep, do the weaving and look after the general welfare of the widows. Should they leave, the conditions of the rest of the community would be such that it would be impossible for us to remain on the island another winter." The letter was signed or marked by twelve of the men.

Having left St. Kilda the MacKinnons settled for a short while at Achabeg near Lochaline before moving to the Black Isle. However, tragedy struck in a different way. T.B., which was very prevalent at the time, took the lives of Donald Ewen, Finlay and Rachel, as well as father, Norman, within a few years of leaving the island. Neil, the last to be born on St. Kilda (on Sept 1st. 1926), after retiring early, due to illness, from the Forestry Commission died in November 1987. Sadly, from this large St. Kilda family, there are now only two surviving members – Christine, married to Mr. Hossack and Mary married to Jimmy Ross.

The Fergusons –
The Postmaster's Family Portrait

ARRIVAL ON ST. KILDA
EARLY REFERENCES
FAMILY BACKGROUND
REMARKABLE FAMILY – Ann, Alex, Neil,
Donald.

ARRIVAL ON ST. KILDA

"It is said that Finlay, the first Ferguson on St. Kilda, came from the island of Berneray, Harris, and was the mate of the boat bringing settlers there (after the terrible small-pox outbreak in 1727-28, D.A.Q.), who fell in love with one of the settler girls and decided to stay on in St. Kilda with her. It sounds a romantic folk-tale but since a relationship is still claimed by some of the Harris Fergusons, who originated from Berneray, there seems no reason in this case to doubt the

"Part of the Great Rock, St. Kilda". Showing the Gap and Conachair. Acland.

romance! This Finlay would be the father of John and so the progenitor of all the Fergusons on the island." (Lawson, 1981)

When Dr. John MacDonald visited St. Kilda in 1922 he recorded in his Journal for Mon. May 23rd, referring back to the Sunday, "After the sermon I baptised a child, the only one in the place needing that ordinance at present, two having died since the Missionary left the island. The child's father, John Ferguson by name, is the only person in the place who can read, at least to any purpose. Found him therefore much better acquainted with the principles of Christianity than his neighbours." (MacDonald, 1823)

In his List of the Inhabitants taken on 23rd. Sept. 1822 MacDonald records only one family of Fergusons, John Ferguson aged 50 with his wife Mary and children Donald aged 18, Neil 15, Finlay 8, Hector 5, Christian, Betsy 1 and Malcolm 1. Lawson comments, "Donald, who was married on the island of Pabbay, Harris, and when that island was cleared for sheep in 1846, was removed to the island of Scalpay, Harris, where he has numerous descendants; Neil, the Ground Officer and great-grandfather of Neil the postmaster at the time of evacuation; Hector and Malcolm went to Australia in 1852; and Finlay, who on the death of his wife and only child, followed his brothers to Australia at the age of 70." (Lawson, 1981)

On the ill-fated voyage to Australia, Hector and his wife survived, as did Malcolm, but his daughter Mary died of measles in Dec. 1852 and his wife Catharine of Scarletina in Feb. 53. Another Ferguson was also on the journey, Kirsty who had married Finlay MacQueen. They arrived safely with their sons Malcolm (the subject of the MacQueen chapter in this book) and John; their daughter Rachel, aged 19 died of measles on the way.

EARLY REFERENCES

Henry Lord Brougham and his party visited St. Kilda in 1799 and in the evening set off in the St. Kilda boat to go across to Boreray. It seems likely that he is referring to Finlay Ferguson in his account. "Our crew talked most infernally and rowed very ill. Seeing that this proceeded from laziness and loquacity, I desired the first (who alone could speak a word of English) to promise them a dram if they rowed better, and to bid them be more quiet. The effect was instantaneous, and immediately the song arose, extempore in composition and far from unmusical in execution; of course, pleasing in point of effect . . . We now weathered the rocks of Boreray, which surrounded St. Kilda to the north and north-east; and as it was now past eleven, I allowed myself to be lulled to sleep by the cadence of the chorus and the oars." (Brougham, 1799).

Another early reference, this time to John Ferguson, occurs in the account of Atkinson who visited St. Kilda in 1831. His party had landed on Boreray on the previous day and on Thurs. June 2nd, they planned to go round to Stac Biorach and Soay. The account is so interesting that it is quoted in full:-

"The Minister told us a deputation of natives had waited on us, to say, if we would give them some tobacco they would take us to the Thumb Rock, and display their utmost skill and dexterity for our gratification. Now our stock of this valuable commodity had only amounted to about three shillings worth, and by the Minister's advice we gave them about half of it in compensation for their trouble yesterday; not, that under ordinary circumstances we should not have given them a liberal pecuniary compensation, but their idea of the value of money is so vague, that Mr. MacKenzie thought that they would be more pleased with tobacco, than with any reasonable sum of money: we were rather sorry to find therefore, from our own boatman John MacDonald, that they had been dissatisfied, and determined this morning to make it perfectly understood how much we intended to give; so we joined them on the beach and with the aid of John Ferguson, the only one who has any English, told them what tobacco we had, they should receive. They exclaimed – very fairly – against it as being so little – but what could we do – money would not satisfy them, so we were making up our minds to take our own boat and row about, when they acceded to our proposition, put their boat into the sea, and away we went to Bioroch.

I never saw any place apparently more inaccessible than this rock, the part of the rock where the thumb is used, is on the left side a little below the slightly prominent part of the rock, the landing being affected rather to the left of the centre of the rock, and a spiral course then adopted; a high degree of celebrity awaits those who have climbed it, as it is considered infinitely the most difficult rock they have, and its ascent is never made but for some weighty consideration in general to gratify the proprietor or his friends, but in this case to obtain a little tobacco of which they then happened to be destitute.

As we drew near the rock, I found that the hearts of some of the crew began to fall, and the rapidity of their rowing and talking to wax faint: the Minister who always went with us, saw it too, but said that he would be astonished if they failed in their engagement. At length we fairly lay alongside the rock, and the crew folded their arms and looked at each other: how it would end we could not divine, and John MacDonald shook his head and looked rather glad of a chance of their not attempting it: well we waited in this solemn state of contemplation half an hour, then one oar dipped and made a kind of involuntary pull towards Soa, and then another, till we were going on more unanimously than we had ever yet done, when a fine lad of 18 jumped up and exclaimed it would never be said by the strangers, that they were inferior to their fathers in skill and courage, and that if any would accompany him, he would lead the way: he was immediately joined by another lad of the same age, and the boat was again brought to the foot of the rock: Rhoderick MacDonald (his companion's name was John MacDonald) then tied the end of a rope round his waist, the other end of which was retained by his

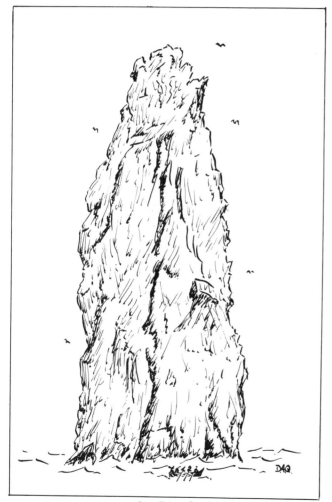

Stac Biorach.

friends in the boat, and succeeded in obtaining a footing on the foot of the rock; the boat then pulled a few strokes off, both to observe his progress, and to be clear of him if he should fall at the corner, which has happened once or twice, though the consequence is only a good ducking, as he is immediately hauled on board the boat by the rope attached to him. In this case the climber succeeded in passing the dangerous point, and then in a manner I have elsewhere described, assisted in hoisting up his companion: we watched them in their ascent, and picked up the fowl they threw to us, captured in their way, and having seen them fairly well established on the top and their operations commenced among the mass of Guillemots there assembled, proceeded to land on the SE side of Soa.

After walking round Soa . . . we joined the boat and picked up the two courageous fellows at Stac Biorach, who had caught a vast quantity of fowl, and then proceeded to coast home along the north side of St. Kilda: this, from the fatigue of the rowers, and their undeviating system of following the winding of the shore, promised to be so tedious, that we got them to land us in the bay on the NW side, and accompanied by the Minister and John MacDonald walked over the hills home." (Atkinson G.C., 1831).

FAMILY BACKGROUND

Refering back to Finlay, the first Ferguson to arrive on St. Kilda, we know that he married a MacDonald and his son John, born in 1772, married Mary MacQueen who was born around 1770. It was through their second son Neil (1807-93) who in 1832 married Catharine MacCrinnon (= MacCrimmon) (1813-99) that the Ferguson line was continued on St. Kilda. Their first son Donald (1833-1918) in 1861 married Rachel Gillies, the daughter of John Gillies and Flora, nee Gillies. They had a large family who were a great influence in the later years on St. Kilda – Ann, who

became known as the Queen of St. Kilda and married John Gillies; Alexander became the prosperous cloth merchant in Glasgow; Neil the Postmaster and Donald who became a Minister in the Free Church.

Neil and Catharine also had a daughter Mary born in 1840 who married Ewen MacKinnon in 1861 but he died in the following year in a fall from the rocks. In 1867 she married Norman Gillies. From this second marriage two children died in infancy before Ann was born in 1872 – she married Calum MacDonald. Two more children died, then Mary was born in 1878 and later went to Glasgow, and Ewen, born in 1891 married Ann MacLeod in 1915 but he died in the following year in a fall from the cliffs at the beginning of the Fulmar Harvest (together with John MacDonald), they had a daughter, Mary Ann, born in 1915. Neil and Catharine had another daughter Margaret born in 1843 who remained unmarried and a son John in 1850 who married Rachel Gillies in 1870.

A REMARKABLE FAMILY

Reverting back to Donald (1833-1918), he had been the Ground Officer before handing this over to

Men at the Jetty, Donald Ferguson, centre front. E. Ogilvie Collection.

his son, Neil. He became the senior elder of the kirk and a respected and powerful preacher. Often he would go over to Harris to preach, getting a passage on a trawler or visiting steamer. They greatly appreciated his ministry and on one visit hid his boots when he was about to return because they didn't want him to go. His influence reached further afield when he went to preach in the Highland Church in Glasgow. He and his wife Rachel produced a remarkable family which was able to make its mark in many spheres, not least on St. Kilda.

ANN (1865-1951) QUEEN OF ST. KILDA

Anne became known as the Queen of St. Kilda and there was great excitement when the preparation for her marriage to John Gillies was announced and planned. Schoolmaster Ross was on St. Kilda in the summer of 1889 and wrote about the event, "Ian Ban is engaged to Ann Ferguson – the Queen of St. Kilda. The only marriageable man is to marry the Queen of St. Kilda and who can blame him. They would have been married before we left but unfortunately the minister did not get a sufficiently comprehensive license to meet the requirements of such a place as St. Kilda and so we had to forego the honour of 'getting the Queen's wedding'. They are going to Glasgow next summer for that very purpose. It must be a sight worth seeing as neither party every left St. Kilda before and the younger man is rather a bashful and excitable fellow, although he has had the experience of passing through the marriage ceremony once already." (Ross, 1889).

In fact the marriage took place on St. Kilda on 24th June 1890, the ceremony being conducted by the visiting Minister, the Rev. Angus Stewart of Whiting Bay, Arran. In the month before the marriage an artist, R. Jobling was on St. Kilda and amongst many splendid sketches he drew a quick sketch of the bride and the groom, the latter he described as Red Gillies on account of the colour of his beard.

Ann and John Gillies also produced a remarkable family of five sons – Donald, John, Neil, Donald John and Donald Hugh (Ewen). Their story is told in the chapter on the Gillies families.

ALEXANDER (1872-1960) GLASGOW TWEED MERCHANT
St. Kilda to Glasgow

Alexander was the first son of Donald and Rachel and he was born in Struth House, Harris. Rachel had not been well prior to this event and had sought proper medical attention there. They soon returned to St. Kilda after the birth of their baby. Alex left the island in 1892 to make a living in Glasgow where he became a prosperous tweed merchant. His daughter, Susan Ogilvie, explained to me the circumstances, "The Missionary advised him to go away. I think my father must have been quite intelligent and he thought he would be just wasting his time. He gave him lessons in Greek and Latin which I don't think he ever needed. He was nineteen when he left. I don't think he had any links with anyone in Glasgow. He was working at Coopers Store in Howard Street, Glasgow, for a while. I don't think he was there for very long, he must have been very enterprising because very soon he started his own Tweed business and had his office at 93, Hope Street, opposite the Central Hotel. It was a wholesale business, he didn't really sell many suits or suit lengths or coat lengths, the big bales of tweed all went to the large firms in London. It was mainly Harris Tweed that went away, and Irish Tweed, too. I think they found the St. Kilda Tweed rather too thick and heavy – it would just be useful for an overcoat. He didn't really sell an awful lot of St. Kilda Tweed although he tried very hard. He used to go up to

London and over to Norway. I remember, as a little girl, him going off in his tile hat and frock coat – he was always well dressed up for business. The tweed was popular in London with the shooting people, the Country people and the game-keepers. I sometimes got a length made up from my father's Harris Tweed – my goodness, I got tired of it before it wore out! He sent to King Edward a suit length of St. Kilda tweed and the King's secretary sent him a photograph of the King wearing the suit."

He disposed of the tweeds which the St. Kildans made during the long winter nights and also of the woollen garments which the women were constantly knitting. "As late as 1928 the St. Kildans produced for export well over one thousand yards of tweed, virtually their only article of commerce." (MaGregor,1969)

Holidays on St. Kilda – The Kearton Brothers

Although Alex left St. Kilda at an early age he still had a tremendous love for the archipelago and always considered it to be home – in fact, on one occasion, gazing, longingly over the sea from Harris, he felt that he was looking, like Moses, over to the Promised Land. Most years he would come over for the summer on his holidays, arriving in May on the first steamer and leaving in August. He was there in the summer of 1896 when the famous Kearton brothers – the Naturalist and the Photographer – were on the islands. They persuaded him to join them on a visit to Boreray.

"The ground officer's eldest son, Mr. A. Ferguson, who a year or two back forsook the lone crags of St. Kilda for the more lucrative and less adventurous life of a Glasgow commercial house, happened to be at home on a holiday at the time of our visit, and we persuaded him to accompany us to Borrera, as he was not only an intelligent and genial companion, but also

very useful to us in interpreting for us in the absence of our friend the factor, who could not go out that day. He was desirous of seeing whether his hand had lost its cunning with the fowling-rod, and one of the men accordingly fastened a rope round him and paid it out from a sure footing as he disappeared over the brink of a fearful precipice. I crawled on my hands and knees to the edge of the cliff, and was astonished to see him pass the noose over the head of a Fulmar and take her off her nest with much skill and deftness that the other birds sitting close around did not appear to be at all disturbed by the fate of their neighbour. By the aid of a rope my brother got into a very hazardous and awkward situation, from which he managed to take a photograph of the ex-fowler in the holiday war-paint of Buchanan Street." (Kearton, 1897)

A little later on in their holiday the young Ferguson invited the Kearton brothers to join him on a fishing expedition in Village Bay. They gladly consented but it didn't develop in the way they had expected. "We commenced operations by the gap dividing St. Kilda from the Doon, and rowed quietly along, hugging the shore until we came to the end of the latter island. As we put about to pull back I noticed a black, ominous looking cloud looming up behind Conagher, and asked the boatmen, who were all of the younger generation and could speak very well, what it meant. "Just a shower," they answered. By the time we had rowed half way back along the Doon it had become so dark that we could hardly see across the bay. This seemed to increase the voracity of the fish, and we hooked one monster after another as fast as we could haul them up. Just as I was in the act of landing one the boat was struck by a blinding deluge of rain. The sea rose directly, and the wind swept the crests of the waves off and twirled them into stinging showers of white spray. Our crew, consisting of four young fellows, pulled away at the oars vigorously, but made no progress so far as I could note by such jutting crags

Alex Ferguson in suit catching a fulmar on Boreray, 1896. Kearton.

of proving a haven of safety, it turned out to be a veritable death-trap. The huge waves lifted our wee craft and flung it forward with such force that it looked perilously like being jammed into the crevice in which the little cave ended.

Our boatmen had hitherto been speaking in English, but the exciting character of the situation soon sent them back upon their Gaelic, in which tongue they yelled at each other furiously . . . Some idea of the danger of our situation may be gathered when I state that more than once, as a wave broke against the overhanging side of the cave on our starboard, it splashed into the boat, and during the back swell we trailed and bumped on the sloping rock on our port.

The whole scene was one of indescribable grandeur from an elemental point of view. Outside, the sea and the descending torrents of rain were mixing in a wild tumult of spray and foam. The waves were leaping against the black basaltic crags, and making fearsome thunder in the great caves that tunnel the Doon in places right through from Village Bay to the Atlantic. Perhaps the strangest thing of all in this scene of gloom and uproar was that afforded by twenty or thirty gentle little Kittiwakes, sitting on their nests in the utmost peace and security only a few feet over our imperilled heads. In from twenty minutes to half an hour the storm blew itself out, and I think we all breathed a sigh of relief when we regained the open water in safety." (Kearton, 1897).

During the First War and afterwards Alex continued to show his interest and love for the islands and the islanders. Lachlan MacDonald commented to me, "Most of the tweed we sold through Alexander Ferguson. During the war we got a very good price from the Navy people who came, a high price, much better than ever before. Some St. Kildans were working at the looms night and day to sell all they could to get good money. But those who sold to Alex Ferguson were able to get what money could not buy –

as were visible through the mirk of the storm. By and by they made the boat creep along, and in a while we came to a cave in which the St. Kildans hoped to find shelter from the wind and the waves. Instead, however,

Alex Ferguson with boys blowing eggs. E. Ogilvie Collection.

white flour and sugar! How he got it I don't know. Others could only get black flour with their money!"

Alex's Family

Alex's daughter, Susan Ogilvie, fills in more details, "My mother was a Glasgow lady, Catherine Sinclair, and her father came from Bendaloch. He was a cabinet maker and joiner and he had a business of his own in the south side of Glasgow. They were married around 1900. My brother Donald was their first child born in 1901 or 02, he became a doctor and moved to Walsall, he was married but had no children. I was the next and was born in 1903 and was followed by Alistair who remained unmarried and by Neil who was married and had one daughter. Donald and Alistair died in their fifties, Neil was about 71 when he died. My father was a tall, good looking man, very determined. My mother had no Gaelic, none at all. Our house was always full of Gaelic speaking people from all over the

Highlands, Islay and other places and they used to argue about different words and their pronunciation – my mother had to listen to all that! Our house became home for all when they came out from St. Kilda looking for a job or if they were in need of hospital treatment. My father couldn't take them to hospital himself – that was always left to my mother to do – he used to faint if he went to hospital – the smell of chloroform or something went for him! My mother had quite a lot of work trotting up to Glasgow on the bus, in the early days it was the tram-car as we didn't have a car in those days. With regard to jobs, my father was friendly with some of the managers in the shipyards, he would always say, 'I've got someone for you.' They always took them because they were conscientious workers and very strong. Even my brother, who was a medical student used to get a job as a rivetter or a rivetter's helper in the shipyards because he wanted to get some money.

I was on St. Kilda several times, and for a whole year when I was only ten – my parents left in 1914 when they knew the war had broken out – they left and I was on St. Kilda until the following summer. I was staying with my Uncle Neil, the Postmaster. They looked after me very well. I can tell you the things I didn't like – the food during the winter. It was very salty – salt fulmars, salt fish, salt mutton – salt everything. My father was always fond of salt fulmar and he used to get them sent out from St. Kilda to Glasgow! We all hated it, we wouldn't touch it – so he got it all to himself! The only thing I liked was the birds' eggs, you could make an omelette with them and use them for baking. The stream at the far end of the Village came down from one of the mountains and in the spring it was just covered with primroses and I used to lie in them and enjoy the sweet scent. The women worked very hard. They went over to the Glen to gather peats and came down with great loads on their backs. In the summer I used to go over with them to the milking in the Glen,

the cows were there for the summer, and then they had to bring the pails back. They made cheese and butter, too. I helped to turn the churn – it was one of the jobs they gave me to do – and they taught me to spin. They weren't going to let me off and be lazy. I was taken to Church to sit through all the Gaelic service – to pass the time I used to count the number of times 'Angus' (Gaelic – 'and') was used during the sermon. We went to visit Rachel MacCrimmon in her oval thatched house. It had a low door, and the window was well into the wall and didn't let in much light. It was darkish inside and the fire was in the middle of the floor. I had a good look round and there was a box-bed and inside it there were about four or five cats – you could see the eyes shining. She made us tea and gave us some great big water biscuits – I don't know where she had got them – not on St. Kilda, anyway. When we were going out my mother handed her a little parcel with a cake she had baked. My mother took a stove out to St. Kilda and she used to bake on it. Rachel thought it was cheese. She wasn't keen on cake or sweet things. One day I landed on Boreray in the mid-summer. What a steep walk up to the huts where the men stayed – they were just like cleits. They would be warmer but being so high up they would get the sea-breezes. My father went to St. Kilda to get me home in 1915 – he had to get permission from the government to go out. It was Captain Walkner (see Chapter on Alice MacLachlan) who went out on a trawler or a minesweeper and brought us to Stornoway and then, I think, to Mallaig. I remember him, he was a very nice man, when we were staying at the Hotel in Stornoway he used to empty the bowls of sugar loaf into my pocket. Coming back from St. Kilda I was sleeping in the deck-house – perhaps it wasn't safe because of mines.

I was twenty-five when I married Allan Ogilvie in about 1928. I took a business training and went to work in a chartered accountants in Glasgow and he was serving his apprenticeship at the time I met him.

He was a graduate of Aberdeen University. My husband started in Montrose and was the first chartered accountant to arrive there – he sat in his office for a whole year before he got any work! He stayed there until he died in 1968 at the age of 78. I have one daughter Elizabeth who was born in 1946, she lectures in drawing and painting at the Edinburgh College of Art. She visited St. Kilda in 1987."

Boating in St. Kilda Waters

Lachlan MacDonald told me how Alex had helped his brother Angus when he left the island just after the war in 1919 or 1920. "He left in Alexander Ferguson's boat which was carrying two tons of dried fish which he would be selling for the St. Kildans in return for provisions; old Finlay Gillies was also. on board after damaging his shoulder in a fall from the rocks near the Lover's Stone, he was going to the hospital in Glasgow for treatment. This was the first time Angus had left the island and half way across to Harris the wind got up, they entered a gale with the waves coming over the side of the boat and they went into thick mist. Alex was all for turning back, but old Finlay said, 'If you are going to turn back, you can say goodbye to St. Kilda and to everyone else – you would never find it in these conditions.' After a very rough, miserable and anxious time they reached the protection of Pabbay and sheltered there over night and later reached Glasgow. After this voyage old Finlay became known as Captain Rimo! Alex Ferguson got Angus a job at Napier and Miller's shipyards."

After the Evacuation Alex continued to return to his native isle. One important visit he arranged was in 1932, instigated by Lord Dumfries, to catch the wild Soay sheep on the island of Soay and to transfer them to the island of Hirta using a small boat which he had left stored away on the island. Malcolm MacDonald was invited to join the party and he recounts the memorable occasion in his chapter in this book.

His yacht was called the "Colonsay". Susan recalled, "My father paid £8,000 for it, which was a lot of money in those days. It belonged to some ship owner who was connected with the island of Colonsay. He could take three or four people and he had two for crew. If he was going to St. Kilda he always took an engineer with him because he didn't know anything about engines. On one occasion they ran into an awful storm and they all thought they were finished – they went into the cabin and got the whisky out. My father was tied to the wheel. They praised him greatly for the way he managed to steer them safely. Instead of going into Village Bay he knew it would be no use – they would get blown ashore – so he went round to the Glen. One of the natives had seen the boat coming so they all came round and took my father's friends ashore and made them comfortable. My father stayed on the boat, he was determined that it wasn't going to be dashed on the rocks. He didn't go often in his yacht after that because of the dangers."

Susan described how his office caught fire on one occasion, "It was his own fault. He was working on a parcel which was to go south and he was using sealing wax and he threw it into the waste paper basket and it must still have been lit. Then he went away out to post it and he was amazed to find smoke coming out of the door when he came back, and all the people along the passage terrified that it was going to spread, but they managed to keep it to the one place."

Alex made many other visits to his old haunts, he was back again in 1933 to help with the catching and ringing of Manx shearwaters, puffins and fulmars. After the Second War Alex made many voyages until his death in 1960.

NEIL (1876-1944) POSTMASTER AND GROUND-OFFICER

Neil, born on the 16th. June 1876, was the second son of Donald and Rachel, he was to become the Postmaster and Ground-officer.

Visitors – Keartons and Heathcotes

When the Kearton brothers visited St. Kilda in 1896 they were fascinated by the idea of the St. Kilda mailboat and were assured that four out of six launched were picked up on the shores of the Long Isle or Norway. Richard Kearton wrote, 'As I expressed a desire to hear from the St. Kildans during the winter by means of their miniature mailboats, they dispatched one containing three letters for me at eleven o'clock on the morning of March 24th, during the prevelance of a north-westerly wind. On the 31st of the same month it was picked up by a shepherd in a little bay at Vallay, North Uist, and its contents forwarded to me by post. The letters had been placed in a small tin canister, and despite the fact that they had become soaked with sea water they still retained a delightful aroma of peat smoke when they reached my hands, reminding me forcibly of my stay on the island." One of the letters was from Neil Ferguson.

St. Kilda
20th. March. 1897

Dear Friend,

I received your letter of the 10th February and I was much pleased to learn that you understood my letter. I am in good health at present, though some of the friends is very sick with a bad cold they got. I was very sorry to learn you were not in good health through the winter. We haven't seen a trawler or liner. I may tell you that I was hunting today at the back of Conicher and killed fifteen Fulmars but four of them was lost. I was thinking of the day I was with you and Cherry photographing when a big stone fell from your feet nearly killed Cherry. I hope to see you yet, this is to be sent in a toy boat by the first north west wind of which Finlay MacQueen is Captain.

With best wishes, remember me to your brother.
I remain,
Yours faithfully,
Neil Ferguson

In 1898 and 99 Norman Heathcote and his sister stayed on St. Kilda, they explored the islands and both climbed Stac Lee. In his book Norman described a particularly interesting boat trip with Neil Ferguson.

"We had a rather interesting expedition towards the end of our stay, right round St. Kilda and Soay in a boat. I wanted to take notes with a view to mapping out the coast-line, but as there was a very big swell coming in from the west, my work was done under considerable difficulties. What made the row specially interesting was that Neil Ferguson, who speaks English very well, told us the names of many places and why they were so called. Unless he could give the meaning of the word, when my sister's knowledge of Gaelic came in useful, it was almost impossible to make anything of the sounds that issued from his lips. Consonants often behave rather oddly in Gaelic, though they do to some extent follow rules; but when a St. Kildan pronounces a word, I never have the least idea whether it begins with a 'c', an 'f' or a 'p': all I can detect is a sort of gutteral sound. However, "Uamh na Ron" (the Cave of the Seals) was intelligible, and the "Hard Cave" recalled to our minds our night in Boreray, when we discovered that a boat, if not quite so hard as a rock, is not as soft as a feather-bed. Then he pointed out the places where they come down after the fulmers, the rock where the great auk used to breed and told us a delightful tale about "the landing-place of the Englishmen." Some gentlemen and two ladies landed here and climbed up the cliffs. Presently they caught sight of some of the natives, and, whether they took them for pirates, cannibals, goblins, or for some other noxious animal, incontinently fled. The men got back to their boat in safety, but one lady, for reasons best known to herself, put her petticoats over her head and tumbled over the precipice. The other lady, being basely deserted by her menkind and having no desire to emulate the example of her sister in misfortune, hardened her heart and waited for the savages. Contrary to expectation, they treated her well, and entertained her on the island for seven years when her friends came and took her away. Why she was left so long without succour is not explained; but when her friends did come and made enquiries as to whether the natives had treated her well, and finding that all had been kind to her with the exception of two, they rewarded the many and killed the two! The narrator of this story stoutly maintained that this had nothing to do with Lady Grange, and, when asked how long ago these interesting events took place, said, "Oh! a hundred years." This I suppose is a synonym for prehistoric times." (Heathcote, 1900)

Postmaster

A sub-post office was established in the Factor's House on the island in 1890 and was administered by the Free Church Minister, the Rev. Angus Fiddes, at a salary of £5 a year with some bonuses. He acted in this position until he left in 1905 when Neil Ferguson took on the appointment which he held until the

Neil Ferguson at the Transmitter, 1st War. Marconi Electronics.

evacuation. The site of the post office was moved from the Factor's House in the summer of 1913 to a corrugated iron hut adjoining the east end of house No. 5, Neil's home. This was done to provide space for the installation of the Marconi Wireless Telegraph Company radio transmitter – the gift of the Daily Mail to the inhabitants. Neil Ferguson and the Missionary were responsible for operating the transmitter in the early stages. It was the aerial masts and the transmitter that the German submarine attacked and put out of action in 1918. The wireless was repaired as part of the necessary defence of St. Kilda but in the February of the following year the Admiralty dismantled and removed it. St. Kilda was once again cut off from the rest of the world.

Neil's task as sub-postmaster entailed stamping and bagging up any letters and parcels and getting them away by a visiting trawler or reliable vessel – no easy task in the winter and often months went by without any mail coming in or leaving the island.

The Approaching Evacuation

As the evacuation approached Neil's feelings and those of several St. Kildans were reported by Eldred Reeve from Glasgow in the Daily Mail in July 1930.

ST. KILDA ISLANDER'S PETITION

"The grim spectre of sickness, semi-starvation, and misery haunts the 35 natives of St. Kilda, the barren sentinel isle of the Atlantic. The inhabitants have sent to Mr. William Adamson (Secretary of State for Scotland) a petition praying for Government assistance to enable them to leave the island and find new homes and occupations on the mainland. Mr. Adamson has promised to do his best to visit St. Kilda soon and Mr. T. M. B. Ramsay, MP for the Western Isles, will go there this month and learn at first hand of the tribulation of his constituents. The hapless islanders, a dwindling remnant of the little race that for centuries has won a meagre livelihood from the bare rock, are faced with a winter of unparalleled hardship.

Tragedy lurked in the first tiny cottage I entered. In a dim corner of the room lay the daughter of Mrs. Donald Gillies, a beautiful but emaciated girl, who is very seriously ill. "We all want to leave the island," Mrs. Gillies told me. She added:– "My daughter has been ill for a long time and will never get well here. We can get the doctor very seldom during the winter and we could not face another winter here. My husband died from appendicitis out on Boreray when a doctor, if one had been available, could have saved his life by operating. One of my daughters died young, and another was taken to Fleetwood by trawler. I would be willing to do any sort of work on the mainland, and I have another daughter of 19, a fine, tall girl who would do well. The young men of the island are going, and we cannot stay alone."

Our steamer brought to St. Kilda tidings of another island tragedy – the death in childbirth of a relative of this family, the wife of Donald John Gillies who lives near. Early in the spring the lighthouse steamer Hesperus, in response to an S.O.S., tried and failed to reach St. Kilda, and later the fishery cruiser Norma landed through the storm and Mrs. Gillies was carried to Oban and taken to Stobhill Hospital, Glasgow. She died on the morning our steamer sailed for St. Kilda. (July 21st. DAQ)

Mrs. MacQueen added her plea to that of Widow Gillies, "It was a terrible hard winter and we did not have enough food. Some of us cannot leave the island without help. I would do any sort of work that could be found for me on the mainland.

A picture of life on St. Kilda was drawn for me by Neil Ferguson, the burly postmaster, and the only St. Kildan who this year has tilled his land and planted potatoes. Many years ago Mr. Ferguson's brother Alexander left the island a poor boy and has now made a considerable fortune in Glasgow. Neil said, "My son is working with Alec now and the rest of us are ready to leave. I think the end of St. Kilda as an inhabited island has come. We have only half a dozen first class men to support the whole community, and some of them are determined to go. That means that the old people and the widows and children must leave too, or they would starve next winter. No preparation for winter has been made and the islanders are doing less and less work. The few men have to cultivate the small patch of arable land, catch the sheep and "pluck" the wool, kill the fulmars (sea birds) for food, weave cloth, do the fishing, keep buildings and walls in repair and do much more heavy work. They are now resolved to leave, and have neglected much work.

No cultivation, little fishing, no building has been done. They are placing reliance on some income from visitors and chiefly upon Government help. The trouble is that they are not fitted for occupations on the mainland and would have to learn. I don't know what work I could get, but I wish to leave with the rest. St. Kilda is no more use.

The trawlers do not call as they used to do, and right through the winter when stores were short we could get no help until February when Captain Quirk, the skipper of a Fleetwood trawler put in and sent us some potatoes ashore and later returned with supplies.

In Mr. Ferguson's family is another example of the hardship caused by infrequent medical service. His wife is ill with influenza, which has affected many of the islanders recently, and although she rose to see the first steamer's arrival she is very weak and obviously needs fairly constant medical attention. The influenza among young and old inhabitants had made heavier the burden on the shoulders of Miss Barclay, the nurse who has worked heroically on St. Kilda for almost three years, and she is eagerly awaiting her recall.

Graphic stories of the island's hardship were told to me by Mr. Munro, the missionary, schoolmaster and advisor-in-chief to St. Kilda. He said, "The winter has been terrible. We have on the island eight able men, five wives, six widows, two old men, three young people, eight children of school age and three under school age. During most of the period between November and April we were without milk and supplies of other necessaries like margarine, tea, treacle, butter, sugar, meal and flour were extremely low or non-existent. Children have come shivering to school through the storm and spray of winter mornings after breakfast only of milkless, sugarless tea and dry bread. For much of the winter the islanders have existed on salted mutton, salted seafowl, and sometimes fish, eked out with a few potatoes."

Typical of the view of the younger St. Kildans who realised the hopelessness of battling against the elements too strong for them, is that of Mr. MacDonald, who told me that he is resolved to leave the island this summer in any case. He told me, "There is nothing here, and I will go to Glasgow. I don't know what work I shall do, but I shall find something. I will do anything but stay on St. Kilda."

"I will leave too, because the others are going," said Norman MacKinnon, a tall young islander. "I don't want to do farm work. Any work, however hard, will be easier than life on St. Kilda, and pleasanter for the women."

The patriarchs of the island, Mr. Finlay Gillies and Mr. Finlay MacQueen, have resigned themselves to leaving, and it now remains with the Government to evacuate the island and settle its inhabitants in gentler, securer conditions, free from unnecessary peril of sickness, starvation and storm."

The Evacuation

To cover the Evacuation the Times sent Alasdair Alpin MacGregor as their correspondent. He stayed with Neil Ferguson and reported that he received a letter from MacLeod's factor at Dunvegan, telling him it is expected that the keys of the houses will be collected from each tenant, and duly sent to him at Dunvegan! He adds, "Neil is overwhelmed with the correspondence that arrived for him yesterday with the 'Hebrides'. Great numbers of people have enclosed to him stamped addressed envelopes in their anxiety to receive a letter bearing the St. Kilda postmark, and arriving with the last outgoing mail from this lone outpost. Others are worrying him for souvenirs and curios, and are inundating him with trifling postal orders that fair bamboozle Neil. There are requests for spinning-wheels, cruises, quernstones, gannets' wings (which make splendid dusters), quantities of St. Kildan wool, and seabirds' eggs . . . In Neil's possession is the nose-cap of one of the shells fired by the U-boat that in 1918 shelled the Village in an endeavour to put the wireless station out of commission. It was found on the hillside after the bombardment."

"Over the turf fire that evening Neil told me much

Neil Ferguson (Senior) outside the Post Office, 1930. A. A. MacGregor.

about life on his native isle, and how altered climatic conditions had harassed the St. Kildans to an increasing extent during their final years. The winters had not changed much: the autumns, on the other hand, had been growing steadily worse. Because of wind and rain and the lack of the sun, corn had not ripened for some years. Often after the harvest had been cut, incessant rains have ruined it. Upon a time the villagers used to sow a good deal of corn. This they threshed with the flail, the two parts of which were joined together by a sheepskin in the days before rope was imported to the island. Neil assures me that that last Great Auk was killed more than a hundred years ago, when seven men were marooned on Stac an Armin for a number of days while fowling there one autumn. Neil then proceeded to tell me how the natives used to go out at night in April, and lie among the rocks to kill the guillemots. By means of ropes they let themselves down the face of the cliffs, and then covered themselves with the white sheets on which the innocent guillemots landed and were caught, mistaking the sheets for guano covered-rocks. He then described how fulmars and puffins were caught with the snaring rod. St. Kilda used to import horse-hair in quantities solely for the making of snares for these birds. When glancing up at the rafters of an old byre

Sheep ready for shipment at the Evacuation. N.T.S.

one day, I noticed quite a hantle of old horse-hair designed for snares. As a momento of our conversation that evening, Neil then presented me with a typical St. Kildan snare which I still have. Weighing no more than a couple of drams, it is one of the neatest pieces of native workmanship I have ever handled. It must have taken hours to pleat and to stiffen it up with bird's feathers . . . I had a light snack before bedtime; and intuition tells me that Neil and his family have not yet forsaken the old custom of reading 'the books' before retiring for the night. I invite myself to remain with them to take part in the Gaelic reading and praying." (MacGregor, 1931)

"From Neil I heard much about the Keartons and their exploits together when Neil and they were comparatively young men. All that had happened while the brothers were on St. Kilda was as clear in Neil's memory as though he had just refreshed it by reading again "With Nature and a Camera". The copy which the brothers had sent to him on publication reposed on the kitchen dresser, carefully wrapped in an abundance of old newspaper, to be brought into the daylight only on very special occasions. Its pages set forth, for all the world to see, the names of himself and his neighbours, with all of whom the Kearton brothers had had so much to do. Richard by this time was dead; while Cherry had attained world celebrity. Neil felt in his heart that, perhaps, without being too immodest, he had had a little to do with their first venture, with their initial contribution to literature, and with Cherry's fame."

"When the missionary is ill or away from home, Neil superintends the village school and preaches the sermon on the sabbath. Furthermore, as ground-officer in the interests of MacLeod of Dunvegan, he sees to the grazings and all matters relating to tenant and proprietor. And then he finds a market in Glasgow for the islander's tweeds, makes time to attend his own flock of sheep, and is the 'Speaker' in the ancient St. Kilda Parliament." (MacGregor, 1969).

On the last full day before the evacuation "The island postmaster, Mr. Neil Ferguson was engaged all day in separating and trans-shipping the community's sheep, but his duties were undertaken by Alasdair Alpin MacGregor, a young Scots writer on the Western Isles who has been on St. Kilda for some days. The post office business did not finish until 2am." (Times, 29/8/30). They had loaded 573 sheep and 13 cattle onto the Dunara Castle together with mails and effects for Oban. The Harebell took the remainder of the furniture and effects with the islanders.

The Times for Aug. 30th. 1930 carried the following article:-

THE RETREAT AT ST. KILDA
None Allowed to Stay on the Island

"The last of the residents on St. Kilda were removed from the island yesterday on board the fisheries cruiser 'Harebell'. There are to be no 'Robinson Crusoes' left on the lonely island: the Government officials saw that everybody left. One young man endeavoured to stay behind when the 'Dunara Castle' was due to sail, but officers from the 'Harebell' insisted on the modern 'Robinson Crusoe' leaving. Similarly, Baron Mackay, heir to Lord Reay, Chief of the Clan MacKay, had intended if possible to remain on St. Kilda to do some exploring, and had brought with him a load of provisions to carry him through his period of isolation. He, however, also left. Shortly after 7 o'clock last night the 'Harebell' steamed into Lochaline Bay. She had on board 33 former inhabitants of St. Kilda. Tenants of the Ardtornish Estate, where the St. Kildans are to settle, gathered on the rocks to give the new settlers a rousing reception. The 'Harebell' anchored in the Bay and a tender brought the St. Kildans ashore. They all appeared to be in the best of spirits.

Passengers on board the 'Dunara Castle'

Rev. Donald and brother Alex Ferguson. E. Ogilvie Collection.

proceeding to Glasgow, were well supplied with souvenirs from the island. One London tourist stated that he was giving a spinning wheel which he brought with him to a museum near his home. On Thursday next the livestock from St. Kilda will be sold at Oban Market."

Interviewed for the BBC Odessey series, "Voices from Scotland's Recent Past", Neil said, "Fine I mind the evacuation of St. Kilda, I was the last to leave the island, all the rest were aboard the steamer early in the morning. I was in charge of the post office and made every excuse to remain as long as I could. I was threatened and pleaded with, but I always made the excuse that I wasn't ready yet, but excuses were of no use. I went for a last walk round the village. It was weird passing the empty houses, it was just like looking at an open grave." (Kay, 1980)

After the Evacuation

Susan Ogilvie, Alex Ferguson's daughter told me, "All Neil's family came over to Kincardine on Forth and they were all working for the Forestry. I visited them there. Neil had three children. Young Neil was always very serious and didn't bother about girls. It was quite a surprise when he married Mary Ann MacQueen, who was always full of fun. (It was the last marriage on St. Kilda). Donald John was working on the lighthouses, he was posted to Arran, he collapsed and died very young. John, Neil's third son, was married in East Kilbride, they had one son, but John died young. The young people, most of them didn't live to a great age. I think it was the change from the lovely clear air."

DONALD (1880-1967) MINISTER OF THE FREE CHURCH

Donald, born on the 7th. April 1880, was the youngest of the family. He left St. Kilda soon after his brother Alex, in about 1896, to serve his apprenticeship with Yarrow Co., the shipbuilders on the Clyde where he qualified as a ship's carpenter and worked as a shipwright. During his time at Yarrow's, with the help of others, he founded the Highland Mission in Partick, Glasgow, where he had a congregation of five hundred. It is now under the auspices of the Free Church.

From 1920-24 he trained for the ministry at Edinburgh University and the Free Church College. He served as a minister at Minard, Ayr, Scalpay (Harris), Fort Augustus and finally Kilbrandon on the Isle of Seil near Oban. On the wall of the Manse at Scalpay there is a plaque noting that Prince Charles slept there while he was on the run.

He was married on 26th. July 1907 to Mary Ann McKinnon who came originally from Grimsay, North Uist. They had six children, John who died aged 4 years, Morag who married Alexander Flemming, Donald married Mary McAulay, Rachel married John Morrison, Dolly and Mary were unmarried. Morag's son, Alisdair, has led several St. Kilda Work Parties.

In conversation with Rachel Morrison, one of Donald's daughters who lives near Oban, I learnt a good deal about this colourful character. "Before he went to College he moved up to Easedale to serve as a Missionary. He was very fond of the sea and while he was there he bought a lifeboat and converted it into a cruiser with six berths. We went on many holidays from there, right up to Tobermoray, where Donald would take over the pulpit for a month or so. We would cruise about from there and visit Lochaline where some of the St. Kildans were living – some were relatives of his own. While he was at Ayr he would take the men from his Bible Class out in his boat – several became very keen on sailing. He was the Commodore of the Yacht Club in Ayr. He had a great sense of humour and he was great with the young people. Let him on the sea and he was in his glory! At his last service before he retired, one man taped the sermon. He was talking about the way he was brought up on St. Kilda as a wee child. He said, "We were always warned that the devil would get us, but if we remembered 'The Lord is my Shepherd' – we would be quite safe. "He was 87 when he died of leukaemia. My grandmother, on my mother's side, was a McKinnon from North Uist, she was over 100 years old when she died."

Lachlan MacDonald remembers Donald with great affection, "He built a boat – a biggish boat by himself – he was on St. Kilda with her. He was a great lad for boats. He had a nerve too. I would trust him in a boat more than his brother Alex, although his brother was very good too. He was a minister – he was jolly and full of fun. One time I took his nephew up to get married. He was great fun. It was a Harris girl who was the bridesmaid, and for a joke I would be making to hold her hand and so forth. Donald turned round and said, 'Here, Lachie, I think I will just make a double wedding of it – and get you married, too!' she said, 'Not on your life' – 'Oh yes, I says.' But I didn't get her – she was a nice girl right enough!"

EPILOGUE

A. A. MacGregor commented, "If you should find yourself at the Lochmaddy Hotel, in North Uist, you may see in the Visitor's Book three significant entries:-

17.7.53 Neil Ferguson 3, West Street, Glasgow C.5
17.7.53 D. G. Ferguson Free Church, Easdale, Argyll
17.7.53 A. G. Ferguson St. Kilda, Old Kilpatrick

These three Fergusons (Neil, Donald, and Alick) are the kindred of Neil Ferguson. In July 1953, nine years after Neil's death, they arranged to meet at Lochmaddy in order to sail from there to St. Kilda aboard a motor launch owned locally. They took with them a stone to mark the grave of my old friend, their kinsman. Immediately after erecting it, they set off on their long return journey. A violent gale sprung up, however, and engine trouble added to their peril. They hoisted as much sail as appeared safe in the circumstances; but the gale ripped it and bore it away. By some miracle they reached Lochmaddy, long overdue and worn out." (MacGregor, 1969)

Two Recent Portraits
Ralph Wright –
A Task Force Portrait

5036798 AC Wright, Ralph was a member of the RAF Task Force "Hard Rock" which landed on St. Kilda in 1957 to begin the preliminary work in the construction of the rocket tracking station on St. Kilda. He took photographs with his little camera which are reproduced here. He has written this fascinating account of his impressions of the island and the work which the Task Force came to accomplish.

"I joined the RAF for National Service in 1956 and entered 5004 Squadron – the works construction unit of the RAF. In May 1957 I was sent with the Task

"Island of Borera and Rock of the Solan Goose 3.30 in the morning July 7th 1812." Acland.

Force "Hard Rock" to St. Kilda. I had no idea where St. Kilda was at the time. About forty of us left by plane from RAF Gaydon in Warwickshire to Benbecula in the Outer Hebrides. We then went by truck to South Uist, then by Tank Landing Craft to St. Kilda – the sea conditions were fair. Our boat beached – we couldn't wait for the tide to go out so we had to wade ashore with our gear. The beach at that time was covered with large boulders of all sizes. Arriving like this, my first impressions of St. Kilda were that it was dull, wet and

rather hostile.

The next day changed all that – it was a nice sunny day. Looking up from the Village Bay to the hills to the north of the island with blue sky and a little mist on top – without any trees around, it seemed a tropical type of weather. Setting up camp was very enjoyable – four of us to a tent. After being there for a week or so, we found out what the weather could be like! The wind got up one night – quite a gale – we had to lash the tents down with as much cord as we could get hold of. In the morning of that particular night, at least half the tents were down and a marquee had disappeared, and lots of our papers were blowing up the hills. We also got rain. when it started it went on for days. Water tumbled down the hills in between the tents and at times through them.

There were goat-like sheep on the island that the people had left when they were taken off in 1930. We explored the island. We went up over the hills and down into the valley below, on the north side of the island, we found aircraft wreckage from the last war. The houses in the Village, what was left of them, were mostly roofless. We repaired the Church and the Manse. Also there were cleits that I could remember all over the island. They were built of stone and were used for all sorts of purposes – drying skins, hay and peat. I had my small camera with me and managed to take some photos. It is now 30 years ago, but the pictures are not too bad.

We had some stormy nights. One night in particular I remember when Russian fishing boats sheltered in the Bay. We also had a large shark in the Bay, one day.

We had a bit of social life on Sundays. We could swim, and we had dinghies out in the Bay to play about in. We had some very hot weather and on one or two occasions there were big rollers coming in onto the beach. By now it was very nice and sandy as we had cleared all the boulders off.

Working on the new army huts. Wright Collection.

We – the RAF – had all kinds of mechanical tools for work. We built roads from the Village up to the highest hill which was about 1,300 feet. The job of 5004 Squadron was to build a radar tracking station and living accomodation. This would be for the Army Signals when we left. I was on St. Kilda from May until September – about four months.

I remember once we didn't get supplies for two weeks, so the bread began to get mouldy. It was because of the weather again. It was so bad that it was impossible for boats to enter the bay. The newspapers we got were always a week or so old. The time we couldn't get supplies by boat, the RAF tried to drop them to us – mail and papers – by plane. The aircraft came in from over the sea on its run and dropped the packages – but, with the upcurrents from the bay to the hills – the first lot went over the top and into the sea on the other side. They managed to get it right in the end!

There were one or two accidents on the island. One airman got crushed between a trailer and a bulldozer – a helicopter came to the rescue. Before it could land we had to clear tons of stones and boulders to make a stand for it to touch down.

We had a cinema – well – we had film shows, anyway, on Sunday evenings in the Church after the service. This was worked very well. To get a seat you had to go to the service first – then you were in your seat!

There were about 300 men and officers. The Commanding Officer, Cookson, was a big man – he used to drive around the island in a landrover with his binoculars to keep an eye on the men!

There was still a lot of bird life on the island and I managed to get some pictures of the gulls, gannets and puffins. The gannets nest on the cliff face on Boreray and were very hard to get to. There were thousands of puffins – very small and pretty little birds. A party from the National Trust – five men and three ladies visited St. Kilda while we were there – they came and stayed in the Manse for two days. The ladies were a pretty sight for us men as you can tell, as this was about three months after we arrived!

Nearly all of us left the island together – just a small party left in the week we were to go. We had a party – some of the boys put on a show – some told jokes they had made up – a verse and rhyme for all the Officers and NCO's. It was quite a laugh! I remember the Commanding Officer's one, it went, "Big brother is

Party leaving, Camp and Village behind. Wright Collection.

watching you. Big brother is watching you – because he's got . . . else to do!" They made up some nice ones as well!

It was a bit sad to leave, but working all the time, we were glad to get home. The day we left was stormy. After leaving we had to pull into Oban. We went round a Force 9 gale, they told us. The L.T.C. boats are flat bottomed and they ride the waves like a cork. We went ashore in Oban that evening and left in the morning after the storm and arrived at Stranraer in the afternoon – then by train to Warwickshire.

This was part of my National Service and looking back on it I would not have missed it for the world."

Richard Castro – A Leader's Portrait

NTS WORK PARTIES – BACKGROUND
CLIMBING STAC LEE
STAC AN ARMIN
VISITING BORERAY

Nesting Gannets on Summit Slope of Stac Lee. R. Castro.

I originally met Richard Castro in Oban, loading up the 'Charna', on my first visit to St. Kilda. He was the leader of our expedition. The voyage was scheduled for 22 - 23 hours, but due to a gale, Force 8, off the Outer Hebrides the journey took 48 hours. Richard, amid groans and distress of his prolonged seasickness, assured us that he would be all right when once we reached the islands. He told us that on his last visit he had been sick nine times on his way out, but, "I had a good return trip – I was only sick five times." In spite of this malaise, Richard is irresistably drawn to St. Kilda and has a tremendous love for the archipelago – no-one radiates more enthusiasm about its glories. He has kindly written his portrait from the point of view of a Work Party Leader with the National Trust for Scotland, referring in particular to Boreray and the Stacs.

NTS WORK PARTIES – BACKGROUND

"St. Kilda's buildings, abandoned in 1930, battered by winter storms, inevitably decayed. Between the evacuation and 1957, when the National Trust for Scotland acquired the islands, cottage roofs came off, chimneys and gables crumbled, cleits, blackhouses and walls collapsed. The Ministry of Defence was dissuaded from converting the houses of Village Street into bottoming for their new road to the top of Mullach Mor and the Trust then turned its attention to the preservation of these historic buildings.

The first two Work Parties went out in 1958 to start the programme of restoration that was to continue for thirty years and bring pleasure and satisfaction to hundreds of volunteers. They were led by George and Irene Waterston and Alex Warwick. There had been fifteen falls of stone into the Village Street and the main task was to clear these and rebuild them as much as possible. They also collected many artefacts and these were sent by the tea-chestful to the Scottish Museum of Antiquities where they are still to be found today. A big fall in the graveyard wall was also rebuilt that first year and George and Irene restored the stone bridge which had collapsed into the Dry Burn.

The St. Kilda Club was formed that summer. Qualification for membership is to have spent at least twenty four hours on the island. Its first reunion was a joint meeting of the first two work parties in the board room of No. 5, Charlotte Square, Edinburgh. This was followed by a public meeting, chaired by Seton Gordon, which was attended by Morton Boyd and Tom Weir. Tom had climbed the Conachair cliff in 1956 with Douglas Scott, some members of these first parties still attend the Club's annual reunions. These were pioneering days with the parties under canvas in the Glebe. The Street provided most of the work for the first three years but other tasks such as the fank wall in An Lag were completed. Allan Aitken was involved with this work from 1959 and made the church his special project from 1969 to 1980 when it was rededicated on the 50th anniversary of the evacuation. Jock Nimlin was drawn to St. Kilda in 1963 and, with Alex, was often on the islands three times a year helping with the restorations but also developing his knowledge of the geology and imparting it to others. Different boats were used each year and in 1960 the 'Avocet', having taken out Alex's first party of the summer, broke its moorings and drifted on to the Village Bay beach where she stuck fast and eventually broke up. Her mast stands at the pier head to this day adorned by the Army detachment's flags.

There are now several work parties each season and the membership of the Club is over six hundred. Over the years these enthusiasts have achieved an astonishing amount. Every summer dry stone repairs are carried out and five 1860 houses, the church, schoolroom and the store have been rebuilt and rerooofed. Each of these twelve strangers, with few building skills, works on projects planned by the

Trust's representative and in two weeks their results are impressive. Cooperation between the Trust parties, the Nature Conservancy Council and the Army personnel has been the corner stone of the successful programme.

It is not all work, of course, and a great camaraderie exists between the three groups. Many social activities are organised and enjoyed by all. There is also ample time off to explore Hirta and savour the views of the other islands of Dun and Soay which are a stone's throw from the main island and, further off to the north-east, the dramatic shapes of Boreray and its stacks. Not many who visit Hirta on holiday get the opportunity to visit the less accessible islands and rocks but during my fourteen visits over the last twelve years I have been lucky enough to have landed on many of them.

I was the leader of the Trust party for the first time in 1977 when one of the enthusiasts in my group was none other than David Quine on his first of several visits to the islands. We couldn't believe our luck, when on a fine calm day, we were invited to join Gordon Ridley and his party who planned to dive Boreray that day from their charter boat – the 'Kylebhan'. David and I and four others landed on Boreray that day and thus heralded the start of a great St. Kilda adventure for us both.

Seen from the high ground of the Outer Hebrides the silhouettes of the St. Kilda archipelago entice those who stare over the Atlantic to visit them. Eight hours wallowing from the Sound of Harris and it's easy to see why the Norsemen named Boreray the 'Fortified Place'. There's nowhere quite like its towering pinnacles and huge stacks which rise vertically from the depths forty miles out from North Uist.

The islands are the remains of a sixty million year old volcano whose crater was four and a half miles across, the distance between the main group of islands and Boreray. There are few weaknesses in the cliffs that skirt Boreray's coastline and to the west they rise awesomely to 1,259 feet. The island and its close neighbours, Stac Lee and Stac an Armin, at first look impregnable but the volcano produced a rough gabbro type of rock that delights any climber who feels it under his fingers and toes. The stacks and cliffs provide high rise accommodation for huge numbers of seabirds and gannets in particular. The precipitous rocks and their inaccessibility are a gannet's paradise and they breed here in larger numbers than anywhere else in the world. And they like to shout about it. They are endlessly blethering, scolding and complaining and their croaking conversations are a constant background din.

CLIMBING STAC LEE

I was leading a work party in 1985 when the warden, Pete More, had to go to Stac Lee to collect some gannets' eggs for research purposes. Three of us landed and climbed this magnificent pillar of rock which rises 720 feet vertically from the sea bed, 564 of them above water. Richard Kearton, who visited St. Kilda in 1897 described it as one of the Wonders of the

Route up Stac Lee. B Marks the Bothy. T. A. Quine.

World. It certainly is breathtaking, but closer study reveals the route that the St. Kildans used when they went there to harvest the gannets. Out of a total of 60,000 pairs, twice the number in any other gannetry, around 12,000 pairs nest on Stac Lee, mostly on the less vertical south face. In summer the combination of birds and guano makes the "Blue Stac" decidedly white.

The St. Kildans often climbed the stack at night and took the birds silently when the colony was asleep. This slaughter of the adult gannet happened in March soon after they had returned from migration. In May there was another expedition to plunder the eggs, and between August and October they annually harvested around 7,000 gugas from this stack alone. Since the evacuation however, only about a dozen people have stood on the summit.

On that fine May day a group of divers were aboard the schooner 'Jean de la Lune' in Village Bay and planned to dive Stac Lee that afternoon. The boat's owners, Dave and Kay Burton, readily agreed to take some of the work party and a few servicemen along too. Wayne Rogers, their crewman, would climb with Pete and me.

Despite the good weather there was a fair swell breaking in Geo Lee – the usual landing place. Tim Edwards, in charge of the Gemini inflatable, tried to land us further round on the south-west side. Although it was more sheltered it proved impossible. There was talk of giving up – possibly my once in a lifetime chance – gone. Wayne was wearing a dry suit and he asked Tim to go back to Geo Lee where, with a rope attached, he threw himself into the water and swam for the landing rock. He made it and scrambled up through the foam on to the great stack. There was no hesitating now.

Once I was tied on, Tim nosed in, I lept onto the rock and he backed out again. The water crashed round my bare legs before I could join Wayne on dry land. What joy to be there at last! Tim repeated the process with Pete and we were off. Our time was limited because we had taken so long to land – we climbed quickly and unroped. The route zig-zags up a series of ledges except for one spot just under half-way where a wee vertical pitch connects a zig and a zag.

The rock was good and warm under the sun. The exposure reminded me of the nose of Agag's Groove on Buachaille Etive Mor and I felt great. The degree of difficulty was about the same. Once the others had followed up we set out along a wide ledge that leads to the summit slope. We were well and truly in amongst the gannets now. The rock fell sheer to the sea and the 'Jean de la Lune' looked a lot less than her 78 feet.

The air was full of noisy, croaking, beautiful birds. They are normally silent but on the breeding cliffs they make up for it in no small measure. In places the ledge was too narrow to pass by the nest and some birds were reluctant to move. Many regurgitated their fish before flying off and the place was strewn with semi-digested haddies. There were a few naked chicks, only a day or two old, and one big downy baby away ahead of the field waiting for his photo to be taken as the first born of the year.

Near the top of this ledge, under an overhang, we came across the St. Kildan's bothy still in good shape. There was a fulmar nesting inside so we didn't go in. The stones were built up to meet the overhanging roof forming a rectangular-shaped building with a window and a door. It might have housed half a dozen men, though not very comfortably, if they had to spend much time there. It would be cold and damp and there wasn't much room to stretch out and sleep. It's situation was spectacular. As it sits in a great rocky ampitheatre it is clearly seen from the south-west in the top left of the face.

Pressing on up the now wide ledge we emerged onto the summit slope which was a sight to behold. Thousands of solan geese perched on their little

Bothy of Stac Lee.

mounds of weed and flotsam packed as closely together as aggressive neighbours would allow, on a huge sloping roof. Incredibly, they were all facing in the one direction - towards the sun - no doubt, dreaming of their winter holidays in the Gambia and such places, only a cheap flight away in November.

As we climbed we found all kinds of rubbish picked up from the sea and built into the nests, including a flip-flop sandal. It was here that the guano lay thickest and I felt for Wayne who was barefoot. The surface was encrusted and, as on ice over snow, our feet broke through with every step. Being so close to these wild creatures was a privilege. They are majestic.

We could have sat for hours enjoying the views of Stac an Armin to the north and the western ramparts of Boreray where many more of the massive colony nest. Standing on top of the remains of the summit cleit we were less than half as high as Boreray's topmost breeding ledges. To the south-west the whole of the

main island group stretched across the horizon from Stac Levenish to Am Plastair. The isolated stacks and huge cliffs over there, including Conachair, the highest in Britain, do not attract a single breeding gannet. Boreray meets their every need at the moment and the birds only go to Hirta, Soay and Dun to fish.

The 'Jean de la Lune' was cruising around the stack waiting for us so we collected our eggs, packed them into two egg boxes, because they are about half as big again as hen's eggs, and set off down through the colony once more. The eggs were well wrapped to avoid breakage. They would be analysed for their chemical content to provide a measure of marine pollution. All went well until we reached the pitch where we had to rope down. Attention on board the boat had been fixed on our progress but it suddenly switched to the other side to watch a school of killer whales go by. She sailed off round the stack to keep them in sight. We quietly coiled the rope, wrapped our cameras in polybags and Wayne put on his dry suit.

Getting off a sea stack is a lot easier than getting on. As the inflatable nosed in on the rise of the swell, we hurled ourselves unceremoniously into it and it backed off as it dropped with the sea. All safely in we sped triumphantly back to rejoin our friends and enjoy a welcome cup of tea.

It had been one of the best days of my life.

STAC AN ARMIN

Stac an Armin, the Warrior's Stack, is the tallest sea stack in the British Isles at 644 feet and is much bigger in area than Stac Lee. Its less steep slopes offer a variety of habitats for birds and therefore it boasts more breeding species. From some angles it's like a big pyramid, but rises 200 feet higher than any in Egypt.

The south face slopes into the sea at a slightly easier angle and modern day visitors favour this as a landing site although it wasn't used by the St. Kildans. The less vertical rock appears more inviting but is just as difficult and even more hazardous for the boatman. The St. Kildans in their clinker built rowing boats could only go close in to vertical rock. To land at this spot an inflatable, powered by a reversible engine, is essential. The boatman must time his approach to nose the stack at the top of the swell and the person poised in the bow must jump before the boat skedaddles backwards as the swell drops, sometimes as much as twenty feet.

These jostlings with nature are extremely exciting but are potentially hazardous. If the boat doesn't get back fast enough it can become high and dry and can capsize on the barnacled rocks. If the man ashore slips off the slimy rocks and can't move up and gets plucked off by the next wave, he is at the mercy of the surging sea, as he bobs about supported by his life jacket until he is picked up. I have seen some close things but never anyone going in, except once on Soay, when a friend

was waist deep before the rope held from above. If landing conditions are not ideal, there must be a serious scientific reason for going ashore. Eggs are sometimes wanted for the chemists, rocks for the geologists and lichens for the botanists.

Stac an Armin has fewer suitable nest sites than its smaller neighbour which is almost exclusive to gannets. Its three colonies have 3,000 fewer breeding pairs. It has large colonies of fulmars, razorbills and guillemots as well as good sites for puffins and petrels and even rock pipits and wrens. The Great Auk bred there nearly 200 years ago but the last one in Scotland is reputed to have been killed on the stack in July 1840. The "guillebills" breed under boulders right up to the summit.

The 15,000 pairs of birds on the stack yielded a rich harvest for the islanders. They provided food, feathers, eggs and oil. This explains the 78 cleits on the stack, identified by Mary Harman during her cleit survey of

Gannets on the summit of Stac an Armin. Wally Wright.

the whole island group in the late seventies. The birds and eggs that weren't needed immediately were stored in them. The birds were gutted out but not salted and the wind, whistling through the cleit walls, dried out and cured the meat ready for consumption during the winter. The harvesters would stay in the bothy perched at over 400 feet up the stack for a week or two.

The accomodation was very basic, but it became home in 1727 for a group of St. Kildans who were stranded there for nine months when a smallpox epidemic broke out on Hirta and decimated the population so quickly that they could not be retrieved. Although no one would choose to spend a winter on Stac an Armin it possibly saved their lives for ninety four died, leaving only four adult and twenty six juvenile survivors. The three men and eight boys, who were marooned from August until the Factor came from Skye in May, survived on fish and the gugas they had gone to harvest. Life must have been hellish for long periods huddled together for warmth in the bothy as the wind and sea raged around them blasting their shelter with rain and salty spray during the long hours of darkness.

Another party of ten men was stranded on Boreray in 1759 when the only boat the islanders had at the time was wrecked in Village Bay on its way home. This was the chance they took from late summer onwards when weather conditions were unpredictable. These men had to live on birds and sheep for nine months of the year until they were rescued in the following June. Tigh Staller was intact at that time so they at least had reasonable accomodation.

VISITING BORERAY

On my first visit to Boreray the conditions were so perfect my granny could have landed without difficulty. Stuart Murray of the Institute of Terrestrial Ecology and Mary Harman, on her cleit survey, went

Boreray from Stac an Armin.

off to work on their own projects. David and I and two other party members made for the summit ridge and the awe inspiring views down the west cliffs where gannets in their thousands drifted back and forth in brilliant sunshine. The great stacks were no less impressive from above.

Although I walked as far as Cleitean McPhaidein and looked at the sheep and the puffins and the views, so overpowering were the sights, sounds and smells that I left after a short visit feeling I had not taken anything in properly and I would need to come again to let it all sink in. I hoped to get back fairly quickly but the opportunity did not arise, so in the intervening years I was more than happy to take my chances to land on Dun, Soay, Stac Levenish and, over by Boreray, Stac Lee and Sgarbhstac. It was not until 1986 that I set out on the 'Jean de la Lune' again specifically to land on my beloved Boreray.

It was a scorching June day and the plan was to dive the arch of Sgarbhstac which had been discovered by Gordon Ridley's team while we were there in 1977.

Landing on Boreray.

parties would live in Tigh Staller, an underground house about 200 feet from the summit, on the southwest facing grass slope. It was not noticeable from the outside, except for a small hole to let smoke out at the top of the 18 feet high corbelled dome. Inside the main room was circular and there were four sleeping compartments off it, capable of accomodating twenty people. By 1860 its roof had fallen in and the stone was used to build new shelters and cleits. Three circular bothies were dug into the steep slope and each had a single chamber about 10 feet long and 5 feet wide and 5 feet high. These made Tigh Staller sound like a palace but they served well until the evacuation. They were still in good shape in 1956 although the roof lintels were exposed. Even at that time all signs of Tigh Staller had disappeared. The remains of the bothies are still clearly visible today and can even be picked out with the naked eye from Hirta when struck by low sunlight.

Dogs were taken to Boreray to run down the sheep one by one and the shearing was a laborious process using only knives. The party lived off rations taken with them but their diet was supplemented by mutton and seabirds. The men worked hard during their stay but the Sabbath was still observed as a day of rest and worship and a service was held exactly as it would have been in the church on Hirta. The blackface sheep were abandoned by the St. Kildans when they left. Completely untended for 55 years they do not appear to me to be the pure blackface we recognise defiantly blocking our roads in the summer months. The adults look as though they have been mixed with a few Soays at some stage but the acrobatic lambs resemble more their mainland cousins. The latest count was done in 1987 when David Miller, the warden, circumnavigated the island and saw 369 sheep.

Cleitean McPhaidein were built at the southerly end of the island above the landing place near Sgarbhstac. Landing could never be guaranteed at any one spot

The divers had the best of both worlds for, after swimming with the seals through the arch, they came ashore to experience Boreray at its best. Low tide and a bit of a swell added spice to this landing but everyone tiptoed up the barnacles to easier ground without mishap. I set out to enjoy the island and try to take in all that it had to offer.

Boreray was considered special and it was every St. Kildan boy's dream to visit it with the parties that went over to harvest the birds. During the summer a group would go for about a fortnight to shear the blackface sheep which had been put out to pasture there. The because of varying weather conditions but there were suitable alternatives. The cleit village, as a group of a dozen or so buildings is known, was used to store the island's produce until the relief boat returned. MacFadyen's cleits are now mostly collapsed and without turf and only provide shelter for petrels, a solitary eider and black-backed chicks hatched nearby.

Other birds were harvested on Boreray. The 38,000 pairs of gannets breed mainly on the north, west and east facing cliffs and, where they can, around 3,500 pairs of fulmar also nest. Guillemots, razorbills, kittiwakes, shag, great black-backed gulls, Manx shearwaters, storm and Leach's petrels breed in varying numbers around the island, but the south-west facing grass slopes are the domain of the puffin. Including two smaller colonies on the east and west coasts there are about 100,000 pairs of puffins going through their enchanting daily routine. The best fertilised grass in the Atlantic, which is heavily grazed by sheep, is perfectly angled for the amusing auks who bustle about gesturing and displayng. Curious calls from underground come from the adult on incubation duty. Occasionally, thousands of puffins whirr by in flypasts that take them out to sea and back round passed the colony again and again. Some with beakfuls of fish peel off into their burrows to feed the young until they are abandoned after six weeks. Mercilessly the puffins were snared in their thousands for meat and feathers. To add to their misfortune around another two or three thousand would be taken by the black-backs each year on Boreray alone but, like all the species harvested, they are great survivors and are still present in huge numbers.

Boreray could have sustained a sizeable human population for fairly long periods. There was plenty of work and food between the birds and the sheep and there was fresh water. Unfortunately, there was no fuel or safe harbour and no permanent settlement was ever built. I wonder what size of work party waiting list would have formed had there been a village in need of restoration on Boreray!

We walked to the summit baked by the relentless sun. The views down to the western gullies, dotted with grazing sheep, of the stacks and the cliffs splattered with gannets, were stunning. A faint breeze carried up the wonderful smell of a big seabird colony reminding me of Stac Lee there far below. Little groups of puffins sat on the rocky edges watching our progress to the top from where Stac an Armin, even from twice its height, is still an impressive fang. From the top of Boreray's sheer west wall, Mullach an Eilein, the views are panoramic. The other islands and stacks across the crater to the south-west float in the ocean which beyond is uninterrupted till the West Indies 2,500 miles away. In the opposite direction you can pick out on a clear day ridges and gullies on the cliffs of the Flannans and, of course, their deserted lighthouse. On such a day the whole of the Outer Hebrides chain, from Lewis to Barra Head, is strung out across the horizon.

I think Kearton was right. This place might well be classed as one of the Wonders of the World, and let us be thankful that, through the National Trust for Scotland and the World Heritage, it will remain so."

REFERENCE MATERIAL

Acland, A. 1981. A Devon Family – The Story of the Aclands. Phillimore, London.

Atkinson, G. C. 1831. A few weeks ramble among the Hebrides. Unpublished Bute Collection. National Trust for Scotland.

Barker Johnson, S. 1973. Childhood Days on St. Kilda, being the reminiscences of Miss Mary Cameron who lived on St. Kilda. Printed by R. and R. Clark Ltd., Edinburgh.

Brougham, H. 1979. An Account of the Island of St. Kilda and Neighbouring Islands. Unpublished. MSS 3051 National Library of Scotland, Edinburgh.

Cooper, J. B. 1931. The History of St. Kilda, Melbourne. Vol.1 1840-1930. Printers Proprietary Ltd. Melbourne.

Heathcote, N. 1900. St. Kilda. Longman's Green and Co.

Holohan, A. M. 1986. St. Kilda: Emmigrants and Disease. Scottish Medical Journal 1986; 31: 046-049.

Kay, W. 1980. Odyssey – Voices from Scotland's Past, Polygon Books Edinburgh.

Kearton, R. and C. 1897. With Nature and a Camera. Cassell and Co.

Lawson, W. M. 1981. St. Kilda Mail – Families of St. Kilda, St. Kilda Club, National Trust for Scotland.

MacDonald, J. 1823. Journal and Report of a visit to the Island of St. Kilda. Edinb. SSPCK.

MacGregor, A. A. 1931 – A last Voyage to St. Kilda. Cassell and Co. 1969 – The Furthest Hebrides. Michael Joseph.

MacKenzie Rev. J. B. 1911. Episode in the life of the Rev. Neil MacKenzie at St. Kilda from 1829-43.

Privately Printed.

Murray, G. 1886. St. Kilda Diary from June 11 1886-87. Unpublished. National Trust for Scotland.

Quine, D. A. 1982. Revised 83, 88, St. Kilda Revisited. Dowland Press.

Quine, T. A. 1986. Thesis An Evaluation of Soil Analysis for Determining Formation Processes on Archaeological Sites. (Excavation in House No.16. St. Kilda).

Report of the Commissioners of Enquiry into the Condition of Crofters and Cottars in the Highlands and Islands of Scotland. Parliamentary Papers 1884 XXXII Appendix p.38 P.P. Evidence Vol.II 1884 XXXII pp. 864-65.

Ross, J. 1889. Diary of the Schoolmaster on St. Kilda in 1889. Unpublished. Bute Collection. National Trust for Scotland.

Troloppe, A. 1878. How the Mastiffs went to Iceland Virtue and Co Ltd., London.

Wilson, J. 1842. A Voyage Round the Coasts of Scotland and the Isles. Vol.2. Adam and Charles Black. Edinb.

NEWSPAPERS AND PERIODICALS

Argos, Melbourne 25th Feb. 1853.
Daily Mail, 1928 and July 1930.
Edinburgh Evening News, Nov. 1927.
Empire News, May 1928.
Port Phillip Herald, Melbourne, 1841.
Scotsman 1927, March 1959.
Sunday Post, Oct. 1927.
Times, 1927, 1930.

INDEX